A Synopsis of the Moral Theology of Peter Dens
by Pierre Dens

Address:
HardPress
8345 NW 66TH ST #2561
MIAMI FL 33166-2626
USA
Email: info@hardpress.net

A SYNOPSIS

OF THE

MORAL THEOLOGY OF PETER DENS,

AS PREPARED FOR THE USE OF

ROMISH SEMINARIES

AND

STUDENTS OF THEOLOGY.

TRANSLATED

FROM THE LATIN OF THE MECHLIN EDITION OF 1838,

BY JOSEPH F. BERG,

FORMERLY PROFESSOR OF LATIN AND GREEK IN MARSHALL COLLEGE.

FOURTH EDITION.

PHILADELPHIA:
LIPPINCOTT, GRAMBO & CO.
1855.

J. FAGAN, STEREOTYPER.

ADVERTISEMENT.

I certify, that the extracts from the " Moral Theology of Peter Dens," translated by the Rev. J. F.
Berg, have been compared by me with the original
Latin, and that I have been unable to discover any
error.   They are faithfully rendered into English;
and in idiomatic sentences the sense is strictly preserved.   The paragraphs or lines under quotation
marks are literal translations; those not so marked
give the sense, or the sense abbreviated, where the
detail at large might not be equally interesting.   And
thus the title of this work is maintained throughout,
" A *Synopsis* of the Moral Theology of Peter Dens."
It is such a translation or Synopsis, however, as fully
warrants our congratulating the English reader, as he
may now thus readily possess the means of ascertaining what are the doctrines and peculiar tenets of the
Roman Church; and that too from a work authorized
and sanctioned as orthodox by the Hierarchy itself.—
Thus "fas est doceri ab hoste;" beyond which, in
this case, there is no appeal.

S. E. PARKER.

The Author is the more fortunate in securing this en-
dorsement of the correctness of his translation, as Mr.
Parker is the person whom Mr. Hughes designated as an
umpire in a dispute relative to the translation of a Latin
quotation, in the course of his controversy with the late
Dr. Breckenridge.

PREFACE.

It has long been the desire of the Protestant public that general access might be obtained to the Moral Theology of Peter Dens; and ever since my attention has been more directly called to the Romish controversy, my mind has been impressed with the importance of the work, which I have at length undertaken. Owing to the pressing duties incident to an extensive pastoral charge, the translation has hitherto progressed but slowly; and I have frequently been constrained to leave it untouched for weeks at a time. Years would probably have elapsed before the manuscript could have been put into the printer's hands, if I had deferred the publication until the completion of the whole work, as it will require no small amount of labour to prepare a synopsis from seven closely printed volumes of from 500 to 600 pages each, with annotations, &c. Protestant ministers have frequently urged me to the work which I have commenced, by reminding me of the important service which a book of this kind would render to them, when attempting to expose the monstrous errors and strong delusions of the Church of Rome. Dens' Theology has long been a text-book in Popish Seminaries on the continent of Europe, and in Ireland especially, from which country our largest importations of priests are made; and I consider myself providentially favoured in having procured from Germany, through the intervention of a friend, the late

Mechlin edition of 1838. The copy in my possession is from the Archbishop's own press, and is therefore stamped with all the authority which the most scrupulous and fastidious Romanist could desire. The work in question is necessarily accessible to few, both on account of the high price, and the extreme difficulty of procuring a copy; and even were these impediments to an extensive circulation removed, it would still be covered with a Latin veil, which must screen it effectually from the eyes of all, except the learned. If I had been writing a book merely for Protestant ministers, I should probably have contented myself with a simple translation; but as I know the common people, both Protestant and Papist, *will* read it, I have thought it best to furnish the antidote with the poison. For the correctness of my translation, I can and shall, at the proper time and place, present the most satisfactory vouchers. In preparing my remarks, I have conscientiously adhered to what I firmly believe to be the truth; and I am persuaded that no one, whether friend or foe, can prove that any of my statements of facts or doctrines have been warped by prejudice. When I can approve a sentiment of Peter Dens, I will do it, not for the love of Popery however, but for the love of God's truth; but when I find doctrines that are an abomination before God and man, no consideration shall hinder me from reprobating them as they deserve.

I am well aware that it is a common thing for Popish priests to deny the authority of any works, even though published by their most approved authors, whenever citations are made from them in illustration of the peculiarities of their system. But if they say that the *Church* is not responsible for the theological opinions of private individuals in her communion, be they Archbishops, Bishops, or Priests, how can they pretend that their church is always "free from pernicious errors," and how will they dare to teach again the words of their authorized catechism, in which they attempt to prove their infallibility by such arguments as the following?

1. "Because as we have seen above, from Matt. xvi. 18. our Lord Jesus Christ, who cannot tell us a lie, has promised, that his church should be built upon a rock, proof against all floods and storms, like the house of the wise builder, of whom he speaks, Matt. vii. 25, and that the gates of hell, that is, the powers of darkness, should not prevail against it. Therefore, the Church of Christ could never cease to be holy in her doctrines, and could never fall into idolatry, superstition, or any heretical errors whatsoever.

2. "Because Christ, who is the way, the truth, and the life, John xiv. 6, has promised, Matt. xxviii. 19, 20, *to the pastors and teachers of his church, to be with them always, even to the end of the world.* THEREFORE THEY COULD NEVER GO ASTRAY BY PERNICIOUS ERRORS. For how could they go out of the right way of truth and life, who are assured to have always in their company, for their guide, Him, who is the way, the truth, and the life?

3. "Because our Lord has promised to the same teachers, John xiv. 16, 17, 'I will pray to the Father, and he will give you another comforter, that he may abide with you for ever, even the Spirit of Truth:' and, v. 26, he assures them that this Spirit of Truth 'will teach them all things:' and chap. xvi. 13, that

1 *

he ' shall guide them into all truth.' How then could it be possible THAT THE WHOLE BODY OF THESE PASTORS AND TEACHERS of the church, who, by virtue of these promises, were to be for ever guided into all truth, by the Spirit of truth, SHOULD AT ANY TIME FALL FROM THE TRUTH BY ERRORS IN FAITH ?" &c.

How then, I ask, could it be possible that Peter Dens, who had received the Holy Spirit by the imposition of the Bishop's hands at his ordination, " should at any time fall from the truth by errors in faith ?" And how is it possible that the Archbishop, who has given to the world the late edition of Dens' Moral Theology, revised and corrected, and who has endorsed and amended it, should have fallen " from the truth by errors in faith," especially when it is remembered that extraordinary spiritual gifts and illumination must have been conferred upon him during his passage from one ecclesiastical dignity to another ?

The *whole body* of pastors and teachers who have received the promise of the infallible guidance of the Holy Spirit, can, of course, not be preserved from error, unless this promise is verified in each individual member. If one may err in matters of faith, two may do the same, and if two, then twenty, and so—a hundred or more, until the *whole body* may finally apostatize from the faith. Hence we see the firm foundation upon which the orthodoxy of the Archbishop and his favourite theologian is based.

Surely, we shall not be told that the Spirit of Truth, (whose infallible direction in matters of faith the priests of Rome claim for themselves as accredited pastors and teachers,) can possibly teach one doctrine in Europe and its opposite in America! No! no!

The ever-blessed Spirit will never accommodate himself to the variations of Popery, for he is what the Church of Rome falsely claims to be, "always and everywhere the same" in the lessons of eternal truth, which he inculcates. The claim to purity of doctrine, to freedom from "pernicious errors," which is so strenuously advocated by the friends of Romanism, will, therefore, appear to be what it really is, *a monstrous, absurd, and preposterous delusion*, when the morals inculcated in some parts of Dens' System of Theology are compared with the pure teachings of the Holy Spirit, as they shine upon the pages of God's blessed word.

I have marked with quotation signs every passage which purports to be as literal a translation of the original Latin, as idiom will allow. Where quotation signs are omitted, I have merely given the sense of the more important paragraphs, and have endeavoured to condense as much as possible. I have been careful to avoid making garbled extracts; and I certainly should deem it a misfortune if I had, in any instance, unwittingly perverted a sentiment by detaching it from its connection. If any such error should be detected, it will give me pleasure to make the correction. It will be observed that my own remarks are distinguished from the Synopsis and Translation by the difference of the type.

I ask a candid and prayerful perusal of the following pages from those individuals in the communion of the Church of Rome, who are not to be deterred by any human interdict from examining for themselves the grounds of their hope of everlasting happiness. I beseech them to pause before they condemn; I pray them to turn " to the law and to the testimony." " If *I* speak not according to this word, it is because there is no light in *me ;*" but if I have the Bible on my side, though "traditions" be against me, all the principalities and powers of earth cannot controvert God's truth successfully until they have overturned his throne! To the Bible I appeal, and by the light of this precious book, I desire to be guided in all *my* inquiries after truth.

I shall probably be accused again, as I have been heretofore, of bearing ill-will to Romanists ; and the publication of this work will perhaps be resolved into a malicious disposition to mortify and perplex persons of a different religious creed from myself ; but this sin will be laid to my charge most unjustly. I can fearlessly appeal to all who know me ; and they will testify that, both in public and in private, I have uniformly treated the private members of the Romish church with kindness and respect ; and the Searcher of Hearts knows that I do most heartily desire that even the bitterest enemies of the Lord Jesus Christ may come to the knowledge of the truth and be saved. But this I avow, and this, in the face of heaven, I shall ever be ready to proclaim,—I hate Popery! I do hate it with a perfect hatred! and whilst God gives me life and strength, I shall exert all the power and influence which his providence and grace afford me, to warn and guard my fellow-men against its insidious errors and its strong delusions.

J. F. B.

PHILADELPHIA, SEPTEMBER 1, 1841.

CONTENTS.

CHAPTER XXII.

xii   CONTENTS.

CHAPTER XXXIV.

CHAPTER XXXV.

CHAPTER XXXVI.

CHAPTER XXXVII.

CHAPTER XXXVIII.

CHAPTER XXXIX.

CHAPTER XL.

CHAPTER XLI.

CHAPTER XLII.

CHAPTER XLIII.

CHAPTER XLIV.

SYNOPSIS OF DENS' THEOLOGY.

CHAPTER I.

CONCERNING MORTAL AND VENIAL SIN.

[No. 153.   Vol. I.]

Concerning Mortal Sin.

" WHAT is mortal sin?

" I. *R.* It is that, which of itself entails spiritual death upon the soul. Inasmuch as it necessarily deprives the soul of sanctifying grace, and charity, in which the spiritual life of the soul consists.

" II. The death of the soul, therefore, which mortal sin induces, is not natural death: because in this sense, the soul is immortal: but spiritual, consisting in the privation of sanctifying grace."

[No. 154.]

Concerning Venial Sin.

" What is venial sin?

" I. That which does not entail spiritual death upon the soul — or that which does not avert from the ultimate end," (*i. e.* which does not create aversion to God), "or which is only slightly repugnant to the right order of reason.

" Is there any such thing as venial sin?

" II. Calvin taught, that all sins are, from their nature, mortal, and worthy of eternal punishment, but that they are not imputed to believers: so that, according to himself, the sins of believers may be called venial, inasmuch as they are not imputed to them, on account of their condition; but not in the sense, as though of themselves they were not worthy of eternal punishment.

(13)

" III. Approximating to this, is the error of Bajus and a few others, who likewise taught that no sin is from its nature venial ; and they differed from Calvin only in this, that they said some sins were venial from divine mercy, whilst Calvin sought this from the condition of sinners. The error of Bajus is published in this his 20th proposition. " No sin is from its nature venial, but all sin deserves eternal punishment."

" IV. Hence it is certain that not only from the divine mercy, but from the nature of the case, there are venial sins ; or (sins) so trivial that they are consistent in just persons with a state of grace, and the friendship of God.

" This is proved from the Holy Scripture. In Prov. xxiv. 16. it is said, " The just man falleth seven times :" and James iii. 2. " In many things we offend all :" which passages are understood concerning just men. Besides, Matt. vii. 5. certain sins are compared to a *mote* (or little splinter); " and then shalt thou see clearly to cast out the mote out of thy brother's eye ;" and 1 Cor. iii. 12. to wood, hay, and stubble ; " But if any one shall build upon this foundation— wood, hay, stubble." Therefore these sins are from their nature light or venial. See other passages from Scripture and the Holy Fathers, in relation to this subject, in Estius, 2 dist. 42. § 4. It is proved also from reason : in all intercourse certain light offences occur, which do not dissolve friendship ; therefore, also, there are such in the fellowship and friendship, which man has with God. Farther, every sin does not create aversion to God : therefore every sin is not mortal.

" *Obj. I.* Christ says, Matt. v. 19. ' Whosoever shall break one of the least of these commandments — shall be called least in the kingdom of heaven ;' therefore the transgression of the least command is mortal.

" *Ans.* We deny the inference : for these commandments are called least only in accordance with the false opinion of the Pharisees ; but in themselves they were important, whether with Augustine you refer the words of Christ to the preceding, or with Chrysostom to the subsequent things, such as anger, injury, &c.

" *Obj. II.* Christ says to Peter, John iii. 8. " If I do not wash thee, thou hast no part with me ;" therefore, &c.

"*Ans.* We deny the inference: because the refusal of Peter, which had preceded, was either no sin, or at least did not exceed a venial offence, but if a refusal had followed the severe reproof of Christ, it would have been a grievous sin of disobedience.

"*Obj. III.* Venial sin is not remitted, except through the mercy of God; therefore, this being set aside, it merits eternal punishment.

"*Ans.* Although the remission of venial sin be through the mercy of God, yet it is in a measure due to a just man, who seeks it; for venial sin does not destroy the divine friendship, nor does it destroy the principle of recovering from the offence.

"*Obj. IV.* Venial sin is a greater evil than eternal punishment, according to No. 149; therefore it merits this penalty.

"*Ans.* We deny the inference. Venial sin is indeed a greater evil in regard to the wrong, as it is an offence against the virtue of God, whereas the punishment would be only against the comfort of nature: but it is not a greater evil in respect of demerit; thus therefore eternal punishment is due to mortal sin alone. See these things more at large in Sylvius & Wiggers."

Our theologian has not been very happy in his selection of proof texts. It is very true "a just man falleth seven times," but Solomon adds what Peter Dens omits, "AND RISETH UP AGAIN." And how does he rise up again? He remembers, whence he is fallen, and repents and does his first works. He looks to the blood of Christ for pardon, and God accepts him. This distinguishes the just man from the hypocrite and the sinner, who fall till seventy times seven, and do not "rise up again," but sink to one depth of degradation after another, until they fall into the perdition of the ungodly. The just man is accepted after falling, not because his dereliction was venial, but because he has risen up and fled to Christ for pardon. But James says, "In many things we offend all.' Yes—truly—and therefore the importance of the Christian's being careful not to pass undue censure upon others, and to bridle his tongue. The consideration that " in many things we offend all," is stated in this connexion to humble us, not to encourage men in sin. But if " we offend in many things" and are still accepted, are not these offences venial? Not more so than any other sins. They must be remitted through the virtue of that blood, which cleanseth from all sin, or we cannot be accepted, but must perish——" The soul that sinneth it shall die."

But some sins are compared to a *mote, i. e.* when, contrasted with other offences, their guilt appears comparatively small.

Christ in this passage, Matt. vii. 5, is rebuking the hypocrisy of those who, whilst they make great pretensions to sanctity, are themselves guilty in a far greater degree of the very offences which they condemn in others; they officiously proffer their services to extract the splinter from a brother's eye, whilst there is a whole beam in their own eye. This does not prove that some sins are *venial*, but it shows conclusively that the guilt of some men is greater than that of others. A splinter in the eye will destroy the vision as effectually as a whole beam, and the soul will be as certainly destroyed by the commission of one act of deliberate hostility against God, as by the perpetration of a thousand crimes. A ship will as infallibly sink through the carelessness of the crew in neglecting a single leak, as though its keel were perforated with a thousand holes.

But where is the justice of God, if all sins are to be punished alike, whilst they differ in the degree of their guilt? God will punish with eternal death all sin, all deliberate transgression, which has not been pardoned for the sake of the Lord Jesus Christ. But some sinners will sink to a lower hell than others, as Christ plainly intimated when he told the Pharisees, " Ye shall receive the greater damnation." The drunkard, who dies in a fit of mania-à-potu, perishes, for " drunkards shall not inherit the kingdom of God ;". but the man who, for the sake of filthy lucre, pampered the cravings of his victim's appetite for strong drink, when he dies in his sins, " receives the greater damnation."

The poor Papist, who is devoted to the superstitious rites of his religion, and who trusts his salvation to the efficacy of penances and alms and masses, will perish unless he repent—but the priest, who taught him to deny the Lord that bought him, and perverted his reason by sophistry and falsehood, will *receive the greater damnation.*—The Judge of all the earth will do right.

As for the allusion to 1 Cor. iii. 12. it is as jejune and inappropriate as an unapt quotation well can be. " If any one shall build upon this foundation,—wood, hay, stubble, if any man's work shall be burnt, he shall suffer loss, but he himself shall be saved; yet so as by fire." As this Scripture is forced in as a proof text to sustain the Romish distinction between venial and mortal sins, I suppose the man's venial sins are to be burnt, and thus he is to suffer loss. Good riddance surely! But he himself shall be saved, yet *so as by fire.* Of course by the fires of purgatory.

The doctrine which is so prominently taught in the standards of the Romish church of the distinction between mortal and venial sin, is *prima facie* evidence, that the whole system is directly at variance with the Word of God. Sin in every form and degree is the abominable thing which He hates. The wrath of God is revealed from heaven against *all* unrighteousness. Fallen man in the pride of his selfish heart graduates the degrees of guilt attached to various crimes, according to the extent to which they affect his comfort and security in this world. Thus, theft and murder are great sins, but profanity and Sabbath-breaking are little sins, because the latter do not so immediately trench upon the rights and interests of society. But God judges by another rule. He looks at the heart, and in the enmity of the carnal mind he sees the secret fountain, from which all the

2

streams of depravity proceed. This alienation of heart is the sin which he hates—and it is developed as clearly to the eye of God in the most secret thoughts, and the most trifling actions of the unregenerate man, as it is to our view in the most appalling exhibitions of depravity.

When the Spirit of God has renovated the heart, changed the bias of the will, enlightened the understanding, and nerved us with moral strength, we are minded to obey—it is our meat and our drink to serve God. We cannot sin as the unregenerate do, who hate God with a perfect hatred, though we may be overtaken in a fault; we may fall as many of the mighty have done, but we believe that though the just man fall seven times, he will rise up again, fly to Christ for pardon, and finally be accepted in the beloved—not because any, or the least of his sins were venial, but because the blood of Jesus Christ cleanseth from all sin.

Our limits will not permit us to follow the author through the intricacies of his nice distinctions between mortal and venial sin. Suffice it to say, that there are no less than twenty-one numbers or chapters relating to this subject. The 156th No. commences with the following words:

" Although mortal sin is far removed from venial, it is extremely difficult to discover, and very dangerous to define, which is mortal, and which venial; so that these are matters which ought to be considered not by a human, but a divine mind, as Enchiridius remarks," &c.

After this statement, we know not whether most to admire the theological acumen or the modesty of the author, portrayed in the twenty chapters, which immediately succeed this avowal of the difficulty and danger of the enterprise. The reader would probably be very little edified by a perusal of Peter Dens' theological prose relative to such points as " The difference between mortal and venial sin," "Rules for distinguishing mortal sin from venial," &c., " The ways in which mortal sin becomes venial, and in which venial becomes mortal," &c.

In the treatise concerning conscience which succeeds the disquisition on mortal and venial sin, the following subjects are discussed: "Rules of human actions." "Definition of conscience." "Division of conscience." "Of acting against conscience." "Of acting according to conscience." "The mode of deposing an erroneous conscience." "The safe rule of action." "Of the conscience, which is the safe rule of acting." "Of conduct, which is safe, safer, and not so safe." "Doubtful conscience." "Perplexed conscience." "Of probability." "Probable conscience." "Of opinions more probable but less safe." "Of the most probable opinion." "Scrupulous conscience." "The causes of scruples." "Remedies of scruples." "The confessor of the scrupulous,"—*i. e.* how the confessor ought to proceed with a scrupulous person. It will be apparent from the preceding captions that there is a considerable assortment of conscience offered to the faithful, and he must be very fastidious, who cannot be accommodated.

CHAPTER II.

[No. 23. Vol. II.]

Concerning the Precepts of the Church.

"I. PRECEPTS of the church necessary to be known are five.

"What are the principal precepts of the church, concerning all Christ's faithful?

"I. Although the precepts of the church are very numerous, both in canon law, and in councils and constitutions of the Popes, yet five are specially propounded in the catechisms as necessary to be known and observed by all: they are the following;

"II. 1. Celebrate the festivals appointed by the church.

"2. On festivals reverently hear the sacred office of the Mass.

"3. Observe the fasts appointed on certain days, and abstinence from some kinds of food.

"4. Confess your sins every year to your own priest, or to another with his permission.

"5. Receive the most holy Eucharist, at least once a year, and that about Easter." * * * * *

This is the Papist's way of salvation; by these meritorious works, heaven is secured to all the faithful! It may well be questioned whether another system of delusion could be invented, which would at once more effectually lead captive the carnal mind and gratify the natural self-righteousness of the human heart. The observance of these five precepts constitutes a good Catholic, and an heir of everlasting life! It is beneath sober demonstration to show that a sinner may observe these five precepts and five thousand more of the same kind, and yet be an utter stranger to the renewing grace of God. Or, are we to suppose that regeneration consists in obedience to these five rules? If so, show us a single one of them in the Bible; or point out even in the corrupted Doway version the authority upon which these five precepts are based. You look for them in vain in God's word—and no wonder, for they are inventions of the Man of Sin.

CHAPTER III.

[No. 27. Vol. II.]

Concerning Infidels and Heretics subject to the Law.

" I. *Infidels are not bound by the laws of the church.*
II. *Heretics, &c., are bound by them.* III. *Whether it is
lawful to give meats to heretics on a fast day.*

" Are infidels and heretics bound by the laws?

"*Ans.* 1. They are all bound by the eternal and natural
law, also by positive divine laws.

" 2. Infidels or unbaptized persons are not held by the positive laws of the church; because they are not subject to the
church; hence the apostle says, 1 Cor. v. 12. ' What have
I to do to judge them that are without?'

" It is inferred if such persons eat meats on a day of ecclesiastical fast, that they do not sin against the law of the
church, nor indeed does he who furnishes meats to them;
unless they should eat these meats in contempt of the church.

" II. 3. Heretics, schismatics, apostates and all such baptized persons, are bound by the laws of the church, which
concern them: because through baptism they have become
subject to the church; nor are they any more absolved from
her laws, than subjects rebelling against their lawful prince
(are absolved) from the laws of the prince.

" Do heretics therefore sin, when they do not observe the
fasts and feasts appointed by the church? -

" Certainly : unless they may be excused for some cause,
as for instance, ignorance.

" *Obj. I.* Heretics are not in the church; therefore they
are not subject to the church.

" *Ans.* It is true, heretics are not in the church as to the
union of charity and the communion of the saints; but
though they are not in the church as to subjection, on the
other hand, by baptism they are subject to the church, and
remain personally subject to the church, wherever they may
have been.

2 *

" *Obj. II.* The church seems to relax her laws in respect to heretics ; because by urging the observance of the rules she can expect no good effect, but rather sins and offences against God on their part.

" *Ans.* We deny the antecedent"—(viz. that the church seems to relax her laws, &c.)—"the contrary is evident from the mind of the whole church. The church accommodates herself to their sins only permissively for higher reasons ; lest, for instance, she might appear to the manifest scandal of the faithful to favour heresy, whilst heretics through their obstinacy obtain an advantage, and are freed from the burdens of laws to which the faithful are subjected. Besides the same reason for relaxing (the laws) would hold good for all the evils of christendom.

" Is it lawful in this Catholic country to place meats on the table before heretics on holidays or fast days ?

" III. We reply with Daelman and Billuart that this is permitted to tavern-keepers, in the case of those heretics who remain in the country through necessity or some important reason : for the consequences of being in the country must be conceded to those, to whom permission is granted to be in the country : thus meats are sold and given to heretical soldiers in time of war.

" But if any heretic should be in the country for purposes of pleasure, trade or any other similar cause, it is not thought that any necessity or sufficient cause is afforded ; whence it appears not lawful for innkeepers, much less for others, to place meats before such an one on forbidden days : but they can properly reply to the heretic that they do not prepare meats to be eaten on that day, in accordance with the laws of the church and the customs of the country.

" The case is different under the government of heretics, when innkeepers give meats to those who ask for them ; because otherwise they might be regarded as disturbers of the republic. See No. 274, on Temperance."

This is not the place to speak of the peculiarity of the Romish church which Paul describes when he tells of some who shall command to abstain from meats, which God hath created to be received with thanksgiving of them which believe and know the truth." That subject will come up in its proper place.　We shall confine ourselves to the main question of the section.　It will be seen from the above that Holy Church considers even Protestants as bound to abstain from meats on the fast days appointed by her.　We are all bound by her laws forsooth, "because through baptism we have become subject to the church;" she claims all the jurisdiction over *us*, which she exercises over her own priest-ridden *subjects*.　WE ARE NOT ANY MORE ABSOLVED FROM HER LAWS, THAN REBELLIOUS SUBJECTS ARE ABSOLVED FROM THE LAWS OF THE PRINCE FROM WHOM THEY HAVE REVOLTED !

The arrogance of this dogma would excite the reader's indignation, if its absurdity did not provoke his ridicule.　If Holy Mother should ever regain the influence she has lost, we apprehend some heretics would continue to commit mortal sin by secretly eating meat on Friday ; and why should they not ? they might readily avail themselves of the expedient, said to have been successfully employed by a Romish priest, whose bowels yearned over a fine roast of beef which had been sent to his Reverence, whether by one of the faithful, or by a heretic, we cannot say.　The priest was in a dilemma as the present was sent on a Friday, and he was hungry and very partial to beef; he adopted an expedient, however, which extricated him from the difficulty without wounding his conscience.　Having procured a fish-hook he took his beef to the river, saying as he let it down into the water, and drew it up, " Go down beef! Come up fish !" The miracle was complete, and the priest eat the beef as fish. To be sure it looked as much like beef and tasted as much like beef as though its nature had not been changed ; but this fact could not possibly disturb the equanimity of a devout believer in transubstantiation.　Certainly it was as easy for his Reverence to change flesh into fish as to change a bit of bread into the body and blood, soul and divinity of the Saviour, by simply saying with the proper intention, " hoc est corpus meum."

CHAPTER IV.

[No. 28.   Vol. II.]

Concerning Just Men subject to the Law.

" ARE just and spiritual men subject to the law ?

" I. Yes : so the Council of Trent has decided.   It is proved by the apostle (Rom. xiii. 1.) where he says, " Let every soul be subject to the higher powers," and Heb. xiii. 17. " Obey them that have the rule over you and submit yourselves."   These texts are general and therefore they include all just men also.

" *Obj. I.* Rom. vi. 14, the apostle says to Christians, ' Ye are not under the law but under grace ;' therefore, &c.

" *Ans.* The meaning is : Ye are not under the Mosaic law, which has now ceased, but under the grace of the new law.

" *Obj. I.* Tim. i. 9, it is said ' The law is not made for a righteous man ;' therefore the righteous is not subject to the law.

" *Ans.* I deny the inference : the meaning is, that the law is not made for a righteous man, that it may terrify him with threats and punishments, and thus compel him to its observance ; because righteous men observe the law of their own accord ; but it consists with this, that the law is made for the righteous man, in order to his direction.

" II. It is to be observed, that men may be said to be subject to the law in a twofold manner ; in one way as to preceptive authority, in the other way as to compulsory authority ; for in every law two things are to be considered ; one, that the law is a rule of morals, because it shows, directs and obliges ; and these things belong to the preceptive authority of the law ; the other, because the law imposes or inflicts punishments, and in so far terrifies and compels ; which relates to the compulsory power of the law."

[No. 29.]

Concerning the Legislator as subject to the Law.

" Is the legislator bound by the laws, which he himself has made?

" I. If the legislator holds monarchical rule, as the Pope, a king, a bishop, &c., or if he is sole absolute lord, he is not held by his laws as to their compulsory power, but certainly in their preceptive authority, at least indirectly, since the laws equally concern himself and his subjects.

" II. That he is not held as to their compulsory authority is manifest: because as he is the supreme prince, he can be compelled by none of those to whom the law is directed, to the observance of his own law.

" III. That he is bound as to their preceptive authority, is proved from this, because right reason dictates, that the head should be conformed to the members. Besides it is proper that a legislator in his own conduct should concur in the common good, and therefore in the observance of his own laws—for as nothing is more injurious than that the legislator should not be the first to observe the law, so nothing is more beneficial than that he should be the first to conform himself to it, &c.　＊　＊　＊　＊　＊

" From this it is inferred that the Pope is obliged to hear Mass on a festival day, to fast on a fast day, and generally to do such things as relate to preceptive authority: yet if excommunication or any other punishment should be appointed against transgressors, he would not incur it; because these things relate to the coercive authority.

" Is the supreme legislator obliged under pain of mortal sin, to observe his law in an important case?

" *Ans.* If the danger of grievous scandal or of manifest injury to a third person, is to be feared from the transgression, according to all (authors) he sins mortally; but whether, apart from these things, he sins mortally is not agreed among authors. Some deny it, *on the ground that the legislator is bound to obey his own law, only by a certain natural propriety, which apart from scandal or some other weighty circumstance, seems a matter of little moment,*" &c.

The reader will learn from the last paragraph, that according to Romish theology, the great cardinal virtue is " to keep up appearances." The Pope or those in authority may do as they list, but they must avoid scandal or else they sin mortally. No doubt his Holiness and his sanctimonious Priests are great admirers of the Spartan rogue, who, rather than betray his theft, suffered a fox which he had stolen and secreted under his robe, to tear out his entrails.

CHAPTER V.

[No. 30.   Vol. II.]

Concerning the Clergy subject to the Laws.

" ARE the clergy subject to human laws?

" I. It is beyond controversy that the clergy are subject to the ecclesiastical laws, which concern them, both as to compulsory and preceptive authority.

" Therefore here is chiefly meant, whether, and how far they are subject to civil laws?

" II. The clergy are under obligation to civil laws, which are not contrary to the clerical order, or to ecclesiastical privilege, so far as preceptive authority is concerned : thus they are obliged to preserve the value of coin ; not to take grain out of the country, if that is forbidden, &c.

" But because a layman has no authority over the persons of clergymen, Suarez and several canonists teach that the clergy are only indirectly obliged by those laws ; as was said in the preceding No. concerning the legislator : forasmuch as in a similar case, a part should conform itself to the whole community, and because the canons teach, that the clergy should observe laws of this kind.

" III. But if the civil laws are adverse to the immunity of the clergy, or if they relate to a matter, in which the clergy are exempt from secular power, by such (laws) the clergy are not held either as to their preceptive or compulsory authority. The reason is, because in such respects, the clergy are by no means subject to the secular power : thus a clergyman is not obliged to stand sentinel, to perform military duty, &c.

"What the matter of ecclesiastical immunity is, &c., see briefly in the treatise concerning Religion, No. 196, &c.

"IV. Persons belonging to religious orders are exempt; and are declared to be so, because in some respects they are exempt from the jurisdiction of Bishops, and are subject immediately to the Apostolic See; but although they are not subject to the Bishop in those things which relate to regular discipline, yet they ought to obey in those things which relate to the administration of the sacraments among the laity; also in those which relate to the preaching of the Word of God, and the performance of public offices, beyond the monastery," &c.

The chapters under the captions "Concerning the obligation of laws," and "The end and ways of fulfilling the law," contain little or nothing of special interest to the general reader. If our limits would admit of it, we would insert a translation of some of the sections concerning "Dispensations," but a brief sketch of a few of the more important principles involved in this Babylonish privilege must suffice.

"What is a dispensation?

"Ans. It is a relaxation of a law in a particular case, by the authority of a superior, the matter and the law remaining unchanged in general."

The right of granting dispensations from the eternal and natural law of God is disclaimed. This, it is affirmed, belongs to God alone, or to him who has received a special commission to that effect. God will grant no dispensation from his laws, because that would be denying himself.

"That the church has the power of absolving from vows and oaths is proved from the general concession of Christ, Matt. xvi. 19. 'Whatsoever thou shalt loose upon earth shall be loosed in heaven.' Besides, the perpetual practice of the church sustains it. Yet this is not properly called a dispensation, but the matter is changed, INASMUCH AS GOD RE-

NOUNCES HIS RIGHT THROUGH THE SUPERIORS OF THE CHURCH, AND THUS THE OBLIGATION CEASES OF ITS OWN ACCORD." !! (See No. 63, towards the close.)

This arrogant blasphemy is a striking illustration of the daring presumption of the Man of Sin, " who exalteth himself above all that is called God or is worshipped."

" The Pope, as he is the Superior of the Universal Church, grants dispensations in all laws which belong to ecclesiastical right; even in the laws of his own predecessors, of Bishops, of all Councils, even general ones, and that independently of the question, whether the Pope is above the Council; because indeed, according to all, he is the head of the church, the guardian of the canons, and the dispenser of the whole economy of the church." (No. 64.)

The dispensing jurisdiction of the Pope it is said extends only to matters of ecclesiastical law and order; cases which belong to faith and morals, are beyond his reach, and belong to the divine right. But what of that? Supposing the Pope finds it to his advantage to transcend these limits, what shall hinder him from doing as his predecessors have done before him? The range of ecclesiastical law is so extensive, and the logic of Rome so subtle and ingenious, that there are few cases which cannot be forced within an ecclesiastical economy, which arrogates to itself all spiritual and temporal supremacy.

The dispensing power of the Bishop is confined to his own diocese, and extends to cases either expressly conceded by the Pope or granted by the general Councils of the church. He gives dispensations from the observance of fast-days, festivals, &c., or in a case of necessity which does not permit the delay of a special recurrence to Rome; hence sometimes when there are impediments in the way of marriage, the Bishop employs his dispensing power. Ordinary priests have not properly the right of dispensation—but in parishes which are rather remote from the Bishop's residence, they may with his consent afford dispensations from fasting, &c. (No. 65.)

There must be a sufficient reason for affording the dispensation ; necessity, or utility, or piety must render it expedient, for if the indulgence is conceded without just cause, it involves the dispenser in guilt proportionate to the nature of the case.

The doctors of the Romish church will differ, however, like other doctors, notwithstanding their matchless unity in matters of faith. Some affirming that arbitrary dispensations entail mortal sin upon the Bishop, others that such offences are merely venial. (No. 67.) It is not for us to decide, when such doctors differ, and we prefer therefore leaving the question to the casuistry of those, whom it specially concerns.

There is also great discrepancy between the opinions of different authors relative to another very important question, to wit : " whether a dispensation obreptitiously or surreptitiously obtained, is valid." A dispensation is said to be surreptitious, when obtained by concealing the truth ; and obreptitious, when obtained by telling a falsehood. Now the Romish doctors cannot arrive at a unanimous conclusion relative to the validity of such dispensations. There are several hairs to be split before any thing like a sound conclusion can be attained. Whether, e. g., the surreption or obreption concerns the *final* or only the *impulsive* cause, will materially affect the case.

The *final* or *motive* cause is " that, which principally moves the superior to grant the dispensation ; so that, in its absence, the dispensation would either by no means have been given, or not without trouble and *compensation*, or at least not in such a form."

" That cause is called *impulsive*, which indeed induces the superior to grant the favour more readily, but in the absence of which, he would have granted (the dispensation) absolutely and in the same form.

" Let this serve as an illustration of both causes : some one gives alms to a poor man, which he affor the more readily,

3

because he believes him to be honest; here, the man's poverty is the *final*, and his probity the *impulsive* cause."

Having given my reader the clue afforded by Peter Dens, I must leave him to find his way out of the labyrinth of "distinguos" as he best can.   Of course, every honourable mind will instinctively venerate the purity of those holy doctors who cannot determine whether falsehood and deceit can invalidate a case or not.   From the premises which some of them assume, the inference is fair that the more proficiency a man has made in deceit and falsehood, the more readily he can be favoured with a dispensation.

For our part we know not which most to admire, the knavery of the man who gives, or the folly of him who accepts, a Popish indulgence.

CHAPTER VI.
[No. 78.   Vol. II.]
The Decalogue, and the First and Second Commandment.

" What is the first precept of the Decalogue ?

"*Ans.* The first and greatest is this, 'Thou shalt not have strange gods before me,' &c.

" What is forbidden by this precept?

" *Ans.* It is forbidden to regard any thing else as God, except the true God, and in any manner to offer to any other thing, that which pertains to God alone; for the words 'strange gods' are equivalent to 'other gods,' as is plain from the text in Hebrew and Greek.

" By this precept, therefore, idolatry, divination, and all superstition of every name, are forbidden.

" ' Before me,' is added: and this denotes that God is everywhere present; and at the same time gives great emphasis in order to signify that the sin is aggravated from the fact that it is done openly and directly in the presence of God.

" What does this part prohibit, 'Thou shalt not make to thyself a graven thing ?'

Ans. The same as the preceding words—*thou shalt have no other gods :* for, as St. Augustine teaches, quest. 71 on Exod., it is only a kind of explanation of the preceding part, prohibiting idols and images to be made in the manner of the Gentiles, who consecrated them, and supposed that by this consecration a certain divine power was included in them; as is plain from Cicero's speech against Verres; and hence they worshipped them also with the veneration of *latria*."*

" From which it is plain that nothing can be deduced from this passage against the worship of holy images; for the Holy Scripture itself does not simply prohibit graven images and pictures : but only in this sense, that no one may adore them, or worship them with the veneration of *latria ;* but in this way Christians do not adore images, neither do they believe that they possess any innate virtue.

" Prove that it was not forbidden to make these images.

" It is plainly proved : for, Exod. xxv. 18., we read, that likenesses and images of cherubim were made by Moses at the command of God, near the ark of the Lord; and, 3 Kings (i. e. 1 Kings) vi. 23, the same was done by Solomon in the temple; also, Num. xxi. 9, by the command of God, Moses erected a brazen serpent, that by looking at it those who had been bitten by the fiery serpent might be healed.

" Moreover, although every kind of images whatsoever had been forbidden to the Hebrews, that precept to such an extent would have been ceremonial, and therefore would now cease, as St. Thomas remarks, &c.

" What is commanded by the first precept of the Decalogue ?

" I answer with the Roman catechism thus : ' Thou shalt worship me the true God ;' or, Thou shalt hold me the only true God, in faith, hope, and charity, and thou shalt worship me alone with the veneration of *latria*."

The division of the commandments of the Decalogue, which obtains in the Romish church, is decidedly objection-

---

* Papists make a distinction between the worship which they offer to God, and that which they give to their saints and images; the former is called " latria," and the latter " dulia." The veneration of the Virgin Mary occupies a kind of middle ground, and is called " hyperdulia."

able. The second precept, which is as distinctly marked as any other, ought not to be attached as a mere appendage or explanation of the first. In Romish catechisms, the first two precepts of the Decalogue are amalgamated, and in order to make out the full complement of ten the last commandment is broken into two. There is something gained by representing the positive and explicit prohibition, " Thou shalt not make to thyself *any* graven image, or the likeness, &c." as a mere amplification of the first precept, because it affords a meagre excuse for omitting the second commandment, in nearly all the Popish catechisms which are published throughout the world. And yet, were it not for the " strong delusions" of this abominable system, it would be a difficult matter for any honest man to reconcile himself to the " due veneration of holy images," required of him by the Romish authorities with the import of such language as that in Exodus xx. 4, 5, 6.

The distinction between latria and dulia is a Popish invention, for which there is no warrant in the Bible. Men are forbidden in the word of God to " bow down *to* or *before* graven images, or likenesses of any thing in heaven above, or on the earth beneath, or in the waters under the earth," and yet the Romish Church, which claims to be *Holy* and *Catholic*, commands all in its communion to bow down to images of saints, and of Christ and the Virgin Mary!

The allusions to the cherubim over the mercy seat, and the brazen serpent, furnish no authority whatever for the worship which Papists offer to their idols. The cherubim were placed in the Holy of Holies, which was accessible to the High Priest alone, and to him only *once* a year. The common people never saw them, and consequently these images could not have been made for the purpose of receiving Popish *dulia*. As for the brazen serpent, if we turn to 2 Kings xviii. 4, we shall find that after the Israelites had been inveigled into the idolatrous practices of the heathen, they actually did bow down to it and burnt incense to it, and for this reason it was that good king Hezekiah "brake in pieces the brazen serpent which Moses had made."

The subject of the veneration of images and relics is discussed at length in my Lectures on Romanism, to which I beg leave to refer my reader.

The exposition of the third commandment (the second in Romish catechisms) contains nothing that is unscriptural.

" What is forbidden in this command?

Ans. " No one," says the Roman catechism, " may despise the divine name, no one may take it in vain, nor swear by it, either falsely, or needlessly, or rashly."

" By the name of God is here meant, not the mere word, signifying God, but the thing signified by it, that is, God himself, or the Divine majesty, or his attributes.

" Whence, observe that this name, although it be placed in the singular, yet ought to be understood as referring to all those things which are usually attributed to God ; thus the Roman catechism (teaches.)

" Therefore by this precept perjury is forbidden : also every oath imprudently or rashly uttered, sacrilege, blasphemy, and every vain assumption of the Divine name.

" What does this second precept teach?

" The Roman catechism replies : 'that the name of God is to be honoured, and that by it we may swear in a holy manner.' The name of God is honoured and praised by acts of faith, hope and charity, and by good works of every kind, especially by the public confession and preaching of the Divine name, by the singing of Divine praises, and by saying as well in adversity as in prosperity : 'Blessed be the name of the Lord ;' by the invocation of the Divine name, and by swearing in a holy manner."

To all this we respond, Amen.

3 *

CHAPTER VII.

[No. 79.—No. 87.]

Concerning the Third Commandment of the Decalogue
(i. e. the Fourth.)

AFTER alluding to the reasons of the change from the seventh to the first day of the week, the following questions are proposed.

"What is taught by this third precept, in the new law? (*i. e.* under the Gospel.)

"*Ans.* Principally these three things; 1. That certain specified days are to be kept holy: 2. That they are to be kept holy by external divine worship, by HEARING MASS,"? &c.: "3. That the same are to be kept holy by abstaining from servile labours."

"Which days are those that are appointed to be kept holy?

"*Ans.* In the first place are the Lord's days, chosen in memory of the glorious resurrection of Christ, and for the religious remembrance of the mercy of creation and redemption by Christ.

"2. Festival days also are appointed, which have been consecrated to religion on account of some particular mystery of our redemption, or which have been devoted to the Holy Virgin, or Apostles, Martyrs or other Saints.

"What is the object of festival days?

"Festival days like the Lord's days have been instituted chiefly to call to mind the mercies of God: moreover, that the goodness and power of God may be praised in the victory and glory of the Saints; and that the Saints themselves may be duly honoured and invoked by us, that we may be helped by their prayers; and that we may imitate the examples of those whose merits we call to mind.

"Besides that the institution and observance of festivals of this kind, and particularly of those which are called the birth-days of the martyrs, are very ancient, is evidently seen from ecclesiastical histories, and from S. Aug. Ambrose,

Chrysostom, and others, who have written sermons to the people concerning them." (No. 79.)

Great stress is laid in this connexion upon the duty of hearing Mass on holy days. It is not quite a *mortal* sin to neglect it, but it is a very grievous offence. Non-attendance at Vespers is a venial sin. "When it can conveniently be done," it is the duty of the faithful to go to hear preaching and the catechism, but this obligation is not binding if there is merely a trifling reason for absence.

"But it is to be observed that whilst some will have it that the church enjoins nothing on the Lord's days and festivals except hearing Mass, and that therefore the faithful do not sin against a precept of the church, if they are present neither at preaching, nor at vespers; yet they admit that those sin venially against the divine command concerning the sanctification of the Sabbath, who perform no act of religion on those days, except the hearing of the Mass."

Moreover, where it can conveniently be done, it is the duty of the faithful to hear Mass and preaching in their own parish. The priest, who without cause continuously neglects to preach for several months, or for one month, sins mortally according to Bonacina — and the Council of Trent rather confirms this opinion.

Acts of faith, hope, charity, contrition, &c., are recommended as highly meritorious. (No. 80.)

The faithful are forbidden to engage on the Lord's days and on festivals in judicial processes, accompanied with noise and confusion, merchandizing and servile labours. Judicial proceedings on the Sabbath or festival days, such as, the summoning of a party, examination of witnesses, formation of a procession, judicial oath, sentence, execution, &c., are null and void. But acts of voluntary jurisdiction, which are done without judicial bustle, are not void—as v. g. dispensation, absolution from censure, election, &c.

By merchandizing, "fairs are meant, such as take place, once or twice a year, or even every week — also contracts of buying and selling, bartering or hiring, &c., whether made publicly or privately."

But yet certain things are usually permitted with the consent of the superiors; such as the purchase of certain small articles of daily food, as salt, pepper, sugar, &c., in a store that is closed. This, however, as the most illustrious Hovius says, for necessity's sake, &c.

For this reason, Layman and Billuart excuse those, who on the aforesaid days sell clothes, shoes and other things to farmers and servants, who cannot provide themselves with such necessaries on other days. So Marchantius for a similar reason excuses those who settle with their workmen on the Lord's day. The more scrupulous, however, by his own admission, are accustomed to do this on the preceding day.

Servile works are those corporeal labours in which one man serves another; such are ploughing, digging, the exercise of mechanical arts, &c. They differ from the exercise of liberal arts inasmuch as the corporeal efforts of the latter are principally directed to the exercise, instruction, or delight of the mind; thus, to teach, read, study, preach, prepare a sermon, &c., are not servile works, neither are they forbidden on a festival day.

To spin and sew being servile labours are forbidden on holy days.

Whether painting is a servile labour is a vexed question. Medina and Layman think it is not, and that it is therefore a lawful employment for the Lord's day. Common opinion, however, is against their decision. But when mere sketches are made, or when persons exercise themselves in painting for the sake of recreation or improvement, it is thought the practice may be more easily connived at.

"It is certain, however, that to dye cloths, colour joists, whiten walls, &c., are servile works."

Notaries and scriveners who consume a great part of a festival in writing on secular business, such as transcribing deeds, accounts, processes, &c., commit sin.

As to hunting and fishing, unless accompanied with great noise or fatigue, they are lawful recreations on the Lord's day. "Many (theologians) suppose that it is not unlawful to fish with a reed, hook, or small nets for the purpose of recreation; and they think the same of hunting on a small scale."

Gathering fruit from gardens or trees is also included among servile labours: but Marchantius excuses from mortal sin those who gather wild fruits, such as nuts, herbs from the meadows, &c., even for purposes of gain, at least on the score of custom.

Whether barbers may keep their shops open or not, is not quite clear—but the decision is rather against the practice, although La Croix and Tamburinus apologize for it; the former excusing barbers if they shave labourers and such as are hindered on other days, or if they shave some from apprehension that they might lose their custom. Tamburinus excuses them on the score of custom — but Sanchez replies that this custom has always been disapproved.

Sports are not forbidden—but are distinctly permitted, nor is it any objection that they are attended with fatigue, as playing at ball, &c., because this fatigue is undergone for the sake of mental recreation, and for rest and recreation from servile labours.

Neither is it forbidden to travel on a holy day, either on foot, horseback, or in a ship, &c., unless the journey is necessarily attended with servile labour, such as carrying merchandize or other burdens, leading beasts heavily laden, &c. But in lawful journeys, venial sin may be committed, if too much time is spent upon them, and the mind is prevented from being open as it should be to divine things. (No. 81.)

Bonacina and Collet consider servile labour on a holy day, protracted to one hour, as sufficiently grave to constitute mortal sin. Marchantius requires three hours; but La Croix fixes on two hours, and is sustained by the more common opinion. It is thought, however, that the quality of the work should be regarded, so that if the work is very servile it will require less, if very light, greater time to make it a mortal offence. (82)

There are four circumstances which may render servile labour on such days excusable: they are, 1. necessity, 2. duty to God or our neighbour, 3. custom, 4. dispensation.

Physicians and apothecaries are excusable for preparing medicines for the sick.

Servants and poor waiting-girls are excusable for mending their clothes, if they have no time on other days, and have no one who can give them to other persons to mend for them. But their masters sin in not giving them the necessary leisure. Cooks are excused in the same way for pre-

paring articles of food on holy days.   Others acquit them
on the plea of custom, even when they prepare delicacies.

Those who make funeral clothes on a holy day are
usually excused on the score of necessity, if they absolutely
cannot be finished on another day — so also blacksmiths
shoeing horses for the convenience of travellers.

Soldiers are excusable for any acts in the line of their
profession performed on holy days.

It is lawful to labour in a servile way whenever the work,
which has been commenced, cannot be discontinued without
loss, as in the manufacture of glass, iron, &c.

So too it is lawful to labour in the harvest or vintage,
when there is danger of damage from rain, &c. But when
this extraordinary labour is performed, license should be
obtained from the bishop, &c.

Likewise, if persons are so poor that they cannot afford
to lose a day, they may labour privately, if they cannot
otherwise maintain their wives and families, particularly if
several festivals concur, and they have not otherwise been
negligent, &c. ; and when extraordinary occasions of profit
occur, they may, according to Pontus and Billnach, be excused for improving them.

" Finally, observe in all cases that nothing be done contrary to law ; that no labour be deferred to a holy day,
which could have been done before, and that more is never
done than necessity to avoid loss, &c. requires." (83.)

Servile labour performed on a festival is not necessarily a
mortal sin, as it may be merely internal and accomplished
in a very short time, and therefore not forbidden by the
fourth commandment. (85.)

Any sin which is in itself mortal is aggravated by the
circumstance of its being committed on a holy day. (86.)

The first objectionable feature in this Romish divinity
which painfully affects a Bible Christian is the insult which
is offered to the God of the Sabbath, by making festival-
days, appointed by the Popish church, of equal authority
with the Lord's Day. God has set apart one day out of
the seven for himself — and the Romish church appoints
we know not how many more for *herself*, and claims for

them the same regard which is due to the Sabbath of the Lord our God. This is arrogance, which is peculiarly and emphatically *Roman*. From the above synopsis of the sections, which treat of the observance of the Sabbath, WE MAY INFER THAT THE INCREASE OF SABBATH-BREAKING IN ANY COUNTRY WILL BE IN EXACT PROPORTION TO THE INFLUENCE WHICH POPERY ACQUIRES. To this fruitful source of the abominations of the earth we may trace all the glaring violations of the Lord's day, which are most commonly practised in our large cities, and indeed throughout our whole continent; not a few of which are tolerated even in the Christian church. Those persons who absent themselves from the church on the afternoon and evening of the Lord's day, after attending in the morning, are involuntarily sanctioning the practice of Papists. Indeed, the deluded Romanist, who conscientiously attends mass on the morning of the Sabbath, and then considers himself at liberty to "find his own pleasure" during the rest of the day, is more excusable than the professed Protestant, who with better knowledge deems himself at liberty to spend the afternoon and evening of the Sabbath in amusement, after having paid his compliments to his Maker by attending the morning service in some house of worship.

The license which is given to many of the grosser forms of Sabbath-breaking will of course find favour with the multitude, who are lovers of pleasure more than of God; but it will be well for those who are in the communion of the Romish church, as well as for such as are somewhat favourably disposed to her doctrines and ritual, to reflect that Jehovah will not suffer his day to be polluted with impunity, and that he will assuredly judge the Babylonish woman for all the Sabbath-breaking which is the legitimate offspring of her unscriptural principles; and if "this mark of the beast" be found on any one, he must receive of the plagues," which God has in store for her.

What can be more explicit than the language of the Fourth Commandment?—" Remember the Sabbath day, to keep it holy.   Six days shalt thou labour, and do all thy work : But the seventh day is the Sabbath of the Lord thy God : in it thou shalt not do any work, thou, nor thy son, nor thy daughter, thy man-servant, nor thy maid-servant, nor thy cattle, nor the stranger that is within thy gates : For in six days the Lord made heaven and earth, the sea, and all that in them is, and rested the seventh day : wherefore the Lord blessed the Sabbath day, and hallowed it."   Exod. xx. 8, 9, 10, 11.

How can we reconcile with this precept the license offered in the Romish church, to engage in trifling pastimes and in sports, such as fishing and hunting on the Sabbath day ? " Thou shalt do *no manner* of work !"   " Ah !" the Papist will tell you, " this is no manner of *work ; it is *recreation* and *pleasure*."   But what saith the Scripture?   " If thou turn away thy foot from the Sabbath, from doing thy pleasure on my holy day ; and call the Sabbath a delight, the holy of the Lord, honourable ; and shalt honour him, not doing thine own ways, nor finding thine own pleasure, nor speaking thine own words : Then shalt thou delight thyself in the Lord ; and I will cause thee to ride upon the high places of the earth, and feed thee with the heritage of Jacob thy father : for the mouth of the Lord hath spoken it." Isaiah lviii. 13, 14.

Here is an express prohibition of such *recreation*. (See also Jer. xvii. 20, 27, &c.)   We are no sticklers for the Pharisaical observance of the first day of the week ; we admit that works of real necessity and mercy cannot desecrate the Lord's day ; for it always has been and ever will be " lawful to do good on the Sabbath day," but it is impious to speak of poor mechanics being compelled through poverty or any other cause to pursue their ordinary calling on the Lord's day.   The poor need rest as much, if not more than the rich; if you deprive them of their Sabbath, you subject them to perpetual drudgery; nothing is better calculated to soothe their distress than the doctrines, consolations and prospects of the Christian religion. Does it not argue an utter absence of spirituality to insinuate that the poor man can possibly be injured by a due observance of the Lord's day? Even in a temporal view, we believe it will be found that in the end nothing can be gained by Sabbath-breaking.

The law of necessity and mercy we recognize as Scriptural, but as for " Custom" and " Dispensation," which constitute two of the four reasons which justify servile labour on the Sabbath, we cannot acknowledge them. They who plead " custom," will do well to remember who has said—— " Broad is the road and wide is the gate that leadeth to destruction, and many there be which go in thereat; because strait is the gate, and narrow is the way that leadeth unto life; and few there be that find it!" And as for " Dispensations," we have no faith in them. We believe them to be devices of Satan, and as such we scorn and abhor them.

CHAPTER VIII.

[No. 87.—94.]

Concerning the Fourth (i. e. the Fifth) Precept of the Decalogue.

THE 87th Section contains some excellent and unexceptionable advice, relative to the honour which is due from children to their parents. We are taught that love, reverence, obedience and assistance are justly to be expected by parents from their offspring; that next to God we are to love father and mother, and manifest our affection " by wishing for them the greatest benefits, praying for their bodily and spiritual health, and manifesting this love by visible tokens."

4

" They are delinquent in this duty of love, who hate or despise their parents ; who rejoice in their adversity, or deplore their prosperity, or who wish evil to them ; also those who distress their parents, frown upon them, speak unkindly to them, &c."

The duty of filial affection is illustrated by the manner in which Joseph honoured his father, Gen. xlvi. 29.——" Joseph made ready his chariot and went up to meet Israel his father, to Goshen, and presented himself unto him : and he fell on his neck, and wept on his neck a good while." And again, by a reference to 3 Kings, ii. 19., (*i. e.* to 1 Kings ; in the Doway Bible the Books of Samuel are called I. and II. Kings,)——" Bathsheba therefore went unto King Solomon to speak unto him for Adonijah. And the king rose up to meet her, and bowed himself unto her, and sat down on his throne, and caused a seat to be set for the king's mother, and she sat on his right hand."

" The Roman catechism also teaches that we honour our parents, when we imitate such actions and manners as are commendable, according to that passage, John viii. 39——' If ye are Abraham's sons, do Abraham's works.' "

Towards the close of this section, however, there is one *dead fly*, which gives the box of ointment a taint of Popery. It is made the duty of pious children to provide a prudent confessor for their parents in the article of death, but there is no Scripture quoted for this, as in the preceding cases. For this omission, we cannot blame Peter Dens, as Moses and all the prophets and apostles, have certainly not recorded any thing about the matter in question.

The 88th Section contains some sound rules relative to the obedience due to parents, mutilated, however, by that unfortunate propensity of distinguishing between mortal and venial sin.

The 89th No. treats of the claims of parents upon filial duty. They are three, viz. — 1. legitimate birth ; 2. a decent education ; 3. proper instruction in the rules of life and in morals.

" Under the third head, parents are obliged to see to it

that their children are baptized as early as possible, and they ought to teach them the first rudiments of the faith, to send them to catechism, and when reason has developed itself, use their endeavours that they may convert themselves to God ; further, by precept and example to direct them, and by reward and punishment restrain them from sins : concerning which, however, parents are to be admonished that they do this not through anger and too many blows, but rather by withdrawing from them their food, play, and other pleasures," &c.

" From this infer that parents should be regularly asked at confession, whether they have children, whether they instruct them properly, whether they send them to catechism and to school, whether they do not permit them to be out at night and to keep dangerous company, &c."

The claims of parents to due regard from their children are sustained by several quotations from the Apocrypha. The genuine Scriptures would have furnished many that are more to the purpose. However, we will not be captious, for if Papists and Protestants follow the advice addressed from the Apocrypha, they will do well in so far as this precept is concerned. Parents, it seems, are required to have their children baptized as early as possible ; to this *we* have no objections, provided the ceremony be performed by a *Christian* minister, with the application of water *only*, in the name of the Holy Trinity. But we cannot understand why it is, if children are regenerated by baptism, (as the priests believe and teach), that parents must use their endeavours that these *regenerated* children may be *converted* when they attain to years of discretion. This to us is even a greater mystery than the practical benefit to soul or body to be derived from the addition of oil, salt, or spittle, which are some of the elements of the Popish laver of regeneration.

" The Roman catechism adds a fourth general reason for honouring parents and all superiors, viz.——that in them, we honour God, because all power and superiority is from God, and God wills that we honour superiors as representing God;

hence the apostle, Eph. vi. 5. — 'Servants be obedient to your masters according to the flesh—as to Christ.   6. Not with eye-service, as men pleasers; but as the servants of Christ, doing the will of God from the heart.   7. With good-will doing service as to the Lord and not to men.'

"Spiritual directors properly present this motive to obedi-ence, in order that they may induce children and others who are in subjection to obey, by proposing to them, whether if God himself should enjoin anything, they would not cheer-fully fulfil it, but that when a command of a superior is obeyed, God accepts it, as though he had himself enjoined it."

We must be permitted to demur here.   When a parent or any one in authority enjoins something that is clearly a *duty*, then from the above Scripture, it is evident that we are bound to do THE WILL OF GOD *from the heart;* but the case is very different when a priest dignifies *his own* will, lust or passion by making it equivalent to the will of God, as priests have done in thousands of instances, to their eter-nal infamy!   There are circumstances in which " we must obey *God* rather than men," as Peter Dens properly remarks in a previous section, (88) but even there, " God and the church" are associated as though of equal authority.   The following is the paragraph to which I allude :

" Should we always and in all things obey our parents ?

" *Ans.* No.   We are not obliged to obey—1. When a precept of a higher power is in the way ; and 2. When in this matter, the son is not subject to his parents : and thus the son is not obliged to obey, if they enjoin anything against the law of God or the church, or which is in any way sin-ful."

" Under the name of parents are included—

" 1, and chiefly, those who have begotten us according to the flesh, &c.

" 2. Ecclesiastical and spiritual superiors, as the Bishop, Pastor, Confessor, &c.—for they produce and promote spi-ritual life in us ; hence Paul, 1 Cor. iv. 15.—' I have begot-ten you through the Gospel.'

" 3. Secular superiors are also meant, as the king, magistrate, masters, &c. Thus the servants of Naaman called him father. (2 Kings, v. 13.)

" 4. Those are meant to whose care we have been committed, such are tutors, guardians, masters, &c. Thus Elisha called Elijah, father. (2 Kings, ii. 12.)

" 5. Aged persons also come under the name of parents, concerning whom it is said, Lev. xxix. 32., ' Thou shalt rise up before the hoary head, and honour the face of the old man.'

" 6. All these persons we honour by the abovenamed acts, by love, reverence, obedience and assistance; but not all equally, but according to the order of superiority, relationship and subjection, as S. Thomas remarks, &c.—' The inferior is bound to obey his superior, according to the order of superiority, as a soldier the general of the army, in such things as relate to war; the servant the master, in those things which relate to the performance of servile works; the son the father, in those things which pertain to discipline of life, and domestic concerns, and so of other things.' "

In case of contracting marriage, children are not obliged to obey their father—but they ought to ask the counsel and consent of their parents.

When two superiors enjoin things which are incompatible, the greater is to be obeyed; the nature of the injunction is also to be considered, &c.

What is to be done, when both are of equal authority is not stated, and we leave the question to perplex some future casuist. (No. 90.)

The 91st Section contains a short dissertation on the promise appended to the command " Honour thy father and thy mother—*that thy days may be long in the land, which the Lord thy God giveth thee.*" The promise is correctly interpreted as including eternal life as well as a long and happy existence upon earth; the dispensations of God's providence which not unfrequently remove good men in early life, are shown to be perfectly consistent with this promise. God may see that a longer life would not be good for them; or they may be taken from the evil to come; hence when premature death overtakes good men, grievous calamities may justly be apprehended. The promise that their days shall be long upon the earth is conditioned by the question

4 *

whether long life upon earth would be to their advantage, and at all events, they are abundantly compensated by an eternity of happiness in heaven. " He cannot be said to be deceived to whom gold is given, when silver had been promised." The doctrine of this section is Scriptural, and we sincerely wish we could endorse every chapter in Dens' Theology as cheerfully as we can this.

The Sections 92 and 93, which treat of the remaining precepts of the decalogue, contain nothing of special interest, in so far as the peculiar dogmas of Popery are concerned. They are sound, logical and Scriptural expositions of the duties enjoined by the Great Lawgiver upon all men ; and there is not a moral sentiment in them which may not be cordially approved by every true Protestant. It is not necessary to insert them, as they may be found in substance in almost every Protestant catechism. The only objection which we have to these sections, is the plea for the division of the tenth commandment ; this is rendered necessary by the forced union of the first and second precepts of the decalogue. The ninth commandment in the Romish catechism is,

" Thou shalt not covet thy neighbour's wife."

" What is forbidden by this ?

" *Ans.* Every secret sin against chastity, such as inclination, desire, a lingering delight ;* for that, which in the *sixth* commandment (the seventh) is forbidden in deed, is here forbidden in desire.

" In the same way, the tenth commandment corresponds to the seventh, (the eighth,) and the things which are there forbidden in deed, are here forbidden in desire."

The tenth commandment then, according to the Romish catechism, is this, " Thou shalt not covet thy neighbour's

---

* I have translated the words " delectatio morosa," *a lingering delight*, rather than *a morose delight*, because the etymological root of the adjective is " mora," which signifies " delay." The meaning is, " an impure delight upon which the mind is permitted to dwell." The reader will please regard the words " lingering delight" as a technical term.

house ———— nor his man servant, nor his maid servant, nor his ox, nor his ass, nor anything that is thy neighbour's."

The plea by which this presumptuous interference with the order and arrangement of the ten commandments is justified is in fact this :——The ninth precept, " Thou shalt not covet thy neighbour's wife," is the counterpart of the sixth, " Thou shalt not commit adultery ;" and the tenth precept, " Thou shalt not covet thy neighbour's house, nor his man servant," &c., is the counterpart of the seventh, " Thou shalt not steal ;" the sins being in the one instance forbidden in *deed*, and in the other in *desire*,——hence the propriety of the division.

Now to this we object——

Because it is an ingenious invention of the Romish church, as is very evident from the simple fact that on the table of stone, the words " thou shalt not covet thy neighbour's wife" FOLLOW the command " thou shalt not covet thy neighbour's house," (see Exodus, xx. 17.) whereas in the Romish catechism the order is inverted. By what authority are the words, which Jehovah wrote with his own finger upon the second table of stone, hewn out of their place, and made to stand in an order different from that which he had assigned them ? Do not the connexion and the very unity of the precept require that they should be left just as he placed them ? The true reason of this violent defacing of the decalogue we have already stated. — *The second commandment is either entirely omitted or else mutilated in almost every catechism of the Romish church published throughout the world !* Now as we must have *ten* commandments in the decalogue, the last precept is hewn into two, in order that the complement may be furnished, and that the fraudulent omission of the precept relative to " graven images," and the " likenesses of any thing, whether in heaven above or in the earth beneath, or in the waters under the earth," may be covered up, and thus the faithful be enabled without conscientious scruple to bow down to all the idols, which the Babylonish woman sets up for them to worship.

This " dead fly" *makes our apothecary's box of ointment stink* again. Whilst we commend the practical duties, which are enforced in these sections, to our own observance and to the regard of our brethren of every persuasion, we must condemn the presumptuous attempt to amend the handiwork of Jehovah.

CHAPTER IX.

Treatise concerning Grace.

THIS treatise contains much that would very generally be considered as sound theology, not a little that involves vexed questions, together with some theories that are peculiar to the church of Rome.

Grace is defined to be " a supernatural divine benefit, given gratuitously to an intellectual creature in order to eternal happiness." Grace thus defined is distinguished from natural endowments, such as, intellect, will, free agency, life, or being, feeling, &c.

It is distinct also from spiritual gifts, such as the gift of tongues, discerning of spirits, healing diseases, prophecy, &c.—all which may be possessed by an individual and he still remain unacceptable to God, as Paul teaches, 1 Cor. xiii. " Though I speak with the tongues of men and of angels and have not charity, I am become as a sounding brass or a tinkling cymbal," &c.

Grace is divided into external and internal. External grace is that which affects a man only outwardly, as the preaching of the Gospel, &c. Internal grace affects a man inwardly.

Internal grace is divided into grace conferred gratuitously, and grace which places its subject in a gracious or acceptable state before God; and this latter species of internal grace is divided into habitual and actual grace.

" Habitual grace is divided into primary, which makes the unrighteous righteous, and secondary, which is an increase of grace and makes the righteous more righteous.

"Actual grace is divided into, 1. operating and co-operating ; 2. into preventing and subsequent ; 3. into exciting and assisting ; 4. into sufficient and efficacious ; 5. into grace of the understanding, and grace of the will ; 6. also into grace of the first state, or state of innocence, and into grace of the second state, or state of lapsed nature."

My readers would probably not wish to follow me through the elaborate treatises on these various subdivisions, and I shall therefore merely note a few of the most striking sections, after giving an outline of the general doctrine.

" Habitual grace is a supernatural gift imparted by God, which, permanently cleaving to the soul by way of habit, renders it formally acceptable to God ; and by this a man is said to become a partaker of the Divine nature."

" Actual grace is a certain divine, supernatural, transient assistance, exciting (us) to learn, will or do things conducing to salvation.

" Actual grace is absolutely necessary to the performance of every work conducing to salvation. This truth is opposed to Pelagius, who denied the necessity of grace, &c.

" It is proved by 2 Cor. iii. 5.—' We are not sufficient of ourselves to think any thing as of ourselves : but our sufficiency is of God.' And again, Philip. ii. 13.—' It is God, who worketh in you both to will and to do ;' and John, xv. 5., Christ says—' Without me ye can do nothing.'

" It is proved by reason : supernatural order exceeds natural power ; therefore for a work of supernatural order, powers exceeding natural strength are required, that is, proportionate, supernatural aid, or grace.

" Besides it is impossible for a human being to do a good natural work without the natural concurrence of God : therefore, a man cannot do a supernatural work without supernatural help, or actual grace ; as no act may exceed the proportion of its active principle.

" What works are called *salutary* ? (*i. e.* conducing to salvation.)

" Three kinds of works are to be noted here, viz., works *deserving of eternal life*, of which, hereafter; works only *morally good*, of which, in the following No., and *salutary* works.

" But those works are called *salutary*, which in some mode conduce to eternal happiness or justification; v. g., works of faith, of hope, and of charity, fasting, alms, &c., if they be ordained to a supernatural end; and these are things, which ought to proceed from actual grace, in order that they may be called *salutary*, &c.

" Whence observe, a sinner before habitual grace may on the whole possess actual graces, and thus be able v. g. to elicit acts of faith, of hope, of imperfect contrition, &c." (No. 4.)

We cannot lay too much stress upon the absolute necessity of the grace of God to qualify us for the performance of any action that shall be good in his sight. No man in a state of nature can be subject to the law of God, because the carnal mind is enmity against God, and this repugnance can be overcome only by grace, working in us effectually to will and to do the good pleasure of God. Grace effects this not by giving them new faculties but by rectifying those which we already possess. It changes the bias of the will, enlightens the understanding, quickens the conscience, and enlivens the affections, drawing them out after God and holiness. As for works which in any way conduce *meritoriously* to our acceptance, we do not believe that *grace* has anything to do with them.

" What works are called morally good?

" *Ans.* Those which are done according to the dictate of right reason through the natural powers only, with the general concurrence of God, without the aid of supernatural grace.

" These works are intermediate between such as conduce to salvation and sinful works: to say that they are such as conduce to salvation, is Pelagian; and to say that they are sinful, is Bajus' error;—of this kind are, to give alms from the natural affection of pity, to love parents and friends, to restore that which belongs to another, &c., merely on account of the natural honesty and rectitude of reason.

"Can a man do a good work without grace?

"1. It has been said in the preceding No. that without actual grace a man can not do a work conducing to his salvation.

"2. Man, even in this state of lapsed nature, may without grace do some works (which are) only morally good: the reason is, because man though he be injured through sin, is still not deprived of all natural good: besides, as these works are of a natural order, they do not exceed the powers of nature.

"3. This conclusion is contrary to Bajus, Jansenius, Quesnel, &c.

"4. Jansenius has followed Bajus, Bk. 3. concerning the state of lapsed nature; also Quesnel, whose 38th proposition, which was condemned, is this: ' Without the grace of him who makes free, the sinner is free only to commit evil.'

"*Obj. I.* John, xv. 5., Christ says: ' *Without me ye can do nothing ;*' therefore, not even a work morally good without grace.

"*Ans.* I deny the inference: for the sense is, that without the grace of Christ, we can not do any work conducing to salvation: for Christ is speaking of those works, through which we abide in him and bring forth fruit; that is, concerning meritorious works, not such as are only morally good.

"Other passages which are objected are understood generally, so that without Christ as God, that is, without the general concurrence of God, we can do nothing, not even works morally good," &c. (No. 5.)

The objections which follow are quotations from an œcumenical council and from Augustine: these we shall not notice.

A mind that is imbued with Scriptural truth will perceive the workings of the Mystery of iniquity in the doctrines stated in the above extracts. We are far removed from the Pelagian view, that works "only morally good" can conduce to salvation; and just as far do we pray ever to be kept from the Popish doctrine that any works are of themselves meritorious. But we believe that poor Bajus, who is condemned under fearful anathemas, had "the secret of the Lord" with him, notwithstanding the Pope's bull of excommunication. With him, we hold that the so called "morally good" works of carnal men are and must be sinful; and for these reasons :—

Because God looks at the heart, and "as a man thinketh in his heart so is he." God always takes into view the motive in which an action originates, when he judges of its character. Now, as the motives of the carnal mind are necessarily selfish, every action proceeding from them must be corrupt, on the principle that "a corrupt tree cannot bring forth good fruit." "Who can bring a clean thing out of an unclean? Not one." We admit that actions "morally good" in common estimation may be performed by the natural man, but that such actions are good in the sight of God, or that they are not sinful, we believe to be unscriptural. "The sacrifice of the wicked is an abomination to the Lord: but the prayer of the upright is his delight." Prov. xv. 8. The unregenerate man walks in his own counsel, and makes self his idol; now though he may do some actions which are apparently praiseworthy apart from the originating motive, he cannot in his unrenewed state do anything that is pleasing to God, because he seeks his own interest exclusively, and not the glory of God. Whether the Christian eats or drinks, or whatever he does, he does all to the glory of God. He walks by faith and not by sight. The unregenerate man walks by sight only; but "without faith it is impossible to please God." Prayer according to Romish doctrine is a meritorious work, and the mere utterance of certain petitions to the Virgin Mary, &c., is made to hide a multitude of sins; but miserably are those poor creatures deceived, who imagine that God hears with complacency the "vain repetitions," which are the offspring either of superstition or slavish fear. So far from purchasing salvation in any measure or degree, they are an abomination in the sight of God.

Whilst we maintain that no man can perform an action that is really "morally good" without the aid of divine grace, and whilst we contend that every thing which is done by the unregenerate man is tainted with *sin*, and is therefore *sinful*, we must not be understood as saying, nor can we suffer the inference to be drawn from our premises, that it is wrong for an unconverted man to clothe the naked, feed the hungry, &c. &c., or perform any other so called "morally good" action. Far from it. But it is wrong for him to do these things from a selfish motive; and so long as the actuating principle is corrupt, he cannot please God by any thing that he does, however specious. Yet if all men will not be religious, would to God that they would all be moral!

I should be very loth to affirm, that the temperance movement among Romanists in Ireland and in this country has done no good. I bless God for every drunkard that has been reclaimed through its agency, and I rejoice that order and sobriety have, to so wide an extent, superseded confusion and intemperance. But as I believe that "a corrupt tree cannot bring forth good fruit," I am confirmed in my suspicion that the glory of God has not been the motive in which this moral reformation has originated. Hence, until the true motive be revealed, I cannot call it absolutely good.

I do not wish to *appear* uncharitable, much less *to be* such, but I shall be most agreeably disappointed if a very short time will not suffice to convince many who differ from me now, that the Romish temperance movement is neither more nor less than a political manoeuvre! A temperance medal will answer quite as good a purpose as a *red cross* on the shoulder, or any other mark by which the faithful have been designated in years gone by.

As to the condemned proposition of Quesnel, that "without the grace of him who makes free, the sinner is free only to commit sin," there is a sense in which I believe it can be successfully maintained. We all agree that the sinner is

5

the slave of sin, — his understanding, his conscience, and, above all, his *will*, are under the bondage of Satan ; how, then, can he be said strictly to be *free* ? If he is led captive by the devil at his will, he is to all intents and purposes despoiled of his liberty, and free only to commit sin : this does not affect his accountability, because he has voluntarily chosen the yoke of Satan ; he hugs his chains, and prefers the pleasures of sin and the service of the devil to the glorious liberty of the children of God. And until the grace of the Son, who maketh free indeed, changes the bent of his will, it is *morally* impossible that his spiritual fetters should be broken, and that he should follow holiness, without which no man can see the Lord. We disown the abstract proposition that any man is under any other necessity of sinning than that which his own imperious lusts and sinful passions impose upon him ; and this necessity, so far from being an excuse, is the very thing which gives the killing emphasis to his guilt.

The necessity of grace in order to love God, to know the truth and to fulfil the law, is taught in the sixth and seventh sections. Man may learn natural truths without grace ; he may arrive at the knowledge of the existence of God by his natural powers alone ; thus Paul says the Gentile philosophers are inexcusable, " because that when they knew God, they glorified him not as God."

" Yet man in this state cannot, without the special aid of grace, understand all natural truths collectively taken on account of the weakness of his understanding and various other hindrances.

" Man cannot understand by true and sufficient assent the supernatural truths of faith, without supernatural grace : the reason is, because these truths exceed the natural power of the human understanding ; therefore there is need of aid exceeding nature in order to understand them by sufficient assent ; and hence the apostle says, 1 Cor. xii. 3—' No one can say that Jesus is Lord, except by the Holy Ghost.' "

The next paragraph justly affirms that any one may learn these supernatural truths, and afford a mere human assent of *opinion*, without grace, such as heretics bestow upon certain arguments accommodated to human understanding.

It is an article of faith that no man can obey any supernatural precept without grace. (No. 7.)   Also, that the commands of God are possible.

" It has before been said, that certain precepts cannot be observed by the powers of nature alone, which yet may be fulfilled through grace ; and thus it must simply be said that no precepts of God are impossible to be observed." (No. 8.)

Grace is necessary to enable us to recover from sins, and to overcome temptations ; but man in his lapsed state may overcome light temptations without grace, by the mere exercise of his will.   His inability to overcome temptations of long standing, and then only by effort continued through a long period, &c., is to be ascribed not to any want of free will, but to its instability and weakness, and the difficulty of these things ; and hence the inability is not physical, but moral. (No. 9.)

Grace is necessary to enable us to avoid mortal sins.   A sinner may escape *single* but not *all* mortal sins in a long time.   " The sin which is not quickly blotted out by penance, by its own weight draws down to another."

" Every one who sins mortally, is bound under pain of mortal sin to confess ;"   " because, otherwise, he exposes himself to the danger of falling into other mortal sins, &c."

" But observe with Sylvius, that the danger is not so pressing with respect to a penitent sinner, although he may prepare himself for confession through one or two weeks, because he has in a certain way been already converted to God in so far as his desire is concerned."

A just man may avoid all and every mortal sin, even during the longest period, &c. (No. 10.)

" A man in a state of lapsed nature may avoid single venial sins by the ordinary assistance of grace ; but yet, though he be a righteous man, he cannot avoid all for any considerable time, except by special privilege." (No. 11.)

" The principal efficient cause, as well of *actual* as *habitual* grace, is God alone.

" The secondary or instrumental efficient cause, are the human nature of Christ, and the sacraments of the church.

" The ministerial cause are angels and men : angels by supplying directions by which we may attain to grace; but men not only by praying and instructing, but also by administering the sacraments.

" The final cause is the glory of God and Christ, and our salvation.

" The meritorious cause is Christ, or the merits of Christ, that is in the state of fallen nature : for in this state no grace is given, except on account of the merits of Christ's passion ; so that we neither have nor perform any thing conducing to our salvation, which does not proceed from the grace given by the merits of Christ.

" The prayers and merits of holy men may be a *meritorious* cause, but subordinate to the merits of Christ, because they are united to his : in this way a just man, by works done through grace, may worthily merit for himself an increase of grace, and properly (merit) primary grace for another.

" The grace of angels, and of the first man in a state of innocence, does not proceed from the merits of Christ ; for Christ died only for the fallen human race." (No. 13.)

To my mind there seems to be a palpable contradiction in the assertion, that the prayers and works of holy men may worthily merit *grace.* What is grace but *undeserved favour?* And how can this be merited? Surely there never was a bolder attempt to mar the grace of God, and make it of none effect, than this device of Satan to persuade men that they can by their prayers and works merit that, which from its very nature can be imparted only as *a free gift.* As for the general doctrine of merit, we shall have occasion to compare that with " the law and the testimony" in a subsequent chapter, and we therefore dismiss it for the present.

CHAPTER X.

Treatise concerning Justification.

JUSTIFICATION is defined to be " A translation from a state of sin to a state of habitual grace and adoption of the sons of God through Jesus Christ our Saviour.

" This definition is derived from the Epist. to the Coloss. i. 13, ' Who hath delivered us from the power of darkness, and translated us into the kingdom of his dear Son.' Also, Council of Trent, sess. 6, ch. 4, where it says, that justification is a translation from that state in which man is born the son of the first Adam, into the state of the grace and adoption of the sons of God. The Council of Trent treats of the primary justification by which any one constituted in original sin, is justified."

The increase of sanctifying grace is wont also to be called justification, according to that passage of Rev. xxii. 11 — " He that is righteous, let him be righteous still." But justification thus taken is called secondary in relation to the former.

" The word righteous is not here taken for a particular cardinal virtue, but for a combination of virtues : and hence it may be defined as being the right disposition of the whole man towards God, his neighbour, and himself.

" What are the principal errors of our heretics in this matter?

" *Ans.* 1. They teach that in justification sins are not truly remitted, but only covered by the justice of Christ, as Jacob was covered with the garment of Esau.

" 2. That justification is not effected through habitual grace dwelling in the soul, but through the alone righteousness of Christ imputed to us.

" 3. That in order to righteousness no other disposition than faith alone is required.

" S. Thomas refuted these errors long before they arose, God so disposing (him)." (No. 26.)

" Prove that in justification sins are truly remitted and blotted out.

" *Ans.* 1. It is proved, first from Ps. l. 2, ' Blot out mine
5 *

iniquity;" Eph. i. 14, 'That we should be holy and without blame before him.' Also, 1 John i. 7, 'The blood of Jesus Christ cleanseth us from all sin.'

"2. It is proved by reason: because, otherwise, it would follow that a man was righteous and unrighteous at the same time: because it is supposed that he is justified, and that the pollution of sin remains besides.

"3. Finally, this was settled by the Council of Trent, sess. 5, can. 5—'If any one denies that the guilt of original sin is remitted through the grace of Jesus Christ our Lord, which is conferred in baptism; or even asserts that that is not altogether removed, which has the true and proper *nature* of sin; but says that it is only erased or not imputed; let him be accursed.' "

"*Obj. I.* It is said, Ps. 321, 'Blessed are they whose transgressions are forgiven, and whose sins are covered;' and v. 2, 'Blessed is the man to whom the Lord does not impute sin:' therefore sins in justification are not blotted out, but are only covered, and are not imputed.

"*Ans.* I deny the inference; for, sins to be covered before God is the same as to be blotted out and destroyed: because 'all things are naked and open to his eyes,' Heb. iv. 13; therefore in order that our sins may be covered before God, it is necessary that they in no manner exist.

"In the second verse, he is called blessed, who has committed nothing which could be imputed to himself as sin: or if the Psalmist treats of him who has sinned, God is then said not to impute sin by remitting it.

"*Obj. II.* Rom. xiii. 14, it is said, 'Put ye on the Lord Jesus Christ;' therefore, &c.

"*Ans.* I deny the inference: for *to put on* is here spoken of, because justification is conferred outwardly through the application of the Holy Spirit by way of ornament to the soul; and this is not effected by a mere external imputation, but by an internal change, by casting away the works of darkness, putting off the old man, &c.

"When is God said to remit mortal sin?

"*Ans.* When he wipes off and blots out the stain of this sin from the mind of the person who has sinned.

"Through what is the stain of mortal sin blotted out?

" *Ans.* Through sanctifying grace, which is imparted by God.

"Can mortal sin be consistent at the same time in the same subject with sanctifying grace? Also, can mortal sin be remitted without the application of sanctifying grace?

"Some suppose that this may be done by the absolute power of God: but it is useless to ask this; because it is certain, according to the present divine order, that sanctifying grace is not consistent with mortal sin, neither can this be remitted without the application of that grace. This is plain from the condemnation of the 31st, 32d, 33d and 71st of the propositions of Bajus. (No. 27.)

"*Imputed Righteousness is repugnant to Holy Scripture.*"

"Prove against the heretics, that justification is formally effected through the application of habitual grace dwelling in the soul; but not through the righteousness of Christ outwardly imputed to us.

"1. *Ans.* It is proved from Rom. v. 5, 'The love of God is shed abroad in our hearts by the Holy Ghost, who is given to us;' concerning which St. Aug. Bk. concerning the Spirit and the Letter, chap. 23, says: 'The love of God is said to be shed abroad in our hearts, not that (love) by which he himself loves us, but (that) by which he makes us lovers of himself; just as that was called the righteousness of God, by the gift of which we are rendered righteous.'

"Hence the Coun. of Trent, sess. 6. can. 11. decreed against the heretics, 'If any one shall say that men are justified either by the mere imputation of the righteousness of Christ, or by the sole remission of sins, that grace and love being excluded which is shed abroad in their hearts by the Holy Spirit and remaining in them; or also (who shall say) that the grace by which we are justified is only the favour of God, let him be accursed.'

"*Obj. I.* It is said 1 Cor. i. 30——Christ, 'who is made to us of God wisdom, and righteousness, and sanctification, and redemption;' therefore we are formally declared righteous through the righteousness of Christ.

"*Ans.* I deny the inference: because these and similar (passages) where Christ is called our peace, life, salvation, resurrection, &c., ought to be received in a causal not a

formal sense : for it is only meant, that Christ is the meritorious cause of our justification, &c.   This is plain, because
when Christ is said to be our wisdom, it is evident that man
is not formally wise with the wisdom of Christ, but with
the wisdom peculiar to himself.

"Conclude that to the justification of every sinner these
two things are required, 1., the application of divine grace,
and 2. the remission of all mortal sins : which is effected in
little children through Baptism, without any previous disposition : not so in adults." (No. 28.)

"What is required for the justification of a sinner?

"*Ans.* For infants before the use of reason, and for
those who have been idiots perpetually, no disposition is required for justification, as they are justified certainly through
the Baptism of water, or of blood.

"For the justification of an adult through Baptism, the
Council of Trent, Sess. 6. chap. 6. requires a disposition
through seven degrees or impulses of the soul.

"The first is the impulse of divine grace, by which the
sinner is excited and assisted, according to Jer. xxxi. 19.,
'after thou didst convert me, I DID PENANCE.'

"The second is an act of faith, 'because he that cometh
to God must believe.' Heb. xi. 6.

"The third is an impulse of fear, useful certainly, yet
not necessary, by which the sinner understanding through
faith that he is guilty of eternal damnation, endeavours to
put away his sins ; according to that passage Eccle. i. 27.
'The fear of the Lord driveth out sin.'

"The fourth : because also through faith, the sinner
considers the sovereign mercy of God, and the infinite merits
of Christ, hence he is elevated into hope, trusting that God
will be propitious to him ; according to that passage, Matt.
ix. 2., 'Be of good heart : thy sins are forgiven thee.'

"The fifth : after hope follows the incipient love of
God, as the fountain of all righteousness ; for when the sinner considers the distinguished goodness of God, that he is
willing to forgive sins even to the unworthy, he begins to
love God before all things (else) ; this act is denoted, Joel ii.
12.—'Be converted to me with all your heart.'

"The sixth act is hatred and detestation of sin, or
an act of contrition ; for he who loves God as the fountain

of all righteousness, cannot but detest sin : this act is expressed, Acts ii. 38.—'Do PENANCE.'

"The seventh is the purpose of receiving the sacrament, of beginning a new life, and keeping the divine commandments, according to that passage of Ezek. xviii. 31.—' Make to yourselves a new heart and a new spirit," &c., &c. (No. 29.)

"Concerning the justifying and special Faith of Heretics."

" What does faith do towards justification ?

" I. I answer with Council of Trent, Sess. 6. can. 8.—' Faith is the beginning of man's salvation, the foundation and root of all justification ; without which it is impossible to please God.'

" Does faith alone justify ?

" II. *Ans.* Thus Simon Magus asserted, against whom St. James says, chap. ii. 24.—' By works a man is justified, and not by faith only.'

" The negative answer is proved also by 1 Cor. xiii. 2.— ' If I should have all faith—but have not charity, I am nothing ;' and from 1 John, iii. 14.—'He that loveth not abideth in death.' Hence, the Council of Trent decreed, Sess. 6. can. 9.—' If any one shall say, that a wicked man is justified by faith alone—let him be accursed.'

" The Lutherans and Calvinists revived this heresy under another explanation, distinguishing a threefold faith : —

" III. 1. Historical faith, by which we believe all those things to be true which are contained in the Holy Scriptures.

" 2. The faith of miracles, by which miracles were performed : through which we implicitly believe, that there is nothing which cannot be done by God.

" 3. The third they call the faith *of promises*, by which the divine promises concerning salvation and the remission of sins are believed. This they subdivide into *general*, by which is believed that God has promised to all believers, salvation and the remission of sins ; and into *special*, by which every man in particular believes, or rather confidently trusts, that his sins have been remitted for the sake of the merits of Christ.

" IV. The heretics affirm that this special faith so justifies, that every one who believes, or confidently trusts that he is absolved from his sins, and that the righteousness of Christ is imputed to him, is by that very act (eo ipso) righteous.

"V. This empty and fictitious faith the Council of Trent condemned, Sess. 6. chap. 9. and can. 12, 13, and 14.

"VI. It is refuted also by the Holy Scripture, in which this rash faith is nowhere found; but that faith by which we believe that those things are true which have been divinely revealed, and to which works are joined—thus, Gal. v. 6, it is said—'Faith which works by love—avails.'

"*Obj. I.* It is said, Acts xiii. 39.—'In him every one who believes is justified.' Therefore, &c.—

"*Ans.* There the question is not concerning special faith, but concerning faith in Christ; but justification is ascribed to faith, not as if it were alone sufficient, but because it is necessary, and (is) the foundation of justification.

"VII. Observe, generally, that the Holy Scriptures attribute one and the same thing sometimes to one cause as the only one, sometimes to another; and this mode of speaking is frequent. Thus, it is said, Luke xi. 41.—'Give alms, and behold all things are clean unto you.' Rom. viii. 24.—'We are saved by hope;' and 1 John, iv. 7.—'Every one who loves is born of God.' In which places, although nothing is said about faith, yet it is still certain that that disposition is still necessarily required for the remission of sins: and hence you may rightly understand similar modes of speech under this condition. If other requisites are present; or in a negative sense: if faith is not present, if alms are not given, if hope is not present, justification cannot be effected.

"*Obj. II.* The apostle says, Rom. iii. 28.—'We account a man to be justified by faith without the works of the law.' Therefore, &c.—

"*Ans.* I deny the inference: because only legal works of the old law are excluded, and works done by the powers of nature alone; not works of charity, penance, &c. Therefore, the opposition is made not of faith against the works of the new law, as heretics pretend, but of the new law against the old law, and the law of nature.—(No. 30.)

"*Concerning assurance of the state of grace and faith.*"

"Can a man certainly know that he has sanctifying grace?

" I. *Ans.* Without special revelation, no one can know with the assurance of faith that he has sanctifying grace. This was settled in Council of Trent, sess. 6. ch. 9, against our heretics, who pretend that all can and ought with divine faith to believe that they are righteous ; and that otherwise, they are neither righteous nor believers.

II. Yet by special revelation a man can know certainly that he is in (a state of) grace. Thus, the Divine Virgin knew this when it was said to her by the angel—' Hail ! full of grace.' The paralytic, Matt. ix. 2.—' Be of good heart, Son, thy sins are forgiven thee ;' and the woman who was a sinner, Luke vii. 47.—' Many sins are forgiven her because she loved much ;' knew that their sins were remitted to them. Concerning St. Paul, it is disputed whether his justification and predestination were revealed to him.

" A man cannot even know from special revelation, with absolute moral certainty, which excludes all fear, that he is in sanctifying grace : because we cannot know any thing certainly unless it is evident, or rests upon infallible authority—but there is room for neither in this case.

" The Holy Scripture frequently asserts this very thing : as Eccles. ix. 1.—' Man knoweth not whether he be worthy of love or hatred.' 1 Cor. iv. 4. — 'I am not conscious to myself of anything ; yet in this I am not justified;' and Phil. ii. 12. — ' Work your salvation with fear and trembling.'

"*Obj. I.* Rom. viii. 16, it is said : 'The Spirit himself giveth testimony with our spirit, that we are the sons of God ;' therefore, we can most certainly know that we are in grace.

"*Ans. I.* With St. Chrysostom I deny the inference : because that testimony is not concerning a particular person, but concerning the assembly of the faithful, or concerning the church : that the church is doubtless the assembly of the sons of God, but not that this or that person is the son of God through love.

" 2. The Holy Spirit gives a certain testimony to every righteous man that he is the son of God, which testimony in itself is most sure, but is not known for sure by the righteous man : because it is perceived only by signs, which make only a probable conjecture. Hence, we are forbidden to manifest too much confidence : for, Eccles. viii. 14, it is said,—' There are wicked men, who are as secure as though they had the deeds of the just.'

"*Obj. II.* It is said, 1 John, iii. 14. —' We know that we have passed from death to life,' &c.—

"*Ans.* I deny the inference ; for this sentence is manifestly general, signifying that they had been translated from death to life who love the brethren ; but John trusted that himself and others were of that number.

" IV. Yet authors generally maintain, that a man may have some moral or conjectural assurance of his own acceptance ; which, though it may not exclude all fear, yet takes away the discomposure and anxiety of mind, according to that, 1 John, iii. 21.—' If our heart do not reprehend us, we have confidence toward God.'

" May a man be certain that he has faith ?

" V. *Ans.* Sylvius thinks that a believing man can be altogether sure that he believes or assents to the things revealed by God : because the church sometimes enjoins that the faithful swear that they believe the mysteries of faith. Besides, faith is in the understanding ; but the understanding can be sure of its own assent, as a faculty may perceive and reflect beyond itself. Add to this, that faith has a certain and infallible external rule, viz. : the creed of the church.

" Yet Herincx and others maintain, that a believer can have no more than a moral certainty ; because, although the understanding may certainly know that it firmly believes: yet it cannot so certainly know whether it believes with supernatural and divine faith ; because *supernatural* does not fall under notice. The creed of the church renders, indeed, believers certain concerning the object which they believe, namely, that it has been revealed by God ; but it does not render them certain concerning the act itself of believing whether it be truly supernatural ; and hence it may be properly said, that the oath which the church sometimes requires, is not concerning the *supernaturality*, but only concerning the act of faith in itself.

" Whether any one may be sure that he has the habit of faith or hope, is not clear as yet. That no one can be sure of his own predestination or election to glory, we have said in the treatise concerning God."

I have given the views of the Romish theologian at length, because the doctrine which is involved in this section has justly been called "doctrina stantis aut cadentis Ecclesiæ." It is in fact the key-stone in the noble arch of divine revelation: take away from any theological system the great truth *that we are justified freely through faith only for the sake of Christ's merits,* and the whole fabric tumbles at once into a chaotic heap of rubbish! Men may prop up the ruins by all the scholastic lore that has been accumulating for ages, and they may seek to cement them by the " unanimous consent of the Fathers," but this *daubing with untempered mortar* will not keep one stone upon another, when the salvation of a single soul is made to rest upon this foundation. " Other foundation can no man lay than that is laid, which is Christ Jesus." This corner stone is broad enough and deep enough to sustain the hope of every sinner, even though all men should build upon *it* alone. We want not the *subordinate merits* of the Saints— for even the holiest of men always have been saved and ever will be saved by *grace.* And if they confessed that they were sinners, justly condemned and ruined, if they fled for refuge to Christ, and plunged into the fountain opened for sin and uncleanness, acknowledging that their righteousnesses were filthy rags, and that the blood of Christ alone cleanseth from all sin, how can their merits assist the sinner ? If Naaman had told the prophet that he would consent to wash in Jordan *first,* on condition that he might complete his ablutions in Abama and Pharpar, think you that Elijah would have said, " Go and be clean ?" No. Because the Lord God was putting the faith of the proud Syrian to the test, whether he would prefer the river of Israel to all the streams of Damascus. And now that he has " opened a fountain in the House of David," shall sinners wash in that *first,* and then go and bathe in the merits of the Saints ? What are the merits of God's Saints ? When they came to:

6

Christ, before ever they could wash and be clean, did they not all with one mouth confess that *death and hell* were their only merits? From these *merits* they prayed to be delivered—and if the sinner will wash in *them*, what is this, but to cast himself into the waves of eternal death, and bathe his soul in the burning lake?

Is not the righteousness of Christ, "the white raiment" in which the saints are clothed? But how did they get this shining apparel? Was it not by confessing with shame, "All our righteousnesses are as filthy rags," and then looking to the finished righteousness of the Lamb of God? And shall the sinner go to Christ *first*, and buy of him without money and without price, the white raiment offered in the Gospel, and then clothe himself in the *merits* of the saints, those "filthy rags," which with tears of shame they have cast off for ever? Satan well knows that some minds would be startled were he boldly to suggest that the blood of Christ is utterly inefficacious for the sinner's redemption, and therefore he craftily seeks to make that blood of none effect, by adding to it, the *merits of the saints.*

Among the principal errors of the "heretics," the first which is mentioned is, that "they teach that in justification, sins are not truly remitted, but only covered by the justice of Christ, as Jacob was covered with the garment of Esau."

In the Word of God, the phrases "transgressions are forgiven," and "sins are covered," are used as parallel and equivalent terms, and they are so used by the Reformed churches generally. We all teach the same thing in matters essential to salvation; and in relation to the sinner's justification before God, with united voice Protestant christendom proclaims in the words which the Holy Ghost teaches, "Being justified by faith we have peace with God through our Lord Jesus Christ." (Rom. v. 1.)

We do truly teach "that justification is not effected through habitual grace dwelling in the soul, but through the alone righteousness of Christ imputed to us ;" whilst we also declare "By grace are ye saved through faith, and that not of yourselves, it is the gift of God. *Not of works,* lest any man should boast." (Eph. ii. 8, 9.) The third error, which is imputed to us "heretics," is, "that in order to righteousness no other disposition than faith alone is required." We should like to see the Protestant Confession of Faith in which these words occur precisely as they are here presented. Protestants are not wont to represent saving faith as existing alone in the heart of a regenerate man. They would tell all who ask them that the faith which links them to the Saviour "works by love," and that "love is the fulfilling of the law." We are no advocates of Antinomianism. We do not believe that the faith, which consists in a mere speculative assent to the doctrines of the gospel, will unite its possessor to the Lord Jesus Christ. We have no confidence in the religion which consists in cold, inert opinions, and we seek no fellowship with any who deny that "faith without works is dead !" But we do exclude our own works and the works of all the saints in heaven and on earth, from all share in our justification before God. We trust alone to the merits of that Saviour, "whom God has set forth to be a propitiation through faith in his blood ;" and to our brethren, who boast of the merit of their saints and of their own good works, we say, "God forbid that we should glory save in the cross of Christ, by whom the world is crucified unto us, and we unto the world !"

But the Council of Trent has settled the matter. We heed the decisions and the anathemas of the doctors and bishops of that far-famed council just as much as the fluttering of an army of bats ! They could not endure the light, but with all their ravings and their curses they were not able to put out the candle of the Lord ! It burned in spite of them, and it will go on kindling into the blaze of the noonday sun, until "the righteousness which is through faith in Christ," "shall

go forth as brightness, and the salvation thereof as a lamp
that burneth." It will burn and shine until the Gentiles shall
hasten to its light, and send back the shout of the redeemed
in glory, "unto him that loved us, and washed us from our
sins in his own blood, and hath made us kings and priests
unto God and his Father; to him be glory and dominion for
ever and ever. Amen!"

But "imputed righteousness is repugnant to Holy Scripture." Where is the proof? "It is proved from Rom. v. 5,
'The love of God is shed abroad in our hearts by the Holy
Ghost, who is given to us.'" A precious text, truly; but
how does this prove that *imputed righteousness* is repugnant
to Holy Scripture? Read St. Augustine's Comment on this
text. But St. Augustine's Comment is not *Holy Scripture*.
Give us chapter and verse, if you please, to sustain the truth
of the caption to this 28th section, "IMPUTED RIGHTEOUS-
NESS IS REPUGNANT TO HOLY SCRIPTURE." Show us the
passage which says, in so many words, or which shuts us
up to the inference, that "the righteousness of Christ is not
imputed to the believer." That "the love of God is shed
abroad in the hearts of the children of God by the Holy
Ghost given to them," we believe; but this surely does not
affect the doctrine of "imputed righteousness."

Yes, but the Council of Trent has decreed (sess. 6, can.
21) against the heretics, "If any one shall say that men are
justified either by the mere imputation of the righteousness
of Christ, &c., let him be accursed."

But, we ask for *Scripture*, not for *anathemas*. And when
we come on such an errand to Holy Mother, and beg for
bread, she ought not to give us a *stone!* If we are "heretics," yet she claims to be the mother of us all, and though
undutiful children, yet we are children still; and now if Holy
Mother will show us the Scripture, which plainly and without possibility of misapprehension teaches *that the doctrine
of imputed righteousness is false*, we will do penance on

the spot, and seek reconciliation without delay ! Do give us Scripture, according to promise.

Well then, " the *heretics* object that this Scripture ' Christ, who is made to us of God, wisdom, and righteousness, and sanctification, and redemption," teaches that we are formally declared righteous through the righteousness of Christ. Now we deny that the *heretics*—

But where is the passage to prove that " *Imputed righteousness is repugnant to Holy Scripture?*" We do not ask you to cavil at the proof texts, which *we* advance to sustain our side of the question, but to produce such as will unequivocally sustain *your* position.

" Conclude that to the justification of every sinner these two things are required : 1st. The application of divine grace, and 2d. The remission of all mortal sins," &c.

But where is the SCRIPTURE ?

Holy Mother is silent. She gives us no texts to prove that " Imputed righteousness is contrary to Holy Scripture." She gives us neither *bread*, nor a *fish*, nor an *egg*, but offers us *serpents*, and *scorpions*, and *stones*, in their place. We cannot digest such food.

But let us endeavour to overcome evil with good ; and since no Scripture has been produced to disprove the doctrine of imputation, let us see if the word of God will not furnish us with this " armour of righteousness on the right-hand and on the left." And first, we will state what we hold to be the Bible doctrine on this subject.

We believe that a man becomes righteous before God only by a true faith in Jesus Christ. His conscience may tell him that he has grievously transgressed, and that he is therefore justly condemned ; he may know and feel that he has always come short of the glory of God, and that the corruptions of his heart are daily causing him to sin ; and yet he is righteous before God, because without any merit of his own, but only of undeserved grace, the perfect satisfaction, righteousness,

6 *

and holiness of Christ, are granted and imputed to him; so
that the believer stands before God as though he had never
known or committed sin; and as though he had himself fully
accomplished all the obedience, which Christ his great Surety
and Substitute has accomplished for him.   His standing is
not in himself, but in Christ.   He is accepted in the Beloved.
There is nothing in the act of faith itself which worthily
merits the divine favour; but the sinner is said to be justified
by faith, because it is through faith alone that the satisfaction, righteousness, and holiness of Christ, can be received
and applied by the believer.

"But now the righteousness of God without the law is
manifested.   Even the righteousness of God, which is by
faith of Jesus Christ unto all and upon all them that believe,
&c."   Rom. iii. 21, 22, &c.

"Knowing that a man is not justified by the works of the
law, but by the faith of Jesus Christ, even we have believed
in Jesus Christ, that we might be justified by the faith of
Christ, and not by the works of the law, for by the works
of the law shall no flesh be justified."   Gal. ii. 16.   See also
Eph. ii. 8, 9; Titus iii. 5.

"If Abraham were justified by works, he hath whereof to
glory, but not before God.   For what saith the Scripture?
Abraham believed God, and it was counted to him for righteousness.   Now to him that worketh is the reward reckoned
not of grace, but of debt.   But to him that worketh not, but
believeth on him that justifieth the ungodly, his faith is counted for righteousness."   Rom. iv. 2—6.   See also 2 Cor. v. 19.
"For he hath made him to be sin for us, who knew no sin
that we might be made the righteousness of God in him."
(2 Cor. v. 21.)

These and similar texts of Scripture we humbly commend
to the special attention of those, who thunder their anathemas upon all abettors of the doctrine of justification through
the imputed righteousness of Christ.

The Protestant will be surprised to learn that the prophet Jeremiah " *did penance*," but if he will turn to the *Doway* Bible, Jer. xxxi. 19., he will find it is even so. The prophet there gives it as part of his experience, " When thou didst convert me, I DID PENANCE." Learn hence the antiquity of this *sacrament*.

So too, Peter on the day of Pentecost answers the convicted Jews, who asked " what must we do?" " Do PENANCE!" To be sure—what else could they do? The penance, which Peter imposed on them, is, however, not recorded. It is to be regretted that Jeremiah does not mention either, in what his penance consisted. That would have settled the matter.

But we are farther reminded that the Apostle James tells us, " By works a man is justified and not by faith." The apparent discrepancy between the epistles of Paul and James will vanish at once, when the circumstances under which the latter apostle wrote are taken into consideration. Already in his day, the leaven of Antinomianism was at work. Even then there were men wicked enough to teach that we are delivered by the Gospel from all obedience to the Moral Law. They who embraced this error of course professed that their faith was sufficient for justification, though it produced no change in the moral character and no reformation in their daily practice. Paul insists upon the necessity of good works being the fruit and evidence of faith, just as strongly as James. Paul commends the " faith that works by love," and says expressly, " With the heart man believeth unto righteousness." And a greater than Paul had taught, " By their fruits ye shall know them." Now a faith that does not produce the great moral results required by the Gospel, cannot be the faith of Christians. Hence the apostle says—" Thou believest that there is one God; thou doest well; the devils also believe and tremble." They are the subjects of speculative belief, but their faith not working by love, is after all but the faith of devils, though they do tremble. He then adds, "But wilt thou know, O vain man! (or hypocrite) that faith without works is dead." Now surely it will not be contended that the faith of the hypocrite is the faith of the Gospel; but it is of this faith that James speaks.

The objection which is made to the distinction between historical faith, the faith of miracles, and the faith of promises, can scarcely be sustained. If the distinction is rejected, and we assume that there is only one kind of faith, then the devils who believe, have Gospel faith!

But it is against "special faith" or "assurance" that the venom of our Theologian is particularly directed. According to the doctrine of the Romish church no man can be sure of his acceptance, except by special revelation—and even then he cannot know it "with absolute moral certainty, which excludes all fear." Now, we know that some good men have frequently not been sufficiently discriminating in relation to this doctrine. We do not believe that assurance is necessary to salvation. It is the privilege, however, of every Christian to know that he has passed from death to life. "Hereby we know that we have passed from death to life, because we love the brethren." To this Scripture objection is made, and the reader may perhaps see more force in Peter Dens' reasoning than I can discern.

St. John says, "Hereby we know that he abideth in us, by the spirit which he hath given us." 1 John, iii. 34. Indeed, it seems as though one of the principal objects of this apostle's epistles is to furnish the Christian with suggestions and texts by which he may try and know his true character.

But the strangest assertion of all is, that "it is disputed concerning PAUL, whether his justification and predestination were revealed to him." How then could Paul say, "I am now ready to be offered up, and the time of my departure is at hand, &c. Henceforth there is laid up for me a crown of righteousness, which the Lord, the righteous judge, shall give unto me on that day, and not unto me only, but unto all them also that love his appearing." 2 Tim. iv. 6, 8. And again, " I know in whom I have believed, and I am persuaded that he is able to keep that which I have committed unto him against that day." 2 Tim. i. 12. And not to multiply quotations or extend these remarks, already too lengthy, any farther, how could Paul without strong assurance of his acceptance, exclaim in that transport of holy boldness, " Who is he that condemneth ? It is Christ that died, yea, rather, that is risen again, who is even at the right hand of God, who also maketh intercession for us. Who shall separate us from the love of Christ ? shall tribulation, or distress, or persecution, or famine, or nakedness, or peril, or sword ? As it is written, For thy sake we are killed all the day long ; we are accounted as sheep for the slaughter. Nay, in all these things we are more than conquerors through him that loved us. For I am persuaded that neither death, nor life, nor angels, nor principalities, nor powers, nor things present, nor things to come, nor height, nor depth, nor any other creature, shall be able to separate us from the love of God, which is in Christ Jesus our Lord."—Rom. viii. 34—39.

Most sincerely do we wish that our brethren would search the Scriptures, and see for themselves whether the Christian is obliged to grope his way by the feeble glimmering of " probable conjecture," or whether his " path" is not as the shining light, which shineth more and more unto the perfect day ? " For we have not received the spirit of bondage again to fear, but the spirit of adoption, whereby we cry, Abba, Father."—Rom. viii. 15.

CHAPTER XI.

[No. 35.]

Treatise concerning Merit.[*]

" WHAT is merit, the second effect of grace?

" *Ans.* It is a good work, worthy of reward or recompense.

" This definition explains merit taken in the concrete for a meritorious action; for merit in the abstract denotes the worth of the work itself, by the power of which it is adapted to induce (any one) to reward.

" How is merit divided?

" *Ans.* Into merit of fitness and merit of worthiness.—A work is called a merit of fitness to which some reward or recompense is ascribed from gratuitous liberality and propriety; a merit of worthiness is a work to which a reward or payment is due from justice. Thus, the actions of a just man working by grace, merit worthily grace and glory : but the supernatural acts of a penitent sinner, merit ulterior graces from propriety.

" Can a man merit any thing?

" Observe, the question is not concerning merit, strictly so called, which is of such a nature, in itself, and from the dignity of the person meriting, that a reward is due to him according to the perfect rigour of justice, for this pertains to Christ alone : but reference is had to merit less strictly taken, and simply to such.

" It is an article of faith, contrary to our heretics, that a person by grace can truly and properly merit.

" This is proved from Holy Scripture. Matt. v. 12, it is said, 'your reward is very great in heaven;' moreover, 2 Tim. iv. 8. 'There is laid up for me a crown of justice, which the Lord, the just judge, will render to me at that day;' also, Heb. vi. 10. 'For God is not unjust that he should forget your work.' But reward corresponds to

---

[*] The reader will please take notice that I quote from the *Douay* Bible, when Peter Dens refers to the Scriptures, and from the *Holy* Bible in my own remarks.

merit; and that which is given by God the just judge, also that which is given from justice is given for the sake of merit : therefore, &c.

" From these passages it is plain that eternal life also may fall under merit, and even on the ground of worthiness : for merit of fitness is not merit of the real kind.

" These points have been settled, Council of Trent, Sep. 6. ch. 16, canon 32. ' If any one shall say, that the good works of a justified man do not truly merit an increase of grace, eternal life, and the attainment of eternal life itself, on condition, however, that he shall die in a state of grace, and even an increase of glory, let him be accursed.'

" *Obj. I.* Rom. viii. 18, it is said, ' The sufferings of this present time are not worthy to be compared with the glory to come, &c. :' therefore our works do not worthily merit eternal life.

" I deny the inference : for the sense of the apostle is, that the sufferings and tribulations of this life are not equal in respect of pain and grief to future glory in respect of pleasure and joy.

" This answer is confirmed ; because, 2 Cor. iv. 17, the apostle says, ' For our present tribulation, which is momentary and light, worketh for us above measure exceedingly, an eternal weight of glory :' whence, although the sufferings, in respect to their pain, are not equal with the celestial glory ; yet, inasmuch as they proceed from a just man through grace, they are worthy of eternal life in respect of merit.

" *Obj. II.* Luke xvii. 10, Christ says, ' When you shall have done all the things that are commanded you, say : We are unprofitable servants ; we have done that which we ought to do ;' therefore, we merit nothing.

" *Ans.* 1. I deny the inference ; because we are called unprofitable servants for the reason that by our works no advantage can accrue to God ; but this is consistent with the fact that they are useful to us, and meritorious before God : whence Christ says, Matt. xxv. 21.—' Well done, thou good and faithful servant.'

" *Ans.* 2. We are commanded to feel humbly concerning ourselves, and to think either that we have done nothing, or that we are worthy of no reward ; as we have done nothing except what we were bound to do.

Obj. III. It is said, Ps. cii. 4.—' Who crowneth thee with
mercy and compassion ;' and Rom. vi. 23.—' The grace of
God (is) everlasting life ;' and viii. 17.—' If sons, heirs also ;'
therefore, no one can merit eternal life.

" *Ans.* I deny the inference.   As for these texts and
others, observe that eternal life is rightly called reward, grace,
mercy, &c.   It is called a reward, inasmuch as it is given
for the sake of merits ; it is called an inheritance, because it
is given to adopted sons ; it is called mercy and grace, because our merits proceed from grace—because God has mer-
cifully and freely promised eternal life to good works ; also,
because election to glory has been made merely of grace.

" Neither do our merits diminish the meritorious virtue of
Christ, as the heretics babble: because our merits derive all
power of meriting from the merits of Christ, just as the
branches (derive) from the vine the power of bearing fruit :
and hence, our merits commend the merits of Christ, inasmuch as by his own merits he has obtained for us the power
of meriting.

" *Obj. IV.* God cannot be a debtor to men, because he is
the supreme Lord : and our works are due to him by various
claims.

" *Ans.* I deny the antecedent : because, although God
cannot be a debtor to men on account of men, he may still
be a debtor to men on his own account, and his own appointment, by which he himself has thought proper thus to ordain.

" In order to furnish (farther) proof (observe), that in case
God should determine to deal with man according to his own
absolute right, then man could merit nothing worthily before
God ; but as God has already resolved to promise a reward
to those works ; hence, now arises the obligation of justice."

Of meriting worthily. (37.)

" What conditions are requisite to merit worthily before
God ?

" Seven are requisite, of which four relate to the action,
namely : that it be free, good, performed from actual grace,
and for the sake of obedience to God ; two relate to the person performing it, viz. : that he be a traveller (upon earth),
and in a state of sanctifying grace ; the seventh relates to

God, viz. : that a divine promise intervenes, by which a re-ward is promised to such work.

" What does the first condition imply ?

" That the work must be free with the liberty of indiffer-ence ;" (i. e. liberty of doing or not doing a thing ;) " and it is an article of faith since the condemnation of the third proposition of Jansenius."

" What does the second condition mean ?

" That *indifferent* works, if such were performed by an individual, are not méritorious.

" What is imported by the third condition ?

" That works only morally good, viz. : those which are performed by the powers of nature alone, are not merito-rious, although they might be done by a good man : because they do not proceed from grace, of which merit is the effect; neither are they proportionate to supernatural merit, as they are natural.

" What is signified by the fourth condition ?

" That a work ought to be referred to obedience to God : because, otherwise, there would be no reason why a reward should be expected from him, especially according to justice.

" Observe, that as well good works, which are (performed in obedience) of a precept, as those which are (in pursuance) of counsel, may be meritorious : for, Matt. xix. 17, eternal life is promised to those who keep the commandments :— 'If thou wilt enter into life, keep the commandments ;' and verse 29, the same life is promised to those who keep the Evangelical counsels : ' Every one that hath left house, or brethren, or sisters,——for my name's sake, shall receive a hundred fold, and shall possess life everlasting.' Indeed, the endurance of diseases and other afflictions can be mer-itorious and satisfactory ; because that endurance may be freely received by the will out of grace and love.

" Prove the fifth condition, namely, that the person must be a traveller (upon earth.)

" It seems that this cannot be proved from natural reason ; but the necessity of this condition appears to proceed from the positive divine decree, manifested to us from Holy Scrip-ture, and the common opinion of the church ; thus, it is said, Ecclesiasticus xiv. 17, ' Before thy death, work justice ; for in hell there is no finding food ;' John ix. 4, Christ says,

7

'The night cometh, when no man can work:' by night, meaning death: after which he asserts no one can meritoriously work.

"Hence, St. Jerome says, &c. 'The time of sowing is the present life; when this has past, the season of working is gone;' and St. Thomas, &c. 'It must be said that merit and demerit pertain to the state of life.'

"Infer that the blessed in heaven, souls in purgatory, and the damned in hell, although the latter do not cease to sin, and the former persevere in good works, yet do not any more merit or demerit by them, so that their happiness or damnation might be increased.

"The Lord Christ, although he was perfect, or blessed from the first instant of his conception, was at the same time also a traveller, (upon earth), and so long only he merited. The saints by their prayers obtain blessings for us from God; but they do not properly merit them, not even on the ground of propriety.

"Who is said to be a traveller, or in a state of wayfaring?

"He who lives in the body in a mortal condition. Hence, it becomes probable that Enoch and Elias do not in fact merit, because they do not live in a mortal state.

"Prove the sixth condition, that a person ought to be in a state of sanctifying grace.

"It is proved from John xv. 4, 'As the branch cannot bear fruit of itself, except it abide in the vine, so neither can you, unless you abide in me;' also, 1 Cor. xiii. 3. 'If I should distribute all my goods to feed the poor, &c., and have not charity, it profiteth me nothing.'

"The same can be proved from Council of Trent, Sess. 6. chap. 16, and from the condemnation of the 12th, 13th, 15th, 17th, and 18th of the propositions of Bajus.

"Therefore, the good works of sinners, even proceeding from actual grace, before the application of habitual grace, are not meritorious on the ground of worthiness.

"Does the sinner therefore in vain apply himself to good works?

"By no means: for although they are not strictly meritorious, yet if they are performed through the incipient desire of converting himself to God, excited by grace, they are preparatory to grace, and are productive of it.

"Show that the seventh condition is necessary, viz. that a divine promise should intervene.

"It is evident; because unless this promise intervened, there would be no title from which an obligation of justice could originate; as God is the Supreme Lord of all, and thus he might exact all our works by various claims, as due to himself."

"Holy Scripture shows that this promise has been made, James i. 12, 'He shall receive the crown of life, which God has promised to them that love him;' and Heb. x. 36, 'That doing the will of God, ye may receive the promise.' Hence the Council of Trent says, &c., sess. 6, chap. 16.

"*Obj.* Many illiterate persons are ignorant of that promise, but yet they do not therefore cease to merit; therefore, &c.

"I deny the inference; because it is not necessary that all the faithful should explicitly know that promise; but it is sufficient for some that they implicitly know it in this, that they believe God to be the dispenser of the reward of eternal glory.

"Are, therefore, any works meritorious on the ground of worthiness?

"I answer with St. Thomas, &c., Every human action which proceeds from free will, moved not only by actual grace, but also instructed by sanctifying grace, if it may be referred to God, is worthily meritorious; and thus not only acts of charity but also of temperance, justice, and every virtue, are meritorious of eternal life, and though merit primarily pertains to charity, as St. Thomas says, yet it pertains secondarily also to other virtues, inasmuch as their acts are enjoined or taught by charity.

"What conditions are requisite to merit on the ground of propriety and by a person in a state of probation?

"These, that the work be free, good, performed through actual grace, and for the purpose of obedience towards God; yet a state of grace is not required, nor a divine promise."

The doctrine of merit as taught in the standards of the Romish church is so directly at variance with the letter and spirit of the Bible that it refutes itself, when simply contrasted with the plain testimony of Scripture, which is, never-

theless, summoned as a witness in its favour. If we are
"saved by grace," as Paul declares, then we cannot be
saved by merit. The texts which have been adduced in the
preceding translation of the two leading chapters on merit,
as heretical objections, cannot be invalidated by the flimsy,
though occasionally plausible arguments which are offered in
reply. It is not worth while to examine them all in detail,
as the general principles which controvert them, have been
mentioned in the preceding chapter, in defence of *Justification by faith ;* but we will briefly instance one or two.
When the following passage is stated in full, the answer
which Peter Dens gives to it, will appear even still more
feeble than in its present form. "Doth the master thank
his servant because he did the things that were commanded
him? I trow not. So likewise ye, when ye shall have
done all those things which are commanded you, say we
are unprofitable servants, we have done that which was our
duty to do." If we were to exhibit angelic obedience to
every command of God, if we had never sinned even in
thought, we could claim no reward on this account—we
should have done no more than our duty, and should simply
have paid a just debt. But who is there that has not offended in many things? And if the least offence is a transgression of a law which is holy, just, and good—if every sin is
committed against a God whose perfections are infinite, and
whose wrath is revealed from heaven against all unrighteousness, how can we lay claim to *merit*, when if saved from
death and hell, it must be alone through the exercise of
sovereign grace and mercy?

In Rom. vi. 23, which our theologian professes to quote
thus, "the grace of God (is) everlasting life," we read these
words : "For the wages of sin is death, but the gift of God
(is) eternal life, through Jesus Christ our Lord." Here the
apostle evidently wishes to contrast "the *wages* of sin" with
"the *gift* of God."

The sinner *merits* death *worthily*, but the believer receives eternal life as a "gift." And lest any one should suppose it to be *given* (to the saint) as a mark of approbation on account of his good works, Paul adds, "through Jesus Christ our Lord." Not only so, but the believer cannot do a good work without *grace ;* this the church of Rome admits, and yet in the very face of this concession, she denounces the heretics who "babble" against the condign merits of the saints !

CHAPTER XII.

TREATISE CONCERNING THEOLOGICAL VIRTUES.

Concerning the Virtue of Faith. (No. 8.)

" THERE are three theological virtues which the apostle mentions, I Cor. xiii. 13, saying—Now there remain faith, hope, charity, these three.

" These virtues are called theological, commonly divine, (in Dutch, Goddelyke Deugden ; in French, Vertus Théologales), principally because they treat immediately about God, or because they have God for their formal and material primary object : farther, because these virtues are made known by revelation alone in the sacred Scripture, and thus were first discovered by Christian theologians, who investigate matters of revelation."

" The word faith is variously received.

" Sometimes it is taken for fidelity in promises, as Rom. iii. 3, ' Shall their unbelief make the faith of God of none effect ?'

" 2. It is taken for the promises themselves and for a vow ; as 1 Tim. v. 12, it is said, concerning certain widows, ' They have made void their first faith.'

" 3. It sometimes denotes conscience ; as Rom. xiv. 23. ' All that is not of faith is sin.' In this sense also, any one is called a possessor of good or bad faith.

7 *

"4. It is taken for confidence; as James i. 6, 'But let him ask in faith nothing wavering.'

"5. It comes also sometimes for the object of faith; thus in the Symbol of St. Athanasius, it is said: 'This is the Catholic faith.'

"6. Omitting other acceptations of faith, it is taken more commonly for the assent of the understanding, or for the disposition inclining to afford assent on account of the authority of another. If that authority is human, it is called human faith; if it is divine, it is said (to be) divine or theological; which, if it respects the truths proposed by the church, is named the Catholic faith. In this signification, we treat of faith in this place."

"What is faith? (No. 9.)

"*Ans.* It is rightly defined by Canisius: A gift of God, and a light, illumined by which a person firmly assents to all things which God has revealed, and proposed to us through the church to be believed, whether these things are written or are not (written).

"It is called, 1; 'A gift of God;' because it is given gratuitously by God alone, and surpasses all the powers of nature: for divine faith, both unformed and formed, (*i. e.* dead and living,) both actual and habitual, is essentially supernatural.

"It is called, 2; 'A light;' that is to say, a spiritual one, by which the intellect is elevated and enlightened to know and believe those things, which are (matters) of faith, &c.

"It is said, 3; 'Firmly assents;' because the assent of faith ought to be firm and certain, without any doubt, hesitation, or fear about its opposite; as it rests upon the truth of God himself.

"It is said, 4; 'To all things which God has revealed;' by which is denoted that it is the adequate material object of faith, that these things are all and alone revealed by God: whence is also signified that the formal object of faith is the highest truth of God who reveals it.

"It is said, 5; 'And proposed to us through the church to be believed;' by which is signified the cause proposing objects of faith; for without the creed of the church it is not plain to us that any article has been revealed by God; and hence the motive of credibility is signified: for the creed of the church makes things evidently credible.

" It is said, 6 ; ' Whether they are written or are not ;' by which is farther denoted that truths to be believed are partly contained in the written word of God, or the Holy Scripture, partly in the word of God (that has been) handed down, or in divine tradition.

" There is another description of faith, which the apostle gives, Heb. xi. 1, in which faith is called ' The substance of things hoped for, the conviction of things that appear not.'

" This description St. Thomas proves to be proper, and reduces it into this form : ' Faith is a habit of the mind, by which eternal life begins in us, making the understanding assent to things which do not appear.'

" It is called, 1 ; ' The substance of things hoped for ;' that is, the basis or foundation upon which our hope, or the whole salvation (for) which we hope, rests : according to others, it is the substance or subsistence ; because it makes eternal blessings (for) which we hope, in some measure subsist in us, by rendering us as certain concerning them as if they were already possessed by us.

" It is called, 2 ; ' The evidence of things, which appear not ;' that is, the conviction ; because the understanding through faith is convinced of the truth of things, which are perceived neither by sense nor by reason.

" *Obj.* Hell is a thing, which is believed by faith : but yet it is not a thing to be hoped for ; therefore this definition is not proper.

" *Ans.* The belief of hell is contained under the last words of the definition, inasmuch as faith is called the conviction of things, which appear not.

" And hence observe, not every object of faith is an object of hope ; or that a person believes some things, which he does not hope for ; such are, evils, or past or present blessings." (No. 91.)

The definition of faith which our author extols so highly, and which with characteristic modesty is placed in advance of the inspired apostle's description, militates against the Scriptural view, and as the theory is unsound, its practical operation must be pernicious. So soon as we make "tradition" of equal authority with the Word of God, we pave the way for the introduction of articles of faith, many of which have no firmer foundation, and no higher origin than the depraved imaginations of designing or deluded men. The church of Rome includes among her "unwritten verities," some of the most monstrous fictions that have ever been fabricated; she has actually recorded among her traditions a vast amount of matter, which cannot be named without exciting derision and contempt, among the more enlightened of her own communion. To make the idle stories, which are registered in the Breviary concerning the immediate disciples of the Saviour, and other saints, of equal authority with the Word of God, to a Protestant at least, appears no better than sheer blasphemy! We put it to the conscience of any intelligent and candid Romanist, whether it does not at least wear the appearance of wanton irreverence, to affirm that the preposterous fables, (we can call them nothing better), concerning the Virgin Mary, Mary Magdalen, &c., are to be regarded as equally authentic with the narratives of the Holy Scripture? Is it likely that Magdalen lived so many years in a cave, secluded from the world, and that once a day she was carried by angels to heaven, to listen to the songs of the glorified spirits before the throne, &c.? Yet this Tradition teaches.

The worship of images is called an apostolic tradition. But is it not strange that all the apostles are silent in relation to the proper veneration, which is alleged to be due to them? And that, when cautioning the Christian converts against the idolatry of the Gentiles, they never stop to make a single distinction relative to image worship?

The kissing of the altar, and the blessing of incense, are enjoined by Tradition. Tradition is the parent of the orthodox turnings and facings and gesticulations of the priests, the swinging of the chalice, the adoration of the host, and other strange ceremonies, which may be witnessed at every celebration of the Mass.

In the Missal, salt is conjured or exorcised, and is said to be done for the salvation of such as believe. And water is blessed in order to expel the power of the great enemy : for the same purpose candles are also blessed, and for all these practices, the priests allege Tradition. Hence too the power to baptize bells ; which by this consecration acquire the wonderful virtue of driving away devils.

Now we appeal to the common sense of every rational man, whether it is not the height of irreverence to ascribe to such traditions as these, the authority which belongs to Scripture ? Since the apostles are gone, we know no surer guide than their written words ; "to which we do well to take heed as to a light that shineth in a dark place ; for if we fulfil the royal law according to the Scriptures, we shall do well."

Surely the canon of Revelation would not have closed with so solemn a caution against adding aught to its words, if important doctrines had been overlooked, or purposely not inserted. Whilst we cleave to the Scripture as our rule of faith, we have a guide that we may trust ; but when men begin to follow the " ignis fatuus" of tradition, they will soon be lost in a quagmire of superstition and folly, and there they will sink, unless God in mercy pluck them from the miry clay, and set their feet upon the rock of Eternal Truth.

CHAPTER XIII.

Concerning the Division of Faith.

" How is the theological virtue, faith, divided?
" I. *Ans.* 1. It is divided into habitual and actual faith.
" 2. Into explicit and implicit faith.
" 3. Into internal and external faith.
" 4. Into formed or living, and unformed or dead faith.

" What is habitual, and what actual faith ?

" II. *Ans.* Habitual faith is the habit of faith itself; actual is the act itself, or the present assent of faith.

" Which faith is called explicit, and which implicit ?

" III. *Ans.* Explicit faith is that by which we assent to some article of faith in itself, and known by its own terms.

" IV. *Ans.* Implicit is that by which certain truths are believed, contained, not in themselves and in their own terms, but in some other as universal or principal, or as cause, medium, figure, &c. Thus, he who explicitly believes that there were two distinct natures in Christ, also implicitly believes that there were in him two wills and operations, proceeding from both natures. Just so, he who explicitly believes whatever God has revealed, or whatever the church proposes to be believed, implicitly believes that there are seven sacraments of the new law, even though he should not know them.

" What is internal, and what is external faith ?

" V. *Ans.* The former is the assent of faith conceived in the mind ; the latter is the external profession of internal faith by words, actions, or other signs.

" VI. *Ans.* What formed and what unformed faith is, appears from No. 2, towards the close, and in what respects they differ from one another from No. 7, towards the close.

The following are the passages alluded to.

" No. 2. What is a perfect or formed virtue ; what is an imperfect or unformed (virtue ?)

" *Ans.* A formed (virtue) is that which is combined with habitual charity ; because charity is the form, the end, and perfection of the other virtues.

" A virtue is said to be unformed which is in (its) subject, destitute of habitual charity, or existing in mortal sin."

" No. 7. The other virtues without charity are unformed and imperfect, because destitute of accidental and extrinsic perfection * * * dead faith is essentially as perfect as living faith ; but charity effects that the act of living faith worthily merits eternal life ; but such is not the act of unformed (dead) faith."

I have given this section concerning the division of faith

at length, for the sake of convenient reference; as the various terms and distinctions of faith will occur frequently in the following chapters.

The material object of faith. (12).

The object of faith is declared to be two-fold—material and formal.

" What is the material object of faith, or what ought we to believe?

"They are all those things which God has revealed to us."

The material object of faith is distinguished again, as "*primary* or *principal*, which is God, and all those things which have been revealed to us in God; and *secondary*, and this, all other things revealed to us by God constitute, such are, the humanity of Christ, the sacraments, &c." * * *

Matters of private revelation, such as v. g. were made known to St. Birgitta, may be a material object of faith to those to whom they have been revealed, if there is sufficient evidence that the revelation was divine; but such things do not properly belong to the Catholic faith. Whatever the *Church* authoritatively enjoins is a material object of faith.

The formal object of faith. (13).

" What is the formal object of faith?

" *Ans.* It is the first or highest truth of God who reveals it, which is founded in this, that God on account of his infinite wisdom cannot be deceived, and on account of his infinite goodness and perfection cannot deceive." * * *

The assent of faith. (14).

" Does the assent of our faith immediately depend upon any reasoning, discussion, or deduction made according to the legitimate form of argumentation?

" *Ans.* No; because the assent, which depends upon discussion, has for a partial motive, the goodness of the inference; as it is an act by which the understanding assents to the conclusion, because it follows clearly from the premises: but the assent of faith by no means rests upon the goodness of the conclusion, but the adequate motive for divine faith is the first truth of God, who reveals it."

External Motives of Credibility. (18.)

" What are the motives of credibility ?

" Some motives of credibility are external, others internal. Very many external motives of credibility are mentioned by S. Thomas, Bellarmine, Wiggers and others, from which we will here submit the principal.

" The authority of the church affords the first and sufficient argument of credibility ; or the creed of the church effulgent by its own marks, (of which hereafter.)

" The second is derived from the miracles and signs by which the truths of our faith have been confirmed by Christ, the apostles and preachers down to these times. For although miracles are the peculiar work of God, and as it were seals of divinity, yet they can be performed in confirmation of the truth : and hence are found never to have been done in confirmation of any other sect ; and if at times such things have been divulged, they have vanished as merely marvellous, or as false and the result of legerdemain.

" Among miracles may be enumerated, the power over devils, by which Christians drive them out of bodies, make them silent, &c.

The wonderful propagation of the faith by a few illiterate fishermen is also mentioned, (and justly,) as properly belonging to the evidence from miracles.

The third motive of credibility is prophecy : evidence is adduced from the predictions relative to the birth, life, death, resurrection, &c., of Christ, the calling of the Gentiles, rejection of the Jews, &c.

" And lest any one should falsely say, that these prophecies were fabricated after the events had taken place, it has been effected by the singular providence of God, that the Jews themselves, the most violent enemies of our religion, have carefully preserved those books and prophecies down to these times, &c.

" The fourth argument is drawn from the antiquity, universality, firmness and continuation of our faith ; these things St. Aug. has briefly and nervously expressed, &c., saying —' There are many things, which most justly keep me in the bosom of the church ; the consent of nations and multitudes, the authority, commenced by miracles, nourished by hope, increased by charity, and strengthened by antiquity : the succession of priests from the very Seat of the apostle Peter, (keeps me) to whom the Lord entrusted the feeding of his sheep, down to the present Episcopacy : finally the very name of catholic, (keeps me) which this church has thus obtained not without reason among so many heresies, as all heretics wish themselves to be called Catholics, &c. &c.—

" To these add the sanctity and purity of the doctrine and members of the church : for those things wonderfully conciliate confidence for our religion, which the church teaches concerning virtues and vices, concerning the reward of good works, and the punishment of sinners, concerning the worship of God and holiness of manners.

" Finally, the constancy of innumerable martyrs of every age, sex, and condition, who have sealed the Catholic faith with their blood, affords an invincible argument of the truth of the faith—"

Internal motives of credibility. (19.)

The internal motive of credibility is two-fold, viz : the supernatural light of faith, and the natural light of the understanding.

" By the natural light of the understanding, a person is led only incipiently towards faith, inasmuch as by it, the things of faith may appear evidently credible on account of extrinsic arguments, whilst they are attentively and dispassionately considered, &c."

" What is the light of faith ?

" It is a certain supernatural internal light, or an inward impression of God, by which the understanding is inclined, so that it attends to the arguments of credibility, and is enlightened so that it more readily apprehends the weight and evidence of the arguments."   *   *   *

That the delusions of the church of Rome are not superficial excrescences, but vital and fundamental errors, becomes more evident as her principles are investigated. Whatsoever the church teaches, is a material object of faith, and must be received without a murmur even of respectful inquiry. The church says so—and let it suffice that " Rome has spoken !" Now, that there are in revelation things, which from their

8

very nature must be received explicitly, we admit; and in so far as they do not fall within the province of reason, and are beyond its ken, they are not properly matters of discussion, and must be believed though they cannot be understood; such for instance are the doctrines of the Trinity, and of the nature and purposes of God, &c. But we are neither required to believe what is clearly contrary to reason, nor yet to shrink from investigations which evidently fall within the legitimate limits of human understanding. The Bible never requires us to receive the "ipse dixit" of a fellow-creature as authoritative; on the contrary, the word of God encourages, commends, and enjoins, the closest scrutiny in those matters of faith which are fairly cognizable. The Saviour blames the Jews for not "judging of themselves what was right." If he had taught that the mere word of a priest was to be regarded as sufficient authority, he would not have asked the Jews, in the language of reproach—"Yea, and why even of yourselves, judge ye not what is right?" It was Christ who bade the Jews "search the Scriptures;" he was willing that *his* claims to Messiahship, should be submitted to that test; and is it not strange, that the sect which claims to be the only and the universal Christian church, should shrink from this ordeal, appointed by the great head of the church, the Lord Jesus Christ himself! The ROMISH CHURCH requires that all her doctrines and decrees, whether contained in the Bible or not, whether contrary to the letter and spirit of scripture or not, whether properly cognizable by reason or not, should be received with explicit faith, and that the mere fact that the church teaches so and so, shall be regarded and received as sufficient evidence of the truth of any doctrine. Now, in this respect, the Romish church claims more than even Christ demanded for himself; Jehovah says, "Come now, and let us reason together;" but antichrist will have no reasoning; and when the most preposterous absurdities are avowed, then it is that the thunder of Holy Church's anathemas is loudest. Under the section which treats of the "external motives of credibility," it will be observed that "the authority of the church" is mentioned as "*the first* and *sufficient* argument of credibility ! !" Then follow the arguments from miracles and prophecy ; these belong to the church of *Christ*, however. But mark : "the truths of our faith have been confirmed by miracles, by Christ, the apostles, and *preachers down to these times*." That Christ and his apostles ever performed a miracle to confirm the peculiar tenets of the church of Rome is, to say the least, a gross delusion ; but that the priests have sought to confirm the *fictions* of their faith by monkish *miracles* and tricks is gravely asserted, and sufficiently proved by many good men ; and we are therefore disposed to allow them all the evidence from "miracles," which is properly their own. As to the arguments from the antiquity, universality, firmness, &c., of *their* faith, we shall attend to them in due time. We will merely observe in relation to the quotation from Augustine, that although some of the peculiarities of the Man of Sin were beginning to develope themselves in his day, St. Augustine would never have been a papist in the nineteenth century.

"The SANCTITY and PURITY of the doctrine and members of the church," will furnish us with materials for a separate chapter, when we come to treat of "the Church" more particularly.

CHAPTER XIV.

Articles of Faith. (22.)

An article of faith is defined as being " a proposition pertaining to eternal salvation, or a certain primary truth among those things, which are to be believed, having a particular difficulty in being believed.   Thus the Apostle's creed embraces twelve articles," &c.

" *   *   *   That Abraham had two sons, one by a bondwoman, the other by a free woman; that by touching the bones of Elisha, the dead man revived, &c. are not articles of faith; but these truths are reduced to one general article by which all things which are asserted in the Holy Scriptures are believed to be true.

"Secondly, it is required that this truth have a special difficulty in being believed; and hence that Christ suffered, died, and was buried, is one article of faith containing three propositions, of which the two latter have not a different difficulty from the former; for if Christ could suffer, he could also die and be buried; but that he rose again on the third day. is a distinct article, because it has a special difficulty.

" Therefore make a distinction between these three things; a doctrine, a point and an article of faith.

" A doctrine of faith is every revealed truth, or every thing that faith teaches.

" And this in like manner is said of a point and an article of faith.

" A point, which others call a proposition of faith is indeed a revealed truth, but a less important one, and not to be explicitly believed by all : for instance that Saul was the first King of Israel.

" An article of faith is a more important truth, and pertaining to eternal salvation; v. g. The consubstantiality of the Word with the Father."

Have articles of faith increased in the lapse of time? (23.)

" From Adam to the times of the Apostles, it is certain that they have increased—for there are many things, which are believed explicitly and in a greater number under the new law, v. g. The incarnation, passion, resurrection, sacraments, &c. of Christ, which were not thus believed under the old law."

" Whether they have increased as to their substance or only as to their explanation is a question.   The latter is the more generally received opinion.

Since the times of the Apostles, articles of faith have

not increased.   " When the spirit of truth shall have come, he will teach you all truth;" "therefore new revelations, which concern the Catholic faith ought no more to be admitted."

" You will say : after the apostles' times many truths were defined and propounded by Councils and Popes as belonging to the faith, which before the definition were not matters of faith ; therefore also, since the times of the apostles, articles of faith have increased.

" *Ans.* I deny the inference : because those truths had been explicitly known and propounded to the church by the apostles ; therefore the church in defining did not establish an article altogether new, but again propounded it particularly ; yet not by a new revelation, but only declaring what things ought to be believed, and had been handed down and believed by the apostles."

" The church is not less learned or intelligent in the mysteries of faith since the apostles' times—' because as in earlier so also in later times, the church is the ground and the pillar of truth,' to which God has promised his assistance even to the end of time.

" And hence this remark of the heretics is to be rejected, &c. that the church may be involved in greater darkness, and may sometimes dote, or fail through old age.

" This indeed may be conceded, that the Fathers nearer the times of the apostles, as S. Jerome, Aug. &c. were more enlightened than the modern ; but yet the same light is found at this day in the whole body of the church, whilst we learn the truths from their writings which they had been taught more immediately through the unction of the Holy Spirit."

That the true church of Christ, consisting of believers out of every kindred and nation and tongue and people, will always be preserved from the darkness of ignorance and the delusions of superstition, is a precious truth.   Even in the gloomiest days, the true light shines in their souls, and though darkness cover the earth and gross darkness the people, God's children always will have peace and love and joy in the Holy Ghost.   But it is not true that there never have been seasons, when religion has fearfully declined, and

8 *

when the visible church has been corrupted.   It was so in
the days of Elijah, and yet God had preserved to himself
7000 who had not bowed the knee to Baal nor kissed his
images.   It was so in the justly called " dark ages," when
the candle of the Lord shone scarcely any where, save
among the persecuted Waldenses and Albigenses and Cul-
dees, who were hunted like the deer of the forest by the
merciless armies of the Pope.

It is not true that the church of Rome never has been
corrupt, and it is equally untrue that she is free from pernicious error now.

It is not true that the Romish church is " the pillar and
ground of the truth," neither is it true that the apostle designated her, when he spoke of the church of the living God.

It is not true that no new articles of faith have been added
by the authorities of the Romish church since the days of
the apostles ; and it is just as untrue that the decrees of
Popes and Councils have always been in accordance with
the faith once delivered to the saints by the apostles of the
'Lord Jesus Christ.

These are all points which will recur for discussion in the
course of the present work ; meanwhile, therefore, we op-
pose a blank denial to the bald assertions of the Romish
Doctor.

Concerning the Symbol of Faith (or Creed). (24.)

A symbol of faith is defined as " A summary or collec-
tion of certain articles of faith, proposing in a compendious
manner the most important things to be believed by all."

The advantages to be derived from this compendium are,

" 1. That the faithful might more easily be instructed.

" 2. That the unity of the faith might more readily be
preserved throughout the world.

" 3. That by the profession of the creed, the faithful might
be distinguished from infidels.

" 4. Lest the faith of the simple might be corrupted by
infidels.

"There are four creeds, viz. ; the Apostles', the Nicene, the Constantinopolitan, and the Athanasian.

"The profession of faith, which Pope Pius IV. prescribed from the decrees of the Council of Trent, and appointed to be uttered with an oath by all who are about to be promoted to sacred offices, academical degrees, &c., has the nature, though not the name of a symbol."

Concerning the Apostles' Creed. (25.)

This is the well-known form of sound words, which is familiar to us all—"I believe in God the Father Almighty, Maker of heaven and earth, and in Jesus Christ his only Son our Lord, who was conceived by the Holy Spirit, born of the Virgin Mary, suffered under Pontius Pilate, was crucified, dead and buried. He descended into hell ; the third day he rose again from the dead ; he ascended into heaven, and sitteth at the right hand of the Father, whence he shall come to judge the quick and the dead. I believe in the Holy Ghost, the Holy Catholic Church, the communion of saints, the remission of sins, the resurrection of the body, and life everlasting. Amen."

" Why is it called the Apostles' creed ?

" Both because it contains the doctrine and articles preached by the apostles themselves ; and also because it was composed by the apostles before they were scattered in the various parts of the world to preach."

In the former part of this answer we can heartily concur, but the truth of the latter assertion is more than questionable, as we will show presently. The creed itself we recognize as orthodox ; it is associated with the first lessons in religion, which Protestants are taught in their childhood, and if we understood it precisely as the church of Rome explains it, there would be less ground for controversy between us than there is. But whilst we acknowledge that it is a form of sound words, we must be permitted to dissent from the opinion as to the extent of the obligation of knowing it by heart, expressed in the following answers.

" Is there an obligation that the faithful should know the Apostles' creed?

" Yes : because by divine command we ought to believe the Gospel ; but the creed contains the principal heads of the Gospel : therefore every one ought to believe it, and therefore to know it.

" How great is the obligation of knowing the apostles' creed?

" I answer with S. Charles Borrom., &c. ' Every Christian if he is an adult is bound to know all the articles of the apostles' creed, under pain of mortal sin :' understand as to its substance.

" Are the faithful obliged to know the creed even word for word?

" Yes ; and this the common opinion of the faithful proves : this obligation has been introduced either by the apostles, or by the custom of the church : and hence it was sanctioned already from the earlier centuries of the church, that boys so soon as they become capable of learning should thoroughly learn before everything else, the creed, and other mysteries of the same necessity.

" Malderes, Wiggers, Sylvius, &c. teach that although the obligation of knowing the creed word for word, is not improper of itself, but only trifling ; yet if any one should not know how to recite it from idle negligence, he could not easily be excused from mortal sin : because such a one for the most part will also be ignorant of the articles as to their substance, and will be found grievously negligent in exercising acts of faith, hope, &c.—Hence St. Aug. says, ' I know not with what face he can call himself a Christian, who neglects to acquire the few sentences in the creed and the Lord's prayer.' "

As to the creed itself, the Romish explanation differs very materially from the Protestant. Thus in the fifth article, " He descended into hell," there is a comment, which strikes us as rather bold.

" What is proposed for belief in the first part of the fifth article, ' He descended into *the lower regions ?*'

" *Ans.* That the soul of Christ separated from the body,

descended to the lower regions, and there remained so long as his body was in the Sepulchre.

" To what place of the lower regions did he descend?

" *Ans.* By the name of the lower regions are meant the secret receptacles in which those souls are detained, who have not obtained celestial happiness : but these as the Roman Catechism teaches, before the resurrection of Christ, were three ; viz. the hell of the damned, purgatory and limbus, in which the spirits of the just fully cleansed (from sin) were kept before Christ's coming to them.

" These things being premised, it is certain that the soul of Christ descended to the ' Limbus Patrum,' and immediately rendered their souls happy ; and afterwards, when ascending to heaven took them with him.

" It is probable that he also penetrated to the place of purgatory, and that he consoled the spirits there detained, and perhaps at the same time liberated at least some from (their) pains.

" That he descended to the abode of the damned is not probable : yet they could feel the virtue of Christ's descending."

Our Theologian speaks like a book upon this subject.

" *It is certain* / that the soul of Christ descended to the Limbus Patrum &c.—'Limbus Patrum?' 'Limbus Patrum!' Where do you find any mention of such a place in the Word of God?

The *Roman Catechism* teaches that " Limbus Patrum" was one of the three abodes of departed spirits—

The *Roman Catechism* / INDEED !

And " it is probable that he also penetrated to the place of purgatory &c.

" *Purgatory ?*" If I had read no other book but the Bible, I should never have seen the word in my life. But as the *Roman Catechism* is again adduced as authority, of course that settles the question. What a blessed thing it is that the Roman Catechism has been framed, and that there is an infallible church, from whose decisions there can be no appeal !

" Observe, that heretics denying the descent of Christ to the lower regions, not less impiously than foolishly understand ' hell,' in this connection for the grave : for the burial has evidently been expressed in the fourth article, and would thus be uselessly repeated here in obscure words."

That the " Apostles' creed," is a symbol of great antiquity, cannot be denied ; though its age has no doubt been overrated by Romish authors.   Tertullian and Irenæus allude to it : and the whole form as it now stands in the English Liturgy, may be found in the works of St. Ambrose, who flourished in the third century ; and also in the writings of Rufinus of the fourth century.   But the following considerations will have some weight in sustaining the belief that the apostles did not compose any such creed.

1. Neither St. Luke, nor any other writer before the fifth century, makes any mention of an assembly of the apostles for composing a creed.

2. The fathers of the first three centuries, in disputing against the heretics, endeavour to prove that the doctrine contained in this symbol, was the same which the apostles taught ; but they never pretend that the apostles composed it.   This they certainly would have distinctly asserted, if they had known it to be a fact.

3. If the apostles had made this creed, it would have been the same in all churches, and in all ages ; and all authors would have cited it in the same manner.   But they have not done so.   In the second and third ages of the church, there were as many creeds as authors ; and the same author sets down the creed after a different manner in several places of his works, which is an evidence that there was not at that time, any creed reputed to be the apostles' : In the fourth century, Rufinus compares together the three ancient creeds of the churches of Aquileia, Rome, and the East, which differ very considerably, not only in tones and expressions, but even in the articles, some of which were omitted in one or other of them ; and amongst these, " the

descent into hell," is one.* As to the meaning of the phrase, " he descended into hell," we do not feel under obligation of any kind to explain it, as we do not acknowledge it to be of divine authority. But lest Romanists should suppose that it is impossible to give any rational and scriptural exposition of it, and that we must after all endorse the Roman Catechism, we will state what we suppose to be meant by the phrase, " he descended into hell."

The Hebrew word, "Sheol," which is rendered *hell*, or *hades*, seems originally to design the whole region downward from the surface of the earth, to an indefinite and inconceivable depth. Thus, Job speaking of the unsearchableness of the divine perfections, says : " It is high as heaven, what canst thou do? deeper than hell, what canst thou know?" and Amos, " though they dig into hell, thence shall mine hand take them ; though they climb into heaven, thence will I bring them down." Now as the bodies of persons dying, are as it were, let down into this pit, which becomes the universal grave of mankind ; therefore to die is frequently termed καταβαίνειν ἐις ἅδου, or κατάρεσθαι ἐις ἅδου, to descend, or be brought down into this *hell*, which, as it happens to all men indiscriminately, is promiscuously attributed to all men without reference to moral character. Hence good Jacob says, " I will go down unto ' hell,' unto my son, mourning," (i. e.) " I will go down to ' Sheol,' this common grave of mankind. In this way, the term ' Sheol' was figuratively used for ' grave,' and so it is translated by the Septuagint in one passage, Is. xxxviii. 28. ' Sheol' (the grave) cannot praise thee ; death cannot celebrate thee ; they that go down into the pit cannot hope for thy truth." If then we understand " the descent into hell," as implying that our Saviour was laid in the common receptacle of the dead, we are sure that there is nothing unscriptural in it ; and the

---

* See Barrow on the creed, and King's history of the apostles' creed.

passage in the Acts, ii. 27, where Peter refers to the words of David, "thou wilt not leave my soul in hell," admits of this interpretation; for our Saviour's soul not being left in hell, and not seeing corruption, is explained by Peter as denoting his resurrection. "DAVID," says he, "FORESEE-ING THIS SPAKE OF CHRIST'S RESURRECTION."

Again, taking "soul" for the *living soul*, or that faculty by which we live, and *hell* for the state of death, the words "thou wilt not leave my soul in hell" will be equivalent to this, "thou wilt not suffer me to remain dead, till my flesh has been corrupted," and this seems to have been Paul's view, for it is remarkable that in the 13th of Acts, he omits the former part, "thou wilt not leave my soul in hell," and mentions simply the latter, "thou wilt not yield thy Holy One to corruption," thereby implying that the two parts of the text constituted a parallelism, so common in the Hebrew idiom, and were to be understood as synonymous, or explanatory one of the other. But then we are told, by adopting this explanation of the words "he descended into hell," we are in fact only repeating what was before stated that "he was dead and buried." To this we reply—

1. For this *we* are not accountable—you must blame those who inserted these words.

2. That to say our Saviour *continued in the state of death for a season, does* add something to the fact that he was dead and buried.

3. That far greater inconvenience results from expounding the words differently. If they contain a separate article of faith, what are we to to think of the negligence of those fathers, Irenæus, Tertullian, &c. who are so much extolled by Papists, but who certainly knew nothing of many practices and doctrines which are now in vogue among Romanists, and who omitted these words? And what are we to think of Paul himself, who in 1 Cor. xv. when declaring the sum and substance of what he had both learned and taught con-

cerning the last grand scenes in the Saviour's history, says, " I delivered unto you first that Christ died for our sins according to the Scriptures, and that he was buried, and that he rose again the third day"? Paul says nothing here of his " descending into hell."

4. If we interpret the word " sheol," or " hell" as meaning a separate abode of departed spirits, whether good or bad, we are involved in a dilemma. It can hardly be supposed that Christ descended to the abode of lost spirits, for you must remember, he told the penitent thief " This day shalt thou be with me in *Paradise*." And it will not do to understand " sheol" as meaning the " Paradise" or separate abode of the departed spirits of the just, because it was " in sheol" or " hades," that " Dives lifted up his eyes being in torments," and besides it is said in the apocalypse that " death and hades (sheol) were cast into the lake of fire," and our Romish friends would hardly suppose that " Paradise" was cast into the burning lake !

And again, this explanation supposes " Paradise" to be located in the lowest depths of the earth. Now Paul tells us that when he was carried away to " Paradise," he was " caught *up*" not *down* " into the third heaven," and that he was caught *up* to Paradise and heard, &c. 2 Cor. xii.

As for the wild vagaries about the Saviour's going to " Limbus Patrum," and taking with him the souls of the good men, who were therein confined, and the " probability" of his having visited purgatory and taken with him at least some of its inmates, having been taught to " refuse profane and old wives' fables," we leave them just where we find them in Dens' Theology and the Roman Catechism.

The ninth article teaches—" I believe the Holy Catholic church," and the question is asked—

" What do we profit by this part of the ninth article : ' the Holy Catholic church ?'

" *Ans.* We believe that there is a true church, which

9

alone is able to hand down and explain the truths necessary to salvation, and the two fountains of Scripture in which the same are found ; but this church is distinguished by its own marks, viz: that it be *One*, *Holy*, *Cátholic*, and *Apostolic* ; as the Constantinopolitan creed has it."

" Concerning the church and its marks, we shall treat hereafter.

" Wherefore is it here said : I believe the church, *and not* in the church ?

" *Ans.* This is plain from what has been said before ; for this reason that to believe *in* any one indicates that he is our ultimate end ; but this, God alone is."

Whilst we cordially acknowledge our belief in the existence of a church which is Holy and Catholic, we must decline believing that the Romish church is either the one or the other.   We neither believe *her*, nor do we believe *in* her.

The tenth article, " the remission of sins," which we also believe, but in a different sense, is thus explained.

" What does the tenth article propose, ' The Remission of Sins ?'

" *Ans.* We are taught in this article, these truths of the faith :

" 1. That no sins in this life, however enormous and multiplied, are unpardonable.

" 2. That in the church, sins are not only truly remitted, but also that the power of remitting sins has been given to the church through the sacraments of Baptism and Penance.

" 3. That out of the church (see No. 71.) there is no salvation, and therefore no remission of sins.

" Observe that under the remission of sins, the remission of punishments also may be included."

We believe that there is provision made for the remission of the sins of all, who come in humble penitence and faith to the Lord Jesus Christ.   But the remission of sins, described above, we cannot recognize.   Many of the sections in this connexion treat upon topics connected with the faith, which are interesting but not essential, and we shall be obliged to omit them, as our limits will not permit us to insert them.

The 45th section is followed by a corollary, from which we learn amongst other things that it is unlawful for Romanists to participate in a Calvinistic celebration of the Lord's supper.

This provision is scarcely necessary, as it is not likely that they would be invited, except on condition of their renouncing their connexion with the Romish church. Farther, to assist at the religious services of heretics, by singing, playing the organ, &c., is not permitted.

" Is it lawful to be present at the preaching of heretics?

" *Ans.* This is forbidden in the following cases :

" 1. If by this act, those present might be deemed heretics.

" 2. If by this, any one may be exposed to danger of perversion ; and for this reason, illiterate common people cannot without sin listen to the sermons of heretics.

" 3. If any one by frequenting (their assemblies) should afford occasion for scandal.

" 4. If any one by his going should afford honour and authority to the minister.

" 5. If all should be compelled to come to the assemblies of heretics. This is plain from the declaration of Paul V., who being consulted by the Catholics of England, whether they might obey such an edict of the king, replied—' It is not permitted you to do these things without detriment to the worship of God and your own salvation.'

" When, therefore, says Steyaert, there is liberty, and it is the custom for Catholics and others to go to the preaching or psalm-singing of such like, apart from the fact that thus they may be supposed to countenance such a religion, then it must be considered, whether any one incurs danger, and how great, or whether he occasions scandal by going to these (ceremonies) ; and also of what nature is the reason of going."

The 47th section discusses the knotty question, whether there is faith in a heretic or not. And the conclusion which is reached is, that he has neither habitual nor actual faith. The decree of St. Thomas is, that " whoever with obstinacy disbelieves one article of faith, has not the act, nor the habit of faith in relation to the remaining articles."

CHAPTER XV.

Concerning Vices opposed to the Faith. (48.)

" What are the vices opposed to the faith?

" Principally these two, *infidelity*, which is opposed to internal faith, and *blasphemy*, which is opposed to the profession of faith, of which hereafter.

" What is infidelity, the vice opposed to the faith?

" It is a defective absence of faith; and thus they are called infidels, who lack faith accompanied with the manifest expression of some defect; for the blessed, (in heaven) although they have not faith, cannot be called infidels, because the absence of faith in them respects perfection, not defect; but little children not baptized are infidels; for they want habitual faith, which they would have had, if (in Adam) they had not sinned.

" But adults not baptized are not always infidels, because through perfect contrition they can be justified before baptism, and thus possess faith.

" It is to be observed, that the infidel is sometimes confounded with the unbaptized person, and the unbaptized with the infidel, &c. &c.

" How manifold is infidelity?

" It is threefold, viz.: *purely negative, privative*, and *positive*, or *contrary*. The first infidelity is also called *involuntary;* the two others, *voluntary*.

" Infidelity is divided into *paganism, Judaism*, and *heresy*, which are called the three kinds of infidelity, of which hereafter.

" What is purely negative infidelity?

" It is the want of faith in him who has heard nothing of the faith, nor been able to hear it; or to whom the faith has certainly not been sufficiently proposed.

" What is privative infidelity?

" It is the want of faith in him, to whom the faith has been sufficiently proposed, or who could and ought have acquired for himself the knowledge of the faith, but neglected (it).

" What infidelity is called positive, or contrary?

" The want of faith, with voluntary error in the faith, through assent of falsehood, or dissent of the truth; or it is the want of faith in him, who, though sufficiently instructed concerning the faith, maintains an error contrary to the faith."

The 49th section treats of the kinds of infidelity which are sinful, and the degrees of guilt to be attached to them. Privative and positive infidelity are both sin. Purely negative infidelity is not sin. Thus, the heathen commit no sin in failing to believe the gospel, as it is not possible that they should believe, owing to their ignorance of it.

" Is voluntary infidelity the greatest sin?

" According to St. Thomas, infidelity, from its very nature, is a more grievous sin than all offences which can be committed against moral virtues : because infidelity is more directly against God than sins which are opposed to moral virtues. Besides, infidelity also takes away the foundation and root of justification.

" Yet hatred of God, which is opposed to love, is more grievous than infidelity, as St. Thomas teaches, &c.

" Observe 1, with St. Thomas, that a sin which, from its very nature, is more grievous, can be less so from certain circumstances.

" Observe 2, that a believing person committing, v. g. adultery, or another sin, sins more grievously, other things being equal, than an infidel committing the same things, both on account of knowledge of the truth from faith, and on account of the sacraments with which he has been imbued, to which he offers contempt by sinning.

" St. Thomas teaches that not every action of an unbelieving person is a sin ; because he may perform some morally good works.

" This is plain also from the condemnation of this proposition, the 25th among Bajus—'All works of infidels are sins, and the virtues of philosophers are vices.'

Concerning the kinds of infidelity. (No. 50.)

" How many kinds of infidelity are there?

" Under the new law there are three, to wit : *paganism,*

9 *

Judaism, and *heresy.* To one of these every other infidelity can be reduced.

"What is paganism?

"It is the unbelief of those who profess Christ neither in figure, nor in the manifestation of the truth; or who do not acknowledge that any Messiah or Christ has come, and do not expect that he will come. Such are idolaters, atheists, deists, Mahometans, &c.

"What is Judaism?

"It is the unbelief of those who confess the Messiah or Christ in figure only; or, who deny that Christ has come, but hitherto expect that he will come.

"What is heresy?

"It is the unbelief of those who indeed profess that Christ has come; but reject his doctrine as proposed by the church, as to some part—Such are Lutherans, Calvinists, &c.

*   *   *   *   *   *   *   *

"Which kind of infidelity is the most grievous sin?

"I answer with St. Thomas, by making a distinction: if infidelity be objectively considered, or with respect to its (subject) matter, then paganism is more grievous than Judaism, and Judaism more grievous than heresy: because a pagan errs in more things than a Jew, and a Jew in more than a heretic. If subjectively, or with respect of the obstinacy of the will, and of resistance against the faith, then the worst is heresy, and Judaism (is) commonly more grievous than paganism: because heretics usually have greater knowledge concerning the truths of the faith than Jews, and Jews than pagans; and thus, heresy is commonly of more grievous guilt.

"Yet if the truths of the faith had been equally credibly proposed to pagans and Jews; then paganism would be a more grievous sin than Judaism, and Judaism than heresy."
&c.

Are infidels to be compelled to the faith. (51.)

"Infidels who have never been baptized cannot be compelled to embrace the faith. Especially, not by the church; because she has no jurisdiction over unbaptized persons, according to that 1 Cor. v. 12.—'What, have I to judge them that are without?' Neither also, by secular rulers, although their superiors : because they have only political power, which regards solely the public peace and tranquillity.

" The examples of Christ, the doctrine and practice of the church, and the rule, Matt. x. prescribed to the apostles in preaching, prove the same thing.

" Yet it is to be observed, that infidels not baptized, although they cannot be compelled to the faith, may yet be obliged by their rulers to observe the law of nature, and thus to abstain from blasphemies against God, idolatry, &c.: the reason is, because right political order is founded in the observance of the law of nature.

" Infidels also, not subject to a Christian prince, may be compelled not to hinder the preaching of the faith in their parts ; the reason is, because the church has the right and power of preaching the gospel through the whole world, which Christ conceded to her. Matt. xxviii. 19, 'Teach all nations ;' and Mark xvi. 15, '.Preach the gospel to every creature.'

" If therefore the church be hindered in this right, Christian rulers can, as the defenders of the church by war or other means, restrain those who endeavour to hinder the preaching of the faith.

" According to Suarez, Herinx, &c., a Catholic ruler can compel infidels subject to him, under pain of exile, to be present at certain times at the preaching of the gospel ; because, according to the constitution of Gregory XIII., Jews living at Rome are compelled every week to be present once at a sermon concerning things of the faith.

" *Obj.* It is said, Luke xiv. 23. ' Go out into the highways and hedges, and compel them to come in ;' therefore, all infidels may be compelled to embrace the Christian faith.

" *Ans.* I deny the inference ; for the words of the parable, according to S. Gregory, are understood concerning compulsion, improperly so called, which is done through preaching, persuasion, showing of miracles, &c.

" But if with St. Augustine you understand the words concerning compulsion, properly so called, then they are understood concerning heretics and schismatics, who have at some time professed the faith, and who can be compelled.

" BAPTIZED INFIDELS, SUCH AS HERETICS AND APOSTATES USUALLY ARE, ALSO BAPTIZED SCHISMATICS, MAY BE

COMPELLED, EVEN BY CORPOREAL PUNISHMENTS, TO RETURN TO THE CATHOLIC FAITH, AND THE UNITY OF THE CHURCH.

"THE REASON IS, BECAUSE THESE BY BAPTISM HAVE BECOME SUBJECT TO THE CHURCH; AND THEREFORE THE CHURCH HAS JURISDICTION OVER THEM, AND THE POWER OF COMPELLING THEM THROUGH APPOINTED MEANS TO OBEDIENCE, AND TO FULFIL THE OBLIGATIONS CONTRACTED IN BAPTISM.

"This also holds good in those who have been baptized in infancy, or who have undergone baptism compelled by fear or some necessity; as the Council of Trent teaches, sess. 7, can. 14, concerning baptism, and the Council of Toledo, 4th can. 55.

"*Obj.* No one believes unless he is willing; but the will cannot be compelled; therefore, no one can be compelled to the faith.

"*Ans.* I deny the inference; for he is not compelled to believe against his will, but from unwilling, to become willing.

"You will insist: no one can be compelled to baptism, therefore, &c.

"I answer with St. Thomas,—'Just as it belongs to the will to vow, but to necessity to perform; so to receive the faith belongs to the will, but to keep it when received to necessity! *However, it is not always expedient for the church to use this right;* as will appear from what is to be said hereafter.' "

The sections which treat of Heresy and of the manner in which heretics are to be punished, speak for themselves. They will be appreciated by every Protestant, and they are respectfully and especially commended to the attention of those liberal and enlightened apologists for Popery, who tell us that Romanism has changed for the better. The preceding and following sections prove it to be the same bloody, persecuting and cruel religion that it always has been. We bring no gratuitous or railing accusation against the private members of the Romish church. The vast majority of them are probably ignorant of many of the vile principles with which the minds of their priests are saturated; but we cannot help regarding every man, who has been trained in the theological schools in which such tenets are inculcated, and who has failed to renounce them and the church which enjoins and practises them, as the foe of God and man, and the sworn enemy of our dearest civil and religious rights. It is only *expediency*, which restrains Holy Church from attempting to enforce these bloody tenets in our own land, and in the experience of American citizens!

In the following sections it is distinctly avowed, amongst other things of scarcely less atrocity, that " HERETICS ARE JUSTLY PUNISHED WITH DEATH." " HERESY IS NOT TO BE TRIED, OR PROVED, BUT TO BE EXTIRPATED, *unless there should be reasons, which may render its toleration advisable.*"

" *If greater evils would follow or greater benefits be hindered,*" then forsooth heretics may find some toleration from Holy Mother Church! Here is an open avowal that so soon as the priests of Rome have the *power*, they will consummate the atrocities, which their *theology* inculcates!

So soon as they can do it, they are bound by their very principles TO COMPEL baptized infidels, such as HERETICS, *i. e.* PROTESTANTS, even by CORPOREAL PUNISHMENTS to return to the CATHOLIC FAITH, and the unity *of the church!*

And yet some of these very men, who thirst for the blood of Protestants like ravening wolves, put on the sheep's clothing of zeal for liberty, and proclaim their attachment to its institutions from the house tops! " They bellow as they'd burst the heavens," Our Country! Our Country! American Independence and Liberty for ever! Out upon such barefaced hypocrites!

But we are accosted by some good men—"Admitting that the principles of Popery are as hideous as the blackness of darkness itself, yet ' where is the danger' to our free institutions, which you seem to apprehend from its existence in this country? The people of the United States are too in telligent as a body to fall in love with the cocked hats and cassocks of the priests and the crude absurdities of Popery, and too enthusiastically devoted to the cause of civil liberty, ever to surrender their freedom to the tender mercies of a few designing foreigners!"

I state in reply: The church of Rome already numbers in her fellowship in the United States, 200,000 members more than the aggregate of all the communicants in the combined Protestant churches! She claims TWO MILLIONS as the number who bow down to her images in this country. The Protestant churches contain according to a late accurate estimate, 1,800,000. In the aggregate of actual professors, therefore, we are according to her own statement outnumbered.

Now, it is true there are millions who avow some of the distinctive principles of Protestantism, who are not in immediate communion with any denomination. But on the other hand, there are not a few, whose predilections are in favour of Popery, though they are not enrolled on the registers of *Holy* Church. And what is the character of the large remnant of our population?

You will find many useful citizens and valuable members of society, who give themselves little or no concern about religion, but whilst we make provision for these more honourable exceptions, is it not true that the patriotism of multitudes, who are living without God in the world, who attach themselves to no place or form of worship, and who care for none of these things, is very questionable? Should any contingency arise, requiring the exercise of self-denying devotion to the country, how much dependence could be placed on them, if they were tempted to surrender some important principle by an appeal to passion or prejudice? Read the history of Europe; and do you not find in repeated instances that the power of the Pope gradually rose from a puny embryo to the stature and vigour of a giant? First, it asks an asylum, and, from sheer pity for its imbecility, an asylum is granted; and when by sycophancy and subserviency it has wormed itself into places of trust and profit, silently and gradually it accumulates a powerful influence; at length with the consciousness of growing strength, it begins to claim immunities, and when it has secured them, it next affects supremacy; and when it has gained this, instead of whispering out of the dust, it commands and threatens with a voice of thunder.

Twenty years ago the man who should have predicted that by this time Popery would be in the ascendency in this country would have been scouted as a fanatic. And with its present power before our eyes, with the voice of history calling to us from every kingdom and empire on the continent of Europe, "Beware of the Beast!" shall we be asked "Where is the danger?"

There is danger in the very nature of the fundamental principles of this monstrous system of superstition and cruelty. Their very enormity screens them by staggering credulity and giving to the truest portraiture the aspect of exaggeration.

There is danger in the insidious and insinuating address of its crafty and unprincipled priesthood, who are the sworn vassals of the Pope.

There is danger in the indifference and supineness of Protestants.

There is danger in the good-natured liberality of " unsuspecting Americans."

There is danger in the vast foreign resources both in men and money, which are at the command of the *Holy Fathers* in this country, and of which they know how to make use.

There is danger in the want of principle and patriotism in many ungodly politicians, who to carry personal or party measures will conciliate the votes of Papists at the expense of the constitution.

There is danger in the corruption and venality of most

of the public journals, whose publishers connive at the ma-
chinations of Popery through fear of losing a little patronage!

And there is danger in the present organized effort to con-
centrate the political influence of the Papacy in this country!

Concerning the intercourse of the Faithful with Infidels. (52.)

There is a threefold intercourse specified under this head.

" The first relates to those things which pertain to their false
religion, in which it is never lawful to communicate with infidels by performing their religious services : for this would
be to profess their sect ; hence it is lawful neither to make
churches, altars, sacerdotal robes, &c."

" The second is in marriage ; and this intercourse is forbidden to the faithful in this manner, that if they attempt to
contract it with unbaptized persons, the marriage is null and
void ; if with a baptized infidel, it is valid indeed, but in
itself unlawful."

" The third is in those things, which relate to civil and
political intercourse, such as buying, selling, feasts, &c. in
which it is lawful to communicate with infidels, unless they
are such, who have by name been denounced by the church
as (persons) to be avoided.   And although anciently all
heretics and all excommunicated persons were to be avoided ;
yet in our day from the moderation of the Council of Constance in the chap. Ad Evitanda, it is commonly taught,
that no excommunicated persons are to be avoided, unless
they have been denounced by name, or are notorious trou-
blers of the clergy.   Hence in our day there is no positive
law, which forbids Catholics to communicate with infidels in
civil affairs.

" Yet from the law of nature an obligation of avoiding heretics and excommunicated persons may arise, viz : on account
of the danger of perversion, or on account of the scandal of
others, or when intercourse with them is in the way of their
conversion.

" Is it lawful to dispute with infidels concerning the faith ?

" Whoever having once embraced the faith, disputes as
though doubting concerning the truth of the faith, sins without doubt ; as St. Thomas teaches, &c.

" The case is different with him, who has never embraced the faith and begins to doubt; such a one lawfully disputes in order to inquire the truth.

" Disputation with infidels has been permitted to some, if namely the disputants are learned and firm in the faith, and it can be prudently judged that the discussion will be profitable: and hence disputation with the obstinate is usually unlawful, unless there may be hope that it will be profitable to some other person, v. g. on the part of the hearers.

" It was said: *It has been permitted to some;* because (by chap. 2. concerning heretics in 6,) it has been prohibited to the laity under pain of excommunication to dispute concerning the faith. The words are: ' We forbid that it be permitted to any lay person either publicly or privately to dispute concerning the Catholic faith; but whoever shall do the contrary, shall be bound in the knot of excommunication.'

" But according to Suarez, Conink, &c. this law seems abrogated by contrary practice, where there is a great concourse of heretics, as in Belgium, Germany, &c. But understand this only of private discussion: for as Henricus declares from S. Ignatius, the holy congregation for propagating the faith decreed A. D. 1664, that it was lawful to no one to dispute with heretics by appointment, except by special license of the Apostolic See, or unless the state of the faith should require it, and there would be danger in delay."

Of tolerating the rites of Infidels. (53.)

" Are the rites of infidels to be tolerated?

" *Ans.* The rites of Jews, although they sin in exercising them, can be tolerated with some moderation; because great good accrues to the church from them, viz: because we have a testimony to our faith from enemies, as by their rites, those things which we believe are represented to us figuratively.

" It was said, ' with some moderation;' because if there be danger that the Jews by their peculiar rites offer scandal to Christians, the church can and ought to restrain or hinder, as shall be expedient: hence it has been decreed, (Bk. 5. Decret. tit. 6. ch. 3 and 7,) that it be not permitted to

10

the Jews to have many synagogues in one state, nor to build new ones in many places.

"The rites of other infidels, viz. pagans and heretics, in themselves (considered), ARE NOT TO BE TOLERATED: BECAUSE THEY ARE SO BAD, THAT NO TRUTH OR ADVANTAGE FOR THE GOOD OF THE CHURCH CAN BE THENCE DERIVED.

"*Except, however, unless greater evils would follow, or greater benefits be hindered.*

"*Obj. I.* The apostle says, Rom. xiv. 5. 'Let every man abound in his own sense;'* therefore liberty of religion is to be left to every one.

"I deny the inference: for the apostle is not treating of the rites of religion; but of the observance, or non-observance of the difference between days and meats according to the law of Moses, both of which could at that time be properly done.

"*Obj. II.* The dilemma of Gamaliel, Acts v. 38, where he says of those things, which the apostles did: 'Let them alone: for, if this design or work be of men, it will fall to nothing: but if it be of God, you are not able to destroy it.'

"*Ans. I.* This is not a dilemma of Holy Scripture, but of Gamaliel, who by this plausible argument wished to deliver the apostles, to whom he was favourably disposed, from present danger.

"*Ans. II.* Admitting that the reasoning of Gamaliel is substantial, there is a disparity, because the case of infidels is not doubtful to the judges of the church, as the case of the apostles was to the Jews: but it is agreed that it certainly is false and condemned; AND HENCE IT IS NOT TO BE TRIED, OR PROVED, BUT EXTIRPATED; *unless there may be reasons, which may render it advisable that it should be tolerated.*"

Concerning Heresy in particular. (No. 54.)

"Heresy is a Greek word, which signifies choice; because a heretic chooses by his own judgment to believe what he wishes.

---

* The Doway translation of the Scripture is unintelligible—the true meaning is given in the *Holy* Bible, "Let every man be fully persuaded in his own mind."

" It is sometimes taken objectively for a proposition containing some error against the faith; however, it is never properly taken objectively for the assent of the understanding, about such a proposition, and formal heresy is usually meant, concerning which in the following (chapters.)

" What is heresy?

" It is an obstinate error in the faith of a person professing Christianity.

" Explain this definition.

" It is said : 'of a person professing Christianity,' that it may be distinguished from Judaism and Paganism.

" It is said : ' an error ;' because heresy is in an erring understanding, as its nearest subject.

" It is added, ' In the faith,' because heresy imports a corruption of the faith, and is an error concerning those things, which belong to the faith.   But something pertains to the faith in a twofold manner : in one way, directly and principally, as the articles of faith ; in the other way, indirectly and secondarily, as that corruption of any article which follows from those things which are denied ; and heresy in the same way as faith may be concerning both.

" But an error concerning other truths or matters of discipline is not called heresy.

" It is subjoined, ' obstinate ;' because heresy imports choice, or that some one knowingly and willingly adheres to an error against the faith ; and hence, without obstinacy, it is not formal heresy, as St. Augustine says, (epist. 16.) ' Without obstinacy I may indeed err, but I shall not be a heretic.'

" And hence the distinction of formal and material heresy, is recognized : for material is an error in the faith without obstinacy.

" How, if to formal heresy obstinacy is required, can heretics, for instance in Holland, be reputed formal heretics, when they out of ignorance persuade themselves that their own sect is the true religion ?

" *Ans.* Although many among them labour under the ignorance by which they think their own sect to be the true religion, yet this very ignorance is usually from an alienation of mind from the faith, and with sufficient obstinacy for heresy ; because the Roman Catholic church had come sufficiently into their notice, shining forth by her own marks of credibility and the incredibility of their own sect; from which they can well enough discriminate that the Roman Catholic church is the true church of Christ, and is therefore to be heard as an infallible rule, according to which the first revealing truth is manifested to us; but this church they either reject, or deny to be the only church of Christ.

"The question is proposed, however, concerning many who have been born and educated among heretics or schismatics, in how far they can be excused from formal heresy.

"Steyaert replies, that in this matter it may generally with sufficient certainty be declared that many such, even after they have in the mean time attained to the use of reason, may be as yet excused: because either they hear nothing about the Catholic faith, or not so, that they are as yet sufficiently capable of discerning its grounds. Afterwards he adds, that it is very difficult to determine any thing specially; nor is it necessary to be too liberal in this respect, when we consider the opinions chiefly of the Fathers concerning the certain destruction of those who have not the true faith of Christ."

Concerning the Division of Heresy.

"How is heresy divided?

"It is divided into *formal* and *material* heresy, which division has been explained in the preceding number.

"Formal heresy is divided into *internal* and *external*, also into *secret* and *manifest*.

"Which heresy is called internal, and which external?

"*Internal* is that which lies concealed in the mind, so that it is betrayed by no outward sign.

"*External* is that which betrays itself by outward signs, from which, if persons were present, they could know that such a one was a heretic, although perhaps no one may be present who sees these signs; such as, trampling under foot the Holy Scripture, images of Christ and the saints, done in an heretical spirit.

"Which heresy is called secret, and which manifest?

"*Secret* heresy is that of him who has not yet been known as such by a considerable part of the community.

" The heresy is called *manifest* of him who is known as a heretic by a considerable part of the community.

" What are the punishments of the crime of heresy ?

" *Ans.* 1. Merely internal heresy in this age has no punishment, nor does it constitute a reserved case.

" *Ans.* 2. External heresy has the annexed greater excommunication of an enacted sentence, and reserved to the Pope.

" The second penalty is irregularity, for which see Tract concerning *Censure* &c.

" The third penalty is disqualification for public benefice and office, &c.

" The fourth penalty is privation of benefices and dignities : &c.

" The fifth is the privation of spiritual jurisdiction as well in the internal as in the external court : however understand this with the qualification appointed in the Council of Constance : (See No. 52 ;) hence so long as they are not denounced by name, or do not themselves recede from the church, they do not lose jurisdiction, and therefore absolve, dispense, &c. validly.   (See Sylvius, &c.)

" 6. Notorious heretics are infamous of course, and are deprived of ecclesiastical burial.

" 7. Their temporal goods are of course confiscated : yet a declaratory opinion concerning the crime from the ecclesiastical judge, ought to precede the execution : because the cognizance of heresy belongs to the ecclesiastical court.

" Finally they are deservedly visited with other penalties, even corporal, as exile, imprisonment, &c.

" ARE HERETICS RIGHTLY PUNISHED WITH DEATH ?

" St. Thomas answers, (2. 2. quest. xi. art. 3. in corp.) YES, BECAUSE FORGERS OF MONEY, OR OTHER DISTURBERS OF THE STATE, ARE JUSTLY PUNISHED WITH DEATH ; THEREFORE ALSO HERETICS, WHO ARE FORGERS OF THE FAITH, AND EXPERIENCE BEING THE WITNESS, GRIEVOUSLY DISTURB THE STATE.

" It is confirmed by this that God under the old law ordered the false prophets to be slain, and Deut. xvii. 12, decreed that, ' He that will be proud and refuse to obey the priest—shall die.'   See also chap. x. v. 19.   ' But he that will not hear his words, which he shall speak in my name, I will be the revenger.'

10 *

" The same is proved by the condemnation of the 14th art. of John Huss in the Council of Constance.

" It is to be observed that persons not baptized do not incur the above-named penalties, which have been appointed by the church, because not subject to the church ; apostates, however incur them, that is, they who after Baptism go over to the Jews or pagans.

" Are those who return from heresy to be received by the church ?

" I answer with S. Thom. quest. 11. art. 4 ; returning heretics are always to be received to penance ; although they may have relapsed frequently : both, because by penance they are brought back into the way of salvation, and because the church closes her bosom against no one returning to her. But they are not always to be restored to their former honours, dignities or offices, neither are they always to be liberated from all punishment, especially when they have relapsed into heresy."

CHAPTER XVI.

Concerning Blasphemy. (57.)

" WHAT is blasphemy ?

" *Ans.* Blasphemy as it is understood by the Fathers and Theologians, is *reproachful speech against God,* or *that by which, through means of reproach, something is detracted from the honour and excellence of God :* and hence you will easily distinguish it from the sin of infidelity, perjury, &c.

" It is said : *Speech,* either external and of the mouth, or internal and of the heart. *Against God,* either against himself, or against his creatures in so far as they belong to God, and the divine holiness and power shine forth in them, &c. *Reproachful ;* because it is done in opposition to God, against whom, as everywhere present, every curse is a real insult.

" Observe, that to constitute blasphemy it is not required, that it proceed from hatred or indignation against God, or that there be an expressed or formal intention of reproaching God; but that it is enough that the words, or the mode of pronouncing them as to themselves, may tend to the reproach or dishonour of God.

" How is blasphemy divided ?

"*Ans.* It is divided into blasphemy of the *heart* and of the *mouth.* Blasphemy of the *heart* is internal or mental ; of the *mouth* it is external, which discloses (itself) externally through words or other signs.

" It is divided into *immediate* and *mediate.*

" That is called *immediate*, which contains a reproach directly and proximately against God ; *mediate* is that which proximately relates to the saints or to other things, in so far as they have relation to God : for then this insult is reflected upon God ; and thus all blasphemy is against God either immediately or mediately.

" It is divided into *enunciative, defamatory,* and *imprecative. Enunciative* blasphemy is committed, either by affirming something concerning God which is repugnant to him, or by denying that which is consistent for him ; or by ascribing something to creatures, which properly belongs to God alone.

" *Defamatory* is committed by affirming any thing which truly pertains to God ; or by denying that which is not consistent for him, but in a reproachful manner, either through contempt or ridicule : for instance, if any one should find fault with Christ that he has suffered, died, &c. ; or should reproachfully mention the blood of Christ, his members, the sacraments, &c.

" *Imprecative* is that, when any one wishes or imprecates evil to God or the saints ; such is that execrable French blasphemy, Mort Dieu, by which they imprecate death upon everlasting life.

" Blasphemy is divided into *heretical* and *not heretical ; heretical* is that which contains heresy like this : ' Je renie Dieu (I deny God.')

" Finally, there is one blasphemy against the *Father*, another against the *Son*, and another against the *Holy Ghost ;* in so far as they are opposed to the appropriation, by which are specially attributed, power to the Father, wisdom to the Son, and goodness to the Spirit : thus, Matt.

xii., that is called blasphemy against the Holy Ghost, by which the manifest works of the Holy Spirit are ascribed to the devil.

Concerning the sin of Blasphemy. (58.)

" To what virtue is blasphemy repugnant?

" *Ans.* All blasphemy is repugnant to the virtue of religion; because it is contrary to the honour and reverence due to God.

" According to St. Thomas, all blasphemy of the mouth is opposed to the confession of faith; but not properly according to Sylvius. It is certain that external heretical blasphemy is opposed to the confession of faith, because by it something repugnant to the faith is asserted; if such a blasphemer inwardly feels with obstinacy as he has spoken, he will be a formal heretic.

" Are all blasphemies sins of the same kind?

" *Ans.* Although scholastics differ in theory, yet they agree in practice, that the quality of the blasphemy is to be expressed in confession, whether it has proceeded from hatred or indignation, or a reproachful spirit against God or the saints, or from an heretical spirit; also, whether it was immediate or mediate, or against the MOTHER OF GOD, or against other saints: the reason is, because one blasphemy may be distinguished from another, if not in kind, at least in degree.

" Moreover, all these things are usually ascertained by inquiring what words were spoken, and in what spirit, or on what occasion; which is the more to be observed in practice on account of the so great ambiguity of this word, *to swear*, among the common people, so that not even the kind of sin is sufficiently expressed.

" Farther observe that they may sometimes use profane phrases with a blasphemous spirit, and blasphemous phrases with a profane spirit.

" Besides, under the word, *to swear*, the common people sometimes include words which sound badly, or curses aimed at creatures, which in themselves contain only venial sin: although one can sin mortally from some other source, by reason of an erroneous conscience, a desire of injuring a neighbour, &c."

In the remainder of this section the question of the greatness of the sin of blasphemy is discussed. It is a *mortal* sin, and cannot under any circumstances be *venial ;* it is worse than homicide, perjury, &c. Blasphemy uttered in a joke is a mortal sin ; " because God is too great, and the saints his friends are too excellent to be exposed to our jokes or derision." But the case is different if for instance, by way of hyperbole, any one should call a woman a goddess ; or if by way of joke or levity a person should speak of the saints, not as saints, but merely as men ; " as if any one should say by way of jest, that St. Crispin was a cobbler," he would sin however by speaking thus irreverently, but not mortally, &c.

Blasphemy in its theological sense is a sin, which from its very nature can be committed against God alone. The word is of Greek origin, and was anciently used as equivalent to " defamation," and applied just as we employ that word to designate an offence against truth or due regard for a neighbour's reputation. In Scripture, the word " blasphemy" designates " reproachful speech against God," and is never employed in an inferior sense. The word of God never speaks of blasphemy against the *saints.* Hence to our mind there appears to be a taint of blasphemy in defining the sin as one which can be committed against other beings besides God. It is a presumptuous addition to " the words, which the Holy Ghost teaches," and therefore it is to be reprobated.

But one of the grossest and most appalling forms of blasphemy which the Devil has ever invented, is that which designates the Virgin Mary, as the MOTHER OF GOD ! Not content with this, Romish authors speak of the Virgin's Mother Anna, as the GRANDMOTHER OF GOD ! And when we shudder at this horrid impiety, the poor Papist looks at us in amazement, and asks, " What ! Do you mean to deny that Jesus Christ is God ? And was not Mary, the Mother of Christ ? And hence is it not clear that she is the MOTHER OF GOD ?"

I know that Jesus Christ is very God — but he was also *very man ;* and his relation to his earthly parent could not possibly extend farther than his human nature. How can the woman Mary, highly favoured as she was, be the mother of the Eternal God? I am pained in my very soul to think that rational and professedly religious men can be guilty of this daring and outrageous blasphemy!

CHAPTER XVII.

Concerning Rules of Faith. (59.)

" A RULE of faith is here called some stable and permanent principle, which applies to us an object of the Catholic faith, or by which the first revealing truth, and things divinely revealed to us are manifested, and infallibly known with sufficient credibility.

" But there are five rules of this kind, of which two are *inanimate* and three *animate.*

" The *inanimate* rules of faith contain the truths of the Catholic faith, in the manner of a deposit, and are Holy Scripture, and Divine Tradition.

" The *animate* rule of faith is that which declares to us the truths which God has revealed, so that it may propose them with sufficient authority, to be believed as it were by a divine faith ; and it is threefold, viz. the Church, the general Council, and the Pope determining " ex-cathedra." The Gallicans deny that concerning the Pope ; yet all admit that provisionally at least, we must abide by his decree.

" Concerning these things, we will treat in order, but briefly : Bellarmine, Sylvius in his Treatise concerning the Controversies of the faith, and others discuss the same at large.

Concerning Holy Scripture. (60.)

" Holy Scripture is usually designated by various names ; by way of eminence, it is called simply *Scripture,* also the

Bible, Sacred Writ, and the Testament of God, also the word, &c. of God.

" What is Holy Scripture?

" It is the written word of God, God inspiring and dictating it.

" The word of God is divided into *written*, and *unwritten*, or into *Holy Scripture*, and *divine Tradition*. Concerning Tradition, we shall treat hereafter.

" Has the Holy Scripture been dictated by God, not only as to matter and sentences, but also as to each word, letter, point, &c.?

" *Ans.* Yes; and it is proved from 2 Tim. iii. 16. ' All Scripture divinely inspired;' also from 2 Pet. i. 21. ' For prophecy came not by the will of man at any time; but the holy men of God spoke, inspired by the Holy Ghost;' and Matt. v. 18. ' Till heaven and earth pass, one jot or one tittle shall not pass from the law till all be fulfilled.'

" This also conduces to the greater dignity and authority of Scripture: nor do we otherwise sufficiently understand, how the Holy Fathers can testify that the tongues and hands of the Sacred writers, and the writers themselves were the pens and amanuenses of the Holy Spirit; also that each word, syllable, and point in the Scriptures are full of import.

" Does it concern the essence of Holy Scripture, that it has been dictated by God, as to single words?

" *Ans.* The affirmative opinion is the more common; because Holy Scripture is the word of God; but that which has not been dictated by God, is not the word of God; therefore if some words were not dictated by God, they do not belong to Holy Scripture.

" Concerning this thing more is to be seen in the censures and justification of Lovanian, and Duacensian Doctors, against these three assertions of Lessius, of which the first is; that in order that something be Scripture, it is not necessary that every word of it should have been inspired by the Holy Spirit.

" The second: It is not necessary that the single truths and sentences were inspired into the writer himself, immediately by the Holy Spirit.

" The third: Any book (such as perhaps the second of

Machabees, is) written by human industry, without the assistance of the Holy Spirit, is made Scripture, if the Holy Spirit afterwards testifies that there is nothing false there.

" *Obj. I.* Therefore our vulgate is not Holy Scripture ; because it was not dictated by the Holy Spirit as to single words.

" *Ans.* I admit our vulgate, (i. e.) that version was not dictated as to single words : I deny that it was not dictated as to single words in its fountain, or in the original, whence our vulgate has been translated, and with which it is considered the same.

" Whence remark, that the question is understood concerning the original, not concerning translations into other tongues, except in so far as by agreement with the original, they are considered the same with it, as to authority, infallibility and equivalence of truth and doctrine : and thus our vulgate is called, and is equivalently Holy Scripture, because the Church in the Council of Trent. Sess. 4. declared our vulgate to be authentic.

" *Obj. II.* The diversity of amanuenses does not make a diversity of style, if the same one is dictating ; but the style of the sacred books which were written by divers individuals is different ; therefore the same person was not dictating.

" *Ans.* I deny the inference ; because God in dictating chose to accommodate himself to the mind and condition of the writers, suggesting such words as were familiar to each ; and thus directing them, as if they had written by his (mind.)

" Hence Solecisms and other defects of writing are not to be imputed to the dictating spirit, but to the writer ; almost in a similar way as if a good writer had made use of a defective pen, the defect of the writing would be imputed to the pen, not to the writer.

" *Obj. III.* The author of the second book of Machabees, xv. 39, begs pardon, if he has not written the history with sufficient dignity and propriety. (' If I have done well, and as it becometh the history, it is what I desired ; but if not so perfectly, it must be pardoned me,') and ii. 24., he confesses himself the abbreviator of Jason the Cyrenian. (' All such things as have been comprised in five books by Jason of Cyrene, we have attempted to abridge in one book ;') the same says, v. 27, that he had undertaken not an easy task, but a business full of watching and sweat, ('and as to ourselves, indeed, in undertaking this work of abridging, we have taken in hand no easy task; yea, rather a business full of watching and sweat;') but all these things could not be said by him to whom all and every word had been divinely given by inspiration; therefore, &c.

" *Ans.* As to the first point, the reason has already been given. As for the second, nothing is said to hinder that the Holy Spirit should select some things from books written by human skill, and cause them to be written down by some one to whom he may dictate the single items. To the third, the answer is given, that the inspiration of the Holy Spirit does not exclude the labour and study of inquiry; for the writers were so moved in writing that they moved themselves: indeed it might be concealed from them, that they were in this manner moved by God; in the same way as it was concealed from Caiaphas, that he prophesied by divine suggestion, John xi. 50. ' Neither do you consider that it is expedient for you that one man should die for the people, and that the whole nation perish not,' to which the Evangelist subjoins, 51. 'And this he spoke not of himself; but being the high priest of that year, he prophesied that Jesus should die for the nation.'

" *Obj. IV.* One and the same voice of God the Father, uttered at the baptism of Christ, is related in different words by different writers; by Matthew iii. 17. ' This is my beloved Son, in whom I am well pleased,' and by Mark i. 11. 'Thou art my beloved son, in thee I am well pleased,' therefore, &c.

" *Ans.* I deny the inference: the reason is, because that voice of the father is alleged only in a relative sense; he who relates the words of another is supposed merely to relate their substance; but Holy Scripture is the peculiar and immediate word of God, in the positive sense, and therefore it ought to be such as to single words."

The divine inspiration of the Scriptures is a doctrine which is dear to every Christian. We believe that " Holy men of God spake as they were moved by the Holy Ghost," and that, thus, the Bible was prepared by the direct sugges-

11

tion of God ; and we know that it is a revelation of his will, from evidence which none of its adversaries can ever gainsay. The heavenly sentiments which the Scriptures contain ; the spirituality of their design ; the majestic simplicity of their style ; the artless and disinterested candour of the writers ; their harmony in innumerable instances in which collusion was impossible ; the wonderful power of the doctrines of Scripture on the hearts and consciences of men of every rank, condition, and country ; their astonishing preservation ; the multitude of miracles wrought to confirm them, and the exact fulfilment of their predictions up to this hour, sufficiently prove the Scriptures to be indeed the word of the living God.   Whether this inspiration is in the most absolute sense, plenary, or entire, has been, and still is a disputed point.   Whilst all evangelical Christians insist upon the inspiration of the doctrines, sentiments, &c. of the Bible ; there are some, who contend that the divine superintendence extended only to them, and not to the language in which they are clothed.

Paul affirms that he and the other apostles spoke not " in the words, which man's wisdom teacheth, but which the Holy Ghost teacheth ;" and a little reflection will suffice to show the importance of a proper selection of these words. We know how easily the beauty and efficacy of a discourse may be marred by impropriety of language ; if then, the sacred writers had not been directed in the choice of words, is it not certain, as many of them were illiterate men, that they would have expressed themselves inaccurately, and consequently have obscured and misrepresented the truth ? How then could our faith rest securely on their testimony ? We must infer, therefore, that the words of Scripture are from God, as well as the matter.   Nor can we recede from this conclusion, on account of the verbal discrepancies, to be found in some texts of Scripture, which contain a repetition of what is asserted in other passages, though it be expressly stated before each that the Lord made the communications *in these words.* We must concede to the Holy Spirit the same latitude in the use of language universally claimed by men in similar cases; and whilst it is obvious that as the words were spoken only once, they could not be communicated exactly under both the forms in which they now appear; yet for every useful and practical purpose the language consists of the identical words spoken on the occasion.

But whilst we agree with the Church of Rome, in the essential points of her theory of the plenary inspiration of the Scripture, we protest against all other rules of faith except the genuine Canonical Scriptures. We cannot recognize the Apocrypha as any part of divine Revelation, because internal and external evidence are both against it. The apology which is offered for the second book of Machabees, appears exceedingly lame; if the reader will recur to the third objection which our author attempts to refute, he will scarcely be convinced by the " answer" which follows it, that Judas Machabæus was inspired. There is a weakness and insipidity about him, which is utterly foreign to the inspired writers; and the excuses and apologies which he offers, are, in fact, equivalent to a direct disclaimer of inspiration. The special plea that " nothing is said to hinder that the Holy Spirit should select some things from books written by human skill, and cause them to be written down by some one to whom he may dictate the single items," is a fair specimen of Romish casuistry. On the same ground, we can prove that Cæsar's Commentaries are inspired. As for the allusion to the *prophecy* of Caiaphas, we need only remark, as it is evident the High Priest was not aware of the meaning which may properly be affixed to his words, that John simply records the fact as worthy of note, that this wicked High Priest should unconsciously have uttered so true a sentiment. God may verify the words of wicked men in a remarkable manner, but does that prove that Judas Machabæus was inspired?

Concerning the Division of Holy Scripture. (61.)

The only point worthy of special notice in this section is that which relates to the Apocrypha. The Scriptures are divided into the Old and New Testament; and the books of both Testaments are distinguished into *legal*, such as Genesis, Exodus, and the four gospels; *historical*, such as Joshua, Judges, and Acts of the Apostles; *doctrinal*, as Proverbs, Ecclesiastes, &c., and the Epistles of the New Testament; *prophetical*, as Isaiah, Jeremiah, &c., and the Apocalypse.

"The books of Holy Scripture are called canonical, because they have been recorded by the church upon a canon or catalogue of divine books; and also because they contain the model or rule which we ought to follow both in faith and customs. These the Council of Trent reviews, sess. 4, viz., of the Old Testament, 45, of the New Testament, 27, and so altogether 72; and commands them, under pain of anathema, to be held for divine.

"The canon of the books of the Old Testament is two-fold: one Jewish, the other Christian.

"Among the sacred books which the church recognizes as such, some are called *protocanonical*, and others *deuterocanonical*.

"The former are those concerning which there never has been any doubt among the faithful.

"The latter are those concerning which, although they are now recorded on the canon of sacred books, yet anciently it was doubted whether they were Holy Scripture; of this nature are, from the Old Testament, the Book of Tobias, Judith, the Book of Wisdom, of Ecclesiasticus, Baruch, the Epistles of Jeremiah, First and Second Machabees, fragments or additions of Esther, from chap. x. v. 4, to the end; and additions of Daniel, viz. chap. iii.; the Song of the Three Children, the History of Susanna, and the History of Bel and the Dragon. From the New Testament, the Epistle of Paul to the Hebrews, Epistle of James, Second of Peter, Second and Third of John, Epistle of Jude and the Apocalypse; also, the last chapter of St. Mark, from v. 9; the history of the bloody sweat, and of the comforting by the angel (Luke 22); the history of the adulterous woman, John viii. ; and v. 7, chap. v. Epist. 1 of St. John : 'For there are three who bear record in heaven, the Father,' &c.

"Farther, as well the deutero as the protocanonical are of equal dignity and authority among Catholics.

"To the canonical books are opposed the apocryphal, which are so called because the church did not receive them into the canon, because it could not find a well-founded tradition concerning them, although some of the Fathers sometimes questioned their divinity ; such are the third and fourth Book of Esdras, the third and fourth of Machabees ; the prayer of King Manasseh when a captive, &c.   Among the apocryphal books some are *positively* apocryphal or *reprobated ;* such are those which Pope Gelasius condemns, &c. ; others are *negatively* apocryphal, *i. e.*, neither approved as divine by the church, nor reprobated.

"Can an apocryphal book become canonical ?

"A positively apocryphal book cannot be made canonical ; but one which is only negatively apocryphal can become canonical : for nothing hinders a book to be sacred, and the fact to be unknown for some time in the church, but afterwards to be known ; as happened concerning the book of Judith, Esther, &c.

"May a canonical book also become apocryphal ?

"*Ans.* Yes; viz., if either the notice of its canonization perishes, or is mixed with so many extraneous additions that the divine can no more be discerned from the human. These things are easily perceived from the manner in which some things can begin or cease to be (matters) of faith," &c.

The ancient writings which are introduced in the foregoing list of Old Testament apocrypha, and which are of equal dignity and authority among Papists as the genuine Scriptures, were never recognized either by the Jewish or Christian church as constituting any portion of the genuine Scriptures. And yet, whoever disputes their authenticity is " anathema," according to the decree of Holy Mother : *i. e., cursed in this world, and damned in the next !* A very severe sentence, we think, for presuming to question the truth of stories, some of
11 *

which the earliest fathers of the Christian church denounced as *fables.* We are not surprised, however, at the zeal of the church of Rome in behalf of the Apocrypha, because she depends on some of these spurious scriptures for important testimony, by which to sustain a few of her corrupt practices. Now, as she can ill afford to lose an iota of such evidence, with our knowledge of her temper we do not wonder that she is indignant whenever the Apocrypha is assailed. Popish anathemas in our day are considered *apocryphal* arguments, and are calculated to excite the mirth rather than convince the judgment of all except the faithful, and therefore with the full knowledge that we incur the curse of Holy Mother, we shall notwithstanding offer our reasons for rejecting the Old Testament Apocrypha.

1. They possess no authority whatever, either internal or external, to warrant their insertion in the sacred canon. Not one of them is extant in Hebrew; all of them are in the Greek language, except the fourth book of Esdras, which is extant only in Latin. Their authors for the most part were Alexandrian Jews, who wrote subsequently to the cessation of the prophetic spirit, though before the promulgation of the Gospel.

2. Not one of them professes to be inspired; and their writings were NEVER received into the Jewish canon, and therefore were not sanctioned by the Saviour.

3. No part of the Apocrypha is at any time quoted either by Christ or any of his apostles; neither does Philo or Josephus, who wrote in the first century, make any allusion to them.

4. The Apocryphal books were not admitted into the canon of Scripture at all, until after the fourth century. They are wanting in the catalogue of inspired writings made by Melito, bishop of Sardis, in the second century; they are not in Origen's catalogue in the third century; and they are omitted in the catalogues of Athanasius, Hilary, Cyril

of Jerusalem, Epiphanius, Gregory Nazianzen, Amphilo-chius, Jerome, Rufinus, and others of the fourth century ; nor are they mentioned in the catalogue of canonical books recognized by the council of Laodicea held in the same century.

5. The Apocrypha, notwithstanding the veneration in which its books were held by the Romish church, was never formally recognized as possessing the same authority as the genuine Scriptures, until the last council of Trent at its fourth session, with characteristic impudence, presumed to place them all (except the prayer of Manasseh, and the third and fourth books of Esdras,) in the same rank with the inspired writings of Moses and the prophets.

As for the epistles and portions of the New Testament, which are included in the list of deuterocanonical books, their authenticity was sufficiently established in the early ages of the church, and there is internal evidence enough to convince all who read them that they are genuine. They need no apology.

Concerning the Meanings of Holy Scripture. (62.)

"What is the sense of Holy Scripture?

"*Ans.* It is that signification, which the words of Scripture immediately, or mediately signify by the intention of the Holy Spirit.

" The sense is divided into literal and mystical.

" Literal is subdivided into *proper,* and *improper,* or *metaphorical.*

" Mystical is subdivided into *allegorical, anagogical,* and *tropological,* or *moral.*

" The *proper* literal sense, is that which the words taken in their proper meaning immediately signify ; such is the sense of these words, ' thou shalt worship the Lord thy God ; thou shalt not kill,' &c. in which no figure, or metaphor, is to be sought.

" The *improper* literal, or the *metaphorical* sense, is that which is immediately signified by words improperly, or figuratively taken ; such as is the meaning in this sentence of Matt. v. 20. ' If thine eye offends thee, pluck it out,'

&c. where eye is not taken properly for the organ of the body, but figuratively for a thing as necessary and acceptable as the eye is.

"It is the same, when an arm is attributed to God; for by it is not meant some corporeal member, but metaphorically divine virtue and power, also, when Christ is called a lamb, vine, &c. these things ought to be taken metaphorically; and generally words are to be understood metaphorically, when a false, impious, or absurd sense would follow from them if properly taken.

"The mystical sense is then defined to be that, ' which is denoted over and above the things signified by the words;' thus this sentence, Ex. xii. 46. 'You shall not break a bone thereof,' was spoken literally of the paschal lambs, and mystically of Christ, as appears from John xix. 36.

"Farther, the mystical sense is threefold, viz., the first is *allegorical*, when the things signified by the words, intimate something pertaining to the church militant, and the instruction of the faith. An example is afforded, Gal. iv. in the two sons of Abraham, Ishmael born of the bond-woman, and Isaac of the free-woman, who prefigured the Old and New Covenant.

"The second, the *anagogical* (sense) is that, when the things signified by the words import something pertaining to the church triumphant, and is referred to hope; thus the entrance of the Israelites into Palestine, after various afflictions, and conflicts, signified that through many tribulations we must enter the kingdom of heaven.

"The third, the *tropological*, or *moral* (sense) is, when actions are the signs of those things, which we ought to do; thus from the command, Deut. xxv. 4; 'thou shalt not muzzle the ox that treadeth out thy corn on the floor,' the apostle proves, 1 Cor. ix. 11, that support is due to the preachers of the gospel from those to whom they proclaim it. 'If we have sown unto you spiritual things, is it a great matter if we reap your carnal things,' and v. 14. 'The Lord ordained that they who preach the gospel should live of the gospel,' &c.

"This one word Jerusalem embraces these four meanings: for in the *literal* sense, it signifies the well-known metropolis of Palestine; *allegorically*, it signifies the church militant ; *tropologically*, or *morally*, the soul of a just man ; and *anagogically*, the church triumphant."

All Scripture has a literal ; but not every Scripture has a mystical sense.

" Besides the already named senses of Sacred Scripture, is there not another, which is called the *accommodatory ?*[*]

" *Ans.* The accommodatory sense is, that which is neither immediately signified by the words, nor mediately by the things designated in the words, but which is applied, or accommodated to signify something else, v. g. by the preacher : and hence, it is not properly the sense of Sacred Scripture, as it was not intended by the Holy Spirit.

" The custom of the church proves, that the use of the accommodatory sense is lawful; the church accommodates very many things from the book of Wisdom, to the blessed Virgin, and various other things to other Saints ; indeed, even Christ himself, Matt. xxv. 7. applies the words of Isaiah, xxix. 13, to the Scribes and Pharisees of his own time ; ' this people honours me with their lips,' (although) spoken to the Jews in the time of Isaiah.

" This use in honourable things for a good object has been permitted, even to private individuals ; hence, the so frequent use of it among the Holy Fathers, and pious preachers. Nor is it doubtful, that the Holy Spirit sometimes has suggested similar meanings to readers, so that on this account, St. Augustine calls them the meanings of Sacred Scripture.

" Yet observe, that many frequently abuse the words, or sentences of Holy Scripture, when they accommodate them in common discourse, or otherwise, to profane things, jests, &c. ; for, this, sanctity and the reverence due to the word of God forbid."

To the " accommodatory" system of interpretation, when *properly, judiciously*, and *scripturally* exercised, there can certainly be no objection.   It frequently happens that a passage of Scripture is peculiarly applicable to circumstances, &c., different in many respects from those under which it was originally given, but yet there is some great leading

---

[*] I am obliged to coin an English word, corresponding to the Latin, *accommodatitius*, which is a monkish fabrication.

feature, which is the same in both instances, and therefore the application may be correctly made to either. Whenever the abstract principle, or truth, contained in the Scripture, is applicable to present circumstances, there can be no reasonable objection to the system of accommodation. But we must protest against the accommodatory meaning in the sense and latitude, in which it is employed by the Church of Rome. To mention one abuse out of many; the whole Psalter, or book of Psalms, has actually been accommodated by one of her Cardinals, to the worship of the Virgin Mary, by substituting the words Mother of God, Virgin, Lady, &c., for the name of Jehovah, and otherwise corrupting the Sacred Text.

The following is an extract:

" Here beginneth the Psalter of the blessed Virgin, made by the Seraphical doctor, St. Bonaventure, bishop of Alban, and Cardinal of the Holy Church of Rome.*

" Blessed is the man that understandeth thy name, O Virgin Mary, thy grace shall comfort his soul. Thou shalt bring forth in him the most plentiful fruit of justice, &c.

" Why do our enemies fret and imagine vain things against us? let thy right hand defend us, O Mother of God, terribly confounding and destroying them as a sword. Come unto her, all ye that labour, and are troubled, and she will give rest unto your souls, &c.

" When I called to thee, thou heardest, O my lady, and out of thy high throne, thou didst vouchsafe to think of me, &c. Blessed be thou, O lady, for ever, and thy majesty, for ever dear.

" Preserve me, O lady, for in thee have I put my trust, &c.

" Blessed be thy breasts, which, with thy deifying milk, did nourish the Saviour, &c.

" I will love thee, O lady of heaven and earth; I will call upon thy name among the nations, &c. All ye cloisterers honour her, for she is your helper, and special advocate.

---

* Canonized by Pope Sixtus, in 1482, and now worshipped as a Saint.

"The wicked man said, &c. Let him depart from his evil purpose; O Mother of God, turn the countenance of God towards us; compel him to be merciful unto sinners, &c.

"My heart is inditing a good matter, O lady, &c.

"Clap your hands, all ye people, &c. For she is the gate of life, the door of Salvation, the reconciler of our life, the hope of the penitent, the comfort of the sorrowful, the blessed peace of hearts and Salvation.

"Have mercy upon me, O lady, have mercy upon me; for thou art the light, and hope of all that put their trust in thee.

"The Lord said unto our lady, Sit here, my mother, on my right hand, &c.

"In the passing of my soul out of this world, come and meet it, O lady, and receive it, &c. Be to it a ladder to the kingdom of heaven, and a right way to the paradise of God &c.

"Except our lady shall build the house of our heart, the building thereof shall not continue," &c., &c.*

How any creature out of hell could ever have dared to utter such horrid blasphemies, is a mystery to me!

Concerning the Obscurity of Sacred Scripture.

"Is Holy Scripture obscure?

"It is agreed against the heretics, that Holy Scripture in various passages is obscure.

"It is proved from Acts, viii., where Philip asks the Eunuch who was reading Isaiah, v. 30. 'Thinkest thou that thou understandest what thou readest?' and he says, v. 31. 'And how can I, unless some one show me?' also, from 2 Ep. of Pet. iii. 16., where speaking of the Epistles of Paul, he says: 'In which are some things hard to be understood.'

"It is proved, also, from the unanimous consent of the Holy Fathers: and more than that, the very dissensions of heretics clearly show it; for why, if Scripture is every-where clear, as they say, do they themselves differ among themselves, and assemble Synods in order to determine con-

* See Fox's Acts, and Mon. p. 185, folio.

troversies? Why do the Lutherans understand Scripture in one way, and the Calvinists in another?

"Wherefore is the sense of Scripture often obscure?

"In the first place, that obscurity arises partly from the mysteries which are there contained, and surpass human apprehension, partly from phrases peculiar to that language in which the sacred books were written, partly from figurative expressions, and partly from sentences apparently contradictory.

"But neither were reasons wanting why it should be proposed in an obscure manner.

"First indeed to rebuke our pride, inasmuch as from this we are compelled to confess our ignorance, and to ask wisdom from God.

"Secondly. For the majesty and reverence of sacred Scripture; for those things which are easily investigated for the most part become contemptible.

"Thirdly. 'In order that a studious mind may be both more usefully exercised in investigating, and more abundantly rejoiced in finding them,' says St. Augustine; for those things which have been obtained by labour and in a long time, are loved more, and remain more permanently.

"Fourthly. That mysteries may be hidden from the derision of infidels."

One of the most common devices which the church of Rome has employed to hinder the circulation and study of the Scriptures, is developed in this section. "The Scriptures are obscure, and are not to be understood by the common people." That there are some passages which are less easily understood than others, is freely admitted, but the texts which present any real difficulty are comparatively few and far between. The argument which is based upon the case of the eunuch, whom Philip found reading Isaiah, is contemptible. Was it any wonder that the eunuch, whose acquaintance with revelation was so slender and recent, should be at a loss to understand the prophecies which related to a Saviour of whom he had never heard? At all events, if the Scriptures had been in an *unknown* tongue, he could not have read them. In relation to the other passage from 2 Peter iii. 16, we would remark :

1. The Apostle Peter does not say ἐν αἷς, but ἐν οἷς, not *in which Epistles* of Paul (as Peter Dens has it), but *in which things* (points or doctrines mentioned before), " many things are hard to be understood." If the *Epistles* of Paul had been intended, then the Greek relative would have been in the *feminine*, as the noun Ἐπιστολη is feminine ; but the relative is in the neuter, οἷς, plainly showing that it refers to the word τούτων, which immediately precedes it ; indeed, the word " Epistles" is not mentioned, though Peter is evidently alluding to them in the preceding verse.

2. Whilst it is admitted that some points are in themselves hard to be understood, we distinctly affirm that all things necessary to salvation are sufficiently expressed and plainly revealed.

3. Those things which are at all obscure in Paul's Epistles, are perspicuously explained in other parts of Scripture.

4. The apostle does not say that these things are *hard* to be understood, simply and to all men, but to the " ignorant and unstable, who wrest other Scriptures to their own destruction ;" and, by the way, the church of Rome is paying a poor compliment to her children by citing this text as a reason for withholding the Scriptures from them.

5. And even supposing that the Scriptures are hard to be understood, and that they are wrested by some to their own damnation, how does it follow *that they are no guide at all, or even an uncertain one ?*

May it not just as well be said that Christ was not an infallible guide, because he spoke parables, and many of his words were wrested by the Jews to their destruction ? For instance, when he spoke of destroying the temple, and building it in three days, John ii. 19.——or when he said he was the Son of God, Matt. xxvi. 64, 65, upon which they

12

cried out he had spoken blasphemy, and they needed no farther witness, &c.

Concerning the reading of Sacred Scripture.

" Is the reading of Sacred Scripture necessary or commanded to all ?

" *Ans.* That it is not necessary or commanded to all, is plain from the practice and doctrine of the universal church ; for which reason, in the Bull unigenitus, the 70th proposition concerning this thing was condemned : ' It is useful and necessary at every time and place, and for every kind of people to study and learn the spirit, piety, and mysteries of Sacred Scriptures.' To this add the 80th, 81st, 82d, 83d, 84th, and 85th propositions, condemned in the same bull.

" It is farther proved, thus : it is the duty of some in the church to teach ; it is the duty of others to seek knowledge of the law from the mouth of the priests, almost in the same way as, in civil affairs, it is not the duty of all to investigate the laws, adjudge controversies, &c.

" This is confirmed : because St. Augustine, Book 1, concerning Christian doctrine, chap. xxxix. reports that certain churches, during two centuries and more, subsisted without the Scriptures ; add to this that many of the faithful do not know how to read, to whom it is not convenient either, to have any one who might read before them.

" Besides, the Sacred Scripture was not read in the church, except in Latin, Hebrew, or Greek, until the fourth century, and in Spain, only in Latin, until the sixth century ; and in England until the seventh century, as Bede attests ; and Harney shows that our ancestors had no Bibles rendered into the vulgar tongue, in the first eight centuries after Christianity was planted here.

" But if the fathers had judged the promiscuous reading of Sacred Scripture to be necessary, as Quesnel and the other heretics boisterously assert, undoubtedly they would have translated it into the vulgar tongue.

" But the study of Sacred Scripture is, by reason of their office and station, necessary to the priests and rulers of the church, on whom the labour of teaching and arguing is incumbent, according to that which is said, Matt. ii. 7. ' The lips of the priest shall keep knowledge, and they shall seek

the law at his mouth;' and therefore John Henry, Archbishop
of Mechlin, in his decree of March 12, 1762, justly resolved
that no one should hereafter be admitted by him to sacred
orders, unless he has diligently perused the principal books
of Sacred Scripture.

"Is the reading of Sacred Scripture permitted to all persons?

"*Ans.* The church does not forbid by any decree, the
reading of Sacred Scripture, even to the laity, in the Hebrew,
Greek, or Latin language.

"Of course, however, this must be abstained from, if this
reading, through defect of capacity, or disposition of the
mind, would be of bad tendency; as it was in regard to
those of whom Peter speaks, 2 Ep. iii. 16., 'which the unlearned and unstable wrest to their own destruction.'

"The church does not absolutely forbid the reading of
Sacred Scripture in the vernacular tongue to the laity, or to
persons of any condition, whatsoever; but it does not permit it except with great caution.

"This discipline of the church which had already been
received by custom in particular churches, was established
for the whole church, by the fourth rule of the index,
towards the close of the Council of Trent, in these words:

"'As it is manifest by experience, if Holy Bibles in the
vulgar tongue are everywhere indiscriminately permitted,
more injury than advantage would accrue, on account of the
temerity of people, let it abide in this point by the judgment
of the bishop, or inquisitor: that with the advice of the
priest, or confessor, the reading of Bibles in the vulgar
tongue, translated by Catholic authors, may be conceded to
those, who they know can derive no injury, but an increase
of faith and piety from such reading: which permission
they must have in writing. But whoever shall presume
without such permission to have, or to read them, cannot
obtain absolution of his sins, unless the Bibles be first returned to the ordinary. But regulars may neither purchase, nor read them, except by permission obtained from
their Prelates.'

"Moreover, if you except certain points, such as (those)
are relating to the obtaining of permission in writing, the
returning of the Bibles previous to absolution, and to be

made to the ordinary, the observance of this law is strenuously urged by the bishops of Catholic Belgium; as may be seen in Harney: and as for this Diocese, See Synod. Diœces. ii. lit. i. ch. 8, &c.

"Indeed, according to Steyaert, this law has been received, and hitherto kept (with some variation, on account of the prevailing spirit of some regions) in by far the greatest part of the Catholic world; indeed, in the whole purely Catholic world: MORE INDULGENCE HAS BEEN GRANTED, ONLY WHEN IT WAS NECESSARY TO LIVE AMONG HERETICS.

"Observe that according to the rule stated (above), the power of granting permission to read the Sacred Scripture in the vernacular tongue, belongs to the bishop, or inquisitor, not to the priest, or confessors, unless this power has been conceded to them.

"The prohibition of keeping, and reading vernacular Bibles, includes the parts of the Old, as well as of the New Testament, which custom does not except; but some of the psalms are excepted by custom, the canticles, and the passion of the Lord inserted in prayer books. The custom has likewise obtained in many places, that the epistles, and gospels, may be read, which are to be sung during the year in the mass; also, the history of the Old and New Testament.

"Sylvius teaches in various explanations, under the word *Bibles*, that pastors, preachers, and others, who are preparing for the office of priest, or preacher, may make use of Scripture in the vernacular language: because this permission has been conceded to them, by the very fact that they are designed for such office; and certainly it has been conceded by the Council of Trent. sess. xxii. ch. 8., where it enjoins that the Sacred Oracles be frequently explained in the vernacular tongue, during the solemnities of the mass, or the celebration of the divine offices. This explanation of Sylvius, common custom approves and confirms.

"He adds, however, that it is not equally agreed, concerning priests, who are preparing for the office, either of priest or preacher, and much less concerning laymen, well skilled in Latin.

"The Quesnellites object: this prohibition is unjust; because a thing, good and useful in itself, is not a matter of prohibition; but Sacred Scripture is a thing in itself good and useful, to be taught, argued, &c., as is said, 2 Tim. iii., therefore, &c.

"I answer by distinguishing the assumption of the proof; I admit the assertion, that a thing good and useful in itself cannot be matter of prohibition on its own account; but I deny the assertion, that it cannot be matter of prohibition through contingency, on account of circumstances, persons, effects, &c.   For instance; communion under both kinds, although in itself it is excellent, is still forbidden to the laity: thus, also, articles of food in themselves good are wisely denied to those, to whom by reason of infirmity, or weakness, they would be hurtful, or dangerous.

"But you will reply: although some persons may abuse food, or drink, as for instance, wine, the use of these things cannot therefore be forbidden, therefore, &c.

" 1. *Ans.* I admit the antecedent, when understood of a law prohibiting universally; because they are of universally necessary use, or simply useful: although even in these things, in order to obviate the abuse, a certain moderation in the use may be prescribed.

" 2. *Ans.* I deny the inference: there is a disparity, because Sacred Scripture has not been ordained, that any one may of himself make use of it like meat and drink; inasmuch as the use of these things cannot be supplied from another source, whilst the reading of Sacred Scripture is supplied more usefully, and without danger of detriment, through the instruction of pastors, &c., from whose mouth the people ought to seek the law of God.   Whence, observe, that Sacred Scripture is a Testament, pertaining, indeed, to all, as to the matter, but not as to the reading of the Testament.

" 3. *Ans.* It has already been stated above, that the reading of Sacred Scripture is not simply prohibited; but in taking away the abuse the church moderates its use, leaving it to the discretion of superiors, (which cannot thus be done in the use of wine), who can judge to whom this use or reading may be good and useful.

" *Obj. II.* St. Chrysostom, Hom. 9, Epist. to Col., speaks thus: " Hear, I beseech you, ye LAYMEN; all of you get Bibles for yourselves, as medicine for the soul;' and Hom.

12 *

3, concerning Lazarus, he says, the reading of Sacred Scripture is necessary to salvation. Likewise, St. Jerome exhorted women also, Paula, Eustochia, &c., to read the Scripture; therefore, Sacred Scripture is to be read by all, even in the vernacular tongue.

" I answer by denying the inference: in the first place, those Fathers do not say that Sacred Scripture is to be read in a language that is not sacred: but those women to whom St. Jerome speaks, were well versed in the Latin tongue.

" It must be said that in this point the discipline of the church has been changed, just as communion under both kinds and daily communion have been changed. For formerly the faithful, more submissive to their pastors, humbly and faithfully derived the sense of Scripture from them without danger of perverse translations; but now, through the example of the heretics, the lust of dissenting from the pastors has arisen; and it is manifest from experience that BY THE PROMISCUOUS READING OF THE SACRED SCRIPTURE, MEN ARE MADE MORE PROUD, MORE DISCONTENTED, AND UNI-VERSALLY MORE CONCEITED. As for that which is objected out of the Holy Fathers, — when they wished to inculcate any thing as proper and useful in their own time, they occasionally used words, by which not only advantage, but also absolute necessity at first appearance was indicated; but that they did not think the reading of the Holy Scripture to be necessary for all, is sufficiently gathered from other passages: and thus St. Chrysostom himself, Hom. 21. on Genesis, says, that the Scriptures are not to be searched by all; and St. Jerome, writing to Paulinus, complains, that all men are presuming to read and interpret Sacred Scripture."

We have sometimes known the advocates of Romanism boldly deny that their church forbids the laity to read the Scriptures; and in the foregoing section it will be observed that notwithstanding all the special pleading in favour of withholding the word of God from the common people, it is expressly stated, " The church does *not* absolutely forbid the reading of Sacred Scripture in the vernacular tongue to the laity, or to persons of any condition whatsoever, but it does not permit it except with great caution." The decree of the

Council of Trent, an infallible œcumenical convention of Romish doctors and bishops, is very explicit in its *conditional* prohibitions, but even there it is not *absolute*, as the Bishop or Inquisitor may permit the laity to read the Bible whenever it is *likely to do no harm*. It is perfectly manifest, however, that the Romish Church is the deadly enemy of the general distribution and investigation of the Scriptures. Her priests hate the Bible; and we are not surprised at the rancour with which they assail the Protestant's Rule of Faith. By their own confession, Popery cannot be sustained by Scripture; they must prop up their system by the pillars of tradition, or it crumbles into dust. But the golden age of Romanism is for ever gone! Thanks to the "example of heretics," there are many in the communion of the Romish Church who claim the right of searching the Scriptures for themselves. Those were palmy days "when the faithful, more submissive to their pastors, humbly and faithfully derived the sense of Scripture from them;" then, like dutiful children, the faithful received all as gospel which the Holy Fathers told them, and piously asked forgiveness and did penance whenever their ghostly counsellors detected them exercising themselves in things that were beyond the apprehension of the laity! Oh! how the bowels of Holy Mother yearn for such a *revival of religion;* how the Holy Fathers sigh, when they are compelled to afford more license to the circulation of the Sacred Scriptures than is consistent with the dignity and true prosperity of Holy Church! And yet, far be it from those holy men *absolutely* to forbid the laity to read the Bible. Any one of the faithful may possess a copy of the Scriptures in Latin or Greek, and he may have the Old Testament in Hebrew, too, provided he does not understand those languages, because then the word of God can do him no harm; it will not make him PROUD, or DISCONTENTED, or CONCEITED, if he cannot discern one word from another, but it will tend rather to augment his veneration for the sacred mysteries of Scripture. The faithful who have never learned their alphabet, are also at liberty to purchase Bibles in the vernacular tongue, especially such as the priest or bishop has blessed; and no doubt they will find them quite as efficacious in driving away the devil as a pot of " holy water."

But now, in all seriousness, what are we to think of the Church whose priests are taught that the promiscuous reading of the Scriptures renders men universally more PROUD, DISCONTENTED, and CONCEITED! That it makes them discontented with popery, we can readily believe; that it causes them to turn even with contempt from its absurdities, we do not doubt; and this very fact furnishes us with one of our strongest arguments. Popery can not stand before the light of Scripture; it shrinks from God's testimony abashed and confounded. The priests well know that the word of God is their most uncompromising enemy. It specifies the corruptions of their church by the voice of prophecy; it reprobates many of her peculiar dogmas by name, and brands her with the marks of apostasy! Its very silence condemns her forms and ceremonies, by proving that they are mere human inventions; whilst the purity, peace, and love, which beam on every page of the sacred volume, rebuke the lewdness and cruelty for which she is notorious. But it is a foul slander on the sacred oracles to assert that their perusal can be pernicious. If the theology of Rome is true, then the inference is irresistible, that the Bible must be a bad book. If it uniformly produces injurious results in exact proportion to the extent of its circulation, we repeat, *it must be a bad book*, and it is blasphemy to assert that God is its author. He cannot be the author of evil.

The opposition of the Church of Rome to the Scriptures, proves that her cause is desperate. "Every one that doeth evil, hateth the light, neither cometh to the light, lest his deeds should be reproved." But without farther introduction, let us briefly state, why the Protestant Churches believe it proper, that the Scriptures should be translated into every language on earth, for the edification of all people.

1. If all Christians are under obligation, according to their capacity, to " search the Scriptures," and by them to test the doctrines of their teachers, then the Scriptures ought necessarily to be translated into the vulgar tongues, that the people may be enabled to do this. But the first is the direct command of God. When the Jews would not believe Christ, he bade them, " search the Scriptures," &c. John v. 39. And in Acts, xvii. 11., the Bereans are commended in these words : " these were more noble than those in Thessalonica, in that they received the word with all readiness of mind, and searched the Scriptures daily, whether those things were so." Therefore it is right that the Scriptures should be translated into the vulgar tongue.

2. Jehovah himself, when he gave a law to the Jews, promulgated it in their *common* language ; and both the Old and New Testaments were delivered in tongues that were most familiar in those times, respectively, to the church ; therefore, from this fact, it is also evident that for the general use and benefit of the common people, the Scriptures may and ought to be translated into the languages, which are most familiar to them.

3. If the Holy Scriptures were lawfully and necessarily translated into Latin, for the use of the Latin Church, then by parity of reason they ought to be translated into other tongues ; unless it can be proved that the Scriptures were more necessary to the Latin, than to other churches. Now that they were thus lawfully translated into Latin for the purposes stated, our adversaries will not deny. Therefore it is right that they should be rendered into every other language.

4. If we lock up the Scripture in unknown languages, we frustrate the very end for which God designed it. He has

given it to us as a revelation of his will, that by hearing reading, understanding, believing, and obeying it, we may be saved. "For whatsoever things were written aforetime were written for our learning; that we through patience and comfort of the Scriptures might have hope." Rom. xv. 4. But how are we to learn these things and thus through patience and comfort of the Scripture have hope,' unless they are translated into a language which we understand?

5. If it be wanton cruelty to deny any one bodily food and sustenance, it is still worse to deprive people of the food and nourishment of their souls. Now as the Holy Spirit frequently declares the Scripture to be the 'word of life,' and compares it to "milk," and "strong meat," the oracles of God should be translated into a language, which the unlearned may understand, because otherwise they are deprived of this spiritual nourishment. The Romish Church is guilty of the utmost cruelty and sacrilege in thus starving the souls, whom she professes to feed.

6. It is wicked to deprive the Christian Soldier of his spiritual weapons; he needs them at all times and everywhere. But the Holy Scriptures are part of the whole armour of God. "Take the sword of the Spirit, which is the word of God." Eph. vi. 17. "For the word of God is quick and powerful, and sharper than any two-edged sword, &c." Heb. iv. 12. Now common Christians are deprived of this great spiritual weapon, if the word of God is given to them in a language which they cannot understand.

7. The Scriptures are compared to a candle or burning torch, set up by God for the very purpose of enlightening all men in the way of truth and salvation; hence David says, "thy word is a light to my feet, and a lamp to my path." But in order that every believer may be enabled by it to direct his steps, it must be translated, otherwise this lighted candle is put under a bushel.

Besides all this, the testimony of the Primitive Church is

on our side in this controversy.   This, Peter Dens and the
priests both know and feel; hence their attempts to explain
away the plain and unequivocal language of the fathers.
Origen of the third century, though his father was a layman, knew the Scriptures from a child.   We learn from
Eusebius (Eccles. Hist. Bk. vi. ch. 2.) that his father Leo-
nidas daily assigned him a portion of them, which he was
to commit to memory; and he must have been a child at
this time, for he was only seventeen years old, when his
father suffered martyrdom.   Origen himself thus writes:
" We beseech you not to content yourselves to hear the
word of God when read in the church, but to apply yourselves to it at home, and to meditate upon it day and night.
Christ has commanded us to meditate in the law of the
Lord, when we walk by the way, and when we sit in our
houses, when we lie down, and when we rise up."*   The
sentence from Chrysostom, is only half quoted by Peter
Dens; let us help him to the latter clause: " Hear, I beseech you, O all ye LAYMEN, provide yourselves with the
Bible, that medicine of the soul; OR IF YOU HAVE NOTHING
ELSE, YET AT LEAST GET THE NEW TESTAMENT, THE
APOSTLES, THE ACTS, AND THE GOSPELS.†   Chrysostom
says also, " the reading of the Scriptures is more necessary
for laymen than for monks."‡   Again he says, " the people
ought as soon as they come home from the church, to turn
over the holy books, and to call their wives and children
together to the conference of those things which are said."§
Jerome, we are told on the testimony of Hosius a Romish
author, translated the Scriptures into the Dalmatian, as well
as the Latin tongue.   Socrates, the Ecclesiastical Historian,
Bk. iv. chap. 33. informs us, that Ulphila, a Gothish bishop,
present at the Nicene Council, translated the Bible into the
native language of his country.   Now what are we to think

---

* Hom. 9, in Levit.   † Hom. 9, in Col.
‡ Com. Matt. hom. 2.   § Com. Matt. hom. 5.

of the honesty of the men who tell us that the primitive fathers reprobated the reading of the Scriptures by the common people! It is well known also, that the Old Testament was translated from Hebrew into Greek, before our Saviour's time. This was done for the special benefit of the Alexandrian Jews, who had forgotten their own language. This translation is familiarly known by the name of the Septuagint, and was used by Christ and his apostles, being then most extensively circulated.

In conclusion, we will notice an objection which is not unfrequently made, and upon which our adversaries in this controversy have laid great stress. They ask us: "If the *main reason* for translating the Bible is that the people may understand it, how comes it that there is so great a difference of opinion among Protestant Ministers and people, and whence the necessity of these numerous comments and expositions, which in many respects vary so much one from another?"

We answer: Admitting that the common people do not understand *all things* contained in the Scripture, they may and do understand *many*. The Bible is a spiritual storehouse, in which there is food accommodated to all ages and constitutions. Here we have "milk for babes," and "strong meat for them that are of full age." Heb. v. 13.

The *simplicity* of many precious Scriptures condescends to our weakness; the difficulty of other passages awakens industry and research. Here we have perspicuity to regulate our duty, and obscurity to teach us humility. We bless the goodness of God in its clear discoveries, and we adore his wisdom in its veiled mysteries. The plain instructions of God's blessed word, we will with the help of divine grace improve to our salvation, and as for "the things that are hard to be understood," if we cannot unfold them to our own satisfaction and the edification of others, we will at least endeavour by God's grace not to wrest them to our own destruction. Whilst we freely admit that there are doctrines of Scripture, which are variously stated and understood by different denominations of the church of Christ, we would remind the advocates of popery that in the essential doctrines of revelation, we are agreed; the truths, which involve salvation we hold in unity of faith; and as to minor points we can agree to differ.

In reading the Scriptures, we wish to be governed by the following rules, which we respectfully commend to the attention of all men, whether Protestants or Papists.

1. *We would read prayerfully.* Christ's precept and promise enjoin this duty. "Ask and it shall be given you," &c. And again, James (i. 5.) says, If any man lack wisdom, let him ask of God, &c.

2. *We would submit our understandings* to the wisdom of God, and subject all our thoughts to the obedience of Christ. "If any man seemeth to be wise in this world, let him become a fool that he may be wise; for the wisdom of the world is foolishness with God." 1 Cor. iii. 18, 19; and also, Matt. xi. 25.

3. *We would lay aside all prejudice,* self-interest or undue prepossession in favour of any system, or the notions of any man, or set of men. We would beware of this *leaven of the Pharisees.* Matt. xvi. 6. 12.

4. *We would search the Scriptures with faith,* and in the exercise of true repentance for all our sins; knowing that in the impenitent and profane, the Spirit of Christ will not dwell. 2 Tim. iii. 7. "They are ever learning, and never able to come to the knowledge of the truth."

5. *We would be filled with love for the truth,* and a sincere desire to know and embrace it, not through mere formality or custom, remembering Paul's words, "because they received not the knowledge of the truth, God shall send them strong delusions that they should believe a lie."

6. We would take up our Bibles with a sincere desire *not*

13

only to know, but also to do the will of God; never forgetting that the great end of Scripture is practical; teaching us, that " denying all ungodliness and worldly lusts, we should live soberly, righteously, and godly in this present world." Tit. ii. 12.

Certain questions concerning Sacred Scripture.
(No. 65.)

" Have any sacred books been lost?

" *Ans.* Yes, this is plain from the Bible itself in which various books are cited, which are unknown to us, &c., &c.

" Are any autographs extant to this time, or primitive and original manuscripts of Sacred Scripture?

" *Ans.* No. Nor is this necessary, as the copies or transcripts approved by the church are of the same authority and use; without whose approbation not even the original manuscripts would have this authority as to us, according to that (declaration) of St. Augustine; ' I would not believe the Gospel, unless the authority of the church constrained me.'

" How great is the authority of the edition of the Latin vulgate?

" *Ans.* It is summary and infallible, because by a decree of the Council of Trent, it has been approved and declared authentic; and so that it is a certain and infallible rule of our faith, because in it nothing is contained contrary to faith or morals, nor any false or erroneous sentiment.

" With this it is still consistent, say Bukentop and others, that our vulgate is not so absolute in all its parts, but that something in it might have been expressed more significantly; some more clearly translated, some rendered into better Latin, and some placed in more correct order: therefore no one can deny but that reference may usefully be made to the Hebrew or Greek text, (although these are not free from errors peculiar to them,) &c. &c.

" Finally, in opposition to heretics, and for the understanding of Sacred Scripture, observe the following things:

" 1. Sacred Scripture is not authentic for us, except through tradition and the teaching of the Church.

" 2. Sacred Scripture is to be received in that sense in which the Church receives it.

" 3. The legitimate sense of Scripture is known to us through tradition.

" 4. From this rule it follows that the true sense of Scripture must be borrowed from the doctrine of the Holy Fathers; for which reason, observe the decree of the Council of Trent, sess. 4, by which it resolved that no one may dare to interpret Sacred Scripture contrary to that sense which Holy Mother Church held and holds, or contrary to the unanimous consent of the Fathers, especially in matters of faith or customs.

" 5. Sacred Scripture is to be understood in the obvious and proper meaning of the words; unless something interposes to the contrary, by which another legitimate sense of Scripture may be proved.

" Finally, by means of the passages of Scripture which are more clear, others which are less clear, ought to be elucidated. The heretics offend against this rule, for whom it is a common thing to catch up some obscure passages, to which they misapply all others, even the clearest texts."

What the papists mean by the unanimous consent of the Fathers, is not easy to determine. One thing is certain, there is as much discrepancy between the Fathers as there is among any other writers on Christian faith and morals. We can defy all the priests in creation to sustain any one dogma which is peculiar to the Romish Church, by the " unanimous testimony of the Fathers." Notwithstanding all the bare-faced interpolations by which many editions of the primitive Christian writings have been corrupted, they are still unable to make out their case.

CHAPTER XVIII.

Concerning Traditions and their Divisions.   (66.)

" WHAT is tradition?

" *Ans.* Generally understood, it is nothing else than un-written doctrine: not as though it could never be found written; but because it has not been written by its author, nor dictated by him that it might be written.

" Tradition, therefore, as it is taken theologically, may be defined : ' a doctrine pertaining to religion, which is commu-nicated orally by its author, and is transmitted to posterity, whether it be afterwards written by any one or not.'

" How is tradition divided?

" *Ans.* 1. On account of its origin or author, into *divine, apostolic,* and *ecclesiastical* tradition.

" 2. On account of its matter, into *dogmatic, ritual,* and *moral* tradition.

" 3. On account of its duration, into *perpetual* and *tem-poral.*

" 4. On account of its place, into *universal* and *par-ticular.*

" What tradition is called *divine?*

" *Ans.* It is the unwritten word of God, or it is a truth divinely revealed to the Church, and transmitted by the Fathers to the latest posterity without the writing of a canon-ical author.   Examples of divine tradition are: that there are seven sacraments, neither more nor less; that there are four gospels; that the Mother of God always remained a virgin; that infants are to be baptized; and various other things, which relate to the substance and forms of the sacra-ments.

" *Apostolic* tradition is that which was instituted by the apostles as the pastors of the Church; such is the observ-ance of the Lord's day, the forty days' fast, and various rites of the mass and sacraments.

" That is called *ecclesiastical* tradition, which was intro-duced by the superiors of the Church or by Christian people after the times of the apostles; such are the observance of festivals, abstinence from eggs and milk-diet on certain days, &c.

"Yet observe, that these terms, *divine, apostolic, ecclesiastical* tradition, are sometimes so confounded that something is said to be of *apostolic* or *ecclesiastic* tradition, which is of *divine* tradition, and vice versa.

"What tradition is called *dogmatic?*

"It is that which treats concerning the doctrines of the faith; as is that by which the existence of Scripture is proved, and that it is the word of God, &c.

"*Ritual* is concerning sacred rites: such is the doctrine of the ceremonies which are observed in the sacrifice of the mass, the administration of the sacraments, &c.

"*Moral* pertains to customs; as that on certain days fasts are to be observed, that the festival of Easter is to be celebrated, &c.

"*Perpetual* tradition is that which is instituted that it may always be kept; such are the divine traditions.

"*Temporal* is that which is instituted for a certain time: as abstinence from blood and things strangled was at the beginning of the Church.

"*Universal* tradition is that which is proposed for observation to the whole Church: as the observance of the Lord's day.

"*Particular* is that which was appointed for one or more particular churches: thus, in the time of St. Augustine, a fast was observed at Rome on the Sabbath, but not at Milan.

"How great is the authority of tradition?

"Divine tradition has equal authority with Holy Scripture; for both are truly the word of God. There is only this difference, that as for Holy Scripture, the creed of the church is more plain to us; from the circumstance that it has fixed the catalogue of canonical books, and has approved the edition of the vulgate as authentic; but the church has not framed a catalogue of divine traditions, but sets forth, sometimes one, sometimes another, as occasion demands.

"*Apostolic* tradition has the same authority; which the decrees of the apostolic institution have.

"*Ecclesiastical* tradition is of the same authority as the ecclesiastical laws and constitutions: and hence the Pope

13 *

may change both an apostolic and an ecclesiastical (tradition.)

"Is tradition a rule of faith, and *which* (tradition is a rule?)

"*Ans.* Merely apostolic or ecclesiastical tradition is not a rule of faith; because neither has been divinely revealed; but divine tradition is truly a rule of faith, as it is the word of God, not less than Holy Scripture. We will especially establish this tradition, as the heretics assail it chiefly."

Concerning the existence and necessity of Traditions. (67.)

" Are divine traditions to be admitted besides Sacred Scripture ?

"*Ans.* Our heretics say no, principally on this ground, that all truths of the faith are contained in Sacred Scripture; against this error, the Catholic faith teaches, that divine traditions are to be admitted in the new law, as the Council of Trent has decided, Sess. 4.

" The existence and necessity of the same are proved, 1. from 2 Thess. ii. 14, where the apostle says : ' hold the traditions, which you have learned, whether by word or by our epistle ;' i. e. whether in word, or writing.

" Hither tends also that which the apostle writes, 2 Tim. i. 13 : ' hold the form of sound words, which thou hast heard from me in faith, and in the love which is in Jesus Christ,' and ch. iii. 14. ' Continue thou in the things which thou hast learned, and which have been committed to thee ; knowing of whom thou hast learned.' God refers also to tradition, Deut. xxxii. 7. ' Ask thy father and he will declare to thee ; thy elders and they will tell thee.' Besides, John says, that not all the things which Christ taught, were written, ch. xxi. 25. ' But there are also many other things which Jesus did ; which if they were written every one, the world itself, I think, would not be able to contain the books that should be written.' Very many things also, which he taught the apostles during the 40 days after the resurrection have come down to us through tradition. Add to this the unanimous consent of the Holy Fathers.

2. It is proved (thus.) Our heretics assert that they believe many things which are no where found in Scripture ; for instance ; the virginity of the divine Virgin, even after

the birth (of Christ) ; that there are four gospels ; that baptism applied to infants is valid, &c.

3. " It is proved from the necessity of tradition : for without divine tradition it cannot be known what books are Sacred Scripture ; why the gospel of Matthew should rather be received than that of Bartholomew ; what is the meaning of Scripture, where there is no other means of discerning those things, at least no ordinary one : although God might show these things in an extraordinary way, as for instance, by a miracle ; but then the course of tradition supplies the (place of a) miracle.

" Hence observe there is more need of divine tradition than of Sacred Scripture, as Scripture cannot be known without tradition.

" The heretics object. One divine tradition can be known without the other ; therefore Sacred Scripture can be known without divine tradition.

" The inference is plain : just as tradition is the word of God orally delivered, so Scripture is the written word of God : but the word of God orally delivered may be known without any other divine tradition, therefore by parity of reasoning the written word of God may be thus known.

" *Ans.* I deny both the inference and the parity ; there is a disparity, because divine tradition is a living witness, and Scripture is a dead witness, which therefore does not prove itself.

" For this reason, it is to be observed that divine tradition must be considered according to its own origin ; but the origin of divine tradition is from the fact that God has revealed some truth to the church by means of speech ; now oral address proves itself: for there is no need when any one speaks that he should also affirm that he is speaking : and thus the church can propose to us one divine tradition without any ulterior one. But the church receives Scripture, not by means of oral communication and speech, but by means of an instrument written by the sacred penman, who might even be ignorant that he was writing the word of God ; hence the church could not know that other Scripture had been dictated by God, unless God should further prove by this revelation that this Scripture had been dictated by God ; and this ulterior revelation is called divine tradition.

" You will reply : but the church without tradition, can define what is Sacred Scripture. The supposition is proved ; the church is infallible, therefore, &c.

" *Ans.* I deny this supposition : the church is indeed infallible in definitions of faith and customs ; but in order that she may define she ought not to proceed in a blind way, but to have sufficient ground for her definition : but the church has not any other sufficient ground by which she may discern Sacred Scripture from that which is not sacred, than divine tradition, therefore, &c.

" Although some divine traditions may have existed, yet they could not be preserved pure and entire to this time ; because that which passes from ear to ear is easily altered and lost : but tradition passes from ear to ear, therefore, &c.

" *Ans.* I admit the assertion, that what passes from ear to ear is easily altered, if there are no causes assisting in its preservation ; but if there are such causes, I deny the assertion ; but these causes are divine providence, which rules and governs the Church, the writings of the ancients, the continuous practice of the faithful ; add to this, that in almost all ages new heresies arise, which God wonderfully employs for the preservation of the doctrine of the Church against them. Learned men also are always raised up by God, who investigate and commend to posterity the doctrine of the Church and ancient traditions."

CONCERNING THE PRINCIPAL RULES OF TRADITION.

1. *Rules for distinguishing Traditions.*

" Are there any special rules for ascertaining traditions ?

" Yes ; and the following are usually assigned :

" 1. If the whole Church embraces any thing as a dogma of faith or customs, has approved by practice something which no one but God alone could institute, and which is not found in Scripture, it must needs be a divine tradition ; thus, for instance, we know that the baptism of infants is valid, and that confirmation and ordination cannot be repeated, &c.

" 2. If any truth not contained in Scripture, has been received in the Church, and the contrary doctrine to it has been condemned as heretical, it is a divine tradition : such is the perpetual virginity of the Mother of God.

" 3. Whatever the unanimous consent of the Holy Fathers and doctors declares the Church to have received from the apostles, has certainly been orally delivered by them.

" 4. ' Whatever the universal Church holds, and which is found to have been appointed neither in councils nor elsewhere, but has always been retained, we most certainly believe to have been handed down by apostolic authority,' says St. Augustine, book 4. against the Donatists.

" It must be observed, remarks Sylvius, that by the third and fourth rule it is ascertained that a thing has been handed down by the apostles, but not whether the tradition is purely apostolic, as it is distinguished from divine; but then it will be known to be such if the thing might have been instituted by human authority, as is, for instance, the forty days' fast.

" 5. ' Whatever the Roman Church holds as tradition, is to be regarded as such,' says St. Jerome. Bk. 3. ch. 3.

" 6. WHATEVER THE CATHOLIC CHURCH HOLDS OR DECLARES AS SUCH IS TO BE REGARDED AS TRADITION."

CONCERNING THE JUDGE OF CONTROVERSIES RESPECTING THE FAITH. (69.)

Besides the inanimate rule of faith there is need of an animate. (rule.)

" Is any other rule of faith to be admitted besides Sacred Scripture and divine tradition ?

" *Ans.* Yes: Because when a controversy arises, which is Sacred Scripture or tradition ; also, what their meaning is ; this controversy Scripture or tradition itself cannot settle, therefore there is need of another rule, viz. an animate one, which may decide controversies : for every legislator who founds any society whatever, ought to leave behind him, those who may represent his authority for establishing the authenticity, sense, &c. of the laws : in the same proportion then as laws are more remote from the apprehension of men, (as in the belief of the mysteries of religion, and the rules of customs), the greater is the necessity of a vicarious authority of the legislator : which certainly in the matter of religion ought not to be of just any kind whatever, but infallible, lest every thing should remain doubtful and uncertain, and thus religion itself become useless.

" Nor is it any obstacle that the church is not above Scripture and divine tradition : for the church does not judge concerning them with the judgment of power, either by changing them, or by deciding whether that which Sacred Scripture teaches is true or false : but it decides concerning them, only with the judgment of discretion, by discerning and declaring which is Sacred Scripture or divine tradition, what is their sense, &c.

" The case is different with respect to traditions merely apostolical or ecclesiastical, in regard to which the church exercises also the judgment of power, with the faculty of changing them, &c.

" Observe, that although, besides Sacred Scripture and traditions a living rule is to be admitted, yet it may rightly be said that our faith rests alone on Sacred Scripture and divine tradition : because nothing is believed with a divine faith unless it be contained in Sacred Scripture, and divine tradition.

" What is the judge of controversies concerning the faith and customs ?

" *Ans.* The church, whether scattered or assembled in general council, and the Pope the head of the church, as will appear from what is to be said hereafter.

" The Lutherans and Calvinists state as the judge, Sacred Scripture alone, or as understood by the private opinion of every man : the English heretics pretend that this judgment belongs to secular judges."

If the Romish Church admits the divine inspiration of the Scriptures, she must of course be prepared to abide by the testimony of God's word.   Now, the Bible, in plain and unequivocal terms, justifies us in asserting that the written word of God is an all-sufficient Rule of Faith.   Paul in his 2 Epist. to Tim. iii. 15, 16, 17, plainly declares, " that the Scriptures are able to make us wise unto salvation.   They are profitable for doctrine, for reproof, for correction, for instruction in righteousness : that the man of God may be PERFECT, THOROUGHLY FURNISHED unto all good works," and what more do we want? The prophet Isaiah says, " To the law and to the testimony : if they speak not according to this word, it is because there is no light in them." Isaiah never would have approved of trying the law and testimony by tradition ; he was for holding up every doctrine and custom before the clear light of revelation, and thus determining its character. If the Scriptures are able to instruct us in every good work, to teach us Christ crucified, to give us light in darkness, to settle our faith, and to teach us the whole way of salvation, then we ask, what do we need more? When the lawyer stood up and asked Christ, " Master, what shall I do to inherit eternal life? He said unto him, What is written in the law? How readest thou?" And when the lawyer replied, " Thou shalt love the Lord thy God, with all thy heart, &c." Christ's answer was, " This do and thou shalt live." If then the Scriptures contain all things necessary to be known in order to inherit eternal life, they must be a sufficient rule of faith and practice. Common sense confirms this verdict. The Church of Rome herself is in fact obliged to appeal to Scripture as the only rule in many cases. She cannot, for instance, prove the doctrine of the Trinity by tradition, either directly or indirectly ; in this case she must refer to Scripture. But if the written word is admitted to be the rule in *one* point, how can it be denied in another? If its testimony is received in one case, it may and ought to be acknowledged in every other in which it is a competent witness, as it claims to be the word of the living God.

But the Romish Church would prove the necessity of tradition by an appeal to the language of Paul ; " Hold the traditions which you have learned, whether by word or by our Epistle." (2 Thess. ii. 14.)

1. To this we answer, that these words do not import that the apostle delivered some things to them as tradition, and others as Scripture, but that he taught them the same truths both orally and in writing.

2. Even supposing that the things which he thus taught them were *different*, this proves only that there are some important and precious truths, which are not contained in this Epistle to the Thessalonians, though all that is necessary to salvation is supplied by other portions of Scripture.

3. Besides if we wish to know the nature of the things which Paul delivered to them by word of mouth, we shall find from Acts xvii. 2, that they were altogether Scriptural. There we are told that when they came to Thessalonica, " Paul, as his manner was, went in unto them, and three Sabbath days reasoned with them OUT OF THE SCRIPTURES," &c.

As for the quotation, Deut. xxxii. 7, " Ask thy father and he will show thee, &c.," Moses is referring the children of Israel to their immediate ancestors, who were yet living, and who could recount to them the wonders of God's providence in former days.

The fact that Jesus Christ did and said many things during his ministry, which are not written in Scripture, is not disputed by Protestants. All that we affirm is that sufficient has been recorded to make us wise unto salvation, and more than this we do not need.

But it is farther asserted that heretics themselves " believe many things, which are no where found in Scripture."

Of this there can be no doubt ; and orthodox Christians do the same.

We know that Romish tradition teaches the virginity of the Mother of our blessed Lord after his incarnation, but the Bible teaches the contrary very plainly, Matt. i. 24, 25. The virginity of Mary previous to the birth of Christ is a doctrine of divine revelation ; her subsequent virginity is a Romish invention, which we decline endorsing. As for the baptism of infants, that does not rest upon tradition ; infants of believing parents had a right to church membership under the Old Covenant, and until we find Scripture in the New

Testament, which disfranchises them, we must consider them fit subjects for Baptism, with all deference to the opinions of those who differ from us. Whenever traditions accord with and sustain the letter and spirit of Scripture, and are well authenticated, we will give them all the weight they deserve. In this case, we know from early ecclesiastical history that Infant Baptism was practised in the Christian church.

We decline the aid of Romish tradition also, in enabling us to ascertain which of the gospels are spurious, and which are genuine. There is internal evidence enough to establish the authenticity of the four gospels.

We do not need tradition to enable us to discover the sense of Scripture; for whilst there are many passages concerning which there has been and still is diversity of opinion, we know that God has promised to give wisdom to all that ask in faith, and the Holy Spirit is pledged to show every sincere inquirer after truth, who searches the Scripture with prayer, what he must do to be saved.

In short, notwithstanding all the specious reasoning of Romanists, their arguments amount to neither more nor less than a *petitio principii*, a begging of the question. They affirm that tradition is part of God's word; and how do they prove it? By Scripture they cannot establish their point; its testimony is decidedly against them; and if they seek to prove their position by tradition itself, or by the authority of the Church, which rests upon tradition, they argue in a vicious circle.

The blasphemous assertion that THERE IS MORE NEED OF DIVINE TRADITION THAN OF SACRED SCRIPTURE, is worthy of the apostate source in which it originates.

The doctrine of the necessity of unwritten traditions is inconsistent with the perfection of the Scriptures, and utterly repugnant to the object for which they were designed. They were intended as the Rule of Faith; but a rule which is not sufficient to answer its purpose is no rule at all. But not

14

only are the Scriptures sufficient in themselves to make men wise unto salvation, thoroughly furnished unto all good works, &c., but God expressly forbids any thing to be added to his word, upon any pretext whatsoever. Paul pronounces an anathema upon any man, and even any angel from heaven, that should preach another gospel. (Gal. i. 8.) And the canon of Scripture closes with a dreadful curse denounced upon any man who should add to, or take from the word. (Rev. xxii. 18.) How then can we receive those traditions, which are declared to be of MORE NECESSITY THAN SACRED SCRIPTURE ?

Whenever God gave laws or directions of any kind to his church, ever since the days of Moses, he has generally caused it to be done in writing : " Go write it in a table, note it in a book, that it may be for the time to come." (Is. xxx. 8.) " To write the same things to you, for you, is safe." (Phil. iii. 1.) In Rev. ii. it is said, " Write" to the churches, not " deliver a tradition to them." Indeed we may rest assured that God would not permit any doctrine or truth necessary to salvation to depend upon the uncertain transmission of traditions, which are liable to be corrupted through carelessness or prejudice.

The notion of the insufficiency of the Scriptures, the addition of traditions or " unwritten verities," was first introduced by the Carpocratians and other heretics, and is directly what the apostle has forewarned us against. " Beware, lest any man spoil you through philosophy and vain deceit, after the TRADITION of men."

The voice of the purest antiquity is against tradition. Justin in Tryphonem, says, If we will be safe in all things, we must fly to the Scriptures ; we must believe God only ; and rest wholly on his institutions, and *not on men's traditions.*

Irenæus, lib. 3. ch. xiii., says of the apostles, that what they *preached by mouth,* they left us in writing, to be the pillar and ground-work of our faith.

Tertullian, de Præscript, speaks plainly, and to the point. It were folly or madness (says he) to think that the apostle knew all things, but revealed the same to few; delivering some things openly to all, but reserving some others to be spoken in secret to some. And again : " We have no cause to be curious after Christ, nor inquisitive after the gospel, (viz. for any other things to be believed in order to salvation.) " When we believe, the first thing which we believe is, that there is nothing further which we ought to believe."

Basil, in Serm. de fide, says ; " It is a manifest defection from the faith to bring any thing that is not written."

And as a counterpart to the alleged quotation from Jerome, " Whatever the Roman church holds as tradition is to be regarded as such," I beg leave to offer the following from the same father, on Hag. chap. i. " All traditions pretended to be apostolic, if they have not their authority from the Scriptures, are cut off by the sword of God."

But we cannot dismiss this point without calling attention to the short and easy method of determining traditions. " *Whatever the Catholic church holds or declares as such, is to be regarded as tradition.*" This settles the apostolic character of the Mass, Extreme Unction, Invocation of Saints, Merit of Works, the Supremacy of the Pope, Holy water, Holy bones, Holy stones, and other Holy relics, Prayers for the dead, Auricular Confession, Penance, Indulgences, Image worship, Celibacy of the Priests, &c. &c. The church of Christ has ever protested against these impious inventions, and has demanded the reason of their introduction. Are they taught by Scripture ? No ! Will you abandon them ? *Abandon* them ? Not we—they are apostolical traditions ! But where is the proof? The proof is here, and let heretics read it and ever after hold their peace ; " WHATEVER THE CATHOLIC CHURCH HOLDS OR DECLARES AS SUCH, IS TO BE REGARDED AS TRADITION !"

CHAPTER XIX.

Concerning the Church. (70.)

" WHAT is the church ?

" The church, generally taken, can be defined for every state, place, and time, (as the) congregation of the faithful united in the true worship of God under Christ their head ; which definition comprehends also the faithful of the Old Testament, not only those who pertained to the synagogue, but also other believers out of the synagogue, as Job, Melchisedeck, &c. ; also the blessed, likewise angels, &c., souls detained in purgatory.

" How is the church divided, generally taken ?

" It is divided into three members, namely, the church triumphant, suffering, and militant.

" The church triumphant embraces all the blessed in heaven, as well angels as men : the church patient or suffering is the assembly of souls detained in purgatory : militant is the assembly of the faithful in a state of pilgrimage, or of such who are as yet travailling upon earth.

" The church militant may be subdivided into the church of the Old Testament, viz. from Adam to Christ, which comprehended both Jews and Gentiles professing the true faith ; and into the church of the New Testament, concerning which in the following sections.

" What is the church of the New Testament ?

" By Canisius it is defined : ' the congregation of all people professing the faith and doctrine of Christ, which is governed under one next to Christ, the chief head and pastor upon earth.' "

CONCERNING THOSE WHO ARE IN THE CHURCH. (71.)

" Are unbaptized persons in the church ?

" No, because baptism is the gate, through which we come into the church, as the Council of Trent, sess. xiv. ch. 2. teaches ; and hence also, (Acts, ii. 41,) those who were baptized were said to be added, as to Christ's mystical body which is the church: 'they therefore that received his word were baptized; and there were added to them in that day about three thousand souls,' therefore, before they were not of the church.

" Cannot Catechumens, indeed, be said to belong to the church?

" No, for the same reason that they have not yet entered through baptism.

" *Obj.* According to the fourth Lat. Counc., no one out of the church can be saved; but a Catechumen may be saved through perfect contrition; therefore he is in the church.

" *Ans.* I distinguish the inference: I deny the inference that he is therefore in the church really; I agree entirely that he is in the church as to vow and desire; but it is enough for a Catechumen to be saved, that he be in the church by vow or desire, (because he is embraced in perfect contrition:) and hence the words of the Lateran Council should be understood of those, who are in the church neither in reality, nor by vow.

" But at least are not those in the church, who are supposed to be baptized, and thus commune in the participation of the sacraments and the confession of faith, although in fact they have not been baptized?

" *Ans.* Wiggers, with some others, says yes: but Bellarmine, Steyaert, Daleman, Danes, &c., say no, for reasons already mentioned: yet such persons although not in reality, yet belong to the church by vow, and thus can be saved.

" Are all baptized persons in the church?

" No: and especially manifest heretics and apostates are not of the church; because they do not profess the same faith and doctrine with those, who are in the church; but this is expressed in the definition of the church.

" *Obj.* The church judges and punishes heretics; but it does not judge those, who are without, according to the apostle, 1 Cor. v. 12. 'What have I to do to judge those that are without?' Therefore they are in the church.

" *Ans.* I deny the inference: for although heretics are out of the church, yet by reason of baptism they remain subject to the church: and hence SHE JUSTLY PUNISHES THEM AS DESERTERS FROM THE CAMP OF THE CHURCH,

14 *

and, therefore, they are under obligation of returning; but the apostle speaks of those, who have never entered the church or have never been baptized.

" Open schismatics are also not in the church: for they have separated themselves from the unity of the church: and hence the church in Parasceve, just as she prays for heretics that they may return to the church, prays also for schismatics.

" Do secret heretics belong to the church? the same is asked concerning secret apostates.

" *Ans.* There is a difference of opinion among authors: if they are secret, merely internal heretics, it seems proper to say that such persons are in the church; because neither has the church separated them, nor have they separated themselves from the visible union of the church; whence it may be said, that they still are members of the church, not indeed living, but dead and dry, as a withered arm may still be called a member of the body.

" But if they are external, secret heretics, then it appears they are not in the church; because by this very fact they have been excommunicated or cut off from the church.

" Yet Daelman plausibly supposes that excommunicated, but not interdicted persons are in the church, although they are deprived of the internal influences and communion of the Saints, not by right, but in fact, and through the indulgence of the church; and hence they are not deprived of jurisdiction, as was said, No. 56.   According to Daelman, therefore, it is probable that those excommunicated persons alone are out of the church, who by a particular sentence have been by name denounced as such.

" From what has been said, it is inferred that all those are out of the church, who either have not entered the church, or whom the church casts from her, or who of their own accord have separated themselves from the church."

The 72d section discusses the question whether all the elect, and they only, are in the church, and concludes with this summary as the result of the investigation.

" From what has been said, you may gather, who are members of the Church militant, viz. all persons truly baptized, externally professing the Catholic faith, and partaking of the sacraments of the church, with due subjection towards the lawful pastors of the church, especially the Roman Pontiff.

"Observe that the doctrine of the heretics by which they assert that the church consists of the elect only, or of the just alone, tends to this that they may make the church invisible, and hence let section 73 treat

Of the visibility of the church.

"Is the church visible?

"1. Yes. This is proved from Matt. v. 14, where it is said concerning the church : ' a city set upon a hill cannot be hid ;' and thus the church is not only visible, but evidently conspicuous, like a city set upon a hill : 'as Augustine, &c. says, ' The church stands forth before all, clear and conspicuous, for it is a city, built upon a hill, which cannot be hid.'

"2. It is proved from Matt. xviii. 16, where Christ commands that the faithful should tell it to the church, that is, to the superiors of the church, when private fraternal reproof does no good : and again he commands, that if a reproved brother shall not hear the church, he must be regarded as a heathen and a publican ; now he cannot be denounced to the church, nor hear her, if the church is invisible; therefore, &c.

"3. It is proved from reason ; all ought to come to the church under peril of eternal damnation ; therefore, it must be visible or cognizable.

Obj. I. Christ says to the Samaritan woman, John iv. 23, 'The hour cometh, and now is, when the true worshippers shall worship the Father in spirit and in truth ;' therefore, &c.

"*Ans.* I deny the inference : for that (phrase) ' in spirit,' does not exclude external worship; but teaches that to external worship internal is to be joined : and hence it is opposed to the worship of the Jews and the Samaritans, most of whom stopped in external rites only ; and the expression, ' in truth,' is opposed to the figures of the old law, or also to the worship of the Samaritans, which was mixed up with many corruptions.

"*Obj. II.* Christ says, Luke xvii. 20, ' The kingdom of God does not come with observation ;' therefore the church cannot be observed or seen.

"*Ans.* I deny the inference : for there the question is not concerning the church, but the kingdom of God is put for the coming of Messiah; and hence the meaning is, Messiah does not come with observation, *i. e.*, with pomp and royal parade, as the Jews expected.

" How is the church said to be visible?

" *Ans.* The church is formally to be seen and known not only through faith and the understanding, but also by physical senses; because the church is not only spiritual by reason of the internal form of faith, hope, charity, &c., but it also is a certain material and sensible body, because it embraces a visible head, visible persons, the external profession of faith, sensible sacraments, the order of a visible priesthood.

" Through what is the church seen sensibly?

" *Ans.* By her own marks, which are so peculiar to our church, that they can be found in no other congregation or sect; and hence the church is visible, not only to the faithful, but also to those who do not hold the faith, as heretics, Jews, and Gentiles."

The arrogant demand of the Romish Church to be regarded as the only and the true Church of Christ, containing in her communion all who shall be saved, deserves no refutation. We pass by this impudent claim with sincere pity for the deluded members of that apostate church, whom " with all deceivableness of unrighteousness," she entices from the way of God's testimonies. Our theologian in contending for the visibility of the Church against " the heretics," is wasting his eloquence and his prowess upon a man of straw. WE believe in a visible church. WE need not be told that the Church of Christ and the private members also of that church are as a city set on a hill that cannot be hid. Surely the church of Rome has sufficient reason both to know and feel that the Protestant church is visible; if she does not know it, the noble army of martyrs, who were slain by the blood-thirsty minions of the Pope, stand forth as witnesses, who being dead yet speak. The flames of persecution, which have reddened the sky of every kingdom and country, which the Babylonish woman has intoxicated with the wine of her lewdness and blasphemy, have made the Protestant church a BURNING and a SHINING light in the world.   We yield the point, however, that the church of Rome has her own peculiar marks.   She bears upon her brazen face THE MARKS OF THE BEAST, mentioned in the Apocalypse.   They are so indelibly stamped upon her brow, that he who reads her history cannot fail to recognise her as the base deceiver and apostate, against whom the finger of divine prophecy is pointed.   These marks are SUPERSTITION, PERFIDY, FALSEHOOD, and BLOOD.

CHAPTER XX.

Concerning the Marks of the Church. (74.)

" What is understood by a mark of the church?

" A certain sign and peculiarity by which the true church can be known, and discerned from all other assemblies.

" How many are the marks of the church?

" Four principal ones are enumerated, expressed in the Constantinopolitan symbol, viz. that she is ONE, HOLY, CATHO-LIC and APOSTOLIC.

" That these are the marks of the true church, the authority of the symbol just quoted, and the consent of the apostles and fathers prove: these reason proves and Scripture attests.

" Calvin and sectarians appoint only two marks of the church, viz. the sincere preaching of the word of God, and the legitimate use of the sacraments.

" These two, although they are found in the true church of Christ, are yet foolishly laid down as marks of the church : for the marks ought to be more notorious than the thing, which they are to characterize : but it is at least as difficult to know which is the sincere preaching of the word of God, (and) which is the legitimate use of the sacraments, as which is the true church.

" But as the four abovementioned marks pertain to the Roman Catholic Church alone, it follows that she is the only church of Christ : and in order that this may appear more clearly, we will consider them one by one."

Concerning the mark of the church by which she is called ONE. (75.)

" Prove that unity is the mark of the true church.

" It is proved from various texts of Sacred Scripture, in which unity is attributed to the church : thus, it is said, John x. 16., ' one fold and one pastor ;' and John xvii. 21, Christ prays for unity for his sheep : that they all may be *one ;* also the apostle, 1 Cor. x. 17., says, ' We being many are one body,' and Eph. iv. 4, 5. ' One body, one faith, one baptism.'

" This unity all the fathers acknowledged in time past, and from it they confuted heretics and schismatics ; amongst them, St. Cyprian wrote his book concerning the unity of the church.

" In what does the unity of the church consist ?

" In unity of head, in unity of faith and doctrine, in the consent of minds, in the communion of the same sacraments, and of other things pertaining to the communion of the Saints.

" Unity of head is found in the Roman Catholic Church ; because in it there is no visible head under Christ except the Roman Pontiff, to whom all the bishops and the faithful are subordinate, and are united as in a centre of unity, and who exercises visible jurisdiction and rule over the whole church.

" This unity of the church is manifestly found in no sect, not even among the Greeks, who obey different Patriarchs.

" Unity of faith and doctrine, equally shines forth in the Roman Catholic Church, in which *all the faithful, although scattered over the whole earth, believe the same doctrines of faith ; neither in any definitions of the church, concerning the faith, can repugnant things be proved ;* but among heretics and schismatics there is no agreement of faith : but there are as many opinions as heads ; as many faiths as wills.

" You will say : In the Roman Church there is also diversity of doctrine, because the doctrines of the Thomists,

Scotists, and Molinists, are opposed to one another in many things ; therefore, &c.

" I deny the inference : for as has been said, the unity of faith and doctrine is in this, that Catholics believe the same doctrines of faith ; to which it is no obstacle that there are different opinions of the school, which, when not injuring the faith, the church permits to be defended for the elucidation of truth, and the exercise of the schools, which are prepared to submit their opinions to one judge, the Roman Pontiff and the church ; but heretics dissent in things pertaining to the faith, nor do they acknowledge any judge to whom they may submit themselves.

" There is also in the church, *a consent, or union of minds,* like the union of sheep of the same fold, and like that of members of the same body.   The same is readily apparent from the communion of the sacraments, and the communion of the saints."

We do most cordially embrace the doctrine of the unity of the Church of Christ ; we believe that Christ has a visible church upon earth, constituting part of the Universal Church to which the innumerable company of angels, and the spirits of just men made perfect, also belong.   The visible church is scattered over the whole earth : but every man, woman, and child, who loves the Lord Jesus Christ, and keeps his commandments, is a member of that church, and shines forth as a constituent part of Christ's mystical body.   Wherever two or three true believers are gathered together in Christ's name, there you have a particular church, inheriting all the promises and blessings of the New Covenant as fully as the largest congregation of believers upon earth.   The word of God designates all as God's children, who love the Lord Jesus Christ ; into their hearts he has sent forth the spirit of adoption, whereby they cry, " Abba Father," giving them in this witness of the Holy Ghost, the seal of their acceptance, and the pledge and earnest of their heavenly inheritance. By whatever name they may be called, the members of Christ's body are ONE ; they love the same Saviour, they have been purchased by the same blood, they are animated by the same hope, they are partaking of like precious faith, contending against the same enemies, and pressing forward to the same eternal and glorious home. They are ONE with Christ, and ONE with each other. In the great doctrines of the Bible involving salvation, they agree entirely. There is not a shadow of difference between the evangelical repentance and faith of any two Christians on the face of God's earth. We care not how they may be called, they are addicted to no master but Christ, whose image they bear. Let a Presbyterian, or a Baptist, or a Methodist, or an Episcopalian, who are the friends of Jesus Christ, be thrown together by God's providence, and, however they may differ in minor matters, they will all testify that they love the Lord who bought them, and that they love one another with a pure heart fervently. Names of human invention cannot separate the true children of God; whenever they meet they coalesce like kindred drops of water, and are ONE in heart, and in all the essentials of faith. "He that is joined to the Lord is ONE spirit," 1 Cor. vi. 17. This is the unity which marks the Church of Christ; this is the unity for which the blessed Saviour prayed, when he was about to be led out as a lamb to the slaughter. I admit there are many who are the professed followers of Christ who manifest none of these traits of Christian character; but what then? all are not *Israel* that are *of* Israel !

There are tares among the wheat, and there are hypocrites within the pale of the visible church, just as there are unfruitful branches on every vine, and withered limbs on every tree; and yet the withered limbs and boughs cannot affect the *unity* of the vine and its branches. In the time of the harvest they will be gathered and thrown into the fire; but meanwhile, we leave them where they are. Christ never meant that his church should be distinguished merely by unity in matters of human invention, which must necessarily be affected by circumstances and expediency. Where did ne ever say that HIS church was to be under the government of a Supreme Pontiff? The word of God tells us that all power is committed to Christ in heaven and ON EARTH; but it nowhere tells us that the Lord Jesus has delegated this power to the Pope! The Romish Church glories in her UNITY! She is known as the true church of Christ, because she is ONE. She acknowledges but ONE head, not many heads, —and that ONE HEAD is Christ's vicar, the POPE!! We envy her not *such* a head. We cleave to Christ, the living head of his body the church; we have no other master, and we never will own another! God is our witness, by his grace we will ever belong to the CHRISTIAN but never to he *Popish* Church.

Oh! but, says the Papist, we acknowledge Christ too as the Supreme Head of the church!. Do you indeed? So you acknowledge TWO HEADS; where then is your boasted UNITY? The Church of Rome claims to have a head in heaven, and a head on earth; we glory in being able to testify, ONE IS OUR HEAD, EVEN CHRIST!

God "hath put all things under his feet, and given him to be THE HEAD over all to the church, which is his body, the fulness of him that filleth all in all." (Eph. i. 22, 23.) "He is the HEAD of the body, the CHURCH; who is the beginning, the first-born from the dead; that in all things HE might have the PREEMINENCE." (Col. i. 18.) We do affectionately and earnestly entreat those, who acknowledge the jurisdiction of the Pope, in the language of Paul, "that *ye* henceforth be no more children, tossed to and fro, and carried about with every wind of doctrine by the *sleight of men and cunning craftiness*, whereby they lie in wait to deceive; but speaking the truth in love may grow up into him in all things, which is THE HEAD, even CHRIST." (Eph. iv. 14, 15.)

But then there are so many sects in the Protestant Church.

15

There you have Methodists, and Calvinists, and *Mormons*, and Lutherans, &c. &c. How does that tally with the unity of Christ's Church? There were sects in Paul's time; one said, I am of Paul; another, I am of Cephas; and another, I am of Apollos; but still they were all of CHRIST after all; they addicted themselves to one teacher in preference to another, just as, in our day, some are of *Wesley*, and others of *Calvin*, and others of *Luther*, and others of *Zuinglius!* And we need to be reminded as Paul admonished the Christians in his day; was *Wesley* crucified for you, or were ye baptized into the name of *Calvin?* But, whilst we acknowledge that there are different denominations of Christians, we deny that there is more than ONE true church, or more than ONE true Head of the church. All believers belong to the Church of Christ, no matter how they are called; just as soldiers of the same regiment, and belonging to the same army, and commanded by the same general, may fight under different banners, wear different uniforms, and use different weapons. Notwithstanding the difference of sects, the Church of Christ stands forth "fair as the moon, clear as the sun, and terrible as an ARMY WITH BANNERS;" and this the Pope's church knows to her cost. As for the Mormons, whom Romish priests take pleasure in enumerating among Protestant denominations, we respectfully decline their fellowship, and we would advise the leaders of those poor dupes to sell the golden plates and the copyright of the book of Mormon to those persons who place great store upon VAIN TRADITIONS, and who believe in revelations, subsequent to the closing of the canon! For our part, we should not know what to do with them, as we do not deal in such merchandise. But, whilst Romanists cry out against the sects of the Protestant Church, do they not forget their own? There are vastly more sects in the Romish than there are in the Protestant Church! I have before me a work, published with the license of that most Catholic monarch, the Emperor of Austria, which contains the history, with painted delineations of some hundreds of orders of *holy* brotherhoods and *holy* sisterhoods, of monks and nuns, black, white, and grey. And amongst them, there are some denominations of *Christians*, who have stranger names than any of the wildest and most fanatical sects of which we have ever heard. Thus in Biedenfeld's history of the different orders of monks and nuns, we read of the "Society of grey penitents," founded, A. D. 1578 ; of the "Reformed grey sisters, at Mons," founded, 1689 ; of "White penitents, at Avignon," and another brotherhood of penitents of the same colour, at Lyons. Then there are "Priests of the holy nail, at Suenia," founded in 1567 ; "Blue penitents at Rome," (1571 ;) Black penitents at Rome, (1577.) "Tailor-brethren," (1647 ;) "Shoemaker-brethren of poor Henry," (1645.) "Daughters of the childhood of Christ," (1657.) "Brethren of stillness and solitude," (1664 ;) "Sisters of stillness and solitude," "Sisters of the child Jesus," (1678 ;) "Brethren of the child Jesus," (1681.) "Daughters of the good Shepherd," (1686.) "Nuns for the continual adoration of the Holy Sacrament," (1653.) "Congregation of the consecrated of the Most Holy Mother of God," (1832,) &c., &c., &c. These are selected out of about 500 different religious orders ; and are presented as specimens of the sects of the Romish Church ; there is probably much more difference between the blue and grey, and black and white penitents, than there is between any of the leading evangelical denominations of the Protestant Church. And certainly amid all the dissensions, which have disgraced Protestant Christendom, there never have been feuds so deadly as those, which have obtained between some of the rival orders of monks in the Romish Church.

A volume might be written concerning the bickerings and jealousies between the Jesuits and the secular priests, during Queen Elizabeth's reign ; if the testimony of the secular priests is to be believed, the Jesuits in those days must have been the very off-scouring of the earth ; and if the Jesuits' declarations are worthy of credit, the secular priests were as bad as themselves.

As for unity in matters of doctrine, it will be as easy to persuade Quakers to become Episcopalians, as to reconcile the Dominicans and the Jesuits ; and all Protestant sects will agree as soon as the Thomists and the Scotists ; Presbyterians and Independents will unite with Episcopalians far more readily than the monastic orders will yield their privileges ; Arminians and Calvinists will be all of one mind when the Jansenists and Molinists are. Our controversies about ceremonies are not quite of as much importance as those which are waged in the Church of Rome concerning *Infallibility.* We find some theologians of the Church of Rome contending that the Pope is infallible, others, that he is anything but infallible ; some insist that he has temporal power, others maintain that his jurisdiction is entirely spiritual. Some maintain that the Virgin Mary was conceived without original sin, others affirm that she was not. Some teach that souls may be delivered out of purgatory, others hold the contrary. The advocates of these various theories have written and railed and preached against one another in a most edifying and *fraternal* manner. Now, when THE CHURCH, the infallible judge in matters of controversy, settles her own disputes, it will be time enough for Protestant sects to invite Holy Mother to be the umpire between them ; as matters stand at present, we must decline her intervention, particularly as some of her own doctors declare that the doctrine of the Pope's infallibility is *heresy.*

Moreover, the UNITY of the Papal Church has been sadly marred by schisms between rival popes ; in repeated instances, there have been several competitors for the chair of St. Peter, and if there is any virtue in anathemas, then many a Pope is doomed beyond recovery. Bellarmine in his chronology confesses twenty-six several schisms in the Church of Rome ; but Onuphrius computes thirty ; of these, some lasted ten, others twenty, and one fifty years, and caused blood to flow in streams. Oh ! how beautifully does the Church of Rome preserve the unity of the Spirit in the bond of peace ; and with what lustre does she shine forth as the ONE and only Church of Christ !

Concerning the Mark of the Church by which she is called Holy. (No. 76.)

"That sanctity is a mark of the Church, is proved, Eph. v. 25. 'Christ loved the Church, and delivered himself up for it, that he might sanctify it ;' hence the faithful are called by St. Peter, 1 Ep. ii. 9, ' a chosen generation, a holy nation.'   Add to this, the Apostles' Creed, in which it is said, ' I believe the Holy Catholic Church.'

"What does this mark, the Sanctity of the Church, mean ?

" It means not only that Christ, the Head and Author of the Church, is holy, but also the sanctity of the persons being in the Church, the sanctity of doctrine, of the sacraments, laws, &c., confirmed by miracles : which sanctity, again, is found nowhere except in our church, which has always had men conspicuous by their sanctity, whom the very champions of the Protestants themselves have acknowledged as holy men : as is to be seen in the history of the variations of the most illustrious Bossuet. (Bk. 3. n. 50.)

" *Obj. I.* Holiness lies concealed in the soul : therefore it does not pertain to the marks of the Church, which ought to be visible.

" *Ans.* Sanctity is not so concealed, but that it manifests itself externally, and becomes visible according to its effects : just as the mind in man is invisible, and yet manifests itself by works : and although the sanctity of each one in particular may not so certainly be known, yet we see the sanctity of the church in the community, when we observe some leading an austere life, others devoting themselves entirely to the duties of piety, &c.   Add to this, that God frequently declares through miracles, the sanctity of private individuals, which beyond the church is never done.

15 *

" *Obj. II.* In the church there are more bad than good : therefore it is not rightly called holy.

" I deny the inference : for the church is not called holy as though all who are in it should be holy ; but because all are holy by their calling and profession ; and because many in it are holy, who are the better part ; and BECAUSE OUT OF IT, THEY CANNOT BE HOLY.

" Besides, that there are bad people in the church, does not arise from the doctrines and principles, which the church proposes, but she is opposed to them : BUT THAT HERETICS ARE BAD, PROCEEDS FROM THEIR DOCTRINES AND PRINCIPLES : for the doctrine of protestants is that good works are not necessary to salvation, that faith alone is sufficient for salvation, that human laws are not binding on the conscience, &c."

That the church of Christ is holy, and that every true member of Christ's body is holy ; in short that there can be no union or communion between Christ and any soul without holiness, is plainly a doctrine of the word of God. There are many in nominal connection with the professed people of God, and in the outward communion of the church, who have never been regenerated and sanctified, but they *are not* members of the church of Christ, though they *profess* to be. The church of Rome claims to be the only society of true believers upon earth. OUT OF IT, MEN CANNOT BE HOLY !

We are prepared to assume the reverse of this proposition, and to *prove* that no man can carry out the principles of the Romish Church, and be *holy.* Holiness consists in the love of God and man. Popery is the enemy of both. When did the Saviour or his apostles either recommend or practise the doctrines which it inculcates relative to the treatment of *heretics ?* They endured persecution and death for the sake of the truth, but they never inflicted either. In meekness they instructed those who opposed them, and being reviled they blessed. But the church of Rome consigns to the dungeon and the stake, those, who cannot violate their consciences by conforming to her idolatry and impiety! The *sanctity* of the church of Rome!! To speak of her as *holy* according to the principles of the Bible, would be resented even by her own priests as merciless sarcasm.   Her history is an accumulation of instances of cruelty, lewdness, perfidy, superstition, and deceit, such as the annals of no other power present.   Surely if the pope were really Christ's vicar upon earth, the men, who have filled the chair of St. Peter would have been addicted at least to no flagrant violations of decorum; the world and the church would not have been disgraced by the execrable lives of some of the nominal successors of Peter, who were notorious for profligacy and crime, from which ordinary criminals recoil with horror.   And yet every one of these men bore the modest title of " His Holiness ;" and thus, we have the strange anomaly of " His Holiness," being at one time an adulterer, at another, a murderer, at another, an avowed sorcerer, at another, a blasphemer.   The instances of popes, who have been merely negatively good men are more than equalled in the number of those, who were notoriously bad.

But even admitting that the church of Rome is not responsible for the character of her Supreme Pontiffs, how is it possible that there should be holiness in that church, whose members are required to believe and endorse such blasphemy as the following: " The faithful must give to the Holy Sacrament of the altar that divine adoration that is due to God only ; and it must be no reason to prevent this, that Christ our Lord gave it to be eaten !" Council of Trent, sess. xiii. ch. 5.

As for the perversions of Protestant doctrine, which are contained in the closing remarks of the last chapter, one of two things is certain.   The writer either did not know that he was misrepresenting the tenets of Protestants, or he did know it.   If the former, we can both pity and pardon him ; and if the latter, he has given a practical illustration of the *sanctity* of the Romish Church. "*The doctrine of Protestants is that good works are not necessary to Salvation, that faith alone is sufficient for Salvation, that human laws are not binding on the conscience,*" &c.   Now the poor papist, who believes whatever his holiness or his reverence teaches, will naturally infer from such language that we Protestants must in strict conformity with our principles be Antinomians, and disturbers of the public peace.   But that we even *doubt* the *necessity* of good works is false. We deny that good works merit salvation, either in whole or in part ; but we affirm that the faith, by which we are justified, works by love, and that whenever there is opportunity of evidencing the existence of saving faith, it will be proved by the holiness of its possessor—and we always testify that the faith which does not produce good works is utterly worthless before God and man.

The assertion that Protestants hold "that human laws are not binding on the conscience," is not true in the unqualified sense in which it is stated.   We *are* bound to obey God rather than man, and if laws were to be enacted, which in their practical operation would be contrary to the law of God, Protestants, who deserve the name, would rather die than yield obedience.   But all governments, which leave us free to worship God according to the dictates of our conscience, will find the strongest supporters of the dignity of the laws in the Protestant portion of the community.   If, however, the Church of Rome should ever gain such an ascendency in this country as to obtain the control of the secular power, and if she were then to attempt to enforce her abominable rites and principles by a political arm, she would find Protestants resisting her tyranny unto death, and rallying around the standard of civil and religious liberty !   Protestants will never entrust their consciences to the keeping of the Church of Rome ; nor will they ever permit the Pope to make laws for them.

Concerning the Mark of the Church, by which she is called Catholic.

" What is signified by the mark of the Church, by which she is called Catholic?

" It is signified that she is diffused over the whole earth, or is universal in place, people, and time ; according to that, Apoc. v. 9. 'Thou hast redeemed us .... from every tribe, and tongue, and people, and nation.' But it is universal as to place and people, because it is diffused through all places and nations. It is universal as to time, because from the time at which the Church of the New Testament began, it shall always endure without any intermission, even to the end of the world.

" But it is predicted that the church would be such, Ps. ii. 8. ' Ask of me, and I will give thee the Gentiles for thy inheritance, and the utmost parts of the earth for thy possession ;' and Mal. i. 11 : 'For from the rising of the sun even to the going down, my name is great among the Gentiles ; and in every place there is sacrifice, and there is offered to my name a clean oblation ;' and Matt. xxviii. 19 : 'Go ye, therefore, and teach all nations ;' and Acts i. 8 : ' You shall be witnesses unto me in Jerusalem, and in all Judea, and Samaria, and even to the uttermost parts of the earth.'

" That this mark of the Church is peculiar to ours is plain ; for in every place, and every nation, Catholics are found, who all, however much scattered, are united under the obedience of the Roman Pontiff : also have been in every time, and will be, Catholics : whereas all other sects are confined to some part of the world, and their time of origin is easily shown, which they, for the most part, also betray by their very name, whilst some are called Lutherans, others Calvinists, &c., from their own authors and inventors, respectively, &c.

"*Obj. I.* The Mahometan religion is more widely diffused than the Christian, therefore, &c.

" Although it were admitted that the Mahometan religion occupies more territory than the Roman Catholic, yet because it is confined in the Ottoman Empire only, and is not found in other parts of the world, it cannot be called universal in every place and in every people. Besides, they who preach that the religion of Mahomet is so widely diffused, consider it with all its sects: and hence it is right against them thus to consider the religion of Christians; but if the Christian religion be regarded with all sects, heretics, and schismatics, the number of those who glory in the Christian name will exceed the number of Jews, Mahometans, and idolaters together.

"*Obj. II.* The Jews are scattered over the whole earth, therefore, &c.

"*Ans.* It is true that the Jews are almost every where, but by the dispersion of their nation, not by the propagation of (their) faith: and hence every where wretched and despised, they bear about with them the punishment of the blood of the Son of God. Besides, there was no necessity that their religion should be either scattered in every place, or embraced by every nation, like the Christian religion."

The prophecies of Scripture plainly predict that the Church of Christ is eventually to extend the knowledge of the truth as it is in Jesus over the whole world; and the Signs of the Times evidently point to this great and glorious consummation as near at hand. The wide diffusion of the principles of the Romish Church is in itself no proof that she is Catholic. Infidelity prevails to a fearful extent, and is to be found in every country which has been or now is under the influence of Popery; but the simple fact of its diffusion is no substantial argument either for or against it. The Bible teaches that truth is *eventually* to prevail; the kingdom of darkness is to be *finally* destroyed, and all the delusions of the Man of Sin are to perish with it; and the providence of God plainly indicates that "the time of the end" is very near. The wane of Popery throughout Europe, and in almost every part of the world, except on the continent of America, and the corresponding increase of Protestant influence, show that the days of Popery are numbered. France is already irretrievably lost; and even Spain is bursting from her shackles; in Italy the very name of the Pope is execrated, and nothing sustains his throne but the bayonets of Austria;

whilst the great cardinal doctrines of the gospel as taught in the word of God and the Protestant Churches, instead of being confined to some few corners of the earth, are daily proving to be the power and wisdom of God to the salvation of multitudes throughout the whole world. The missionaries of Christ are proclaiming salvation through faith in the Redeemer's blood to the kindreds and nations of the earth, and the mighty angel having the everlasting gospel to preach, is flying through the midst of heaven. Moravians and Methodists, Presbyterians and Reformed, are scattering the precious seed of revealed truth stripped of Romish inventions, and however industriously the enemy may sow tares with the wheat, he cannot stay the approach of the harvest. It is ripening amid the snows of Greenland and on the burning sands of Africa; India and China and the isles of the Sea are stretching forth their hands to God, and we look and long for the dawn of the day when the heathen shall be given to Christ for his inheritance, and the uttermost parts of the earth for his possession.

Concerning the Mark of the Church, by which she is called Apostolic. (78.)

"The fourth mark is that the true Church is apostolic, concerning which, as Christ says, Matt. xvi. 18: 'Thou art Peter, and upon this rock I will build my church;' and Matt. xxviii. 20: 'I am with you always, even to the consummation of the world;' likewise the apostle, Eph. ii. 20: 'Built upon the foundation of the apostles;' and ch. iv. 11: 'And some, indeed, he gave to be apostles,—and others pastors and teachers;' and ver. 12: 'for the perfection of the saints, for the work of the ministry, unto the edification of the body of Christ.'

"For what reason is the Church called apostolic?

"*Ans.* 1. On account of the doctrine received from the apostles, the same which our church always has received, and always will receive, SO THAT FROM THE TIME OF THE APOSTLES UNTIL NOW, IT CANNOT BE SHOWN, IN WHAT RE-

SPECT, WHEN, WHERE, AND BY WHOM ANY THING CON-
CERNING DOCTRINE HAS BEEN CHANGED.

"2. Because it was propagated by the apostles.

"3. Because it has a legitimate and uninterrupted succession of bishops, especially in the very seat itself of Peter,
concerning which St. Aug. says: 'The succession of priests
from the very seat of the apostle Peter, to whom the Lord
entrusted his sheep to be fed, down to the present Episcopate,
keeps me in the church.'

"4. Because she adheres inseparably to the chair of St.
Peter, or to the Roman See, founded by Peter; and hence
she is called Papal by her enemies, &c.

"From the mark of the Catholic and Apostolic Church,
it will be proper to use the argument of Tertullian in his
book concerning Prescriptions, ch. 37, and to accost them
in his words: 'Who are you? When and whence do you
come? The possession is mine; I possess it of old, I possess it before (you), I have firm origins from the authors
themselves.' And ch. 32. 'Let them publish the origins of
their churches, let them develope the order of their bishops,
running through successions from the beginning, so that the
first bishop shall have some author from the apostles or
apostolical men.'

"From these remarks you will gather, that NOVELTY IN
THE CHURCH IS ODIOUS, and antiquity venerable; and therefore that the antiquity of the church is not a sign of debility
or defect, but of strength, firmness, and perfection."

There are several remarks in this section, which are calculated to startle by their boldness even those who are prepared for the exhibition of no small degree of assurance on
the part of Romish writers. There is not a greater farce
extant than the pretensions of the Papal Church to apostolicity, as we hope to show in the course of this chapter. We
join issue on the following proposition, " *that from the time
of the apostles until now, it can not be shown, in what respect, when, where, and by whom anything concerning doctrine has been changed.*"

A comparison between the doctrines taught in Paul's

Epistle to the Romans and those now maintained by the
Church of Rome, and prescribed as articles of faith by the
Council of Trent, will suffice to show the impudence and
absurdity of her claim to apostolicity.

1. The Church of Rome represents the Eternal Father,
the first person in the Trinity, under the figure of an old
man, and teaches that it is proper to bow down to images
representing the Deity. Paul condemns it as heathenish
idolatry, and as entailing the judgments of God. Rom. i.
23—32.

2. The Church of Rome teaches that the Virgin Mary
was without sin. Paul asserts no *such* doctrine, but on the
contrary, affirms, of both Jews and Gentiles, that "all are
under sin;" and that " all have sinned and come short of
the glory of God." Rom. iii. 9 and 23. From this charge
he exempts no common member of the human family.

3. The Church of Rome teaches that the " faithful" are
justified by works; Paul, on the contrary, proves that we
are justified freely by grace. " For we conclude a man to
be justified by faith without the deeds of the law." (Rom.
iii. 28.)

He tells us explicitly that Abraham's faith was counted to
him for righteousness, and then adds, " Now, it was not
written for his sake alone, that it was imputed to him ; but
for us also, to whom it shall be imputed, if we believe on
him that raised up Jesus our Lord from the dead." Whilst
he uniformly teaches that good works are the fruit of faith,
he as uniformly denies that they can have any share in our
justification.

4. The Church of Rome would have us believe, not only
that a man may perfectly fulfil the law, but also do works
of supererogation, and thus make Almighty God his debtor,
and that a draft upon this fund of merit will always be
honoured by Him. Whereas, Paul in all his writings ac-
cords with the doctrine taught by the Lord Jesus Christ, that

16

when we have done all things that we are commanded to do, we have done no more than our duty, and are unprofitable servants.

5. The Church of Rome teaches that holiness consists, in some considerable measure at least, in the observance of festival days of her own appointment, and in abstinence from meats at certain times, under pain of *mortal* sin.   But Paul declares that " the kingdom of God is *not* MEAT and DRINK, but righteousness, and peace and joy in the Holy Ghost," Rom. xiv. 17.   We commend this whole chapter to the devout attention of those " who command to abstain from meats, which God hath created to be received with thanksgiving of them which believe and know the truth." 1 Tim. iv. 3.

6. The Church of Rome teaches that the reading of the Scriptures by all classes, is productive of more harm than good ; and that the invariable tendency of this practice is to make men *proud, discontented*, and *conceited*.   But Paul tells us, that " whatsoever things were written aforetime, were written for our learning, that we through patience and comfort of the Scriptures might have hope." Rom. xv. 4.

7. The Church of Rome teaches that the sufferings of the saints upon earth are worthy of eternal glory.   Paul affirms that " the sufferings of this present time are not worthy to be compared with the glory that shall be revealed in us." Rom. viii. 18.

8. The Church of Rome enjoins upon the faithful the worship of saints and angels, and of the Virgin Mary ; and prescribes that the same veneration be paid to the consecrated host which is due to God ; and that divine images, holy relics, &c., are also to be worshipped.   Paul inculcates the contrary, and shows that the judgments of God were inflicted upon the Gentiles on account of their idolatry. (Rom. i.) He never desired the brethren to secure an interest in the prayers of the saints in heaven in his behalf, but he be-

seeches them, " for the Lord Jesus Christ's sake, and for the love of the Spirit, that they strive together with him in their prayers TO GOD for him," &c. Rom. xv. 30.   And yet Peter Dens has the effrontery to assert that, " from the time of the apostles until now, it cannot be shown in what respect, when, where, and by whom, any thing concerning doctrine has been changed ! !"

With Roman assurance those are challenged who ground their faith upon the word of God alone, and who " build upon the foundation of apostles and prophets, Jesus Christ himself being the chief corner-stone," " Who are you ?   When and whence do you come ?   The possession is mine ; I possess it of old ; I possess it before you ; I have firm origins from the authors themselves."   Now, that the Church of Rome may have " firm origins from the authors themselves," of many of her strange inventions, we are not disposed to dispute, but the apostles certainly are not the authors in question.   *They* never said mass ; *they* never sold indulgences ; *they* never manufactured holy water ; *they* never worshipped images ; *they* never imposed penances ; *they* never offered prayers for the souls in purgatory, &c., all which things, and a thousand more equally impious and absurd, are practised in the Romish Church.

But we are farther challenged.   " Let them publish the origins of their churches, let them develope the order of their bishops, running through successions from the beginning, so that the first bishop shall have some author from the apostles or apostolical men."   Our main concern is whether the doctrines which we receive and preach are those which Christ and his apostles taught ; this we hold to be the true apostolical succession, and this is all the apostolicity which we seek.   Yet we cannot but admire the zeal with which Romish priests insist upon their apostolical succession. Although it is notorious that there have been repeated schisms in their church ; that one pope has anathematized another, and has in turn been deposed and anathematized by a competitor; though the line of apostolical succession has been entangled and broken by the acts of three rival contemporary popes, who all cursed each other, and mutually pronounced their ordinations, and all other official acts, invalid, yet forsooth they can trace the order of their clergy from the present day down to the times of the apostles! A hiatus of a few centuries is a mere *circumstance* — and the occasional breach of a century in the chain of apostolical succession cannot impair either its continuity or its strength!

Besides, when we come to the investigation of the practical benefits to be derived from this boasted succession, what are they? where are they? A Romish bishop professes to confer the gift of the Holy Ghost upon the priest whom he ordains. The mere imposition of the bishop's hands, with the proper intention by virtue of the apostolic succession, imparts the Holy Spirit to the candidate. He rises from his knees duly ordained. But how is it manifest that he has actually received the Holy Spirit? Is he a holier man? Has he become more apt to teach, or has he received a single endowment more than the Presbyterian or Reformed minister, who is set apart by " the laying on of the hands of the presbytery?" Now, if he has received no additional gift, we cannot conceive of what practical benefit the apostolic succession has been to him. The very fact that God sets his seal alike to the testimony of all ministers who preach the gospel in its simplicity, is a standing evidence that the residue of the Spirit is with him, and not with the BISHOP.

But we are told in the last paragraph, " NOVELTY IN THE CHURCH IS ODIOUS." So it is. Peter Dens occasionally presents important truths in vigorous language. " Novelty in the Church *is* odious," and for this very reason we abhor the leading tenets and principles of Popery.

The section which treats of the duration of the Church, we omit, with the general remark, that we hold as a precious truth the doctrine that the Church of *Christ* has always been preserved, has never been extinct since its foundation, and never will be overthrown, though the gates of hell and of Rome should move against it.

CHAPTER XXI.

Concerning the Infallibility of the Church.   (80.)

" Is the Church infallible ?

" 'That the Church in matters of faith and customs can in no respect err, is a doctrine of the faith.   It is proved from Matt. xvi. 18. ' The gates of hell shall not prevail against her,' and chap. xxviii. 20. ' Behold I am with you always, even to the end of the world.'

" Observe against our heretics, that they indeed admit that the Church can not fail ; but then they recur to the invisible : but that the Church is visible, has been already proved, No. 73.   Besides, 1 Tim. iii. 15, the apostle says : ' That thou mayest know how thou oughtest to behave thyself in the house of God, which is the church of the living God, the pillar and ground of the truth ;' there, manifestly, the discourse is concerning the visible church ; for Timothy is not receiving instruction how he ought to behave in a church which he did not see, but which he saw : but now that church is the pillar and ground of the truth ; therefore the visible church is indefectible.

" Moreover, a twofold infallibility may be considered in the Church : one active and authoritative, which is called infallibility in teaching and defining ; the other passive, or obediental, which is called infallibility in learning and believing.

" Infallibility, considered in the former mode, belongs to the church by reason of its head or supreme P***** and the

16 *

prelates of the Church; although this infallibility does not belong on account of the laity or inferior pastors; for just as a man is said to see, although vision does not pertain to him by reason of all his members, but only by reason of the eyes, so the Church is said to be infallible in this way, although this infallibility belongs to her only by reason of the superiors.

"But if the church be regarded not with reference to her head, but as she embraces all the faithful, even the laity under obedience, she ought not thus, properly to be called infallible in teaching and defining, because in this respect her office is not to teach, but to learn and believe: wherefore the church considered in this way may either be called passively infallible, or in learning, believing, practising, &c.

"Hence it cannot be that the Universal Church obeying the Pontiff may believe something as revealed, or may practise any thing as good, which is not such: and hence it is commonly said that the opinion of the Universal Church is always true, and her practice or custom always good."

Concerning the authority of the Church. (81.)

"Is the Church the judge of controversies respecting the faith?

"*Ans.* The Church, whether assembled or scattered, is an infallible judge of controversies respecting the faith, as is plain from Nos. 68 and 80. It is farther proved (thus); if all the pastors of the church scattered over the world could teach any thing false, the Christian people scattered every where would also be bound to admit and believe that which was false; and thus the error of all the pastors would be the error of the whole church; and so even its passive infallibility would vanish, which even our adversaries themselves acknowledge.

"It is proved also from the practice of the church, which although scattered, has condemned many heresies without councils, as Eusebius attests, and St. Augustine teaches, (Bk. 4 to Bonifacius, last chap.) 'As if,' says he, 'no heresy has been ever condemned without the assembly of a Synod; when rather those (heresies) are very rarely found, in order to condemn which such a necessity has existed; and there are much and incomparably more which deserved to be disapproved and condemned there where they have arisen.'

" 'To whom does the authority of judgment in controversies respecting the faith belong?

" *Ans.* To the Superiors of the Church, namely, to the Bishops, and above all, to the Supreme Pontiff.

" These Christ means when he says, Matt. xviii. 17 : ' Tell the Church ; but if he hear not the Church,' &c. ; also Luke x. 16 : ' He that heareth you heareth me ; and he that despiseth you despiseth me :' to these also Paul says, Acts xx. 28 : ' Take heed to yourselves, and to all the flock over which the Holy Ghost hath placed you Bishops, to rule the Church of God.'

" Does this judgment, in matters of faith, not appertain to theological doctors, or other ecclesiastics ?

" *Ans.* No : and hence in general councils they have not a decisive vote : but they are admitted to them only for the examination of subjects and for consultation ; much less therefore are laymen judges in matters of faith.

" From these things, observe, the government of the church is indeed monarchical by reason of its head, the Supreme Pontiff, but it is at the same time tempered by an aristocracy : and, because there is likewise a subordination of the ministers of the church among themselves, hence, also, it is a hierarchy.

" From these remarks it is plain : that this is a vain subterfuge of the Quesnellites, who say that the Bull Unigenitus was not accepted by the bishops assembled in one place: their appeal to a general council is also vain, as the church dispersed is equally infallible, as if assembled in general council, and is the same tribunal. And hence not even that appeal is legitimate according to the principles of the French, who maintain that the pope is fallible and inferior to a general council : because from an infallible judgment, such as is that of the church dispersed, no appeal is admitted.

" Is it necessary in order to the unshaken and infallible authority of a definition, that all the bishops throughout the whole world should be of one and the same opinion ?

" No : but a moral unanimity of the bishops is sufficient, or the greater part of them agreeing with their head, the Supreme Pontiff.

" It is proved (thus): It is the common and received law
of all tribunals, that an opinion be pronounced according to
the plurality of votes : but here a plurality of votes is obtained of those, who agree with their head, the Supreme Pontiff: therefore if a definitive opinion be pronounced by them,
this is the legitimate opinion of the tribunal of the whole
church.

" This is confirmed : for otherwise the church would fail
and be rendered invisible: for it would not be known to
which party it would be right to adhere: but to both parties
we could not adhere, as between them the unity of the church
could not subsist : nor could it be known which church was
the pillar and ground of the truth.

" Finally that smaller number of bishops dissenting from
their head, can not constitute or represent the church.

" Hence it follows, that in order that it may be known
that the whole church has accepted any pontifical bull, it is
sufficient that the greatest and the principal part accepts it :
but by no means (as the Quesnellites pretend), is it necessary that all the bishops of the whole world receive it, in
order that the church may be known to receive any doctrine
as Catholic, either to propose it, or to condemn the contrary
as heretical.

" This is demonstrated : (thus) otherwise the church would
not be able to condemn heresy, when some bishops were
infected by it : thus, for instance, the impious doctrines of
Arius, Macedonius, Pelagius, &c., could not be condemned
by the church, because they were defended by many bishops :
but yet the decrees of the church against said heretics have
remained firm and unshaken, and so they are held by the
Quesnellites : therefore, it by no means obviates the condemnation of the Quesnellites that some bishops in France have
been refractory against the Bull Unigenitus."

Of what nature the consent of the Bishops ought to be. (82.)

" Is the expressed consent of the bishops required in order
to the infallible authority of a decision that is passed, or for
a definition of the universal church ?

" No : but a tacit consent is sufficient, bestowed in silence
and without demurring, after the decree has passed, which
has sufficiently come to the notice of the bishops ; for to be

silent in this case is to consent: for an error to which no opposition is made, says Felix III. is approved, and truth, when it is not defended, is oppressed. And St. Augustine (epist. 119. alias 55 to Januar. chap. 19. n. 35,) says : ' the Church of God neither approves nor passes over in silence those things which are contrary to faith and a good life.'

"It is proved 2d, from the sense and practice of the Church ; for many heresies have been condemned by the Pope alone, without the expressed consent of the bishops, and yet the condemnation of these has been considered as an infallible decree of the Church, and therefore those who dissented have been regarded as heretics : thus, for instance, the condemnation of the errors of Jovinianus, made by Pope Siricius, also the Bulls of Pius V. and Gregory XIII., against the errors of Bajus, are considered as an infallible rule of thinking and speaking, although few bishops have received them by an expressed and public record.

" Observe, independently of the question concerning the infallibility of the Pope, that it is certain, that, when the Supreme Pontiff defines anything, and a plurality of bishops does not demur, it is not possible that that definition can contain any errors, and consequently it cannot favour the Quesnellites, even if the Bull Unigenitus had not been accepted by an expressed consent of the bishops ; although, at the same time, no pontifical Bull has ever been received in the Church as expressly and solemnly as this.

" *Obj. I.* Many opinions of authors are circulated, against which the bishops do not demur ; but yet they are not supposed to assent to them, or to approve the same ; therefore, &c.

" *Ans.* I deny the inference : there is a disparity, because the doctrine of *one* or of several authors is not published as a decree, but as an opinion ; and this also is sometimes not known by the bishops, nor can it involve the faithful generally in an error. The case is different concerning a Constitution of the Supreme Pontiff, pertaining to faith or customs, directed to all the faithful as a model and rule to be observed.

" *Obj. II.* There may be various reasons for the silence of the bishops, v. g., the fear of incurring the indignation of Rome, the fear of the tribunal of the Inquisition, or also the opinion of the pope's infallibility, &c.; therefore their silence cannot be considered as consent.

"*Ans.* Whatever there may be of these or similar motives for silence, the inference is denied; for this always is firm, that the Spirit of Truth never will permit that the church should in any way whatever approve any error in faith or customs, lest the gates of hell might prevail against the church, if silent in such a manner.

"Wherefore, observe, that the infallibility of the church does not depend upon the question of giving consent from these or similar motives: because infallibility has been given to the church absolutely: not as if the church could proceed in a blind way in her definitions, but when the church defines, it must be undoubted that the pre-requisites also have been afforded.   Besides, otherwise, all the definitions of the church might be called into question," &c.

The 84th section treats of the authority of the church about questions of fact. The main proposition is thus stated.

"It is to be premised, 2d, that a threefold fact is distinguished: for one is *immediately revealed;* for instance, the incarnation of the Word; another is *merely historical* and *personal*, and this has respect to the truth of some occurrence, or the state, condition, inward opinion of the mind, crime or innocence of some person: the other is dogmatical, which attributes some dogma of the faith to some book or person.

"All acknowledge that the church is infallible in matters immediately revealed.

"All admit that the church may err in facts purely historical and personal; and hence it is inferred that when it is asked, whether the judgment of the church concerning propositions or books is infallible, the question is not whether the church infallibly decrees that this book is this or that author's, for this kind of fact, the church, which judges concerning books just as they are circulated under the name of a certain author, supposes, but does not determine," &c.

Concerning the infallibility of the Church in the Canonizaton of the Saints. (85.)

" What is the canonization of the saints?

" *Ans.* According to present use, it is a solemn judgment of the pope, with the concurrence of the church, concerning the sanctity and the fruition of celestial glory of a departed person with the provision that he be considered by all as such, and be honoured with due veneration.

" But, Beatification is a permission of the worship of some person deceased, in the communion of the Catholic Church, given only to some particular places, or to a regular order, until his solemn canonization may take place.

" And hence, Beatification differs from canonization.

" 1st. That in Beatification, worship is only regularly permitted ; in canonization, worship is decreed by enjoining through a definitive sentence.

" 2d. That the worship permitted in Beatification is usually confined within particular places, or a religious family ; the worship of a canonized person extends to the whole church.

" 3d. And principally, canonization is the decree of the Supreme Pontiff, ultimately definitive, concerning the sanctity of a deceased person : not so Beatification.

" But because the canonization of the saints is a certain kind of fact, the question is asked, whether in it the church is infallible, or the pope?

" *Ans.* The doctors commonly affirm with St. Thomas, &c., because this is a question not simply of fact, but of dogmatical fact : for it has relation to the customs of the whole church, which would thus without remedy be involved entire in a superstitious worship, if at any time, one should be invoked as a saint, who is associated with the damned in hell.

" *Obj. I.* The sanctity of a man depends upon this fact, whether he has died in a state of grace : but this neither the pope nor the church can know. No one short of a divine revelation can know this of any man living : therefore, &c.

" *Ans.* I deny the inference : for this is judged from various signs and miracles, especially after the decease of the person to be canonized, performed by his intercession, with the superadded assistance of the Holy Spirit, which in a matter so grave and affecting the whole church preserves the pope free from error.

"For the proof, it is to be said that it does not belong to the rule of the church that she should bear testimony concerning a man still living, who may also continually fall from holiness.

"*Obj. II.* In order that any one may be prudently worshipped as a saint, moral certainty seems to suffice; therefore in this point, the infallibility of the church is not necessary.

"It is proved before: such certainty is sufficient for any one to adore the consecrated host.

"*Ans.* There is a disparity, because the worship of Latria exhibited in the adoration of the host, terminates on Christ; and, although in reality through want of valid consecration he might not be present, he is nevertheless the object of adoration: and therefore it will not be an error of the object, but of the place: but in the worship of a person, who should not be holy, it would be an error of the object.

"Is it to be believed with a divine faith that a canonized person is a saint?

"*Ans.* This is not clear. To Silvius, in his controversies, and to various other persons, this thing seems not to be in assured confidence; yet they add that it must nevertheless be firmly held; so far that to say that the Pope can err in the canonization of Saints, is scandalous, rash, and smacking of heresy. Thus also thinks Benedict XIV. lib. 1, concerning the canonization of Saints, &c.

"Is the Church or the Pope infallible in Beatification?

"I answer with Benedict XIV., &c., that when the judgment of the Pope, in Beatification, is not ultimately defining or enjoining, but only indulging and permitting, it must not necessarily be infallible; but it may suffice that it is certain with that moral certainty, by which the Pope acts prudently and wisely, indulges and permits.

"Whoever wishes more, let him refer to that excellent work of Benedict XIV., filled with every variety of learning, which is inscribed, *Concerning the Canonization of the Saints.*"

The arguments by which Papists attempt to prove the infallibility of the Romish Church, are perfectly ridiculous. They tell us that it is impossible that all the pastors of the church should at one and the same time depart from the faith. Why so? Because they have all received the Holy Spirit, and he is a Spirit of truth. But where is the proof that all her priests have been thus highly favoured? Because Christ promised to give the apostles the Holy Spirit, and the priests of the Church of Rome can trace the validity of their ordinations, through a long succession, down to the very apostles themselves; and because the Saviour has declared " Lo, I am with you alway, even to the end of the world," and " the gates of hell shall not prevail against *her*," i. e., the Church. But now, the priests ought to know that these promises belong to the Church of *Christ*, and not to the Church of Rome. The gates of hell shall never prevail against *his* Church; and he always will be with his people to the end of the world; but these two great and precious truths certainly do not establish the infallibility of the Church of Rome. Christ has never promised his Spirit to *her*, and to the papal apostasy as such he never can give his Spirit. We have already shown that error abounds without limit in the Romish system, and this fact is proof enough that the promises which Christ has given to HIS Church are misapplied when claimed by the Pope and his priests for themselves, for according to their own theory it is impossible that those should fall into gross errors to whom Christ has given the Spirit of truth. And even supposing that the Romish Church were part of the Church of Christ, which we utterly deny, the texts of Scripture which are adduced establish her infallibility only when she is permitted to beg the question, and assume at once that her interpretations of Scripture must necessarily be correct. She claims to be the judge of controversies respecting the faith; from her deci-

17

sion there is to be no appeal, and it is only by her approbation and authority that the Scriptures are to be known or received as authentic!

The Church of Christ has four special offices relating to the Scriptures.

1. She is their witness and keeper. If a friend sends a letter to us by the hand of a second person, and he delivers it, we do not credit the contents for the sake of the bearer, but because we recognise the hand and seal of the writer; neither do we receive the Scriptures as the word of God only or chiefly upon the recommendation of the Church, though conveyed to us by her ministry.

2. The Church is to preserve and vindicate the Scriptures, to exclude that which is spurious from the genuine word. And to this end the Church is assisted by the Spirit of Christ, through whom she recognises the " voice of the Bridegroom." But the Church does not make the Scriptures genuine, any more than the jeweller makes the gold, whose nature he determines by his chemical tests.

3. The Church is the herald to proclaim the Scripture, and is bound to promulgate it just as she has received it. Now when is a royal edict credited for the sake of the herald who proclaims it ?

4. She is the interpreter of the Scriptures ; she must expound them, without mixing any thing of her own, and explain Scripture by Scripture.

But without the internal evidence of the Holy Spirit, the testimony of the Church will be of little efficacy. The Scriptures are in themselves worthy of belief, and are received by us as the word of God, not *only* or even *principally* because the Church so directs, but because they proceed from God. Now that they do thus emanate from God, we know from the testimony of the Holy Ghost, who always makes use of the sacred truths of God's word for the conviction and conversion of sinners.

We know that the Scriptures are divinely inspired.

1. By the testimony of God speaking in the Scriptures.

2. By the inward witness of his Spirit. "We have received the Spirit which is of God, that we might know the things that are freely given us of God." 1 Cor. ii. 12; and ver. 15. "He that is spiritual judgeth all things."

3. By the virtue and power which proceed from every page of the Bible; by its pure and perfect morals; by the majesty of its style; by the awe with which it inspires the conscience; by the literal fulfilment of its prophecies; by its admirable preservation; by the harmony of all its parts; by the rage with which Satan pursues those who make it their rule of faith and practice; and by the success which has attended the promulgation of its principles.

The Scriptures had authority with believers before the judgment of the church, with respect to the canon, had been passed, and consequently the authority of the word of God did not then depend upon her testimony. The judgment of the Fathers is comparatively but of yesterday. If the books which the Fathers and council cite as canonical were not authentic before, then for several centuries there was no authentic Scripture at all.

If the authority of the Church, as it respects us, depends on the testimony of Scripture, then the authority of Scripture does not depend on the voice of the Church. But it is plain that the Church can have no authority, except what is conferred by Scripture. If I ask, how am I to be sure that the Church did not err in preparing the canon of Scripture? a Papist will answer:—Because she is guided by the Holy Ghost. But how shall I know that she is so directed? He replies:—Because Christ has given a promise to that effect. I ask, where? He tells me, in the Scripture, Matt. xxviii. 20, &c. "Lo, I am with you alway, even to the end of the world." And thus, even the Papist must confess that it is Scripture which gives authority to the Church.

There can be no greater or more certain evidence to us than that of a divine testimony; and such is the voice of Scripture, which is the word of God; whereas the declaration of the Church is but the word of man.   If the authority of the Church were paramount, then the truth of all the promises of salvation would stand on the sandy foundation of human judgment, and our faith must ultimately be resolved into the voice of the Church, which would be arrant absurdity, and gross impiety.

As for the presumptuous claim of the Romish Church, that she has the promise of the Holy Spirit to preserve her bishops and pastors from error, we have already remarked that this promise pertains to the Church of Christ.   Every pastor, and every private member of that church, who seeks the aid of the Holy Spirit in fervent and believing prayer, shall be guided into all truth necessary for salvation.   No man, who in honest simplicity places himself under the guidance of the Blessed Spirit, and asks of God, shall fail to know which doctrine is divine, and what he must do to be saved.   "If *any of you* lack wisdom, let him ask of God, who giveth liberally to all men and upbraideth not, and it shall be given him." James i. 5.

According to the Romish theory, her bishops, assembled in council, who all have the infallible direction of the Holy Spirit, may nevertheless differ *toto cœlo* in their opinions and decrees; and the decision of a case depends upon a plurality of votes, though all are equally infallible!   Was there ever a more senseless and stupid plea set up in behalf of any absurdity ?

The contradictory decrees of councils have made the Romish claims to infallibility a laughing-stock and a byeword of reproach.   The contests in relation to image-worship alone are sufficient to brand it as a gross imposture. In the fourth century, the Council of Elvira decided against the practice; thus also, in 754, a council at Constantinople condemned image worship by a formal decree. In 787, the Second Council of Nice declared the former council at Constantinople to be illegitimate. In 794, another council reversed this decree of its predecessor; and its act was confirmed by another, held in 814; but in 842, image worship was re-enacted.

As for the pope's infallibility in the canonization of saints, the statement of a few facts will be sufficient to show how much dependence is to be placed upon the judgment of his holiness in the manufacture of the gods of Rome. We are struck at once with the resemblance of the canonization of saints to the deification of the heathen. Plutarch tells us that "the ancient priests, in order to the credit of their system, felt it necessary to persuade the people that certain characters, many of whom had, however, been the most ambitious and sensual of mankind, were honoured by the special favour of heaven; were deep in its mysteries, and even worthy of being placed among the gods themselves; in consequence of which their public deification took place, with all the pomp and circumstance so well calculated to impose upon a gross and idolatrous people. In order, however, to this ceremony, some miraculous intimation of the favour and will of heaven, as to the individual in question, was required to be duly attested as necessary to the ceremony. Thus, in the case of Romulus, one Julius Proculus took a solemn oath, "That Romulus himself appeared to him, and ordered him to inform the senate of his being called up to the assembly of the gods, under the name of Quirinus." In papal as in pagan Rome, the evidence of miracles is required, with this difference, however, that in the case of the pope's idols, the miracles are alleged to have been performed by the saints themselves. The matter of procuring the necessary attestations, is a mere trifle; hence the canonization of saints has become almost as common as the creation of cardinals, and the calendar of the

17 *

saints is continually enriched by the addition of new names. The most common miracle which saints perform after their death, is to impart a delightful perfume to their carcasses; and it is an especial recommendation if they can preserve it for a long course of years, so that, when their graves are opened, all may be sensible of it. Collin de Plancy, (a French author, who I am sorry to say is not much admired by Romish priests), in his critical dictionary of miraculous relics and images, mentions a large number of wonderful miracles, which are duly attested by reverend monks and others, who were eye-witnesses of them, or at least *said that they were*. I will translate a few paragraphs as specimens.

" VICTORIA, a Roman Martyr of the third century. Her body is at Monte Sione, and at Plaisance. She had a third at Paris, in the Convent of the Daughters of God. This third body was sent from Rome, in 1784 : when it was exposed, people were surprised to see a saint, who had been dead for so long a time, preserve a fresh colour, and a beautiful skin. Some incredulous persons opened other eyes than those of faith ; and it was ascertained that the Daughters of God, in order to hide from their devotees the hideous spectacle of a skeleton, and to give a better grace to their saintess, had covered the head with a mask of silk, and the rest of her bones with a long robe."

" VICTOR, a martyr of Marseilles, in the third century. Whilst the Emperor Maximan Hercules was in this city, Victor overthrew with a kick an altar consecrated to idols. Although he was an officer of the troops of the emperor, he was immediately arrested ; he was tied to the tail of a horse that had never been trained : this punishment did not kill the saint ; he was whipped with cowhides, without seeming to feel it ; he was crucified, without appearing in the least incommoded. As he sung upon the cross, they put him in prison ; during the night, he converted his jailors, baptized them, and was whipped next day more cruelly that the first time.

" He was afterwards led before the statue of an idol, to which he again gave a kick. This holy foot was cut off by order of the tyrants, and Victor walked not a whit less straight for the want of it. They were obliged to put him to death under a millstone.

"The remains of Saint Victor were honourably interred; they possessed in an eminent degree the virtue of driving away devils. A vast number of blind, deaf, and dumb, is enumerated, whom he cured.

"At Marseilles there were formerly sold, bottles of holy water in which some bones of Saint Victor had been steeped. It was a sovereign remedy against all sorts of diseases.

"The body and the head of Saint Victor are at Marseilles; but he had a second head at Sens, and a third cranium at St. Victor, of Paris. The venerable foot with which Victor overthrew the idols, is also shown in this latter abbey. It is said that he has a second body at Rome in the church of Saint Pancrace," &c., &c.

The evidence of such wonders would certainly constitute some recommendation to a saintship, but unfortunately it is not always that the miracles are so fully attested as in the present instance. I am aware that it is " scandalous and rash," and that it " smacks of heresy" to question the infallibility of his holiness in the canonization of saints; and therefore, in the first instance, I will show merely that the faithful may be deceived. Middleton, in his Letters, makes the following statements.

"The Spaniards, it seems, have a saint held in great reverence, in some parts of Spain, called Viar; for the farther encouragement of whose worship, they solicited the pope to grant some special indulgences to his altars; and upon the pope's desiring to be better acquainted first with his character, and the proofs which they had of his saintship, they produced a stone with these antique letters, S. VI A R, which the antiquaries readily saw to be a small fragment of some old Roman inscription in memory of one who had been *Prefectu* s. viarum, or overseer of the highways."

"We have in England," says Middleton, " an instance still more ridiculous, of a fictitious saintship, in the case of a certain saint, called Amphibolus, who, according to monkish historians, was bishop of the Isle of Man, and fellow-martyr and disciple of St. Alban; yet the learned Bishop Usher has given good reason to convince us that he owes the honour of his saintship to a mistaken passage in old acts or legends of St. Alban; where the Amphibolus, mentioned and since reverenced as a saint and martyr, was nothing more than a cloak which Alban happened to have at the time of his execution; being a word derived from the Greek, and signifying a rough, shaggy cloak, which ecclesiastical persons usually wore in that age."

All this, however, does not necessarily affect the pope's infallibility; because we have not proved that his holiness had really canonized the cloak in question; but, however loth I am to soil my pages with any thing that is really "scandalous, rash, and smacking of heresy," I may as well say at once that his holiness's infallibility in this respect is at least *suspected*. The same author to whom I have just referred, says farther:

"They pretend to show here at Rome, two original impressions of our Saviour's face, on two different handkerchiefs; the one, sent a present by himself to Agbarus, prince of Edessa, who by a letter had desired a picture of him; the other, given by him at the time of his execution, to a saint or holy woman, named Veronica, upon a handkerchief which she had lent him to wipe his face on that occasion; both of which handkerchiefs are still preserved, as they affirm, and now kept with much reverence; the first in St. Sylvester's church, the second in St. Peter's; where in honour of this sacred relic, there is a fine altar, built by Pope Urban VIII., with a statue of Veronica herself with an inscription. There is a prayer in their book of offices, ordered by the rubric, to be addressed to this sacred and miraculous picture, in the following terms: 'Conduct us, O thou blessed figure! to our proper home, where we may behold the pure face of Christ.' But notwithstanding the authority of their popes, and this inscription, this Veronica, as one of their best authors has shown, like Amphibolus before mentioned, was not any real person, but the name given to the picture itself by old writers who mention it; being formed by blundering and confounding the words, VERA ICON, or true image, the title inscribed perhaps, or given originally to the handkerchief by the first contrivers of the imposture. 'Haec Christi imago a recentioribus Veronicæ dicitur : imaginem ipsam veteres Veronicam appellabant,' &c. Mabill. Iter. Ital. p. 88. 'This picture of Christ is called Veronica's by more recent (writers); the ancients called the picture itself Veronica.'"

It is certain that not a few of the saints whom Papists devoutly invoke, never had any existence at all, and some who did live were persons of very doubtful reputation.

On the 21st of October, they who follow the Romish calender, make mention of St. Ursula and the 11,000 virgins, in these words : —— "Permit us, we pray thee, O Lord our God, to venerate with unceasing devotion the triumphs of the holy virgins and martyrs, Ursula and her companions; &c."[*] And yet some Romish authors doubt the authenticity of her story; and well they may. For why so many virgins should ramble away from Cornwall to Rome, without any business, is certainly hard to determine; and still more difficult is it to say what motive the Huns should have had for putting them all to death. It is said also that Pope Cyriacus went with them, and yet Baronius denies that there ever was a Pope of that name.

So on July 27th, some simple souls pray to the Seven Sleepers, and worship them as saints. But any one who can believe that they slept in a cave from the time of Decius to the reign of Theodosius, a period of 362 years, and then, to confute some heretics that denied the resurrection, woke up and looked as fresh as a rose, certainly deserves to be canonized as an *eighth* sleeper. What confirmation the doctrine of the general resurrection could derive from the sleep of

---

[*] See Breviarium Monasticum of Pope Paul V. p. 676. Paris, 1671.

these seven persons, who it seems were not really dead, of course is not for heretics to conceive.

St. George is also a renowned saint, and yet his very existence is problematical. St. Christopher, one author tells us, was a gentleman who measured just twelve feet, but another veracious historian stretches his stature to twelve cubits that is at least eighteen feet. This tall saint converted just 48,000 Gentiles to Christianity; and it is further reported of him, that he carried Christ over an arm of the sea on his back.

On the 15th of March, St. Longinus receives due veneration. This is the Roman soldier who pierced the Saviour's side.

The 29th of March is the day of Marcus Arethusius; yet Baronius condemns him as an Arian heretic.

Thomas à Becket, the wicked Archbishop of Canterbury, is invoked in Latin verses to this effect:

> " By that same blood shed for thee, O Thomas,
>   Christ, raise us to that place to which he has ascended !"

And yet history represents this *saint* as a vile traitor to his country. And though we do not justify the manner of his death, all that can be said in his favour is, that he died the Pope's martyr.

CHAPTER XXII.

Concerning Ecclesiastical Councils.   (86.)

" What is meant by an ecclesiastical council ?

" An assembly of the chief priests or ecclesiastical rulers, convened by legitimate authority, in order that the opinions concerning things pertaining to the church being collected into one, that is, concerning faith, customs, or discipline, it may be determined what is to be thought or done.

" How are ecclesiastical councils divided ?

" They are usually divided into four kinds, viz., into *diocesan*, *provincial*, *national*, and *general*.

" A *Diœcesan* is that which the Bishop celebrates with the clergy of his own diocese.

" A *Provincial* is that which is celebrated by the Bishops of some ecclesiastical province, their Archbishop or Metropolitan being president.

" That is called *National* to which the Archbishops and Bishops of a single kingdom or nation are convoked, the Patriarch or Primate of that nation presiding.

" A *General* council is that to which the Bishops of the whole world are assembled, and over which the Pope himself presides, either in his own person or by his legates : it is called also universal, œcumenical, and also plenary.

" Among the ancients a national council is sometimes also called plenary and universal ; because it is such as to the kingdom and nation, although it is not absolutely such."

In order to a general council it is not necessary that all the Bishops should, without exception, be present. Sometimes a National is more numerous than a General council. Thus at the first Constantinopolitan council there were not more than 150 Bishops present ; whereas the National Carthaginian Synod, at which St. Augustine was present, consisted of 217 Bishops.

It is sufficient that it be lawfully assembled out of the whole Christian world.

" By right, Bishops alone should be called to a General Council, and they are present by divine right as ordinary judges, who, therefore, alone have by right a decisive vote. This is proved from the fact that Christ entrusted to them the government of the church, according to Acts xx. 28 : ' Take heed to yourselves and to all the flock over which the Holy Ghost hath placed you Bishops, to rule the Church of God.'

" Therefore Bishops in councils are as judges, and not only as counsellors of the Pope, and therefore they are accustomed to use these words, ' We decree, we resolve,' &c., and as decreeing they subscribe the council : hence also the things defined in councils are not wont to be called decrees of the Pope but of the council.

" Observe, however, that the Supreme Pontiff is not obliged

to follow the greater part of the Bishops in delivering his opinion, for although the Bishops are true judges, yet the supreme judgment has been committed by Christ to his vicar upon earth, and has been entrusted to him that he may confirm and direct his brethren: and thus a king is not obliged to follow the greater part of the judges.

"Observe, that by privilege, Cardinals who are not Bishops, and certain Abbots, and the Chiefs of Regular Orders, may be present at councils as judges, and have a decisive vote," &c.

From No. 87 we learn that it is the Pope's right to convoke a general council, to continue and dissolve it, and to preside over it, and approve its proceedings. Whenever Emperors presided at Oriental councils, their presidency was not authoritative but honorary: they were there merely as favourers, defenders, and witnesses of those things which were done. When they subscribed the decrees of councils, they did it not as decreeing, but as consenting, as witnesses, and as obeying.

"It also belongs to the Supreme Pontiff to approve general councils as such, when he is not personally present at them : so that without his approbation, they cannot have the authority of a general council : and therefore we find it recorded that general councils, and the Council of Trent itself so earnestly sought confirmation from the Apostolic See.

"If the Pope presides by legates, then, if the legates have instructions from the Pope, concerning questions to be settled, and follow them according to the rule in decreeing with the council, then this council appears to be firm and infallible before the Pope's confirmation; however then, there is in so far need of confirmation, that there may be no dispute concerning the legitimacy of the council, and the consent and approbation of the Supreme Pontiff; but if the legates either have no instruction, or do not follow it, then whatever the council defines is not of infallible authority before the pontifical confirmation.

"Hence arises another division of councils, by which some are called approved, others reprobated or rejected, some partly approved, partly rejected; others neither approved nor reprobated."

Concerning approved General Councils. (88.)

" The approved general councils from the time of the apostles number eighteen.

" The first is the *First Nicene* Council, celebrated in the year 325, under St. Sylvester, at which 318 Fathers were present, in which it was definitely settled against Arius and his followers, denying the divinity of the Son, that in divine things, the Son is consubstantial with the Father, &c.

" The Sardicensian council under Julius I., which is usually considered as an appendix of the Nicene council, followed in confirmation of this Synod in the year 347, &c.

" The second is the *First Constantinopolitan*, in the year 381, assembled under St. Damasus, at which 150 Bishops were present. Gregory Nazianzen, the Prefect of the Constantinopolitan Church, presided partly, and partly also Nectarius, Gregory's successor, in the Constantinopolitan See. In this, the Nicene faith was confirmed, and the heresy of Macedonius who denied the divinity of the Holy Spirit was condemned ; and hence to the Nicene Symbol those things were added in this council, which pertain to the divinity of the Holy Spirit.

" The third is the *Ephesian*, in the year 431, held under S. Cælestinus, in which more than 200 Bishops were numbered ; and Nestorius, the Constantinopolitan Bishop, was condemned, asserting two persons in Christ, a divine and a human, and consequently denying that the divine Virgin is the mother of God.

" The fourth is the *Chalcedonian*, of 630 Bishops, and convened A. D. 451, under St. Leon, in which Eutyches was condemned, teaching that there was only one nature in Christ combined from a divine and human nature.

" The fifth is the *Second Constantinopolitan*, A. D. 553, under Vigilius, celebrated by 255 Bishops, in which the Nestorian and Eutychian heresies were again condemned with three renowned chapters, and the errors of Origen rejected.

" The sixth is the *Third Constantinopolitan*, under St. Agatho, of 299 Bishops, begun A. D. 680 ; in this the heresy of the Monothelites was condemned, professing that

18

there was but one will and operation in Christ, and thus restoring the heresy of Eutyches.

" The seventh is the *Second Nicene*, of 350 Bishops, A. D. 787, under Adrian I., celebrated against the Icooomachists, or Iconoclasts, i. e., the assailers of the images of Christ and the Saints.

" The eighth is the *Fourth Constantinopolitan*, A. D. 869, held under Adrian II., at which 383 Bishops assembled : in this their own honour and worship was restored to the sacred images, and Photius, a most crafty man, and who had intruded himself into the patriarchate of Constantinople, was deposed ; by his persuasion and influence the Greeks began to assail the primacy of the Supreme Pontiff, and to follow the Latins with deadly hatred, turning many things into accusation against them, and particularly that they taught that the Holy Spirit proceeds from the Father and from the Son, and that they had added the words ' and from the Son' to the Constantinopolitan creed ; and hence that foul schism of the Greeks took its origin.

" No general councils were afterwards held in the East : the others were celebrated in the West.

" The ninth general council is the *First Lateran*, A. D. 1123, celebrated under Calixtus II., in order to obviate a grievous dissension between the popes and emperors concerning the right of investiture, which concerned the institutions of the bishops, chief priests, and those who held benefices : this right the emperors arrogated to themselves ; but the popes wished this to be reserved to the church. In the same council, provision was made for affording supplies to the holy land and Spain against the Saracens. There were present more than 300 bishops.

" The tenth is the *Second Lateran*, A. D. 1139, held under Innocent II., by about 1000 bishops, on the occasion of the schism of Peter Leo, the anti-pope, also against the errors of Peter de Bruis, and Arnold of Brixia, and for the restoration of discipline. But this Peter and Arnold were in error concerning the real presence of Christ in the eucharist, and taught that temples and crosses were to be destroyed, and that the dead were not helped by prayers.

" The eleventh is the *Third Lateran*, A. D. 1179, celebrated under Alexander III., by 300 bishops, against the

Schismatics ordained by Victor IV., the anti-pope, also, against the Waldenses, who taught that the Supreme Pontiff was not to be obeyed, that swearing was unlawful, that all were priests, that robbers should not be put to death, &c.

"The twelfth is the *Fourth Lateran*, celebrated in the year 1215, under Innocent III., against the Abbot Joachim, Almaric of Bena, and the Albigenses, who renewed the errors of the Manichæans. There were present 412 bishops, and upwards of 800 abbots and priors, numerous procurators of the absent, and legates of a great many princes, for which reason it is usually called the great Lateran Council.

"The thirteenth is the First Council of Lyons, of 140 bishops, in the year 1245, assembled under Innocent IV., against the emperor Frederic, who ruled tyrannically, and who also was deposed. Various measures also concerning the reformation of morals were passed.

"The fourteenth is the *Second Council of Lyons*, A. D. 1274, held under Gregory X., for the recovery of the holy land, and that the Greeks might be called back to the faith and communion of the Roman Church : peace was agreed upon by the Latins with the Greeks ; but was not long kept by the latter.

"The fifteenth is the *Viennensian in France*, A. D. 1311, under Clement V., of about 300 bishops, against the errors of the Beguardians, and Beguinians, and Fratrieuli, who taught that man in this life may attain to the highest perfection, so that he may become impeccable, and not be able to advance any farther ; and, that, therefore, he should then neither pray nor fast, nor be subjected to any laws. In it, it was also settled that the rational or intellectual soul, is in itself and essentially the form of the human body : the order of the Templars also was abolished.

"The Council of Constance followed in the year 1414, in order to abolish a schism which had long troubled the church, several claiming to be Pope ; also against the errors of Wicklif and John Huss, who taught that all things happen by fatality, that the church consists of the predestinated only, that no one is Lord, Prelate, or Bishop, while he is in mortal sin, &c. It was dissolved under Martin V., elected in this same council. The French reckon this council among the œcumenical, but others admit it only as to the last sessions, and as to those actions against the errors of Wicklif and others, which the same Martin V. approved.

"The sixteenth is the *Florentine*, commenced at Ferrara, A. D. 1438, under Eugenius IV., but transferred to Florence on account of the plague, and there dissolved, A. D. 1439; in it the Greeks agreed with the Latins concerning the procession of the Holy Spirit from the Father and the Son, concerning purgatory, concerning the Supremacy of the Roman Pontiff over the whole earth, concerning the Eucharist, that it may be prepared equally with unleavened and fermented bread, and concerning various rites. The union of the Armenians with the Roman Church followed the reconciliation of the Greeks with the Latins, (which, however, did not last long;) who (the Armenians) received from Eugene IV. letters of union, containing in a compendium the Catholic doctrine.

"The Seventeenth is the *Fifth Lateran*, commenced in the year 1512, under Julius II. and Leo X., of 114 Bishops, against the Conventicle of Pisa, and for the reformation of morals; in this it WAS SETTLED THAT THE RATIONAL SOUL IS IMMORTAL.

"The eighteenth is the *Council of Trent*, commenced Dec. 13, A. D. 1545, under Paul III.; on account of a pestilence affecting the city of Trent, it was transferred to Bononia; afterwards it was brought back to Trent; on account of threatening wars, it was again interrupted; finally, on the 4th day of December, A. D., 1563, it was dissolved under Pius IV.; 255 Fathers subscribed. This council was celebrated especially against the errors of the Lutherans, Calvinists, and other heretics, at that time rampant."

Concerning the authority of Councils. (89.)

" May ecclesiastical councils err?

" All admit that particular councils, or such as are not general, may err; yet even they themselves have seldom erred, if their great number is considered, and if reference is made to councils of Catholic Bishops.

" If a particular council, in which heresies are condemned, is approved by the Supreme Pontiff for the whole church, it obtains infallible authority in the faith, founded indeed on the infallibility of the Pope himself; and thus the Roman See has approved two African provincial councils, the Milevitian and Carthaginian, against Pelagius and Celestius; and hence St. Augustine, in discourse 131, concerning the words of the apostle, judged that the matter against the Pelagians was altogether concluded, saying ' Answers have come from Rome, the question has been decided, would that an end might sometime be put to error!'

"In our day, says Benedict XIV, bk. 13, concerning the diocese, synod, ch. 3. (vol. 3, p. 287 and 290, Mechlin edit.) in particular councils, questions of faith are not wont to be discussed, but decrees are passed, relating merely to discipline; yet it happens sometimes, that these also are approved by the Apostolic See; and hence it might be doubted whether from this confirmation, they acquire the power of obliging the whole church? To which the same Pontiff replies, that confirmation, indeed, adds strength to these confirmed decrees, but that they by no means extend to other dioceses, unless the Pope has otherwise expressed: hence the Provincial Synod of Mechlin, in the year 1607, although confirmed by Paul V. does not transcend the limits of the province.

"Can general councils err?

"General councils, without the confirmation or approbation of the Roman Pontiff, are fallible, and have frequently erred, as is plain in the Ariminensian, Second Ephesian, &c. because thus they do not represent the Church, but a body without head, to which Christ has not promised infallibility.

"But if the assent and confirmation of the Pope is afforded only to some decrees of the council, then they alone will have plenary authority; as was done in the case of the decrees of the Council of Constance.

"Yet the promises of Christ, made to the Church, appear on the whole to require that a general council, held when the Pope is dead or doubtful, may have passive infallibility, or guard the faith and customs, and not define anything contrary.

"That general councils, approved by the Supreme Pontiff, cannot err in defining matters of faith and customs, is certain as a matter of faith; and hence they are immediately regarded as manifest heretics, who presume to call in ques-

18 *

tion any things decreed by such councils : hence St. Gregory, bk. i. epist. 24, says ' THAT HE RECEIVED AND VENERATED THE FIRST FOUR COUNCILS JUST AS THE BOOKS OF THE HOLY GOSPEL.'

"This infallibility is proved by No. 80, from which it is plain that the Church is infallible in matters of faith and customs : but a general council represents the whole Church, therefore, &c.   Hence the statutes of a general council are said to be from the Holy Spirit, according to Acts xv. 28. ' IT HATH SEEMED GOOD TO THE HOLY GHOST AND TO US.'

Moreover, if a general council, approved by the Pope, has not infallible authority, it would follow that there is not a certain and undisputed authority in the Church for settling controversies ; which is against No. 69.

" *Obj.* St. Augustine, bk. 2, concerning baptism against the Donatists, chap. 5, says that the former plenary councils themselves, are frequently amended by later ones ; but that which may be amended is not infallible ; therefore, &c.

" *Ans.* Several answers to this passage may be given :

" 1. That St. Augustine is speaking of plenary councils in general, as well of those not approved, as of the approved : and thus it can happen that the former, which had not been approved, and contained errors, may be amended by later approved (councils).

" 2. St. Augustine appears not to speak concerning general councils properly, but improperly, just as national councils are called general, and as he calls the Hyponeusian Synod plenary.

" 3. If it be understood concerning councils truly œcumenical, it must be said that St. Augustine only means, that the former may be amended by subsequent ones in simple facts, and in those things which relate to discipline, ceremonies, and other ecclesiastical customs ; and hence he subjoins to the same passage : 'As in the course of experience that which had been hidden is opened, and that which was concealed becomes known ;' but these things which belong to the faith, are known not by experience, but by the Word of God written or handed down.

" Yet do not infer from this that it can happen that the church may introduce or approve a general discipline that may be hurtful to the salvation of her own.   In the apostolical decree already cited, abstinence from blood and things strangled, was a mere point of discipline, and indeed not to be of long duration; and yet, in enjoining it, the apostles say: 'It hath seemed good to the Holy Ghost and to us:' by which words they sufficiently intimate that the church, in sanctioning general discipline, has the Holy Spirit as president and assistant. Therefore, although the reason of acting is various, yet it is always wisely accommodated to the various circumstances of times and persons.

"4. Finally, certain subsequent councils, define more clearly some things which were not yet sufficiently settled in former ones; and thus the former councils are elucidated by subsequent ones.

"It is here to be observed with Estuis, in Bk. 2, &c., 'Not all things which are said in any way whatever in the decrees of councils, are to be considered as settled; but those things only to which the intention of the persons resolving and defining is properly directed. But this is known from the circumstances of the case, and from the causes or occasions of framing the decrees.

"Melchior Canus gives the following rules, by which a definition of a council pertaining to the faith may be discriminated, Bk. 5. de locis theol. ch. v. 9, 4.

"1. The first is, if those who assert the contrary are considered heretics.

"2. When the Synod prescribes decrees in this form, 'If any one shall think so and so, let him be accursed.'

"3. If sentence of excommunication is passed by the law itself against those who shall contradict.

"4. If it is said that any thing is to be firmly believed, expressly and properly, by the faithful; or is to be received as a doctrine of the Catholic faith, or, in other similar words, that any thing is contrary to the gospel, or the doctrine of the apostles. But it must be said, not as opinion, but as a certain and firm decree."

I presume my readers will excuse me for not offering an elaborate refutation of the infallibility of the general councils of the Romish Church. They were composed of frail and fallible men, as was but too often signally manifest in the intrigues and animosities by which they were marked, and in the preposterous absurdities, which were defined and decreed as the results of infallible deliberations and disputes.

Not a few of these councils, so far from being assemblies of pious and learned divines, were mere cabals ; the majority of which were quarrelsome, fanatical, domineering and dishonest prelates, who, as Dr. Jortin says, " wanted to compel men to approve all their opinions of which they themselves had no clear conceptions, and to anathematize and oppress those, who would not implicitly submit to their determinations."

The audacious attempt to make the statutes of such councils equivalent in authority to the precepts of the Word of God, and the impious assertion that these quarrelsome cabals were directed in their deliberations by the Spirit of God, so that they might properly say in the language of the apostles, " it hath seemed good to the Holy Ghost and to us," are nothing short of rank blasphemy !

To the faithful, it would no doubt be consolatory to know that in the sixteenth century, the *immortality of the rational soul was definitely settled*, by the Fifth Lateran Council, were it not, that they, alas ! expect their immortality to be verified and almost eked out in purgatory.

For a succinct vindication of the doctrines and practice of the Waldenses, and a narrative of their persecutions and sufferings, I refer my readers to a little work by Dr. Brownlie, recently published at the office of the Protestant Reformation Society of New York.

CHAPTER XXIII.

Concerning the Supreme Pontiff. (90.)

" What is the Supreme Pontiff?

" He is Christ's Vicar upon earth, and the visible head of his church.

" Christ instituted the church of the New Testament upon earth, not on the plan of an aristocratic or democratic government, but on the plan of a monarchical government, yet tempered by that which is best in an aristocracy, as was said No. 81.

" But when Christ was about to withdraw his visible presence by his ascension into heaven, he constituted his Vicar the visible head of the church, he himself remaining the supreme, essential and visible head.

" Who is called Supreme Pontiff, and wherefore ?

" The Roman Pontiff, not only because he holds the highest honour and dignity in the church, but principally, because he has supreme and universal authority, power and jurisdiction over all bishops and the whole church.

" He is also called the pope, which word signifies either father, or by antonomasia the father of fathers ; also the Chief Priest of the Apostolic See ; so that the Roman See by way of eminence is called without any addition the Apostolic See."

Concerning the Supremacy of Peter. (91.)

" As heretics can not only deny the superiority of present popes, but also the supremacy of the apostle Peter himself, therefore this must be asserted against them.

" I. But it is proved that Peter received supremacy from Christ above the other apostles, from Matt. xvi. 18., where the supremacy is promised, and John, ch. xxi., where it is conferred.

" Christ says, Matt. xvi. 18 : ' thou art Peter, and upon this rock I will build my church, v. 19., and I will give to thee the keys of the kingdom of heaven ; and whatsoever thou shalt bind upon earth,' &c.   Here although the name of supremacy is not expressed; yet it is manifestly promised under two metaphors: the former metaphor is taken from the plan of a foundation and a building: but what the foundation is in a building, this the superior is in a community, the king in a kingdom, &c.: the other is borrowed from the delivery of keys: for he to whom the keys of a city are delivered is constituted or declared king or governor of the city.   Add to this, the interpretation and authority of the Holy Fathers, as may be seen in Bellarmine, Sylvius, Tournely, &c.

    " Calvin objects: that by the word, rock, upon which it is said the church shall be built, is to be understood not Peter but Christ, and therefore the Evangelist changes the term, and afterwards said, ' Thou art Peter,' by saying ' not upon this *Peter*,' but ' upon this *rock*.'

    "*Ans.* I deny the antecedent: how foolish this observation of Calvin is, is plain from the Syriac, which idiom Christ used, in which the difference of gender is not found, which is in the Latin and Greek: and hence Christ said with one and the same word: ' Thou art Cephas, and upon this Cephas,' which in Latin should be rendered, ' thou art a rock, and upon this rock;' but the Latin translator renders, ' Thou art Peter,' in the masculine, because the remark was made concerning a man, having followed the rule of the Greeks, among whom the word *Petra* received a masculine and feminine termination, (πέτρος, m. and πέτρα, f.,) which the Latin word, *Petra*, does not receive; therefore when Christ says, *upon this rock*, the pronoun *this* manifestly refers to the rock, concerning which mention was just made; but immediately before, Christ had called not himself but Peter the rock; therefore, &c.

    " Hence the mystery of the change of the name Simon into Peter, or a rock, John i. 42.   Besides, if these words, ' upon this rock,' should be referred to Christ and not to Peter, Christ would in vain have said to Peter; ' I tell thee because thou art Peter;' nor ought he to have said, I will build, but I have built, or I build. •

    " You will urge, St. Aug. in the last treatise upon John, by this rock understands Christ.   It is confirmed by his opinion, Bk. I. Retract. chap. xxi., where he says; ' For it was not said to him, thou art a rock, but thou art Peter; but Christ was the rock.'

"*Ans.* St. Augustine formerly proposed this interpretation, pleading against the Donatists, who deduced the power and efficacy of the Sacraments from the holiness of the minister, and hence he preferred placing this foundation in Christ rather than in Peter, lest the Donatists might thence have deduced a confirmation of their error.   Yet he admitted our interpretation, which is the common one; indeed in the passage adduced, mentioning both he subjoins: 'Of these two opinions, let the reader choose that which is the more probable.'

"This doubt of St. Aug. arose from ignorance of the Hebrew or Syriac and of the Greek; to those skilled in which, it is known that the phrase 'Thou art Cephas,' is the same as 'Thou art a rock.'

"You may rejoin: Christ alone is the foundation of the Church, according to that 1 Cor. iii. 11. 'For no one can lay another foundation but that which is laid, which is Christ Jesus;' therefore, by this rock Peter is not meant, but Christ.

"*Ans.* I deny the antecedent: Christ alone is indeed the essential and primary foundation which consists in itself and depends on no other, but sustaining all those things which belong to the building of the church, and, therefore, Peter himself: yet it is consistent with this that Peter is the secondary foundation, founded on Christ by the virtue and authority received from himself.

"The Lutherans object: by the rock upon which the Church is said to be built, Peter is not meant, but the faith or confession of Peter.   They confirm it from St. Chrysostom, St. Ambrose, St. Hilary, &c.

"*Ans.* I deny the antecedent: for it is plain from what has been said, that the person of Peter ought to be understood, which the following words, 'I will give to thee the keys of the kingdom of heaven,' evidently show.

"To the confirmation from the Holy Fathers, it must be said, that they sometimes speak thus in a causal sense; because, indeed, Peter confessing the divinity of Christ, obtained for the sake of the merit of his faith, that he should be the foundation of the Church.

"Besides, those saints do not mean that the Church is

founded upon the faith in itself considered, without relation to the person of Peter, but upon his personal faith, which is the same as upon the person itself of Peter having faith: and hence, when they say, that the Church is founded upon the faith of Peter, or that Peter's faith, or confession of faith, is the foundation of the Church, they mean it in this sense, that Peter by reason of his own indefectible faith, indefectibly sustains and confirms all in it.

"Against the argument deduced from the delivery of the keys, the heretics object: the keys are promised immediately to the Church, and not to the person of Peter.

"The antecedent is proved from St. Augustine, treatise 50 upon John, where he says thus, 'Peter, when he received the keys, signified Holy Church;' therefore, &c.

"*Ans.* I deny the antecedent: for it is evident that from what was before said, it is clear that the remark was directed to the person of Peter.

"As for St. Augustine and the other fathers, it must be said that they only mean that Peter did not receive the keys as a private person, but on the condition of the Supreme Pastor, and for the advantage of the Church, from whom, by ordinary right, the power of the keys was to be conferred upon the other superiors of the Church, the bishops and pastors.

"Add to this, that the fathers do not always quote Sacred Scripture in the literal sense, but often in the mystic sense, and sometimes in the accommodatory sense.

"*Obj.* The same which is promised to Peter, Matt. xvi. 19. 'I will give thee the keys,' &c. is promised to the other apostles, Matt. xviii. 18. 'Whatever ye shall bind upon earth,' &c.

"*Ans.* I deny the antecedent: for the power of the keys promised to Peter alone, Matt. xvi., and given, John xxi., is something greater and better than the power of binding and loosing, which is only an inadequate act of the keys.

"Observe, although the other apostles received the power of preaching everywhere, and founding churches, and thus a certain universal jurisdiction through universality of place, that this, although such, was still only extraordinary, and with subjection to Peter, and to become extinct with themselves: hence the proposition which placed St. Peter and St.

Paul as the two-fold head of the church, was justly condemned as heretical by Innocent X.

"Prove that the primacy of Peter is gathered through those words, John xxi. 17, 'Feed my sheep!'

"II. Because, by these words, under a metaphor deduced from the pastor of sheep, the office of pastor and ruler of the universal church is enjoined upon Peter, &c., therefore the power is conceded to the whole church. It is proved: because to feed signifies not only to teach, but also to have authority and to rule: just as it belongs to a pastor of sheep, not only to afford food, but also to conduct and bring back, to defend and restrain.

"By 'my lambs—my sheep,' is signified the universality of Christ's faithful, for the pronoun *my* is equivalent to a universal sign, as Christ speaks indefinitely and all the faithful are Christ's sheep or lambs.

"The heretics object: it was not said to Peter alone: 'Feed my sheep,' therefore, &c.

"They prove the antecedent from St. Augustine, Book concerning the Christian Combat, chap. xxx, where he says, 'When it is said to him (to Peter), it is said to all: Lovest thou me? Feed my sheep.'

"I deny the antecedent: because circumstances show that those words were spoken to Peter alone: for Christ addresses Peter alone, accosting him by his proper name, 'Simon, son of Jonas;' so that indeed others are excluded by these words: 'Lovest thou me more than these?'

"As for St. Augustine we reply, that it may be said to all other superiors of the church, 'Feed my sheep,' in so far, namely, as the part of the flock which was committed to them is concerned; or according to the accommodatory sense, inasmuch as they ought to imitate the model of Peter in feeding and governing.

"III. The third argument in order to prove Peter's supremacy from Sacred Scripture can be borrowed from various prerogatives, with which Peter was endowed before the other apostles.

"The first prerogative is the change of name: 'Thou shalt be called Cephas.' John i. 42.

"The second is, that in the order of the enumeration of the apostles, Peter is always named in the first place by the

19

Evangelists, notwithstanding the change of the order of the others. Thus it is expressly said, Matt. x. 2., 'The first Simon, who is called Peter.'

"The third, tribute is paid for Christ and Peter. Matt. xvii. 26.

"The fourth, Peter alone walks with Christ upon the water. Matt. xiv. 29.

"The fifth, Christ says specially to Peter. Luke ch. xxii. 32. 'I have prayed for thee that thy faith fail not; and thou being once converted, confirm thy brethren.'

"The sixth, Peter, Acts i. 15, proposes and teaches that a new apostle must be chosen in the place of Judas; Acts ii. 14, after the Holy Spirit had been received, he first promulgates the gospel; Acts iii. 6, he does the first miracle in proof of the faith; Acts x. 28, he first begins to preach to the Gentiles; Acts xii. 5, for Peter prayer was made without intermission by the church; Acts xv. 7, he speaks first as though president of the council at Jerusalem, and all follow his opinion. These and other prerogatives, with the interpretations of the Holy Fathers, Bellarmine rightly deduces, Bk. I., concerning the Roman Pontiff.

"Against these, the heretics again object, I. Paul saying, Gal. ii. 7: 'To me was committed the gospel of the uncircumcision, as to Peter was that of the circumcision,' signifies that he is the apostle of the Gentiles, as Peter of the Jews; therefore jurisdiction was divided between them.

"*Ans.* I deny the inference: for that was a division, not of jurisdiction, but of nations, in order to the work of preaching; viz., that as Peter had been principally destined for preaching to the Jews, so Paul had been specially destined by Christ for preaching to the Gentiles.

"They object II. Paul in the same place, v. 11, resists Peter to his face, therefore he was not subject to him.

"*Ans.* I deny the inference: because Paul does not blame Peter by authority as a superior, an inferior, but by fraternal reproof, which is sometimes lawful for an inferior with respect to a superior. *Some maintain that Cephas, concerning whom Paul there speaks, was not Peter, but another disciple.* Kerkherdere may be consulted concerning the reproved Cephas.

"They object III. If Peter was the head of the church,

the church must perish at the death of Peter; for the head dying, the body dies.

"*Ans.* I deny the inference: for that the body separated from the head must die, is true of that head from which the members derive sense and motion: but Peter was not thus the head of the church, but Christ: but it is not true concerning the head of which the loss is merely external according to external government; such was Peter, and such are his successors; for when the Pope dies, Christ the invisible head remains, from whom the church derives life and sense, and is prepared to receive another visible head."

If the doctrine of *Peter's* supremacy were taught in the word of God, it would still be incumbent upon Papists to show by incontestible evidence, that Peter was bishop of Rome, and that he had divine authority to invest all his successors in that See with pre-eminence over all their brethren. If the proof fails in any one of these three points, the rock upon which popery is built is broken, and the whole fabric falls into ruins. Against the foregoing arguments, we offer the following as our reasons for disbelieving the first proposition, viz., that Peter was invested with supremacy.

1. If such authority was really conferred upon Peter, the Evangelists who by the inspiration of the Holy Spirit recorded all things necessary for faith and salvation would have mentioned it in plain and unequivocal language. But do they ever say that one of the apostles was to have and to claim authority over all the rest? If so, when and where? Do they not on the contrary explicitly affirm that equal authority was given to all the apostles? John xx. 23. When the question who should be greatest was started among them, there is no mention made of any preference given by Christ to Peter; but the Saviour evidently condemns the lust of power, and says, " ye know that they which are accounted to rule over the gentiles exercise lordship over them; and their great ones exercise authority upon them. BUT SO SHALL IT NOT BE AMONG YOU; but whosoever will be great

among you shall be your minister, (or servant.) Mark x. 42, 43.   On another occasion he said to his disciples, "Be not ye called Rabbi, for one is your Master, even Christ, and all ye are brethren." (Matt. xxii. 8, 9.)   Could there have been a plainer intimation of the equality of the apostles ?

2. When the Apostle Paul enumerates the various orders in the churches, he says, "God hath set some in the church, *first*, APOSTLES ; secondly, prophets ; thirdly, teachers ; after that miracles, then gifts of healings, helps, governments, diversities of tongues." (1 Cor. xii. 28.)   Strange omission! Not one word of Christ's Vicar ! FIRST *apostles*, not FIRST, *Peter !*

3. If Peter had really possessed the supremacy ascribed to him, how could Paul have said, (2 Cor. xi. 5.) "I was not a whit behind the very chiefest apostles ?"   What ?   Not a whit behind *Peter ?*

4. It is natural to suppose that if Peter had been the acknowledged chief of the apostles, he would have been called upon to decide controversies, but this was never the case. In the debate between Paul and Barnabas and others, about circumcision, they referred the point, not to Peter, but to the Church, and the apostles and elders at Jerusalem.   The conclusion to which they arrived was recorded, not as the decree of Peter, (for he did not even preside,) but as that which "seemed good to the Holy Ghost and to us," i. e. to the apostles, elders, and brethren, who met at Jerusalem on that occasion. (Acts xv. 2—29.)

5. Paul would not have had occasion to withstand Peter to his face, had his erring brother been infallible ; and if he had possessed the supremacy ascribed to him by the Church of Rome, it would scarcely have been decorous in Paul to expose the failing of his superior.   Neither can this be regarded as an ordinary fraternal reproof, (as Peter Dens intimates,) because that is to be administered privately, as a re-

ference to Matt. xviii. will show.   Nor will Kerkherdere, to whom we are referred, extricate Romanists from this difficulty, by suggesting that the "Cephas, concerning whom Paul there speaks, was not Peter, but another disciple." The connexion shows it could be no other than the *infallible* apostle himself.   Besides, if it had been another disciple, it would have been an unpardonable omission in the sacred writer, had he neglected to state the fact in emphatic language. There were two of our Lord's twelve disciples, who were called Judas, but the evangelists are careful in distinguishing between them.   Hence we read of "Judas Iscariot," and Judas ("not Iscariot,") and if anything disparaging was to be mentioned, which affected another disciple of the same name as Peter, and not the apostle himself, in common justice it would have been stated.

6. Again ; we find the apostles sending Peter as their messenger, in company with John, (Acts viii. 14 ;) if he had been Pope among the apostles, he would have *sent* them. Would not his Holiness marvel greatly if his Bishops should send him on a missionary tour with one of their own number ?

7. If Peter had possessed the supremacy ascribed to him, is it probable that he would have been accosted by his brethren as we read in Acts xi. 1—4 ?   Would he have deferred to the judgment of private brethren so far as to vindicate himself before them ?   The brethren did not bow down reverently and kiss the apostle's sandal, and address him with the blasphemous title which Romish writers have conferred upon their Pontiff—"Dominus Deus noster, Papa"— "Our Lord God, the Pope !"

8. In short, if Peter had been appointed by Christ as his vicar upon earth ; had he been clothed with supreme authority, he would certainly have been called upon to exercise it, and his decisions ex cathedra would as certainly have been recorded.   But he never claimed this authority, either when

19 *

present with the churches or in his epistles; he claims no more than an equality with his brethren, the apostles, and pastors of the church; " The elders who are among you I exhort, whom am also an elder." The language of Paul is far more authoritative than that of Peter, 1 Cor. vii. 10; 1 Tim. v. 14. 21. Peter, at the close of his first epistle, (v. 1—3.) warns those in authority against being " lords over God's heritage,"—as though he had been divinely directed himself to confound the claims of Anti-Christ.

But there are a number of special prerogatives ascribed to Peter by the evangelists.

The first is the change of name, " Thou shalt be called Cephas;" John i. 42. We must admit this *prerogative*, and we do it cheerfully—but what then ? Therefore Peter is Christ's Vicar upon earth !

The second is, " Peter is always named first, where the apostles are spoken of." He is not always named first, Gal. ii. 9, " When James, Cephas, and John, &c." Supposing he is generally named first, he was probably the oldest : what does this prove ? Peter's supremacy !

The third is, " Tribute is paid for Christ and Peter." Admitted. Does that prove that Peter's successors are above all the kings of the earth, and should pay no tribute ?

The fourth is, " Peter alone walks with Christ upon the water." True—and " when he saw the wind boisterous, he was afraid, and, beginning to sink, he cried, saying, Lord, save me." Therefore Peter was the first Pope !

The fifth is, Christ says specially to Peter, " I have prayed for thee that thy faith fail not," &c. But did not Christ pray thus specially for Peter because he knew that his disciple was about to deny him under aggravating circumstances ? And if so, is not this a singular proof text of Peter's infallibility ?

The sixth, " Peter proposes the election of an apostle in the place of the traitor Judas." He does. This establishes his supremacy!! After the Holy Spirit had been received, he first proclaims the gospel, does the first miracle, first begins to preach to the Gentiles! And for Peter prayer was made without intermission by the church: and why? Because Peter was in prison. If any other apostle had been there, they would have wrestled with the Lord in his behalf just as they prayed for Peter's deliverance. This beloved apostle was naturally ardent and impetuous; Christ had loved him much and forgiven him much, and this was enough to make him bolder than his brethren, who had never denied the Lord as he had done. But now, if these reasons constitute an argument for *Peter's* supremacy, we may adduce others which will make John a rival candidate.

1. John was the only disciple who leaned on Jesus' breast at the last supper.

2. John is called the disciple whom Jesus loved.

3. "*Peter* beckoned to him that he should ask who it should be" that should betray the Lord.

4. John alone, of all the apostles, is said to have died a natural death, and he survived all his apostolic brethren. Thus, too, we might prove the supremacy of Paul and James by facts peculiar to their history: but we have neither time nor space to imitate the trifling of Romish Theologians.

The text upon which Papists place their main dependence is that which is so elaborately discussed in the preceding sections: " Thou art Peter, and upon this rock I will build my church." They appear to lay almost as much stress upon these words as upon the declaration of Christ at the institution of the Lord's Supper—" This *is* my body." If the words, "Thou art Peter," &c., are to be understood at all figuratively, they tell us that the metaphor of which Christ makes use is realized in the person of Peter. He, personally, is the *rock*. We may, therefore, adopting the very principles of interpretation by which they seek to vindicate the strange doctrine of transubstantiation, require them to prove that Peter was literally and truly a bona fide rock, and that the Church of Christ was built upon the body and blood, bones and sinews of the good apostle. " Thou art a rock, and upon this rock I will build my church ;" most unquestionably, this interpretation will find readier belief than that Christ gave his own body and blood, soul and divinity to the faithful to be eaten to the end of time. The explanation to which Peter Dens alludes, and which he professes to refute, is briefly this. In the preceding verses, Christ asks his disciples, " Whom say ye that I am ?" Peter replies, " Thou art Christ, the Son of the living God." This good confession Christ calls the rock upon which his Church should be built, alluding at the same time to the signification of Peter's name. He could not have intended that Peter should be literally and truly the foundation of his Church, because we are expressly told, " Other foundation can no man lay than that is laid, which is Christ Jesus." If Christ is the foundation of his Church, and Peter is the foundation also, then there are two foundations to the same building ; but this cannot be. As to the distinction which Peter Dens makes in noticing this objection, between the primary and secondary foundation, when we find it in the Scriptures we will cheerfully endorse it. It is remarkable that not a single passage is adduced from any one of the primitive fathers to sustain the Romish interpretation of the passage in question ; Augustine declares in so many words, when commenting on this text, " For it was not said to him, thou art a rock, but thou art Peter : but the rock was *Christ*."

The apology which is offered for Augustine is creditable neither to the Saint nor to the person who offers it. According to Peter Dens, Augustine equivocated somewhat, in order to prevent the Donatists from retorting unpleasantly ! The testimony of the fathers, however, must always be considered of secondary importance ; the best means of ascertaining the sense of Scripture is to collate one passage with another, after examining the scope of the writer.

But, " the keys were given to Peter." So they were, and Peter used them by opening the door of the gospel on the great day of Pentecost, when the first fruits. of the Spirit were manifested in the conversion of three thousand souls. When the pope becomes a preacher of the gospel of Christ, and employs. himself in laying the foundations of churches by his personal ministry, we will acknowledge his claim to be Peter's successor as more valid than it is at present. II. The second point, which Papists must prove, is that *Peter was bishop of Rome*.

1. If Peter really held this office by the tenure and for the purpose, for which the church of Rome contends, then it certainly ought to be considered as an article of faith, and as such it would have been distinctly taught and enjoined in the word of God. But the Scriptures are entirely silent on this subject.

2. The utmost that can be said in favour of Peter's having resided at Rome, is that it is *probable*, and even this can scarcely be admitted as proved. But in a case of this kind the utmost certainty is requisite. Peter dates his Epistle from Babylon. Some suppose that this was the Babylon in Assyria ; others understand it as a figurative name of Rome ; and whatever reason there may be for supposing the latter interpretation to be correct, we may rest assured that Romish writers would, of all persons, be farthest from pleading that Babylon is used figuratively for Rome, were it not that they are sorely pressed for evidence to sustain a darling hypothesis ; for by this admission, the Babylon of the Apocalypse must likewise be understood as designating Rome. Luke, who wrote the travels of the apostles Paul and Peter, takes no notice of Peter's going there. And when the former apostle writes to the Romans, and sends greeting to about forty by name, he says nothing of Peter, whom he

would scarcely have forgotten, if he had been the Pope's prototype; so too when Paul writes from Rome, he says not a word of Peter. He even complains when writing from that city to the Philippians, (ii. 20.,) that "all sought their own, not the things which are Jesus Christ's;" and when addressing the Colossians, (iv. 11.), he names a few, who "were his only fellow helpers there." Writing to Timothy from the same city, 2 Tim. iv. 16., he declares that "at his first answer all men forsook him." Now Peter would surely have proved himself a true yoke-fellow, had he then been bishop of Rome. Indeed, the very nature of Peter's apostolic office constrained him to go from place to place, to preach the gospel, and it will hardly be asserted even by Papists that the pretended chief of the apostles would act contrary to his commission, and take upon him the charge of a church in any particular city, which would necessarily require such a residence there as was inconsistent with his duties as an apostle. Besides, how could he, who was *the* apostle of the *Jews*, take upon him the charge of a Gentile Church? And supposing that he was bishop of a church of Jewish converts, Peter must have been strangely negligent of his charge to have been absent from them for so many years, and never write to the Romans as Paul did to establish their faith, and not even mention them in his Epistles.

Such is the silence of Scripture relative to Peter's residence at Rome, and such the obscurity of primitive antiquity about it, that whilst we will not affirm that he never was in that city, it is highly improbable that he lived there so soon after the death of Christ, and for so long a period as Papists would have us believe. There is not a particle of positive proof extant to show that Peter was ever bishop of Rome, whilst there is abundant evidence of the contrary. The third point, whether the Popes are Peter's successors, we reserve until the close of the following sections.

CHAPTER XXIV.

Concerning the successor of Peter in the Primacy. (92.)

" DID any one succeed Peter in the primacy of the church?

" The affirmative is a matter of faith, and is proved in this way : Christ the Lord instituted the church, so that it should endure to the end of time; therefore, he must have instituted in it a perpetual form of government; and thus at the death of Peter another must, by divine appointment, succeed, who should be the visible head of the church, and Christ's Vicar.

" Besides, Peter was appointed the foundation of a church that was to endure perpetually : therefore, the foundation should be perpetual ; the keys also and the government must continue, whilst the kingdom endures ; a pastor and ruler are necessary for the sheep ; therefore the primacy of Peter must continue whilst the church continues.

" Nor is it any objection that S. Gregory the Great, Bk. 5. Epist. 20—alias 32, condemns the name of universal bishop, saying that it is a blasphemous name. For St. Gregory means that it is blasphemous in this sense, as though one man were bishop of the whole church, and the rest were not true bishops of their own churches ; and hence, Bk. 7. Epist. 79, he speaks thus : ' If one man is universal (bishop), it remains that you cannot be bishops.' Otherwise, if by the universal bishop, you understand the Supreme Head, even of Bishops, you will properly call the successor of Peter, universal Bishop.

" It is to be observed, however, that St. Gregory lays great stress upon the novelty of this name, principally because the Constantinopolitan bishop arrogantly usurped to himself the name of universal bishop, to whom it certainly by no means pertained.

" Who is this successor of Peter?

" It is a matter of faith that he is the Roman Pontiff. It is proved from the unwavering decree of general councils and of the church, and from the doctrine of the Holy Fathers ;

so that on this account St. Augustine says, that this continuous succession from the very seat of Peter kept him in the Catholic Church.

"This succession, down to this day in which Gregory XVI. reigns, is continued in a series of 258 Pontiffs.

"As the primacy of the church is by divine right, has it also been annexed by divine right to the Bishopric; so that the particular Roman Episcopate cannot be separated from the Supreme Pontificate, but to the end of the world, is the succession of Supreme Pontiffs to continue in the Roman Bishops?

"*Ans.* This is a controverted point: some suppose that the primacy is annexed to the Roman Episcopate only by human right; they say indeed that it has been merely ordained by Christ, that the Episcopate should have the primacy, which the church should designate: but the church has designated the Roman Episcopate; and hence, they say, it may happen by the disposition of the Church, that the primacy may be taken away from the Roman Episcopate.

"But it is more commonly maintained that the primacy has been annexed to the Roman Episcopate by divine right; because, although the most weighty reasons were urgent, such as were the persecutions of the Gentiles, and the devastations of Rome, yet the thought never was harboured of separating the Pontificate from the Roman Episcopate; therefore the church has thought that the primacy has, by divine right, been annexed to the Roman Episcopate.

"Observe, that this question is different and independent from these two, which are settled in the faith, that the primacy of the church is of divine right, and that this primacy should continue in the Roman Bishop, or Pope."

Concerning the Power of the Supreme Pontiff. (93.)

"From whom does the Pope, legitimately elected, receive his power and jurisdiction?

"*Ans.* He receives it immediately from Christ as his Vicar, just as Peter received it.

"Nor is it any objection that the pope is elected by cardinals; for their election is only an essential requisite, which being supplied, he receives power and jurisdiction immediately from Christ.

" From whom do the Bishops receive the power of jurisdiction ?

" *Ans.* The French contend that they receive it immediately from Christ; but it seems that it ought rather to be said that they receive it immediately from the Roman Pontiff, because the government of the church is monarchical, &c., &c.

What and how great is the Power of the Supreme Pontiff. (94.)

" What power has the Roman Pontiff?

" We reply with St. Thomas, &c. : ' THE POPE HAS PLENITUDE OF POWER IN THE CHURCH ;' so that his power extends to all who are in the church, and to all things which pertain to the government of the church.

" This is proved from what was said before : because the Roman Pontiff is the true Vicar of Christ, the head of the whole church, the pastor and teacher ; therefore, &c.

" Hence it follows, that all the faithful, even bishops and patriarchs, are obliged to obey the Roman Pontiff; also, that *he must be obeyed in all things which concern the Christian religion,* and therefore, in faith and customs, in rites, ecclesiastical discipline, &c.

" Hence, the perverse device of the Quesnellites falls to the ground ; namely, that the pope is not to be obeyed, except in those things which he enjoins conformably to Sacred Scripture.

" Has the Supreme Pontiff not only directive, but also compulsory power over all the faithful?

" *Ans.* Yes ; because, Matt. xvi. 19, the power of binding, which pertains to compulsory authority, is given to Peter and his successors. Perpetual custom also confirms this, hence, the power of suspending, excommunicating, &c., belongs to the Supreme Pontiff.

" *Obj.* Christ says, Luke xxii. 25, ' The kings of the Gentiles lord it over them'—v. 26, ' But you not so ;' therefore, coercive power does not belong to ecclesiastics.

" *Ans.* I deny the inference : for it is merely forbidden that they govern in the manner of Gentile kings ; and hence he adds : ' But you not so ;' that is, they should not rule

20

tyrannically and haughtily, seek their own advantage, glory, &c. in ruling."

The following section (95) discusses the question *whether the Pope is superior to a general council.*

"The question is not concerning a council assembled together with the Pope : for in this case the pontiff cannot be above the council, as he must then be superior to himself; but he is of equal authority with the council.

"It is asked, therefore, whether a general council taken by itself without the Pope, but yet lawfully assembled, is above the pontiff?

"The French maintain the affirmative : out of France it is commonly affirmed that the Pope is superior to a general council, so that he may transfer, dissolve it, &c.

"This is proved : Christ said to Peter, not to the council : ' I will give to thee the keys of the kingdom of heaven; feed my sheep,' &c. Peter, therefore, and his successors are the head and pastor, not only of the church in its dispersed state, or of single believers, but, also, of the church assembled in council : for the head is superior not only to each member particularly but taken together : the shepherd governs and is superior not only to each sheep in particular, but to the whole flock : and hence the Chalcedonian Council in a letter to Pope Leo acknowledges him as their head and father," &c.

Concerning the Infallibility of the Supreme Pontiff. (96.)

"It is to be premised that the Pope is sometimes said to speak or determine ex cathedra, but sometimes not, but as a private doctor, or as replying to a particular question or case.

"He is regarded as speaking ex cathedra, (from the throne) when he speaks from the plenitude of power, prescribing to the whole church anything as a doctrine to be believed by faith, or observed in customs, or accepted as good or religious.

"Is the opinion of the Supreme Pontiff of infallible authority?

"The Supreme Pontiff just as an entire general council may err in mere facts, or in things not concerning faith or customs : because infallibility in such things is not necessary for the government of the church, nor does a mistake injure the integrity of religion.

" He may also err, when he does not speak ex cathedra: and thus, if a work on theology or law is published by the Supreme Pontiff, there may possibly be errors in it : because it bears no other authority before itself than that of a private doctor; as Benedict XIV. declares concerning his own works in a brief to James Facciolatus, which he wished to have prefixed to the first volume.   A mistake may possibly be found in some decrees entered upon the canonical law : because, although those decrees are entered upon the canonical law, that the judges might have some rule in judging, yet the pontiffs do not present them all as definitions of the faith.

" The Supreme Pontiff determining from the throne matters relating to faith or customs is infallible: which infallibility proceeds from the special assistance of the Holy Spirit."

The three following passages of Scripture are then adduced as proofs that the pope is infallible.   Matt. xvi. 18. " Thou art Peter," &c.   Luke xxii. 32. " I have prayed for thee that thy faith fail not, and thou, when once thou art converted, strengthen thy brethren ;" where Christ promises Peter indefectibility that he may confirm his brethren in the faith : which belongs to the office of pastor and head, and thus, also, to the successors of Peter.

" It is proved 3d from John xxi. 17., where it is enjoined upon Peter and consequently on his successors that they feed and rule the whole church : therefore the whole church is bound to hear and to follow the doctrine of the pontiff: and hence if he can err, the whole church will err, which cannot happen, according to No. 80, &c., &c.

" *Obj. I.* The Pope may err in matters of faith and customs if he does not apply the necessary diligence : but it is possible that he may not apply the necessary diligence : therefore he may err.

" *Ans.* The same arguments may be framed against the infallibility of a general council, which yet by the confession of our adversaries would not be conclusive : therefore, it is also not conclusive against the infallibility of the pope.

" We say, therefore, that the Pope, just as the general council, ought to apply the necessary diligence to proceed prudently : but yet that the infallibility neither of the pope nor of the council depends on the condition that they have proceeded carefully : it is justly taken for granted, however, that all diligence has been applied in determining.

" *Obj. II.* Therefore, general councils are useless : for the Pope, as he is infallible, may by himself determine all controversies about faith and customs by a judgment that cannot be improved.

" *Ans.* I deny the inference : by way of proof, it is to be remarked that, although the Pope is infallible, yet he ought not to neglect human and ordinary means, by which he may arrive at the knowledge of the truth of the thing in debate : but the ordinary means is a greater or less council as the importance of the case demands, &c., &c.

" Various pontiffs are cited as objections, who are accused of error in decrees concerning the faith or customs.

" *Ans.* It is to be observed generally for the solution (of this difficulty,) that this error is either in mere facts, or in things not pertaining to faith and customs, or in decrees which are not ex cathedra, and, therefore, they do not at all hinder the conclusion, just as, also, the personal failings of the Popes are no objection."

Whether the Pope at least as a private person may be a heretic ? (97.)

" Although this would be no impediment to the preceding conclusion, as has been said, yet the negative opinion seems the more probable, so that the privilege of Peter, Luke xxii. 32 : ' I have prayed for thee that thy faith fail not,' may also be transferred to the successors of Peter : and it is agreeable to divine providence, that he who is a teacher of the faith, should himself not fail from the faith.

" It is proved also by this, that it could never yet be proved concerning any Pope, that he was a formal heretic ; and this, St. Augustine, Epist. 165, concerning the Popes, attests up to his own times.

" *Obj. I.* Marcellinus, under Dioclesian, burnt incense to an idol, therefore, &c.

" *Ans.* Augustine, and after him, Baronius, Bellarmine,

Christianus Lupus, &c., say, that this lapse of Marcellinus is a fiction fabricated by the Donatists; Binius Schelstratius and others, who admit the lapse, say that Marcellinus burnt incense to idols through fear of death, and therefore that he sinned against the profession of faith, but did not lose the faith internally.

"*Obj. II.* Pope Liberius subscribed to the Syrmian formula of faith, prepared by the Arians, and the condemnation of Athanasius, who held the true faith; therefore he was a heretic.

"*Ans.* I deny the inference: it is indeed true that Liberius was sent into exile on account of the Catholic faith, and that at length, overcome by calamities, and protracted misfortune, he communicated with the Arians, and subscribed the condemnation of Athanasius, not for the sake of his faith, but on account of accusations falsely laid to his charge by the Arians.

" He afterwards subscribed to the Syrmian formula, which, (notwithstanding it did not sufficiently explain the faith,) contained nothing contrary to the faith, although in it the word *consubstantial* was suppressed; from which, therefore, it cannot be proved that Liberius was a heretic, although he may not be excused from sin in the manner of acting.

"There are not wanting some, however, who regard the lapse of Liberius as a mere fable, circulated by the Arians, and believed by a few Catholics, as is commonly the case. See Collet, &c.

"*Obj. III.* Honorius I. was a Monothelite; therefore, &c.

"The antecedent is proved; because, in a letter to Sergius, he teaches that in Christ there was one will and not two.

"*Ans.* I deny the antecedent: for proof, it is said that in these letters, he did not deny that in Christ there are two wills, divine and human; but he only denied that there were two human wills warring against each other, the one of the flesh, the other of the spirit; such as we find in ourselves, by which, from our depraved nature, the flesh lusts against the Spirit: and he enjoined that they should abstain from the words, ' one or two wills,' lest from the different interpretation of the words, a schism might arise.

20 *

"You will urge: the Sixth Synod condemned Honorius as a heretic; therefore, &c.

"*Ans.* Sylvius, with some others, contends that the acts of this Synod have been corrupted, and the name of Honorius substituted in place of Theodorus: but this plea, Thomassinus refutes in a learned manner, in his 20th dissertation on Synod 6.

"Others say that the sixth Synod, in condemning Honorius, erred, namely, by a mistake of a merely personal fact, not about the literal sense of the dogmatical texts; for, they say, the judgment of the Synod was merely criminal, not dogmatical: for the question was principally concerning the person of Honorius; and hence, his letters were not primarily discussed, in order that inquiry might be made concerning doctrine, but only that the person might be judged; in which judgment it was admitted, No. 84, that the church might err.

"Others say, that Honorius, in the sixth Synod, was condemned as a favourer of heresy, but not as a heretic; and the fact favours this opinion, that Leo II., who confirmed the Synod, in various passages, blames only the negligence and imprudence of Honorius, by which he permitted the immaculate faith to be stained; also that Constantine Pogonatus, the emperor, who was present at this Council, condemns Honorius as the favourer, abettor, and confirmer of heresy. It is indeed true that an anathema was pronounced upon Honorius as a heretic; but the Fathers seem not to have distinguished between heretics and the favourers of heresy; at least, the very words of the Fathers blame the connivance of Honorius, rather than his open profession of heresy.

"*Obj. IV.* Dist. 46 Can. IF THE POPE, &c.: the Pope is said to judge all persons, and to be judged by none, unless he shall be detected deviating from the faith; therefore, he may be a formal heretic.

"*Ans.* I deny the inference: for it is only said what may be done in case that the Pope fails from the faith; but we think that this case never has happened, and never will occur."

Concerning the Temporal Power of the Supreme Pontiff. (98.)

" Has the Supreme Pontiff also a certain temporal and civil power?

" *Ans.* It is certain that he has even direct power in places subject to him by temporal dominion. For it is no objection that the same person is an ecclesiastical chief, and a political one in temporal things, as appears in Melchizedech, the Machabees, &c.

" Has the Pope also temporal power over all kingdoms of the world?

" *Ans.* There have been those, as Bellarmine shows, Bk. 5, concerning the Roman Pontiff, who ascribed to the Pontiff by divine right the most plenary and direct power over the whole world, as well in temporal as in spiritual things; but this opinion is rejected by all.

" Bellarmine, Sylvius, and others, say that the Pope has not by divine right *direct* power over temporal kingdoms, but indirect; that is, *when the spiritual power cannot be freely exercised, nor his object be attained, by spiritual, then he may have recourse to temporal means, according to St. Thomas, 22, 9, 10, a 12, s. q. 12, a 2, who teaches that princes may sometimes be deprived of their rule, and their subjects be liberated from the oath of fidelity ; and thus it has been done by Pontiffs more than once.*

" The other opinion teaches that kings and princes in temporal concerns are by no means subject to pontifical and ecclesiastical power, and that they cannot be deposed directly or indirectly by the authority of the keys, and that their subjects cannot be relieved from faith and obedience, or absolved from the oath of fidelity which they have taken. Thus the declaration of the Gallican clergy, in the year 1682, asserts, which many foreign (clergy) follow. The treatise of Bellarmine, concerning the power of the Supreme Pontiff in temporal concerns, against Barclay, the Parisian senate had condemned already in 1610, as may be seen in Tournely."

The claim of the Pope to universal spiritual supremacy upon earth, is, if possible, even still more absurd than the

plea which is offered for the primacy of Peter.   If the Pope
is the successor of Peter, it must be either in his peculiar
office as apostle, or as Bishop of Rome, or as the Head of
the Church : but he cannot succeed Peter as an apostle, for
the apostolic office was not continued after the death of the
twelve, whom Christ himself appointed, as they neither constituted any others to succeed them in that office, nor had they
authority to do so.   He cannot succeed him as Bishop of
Rome, for it never yet has been proved that Peter held that
office, but on the contrary there is abundant presumptive evidence of the very strongest character to show that he could
not have been the Bishop of any Church at Rome.   The
Pope cannot succeed Peter as the Head of the Church, for
Peter never was appointed as such, and never claimed to be
Christ's vicar upon earth.   He expressed his concern that
the things he presented might " always be had in remembrance after his decease," but neither he nor any other inspired writer alludes even in the most distant manner to his
giving a commission to the Bishops of Rome to succeed him ;
but he certainly would not have failed to mention in precise
and explicit terms the nature of his supremacy, nor could
the other apostles have been utterly silent in relation to it, if
he and his successors had been appointed as Christ's vicars
upon earth to the end of time.   We may rest assured that
if the doctrine of the Pope's supremacy were really taught
in the Bible, it would have been declared in terms as precise
and definite as justification by faith or the resurrection from
the dead.

But not only are the Scriptures silent in relation to this
subject, but no authority can be gathered from the testimony
of the purest antiquity to sustain this strange and presumptuous claim of the Romish Church.   Which of the early
fathers plainly declare in so many words, or in language that
unequivocally imports that Christ constituted Peter the uni-

versal Bishop of his Church, and the Bishops of Rome his successors in that office?

How strange it is, if they recognised an infallible Head upon earth, that they should have toiled and laboured so assiduously to compose elaborate confutations of heretics, when there was a visible infallible guide to whom every difficulty might have been referred, and from whose decision none who professed to acknowledge the authority of Christ and the Holy Scriptures could possibly appeal? But when do they ever refer heretics to such a judge of controversy? When? The testimony of many of the writers, whom Papists designate as belonging to the Fathers of the Church, is of very little value, inasmuch as they were interested in sustaining abuses which they had themselves assisted in bringing into the church; this remark will not generally apply to the standard-bearers of the First and Second and some of the Third and even Fourth Century, but after that period very many of the Fathers are witnesses of very doubtful reputation.

It is amusing to see the perfect nonchalance with which Peter Dens passes over the most formidable objections of writers, for whose authority Romish Priests profess the greatest deference. Thus, when Gregory the Great condemns the name of universal Bishop as blasphemous, there is a "distinguo" at hand, which explains the difficulty at once. The whole secret of the case was that Gregory conceived it to be blasphemous in the Bishop of Constantinople to affect a dignity, for which he was himself an aspirant. We care not for his opinion except in so far as his indignant rebuke of the Constantinopolitan Bishop is some proof that the claim to universal supremacy was a novelty in his day.

As for Peter's supremacy, it is plain that it did not exonerate him from subjection to his brethren, before whom he pleaded his cause, and by whom he was sent as a messenger, Acts viii. 14, and xi. 3. Nor did his infallibility render him proof against error, for which Paul withstood him to his

face, Gal. ii. 11.   And though Christ prayed for Peter, that
his faith might not fail, and thus rendered him and his successors indefectible, yet it was but a very few hours after the
Saviour had thus prayed that Peter denied him—denied him
thrice, and with an oath!   This shows surely that the Lord
Jesus did not intend by this expression to intimate to his disciple that he never should commit an error, much less that
his successors should have this privilege; but he told him
that he had prayed for him that his faith might not fail, or
in other words, that he might not perish as a castaway.   It
is evident that if Christ had prayed that Peter might not err
either in faith or practice, his disciple would not have fallen
into the sin of a gross and aggravated perjury only a few
hours after the annunciation of his confirmed indefectibility.

But the Pope claims " plenitude of power in the church, so
that his power extends to all who are in the church, and to
all things which pertain to the government of the church."
" He must be obeyed in all things which concern the Christian religion."   These assertions, although extravagant
enough, are not quite so audacious as the language of some
other approved writers of the Romish Church.   Cardinal
Zabar, speaking of the Popes, affirms—" That they might
do all things which they choose, even things unlawful, and
so could do more than God himself."   The canonists re-
peatedly compliment the Pope as " Our Lord God, the Pope!"
This title was given to the Pope by the Council of Lateran,
Sess. 4.   Gratian asserts, " That all mortals are to be judged
by the Pope, but the Pope by nobody at all."   It would indeed be a hard matter to judge him, if Massonus be good
authority, for in his third Book, in the life of Pope John IX.,
he tells us " That the Bishops of Rome cannot commit even
sin without praise!!"   Now, I do not wish to imply that
every Romanist would approve of such horrid blasphemy as
this; it is more than enough to brand their church with infamy, that there has been a time in her history when such

writers were permitted to express these and similar sentiments
without rebuke!

The supremacy of Peter did not exempt him from paying
tribute even to a heathen, Matt. xvii. 27. Strange as it is,
it is nevertheless true that this fact is mentioned as one of
the prerogatives of Christ's vicar; Peter Dens actually bases
an argument for the supremacy upon this fact!! If the Pope
were to follow Peter's example in this respect, what would
become of the Apostolic See! In his epistles, Peter urges
many precepts of obedience to princes—"Submit to every
ordinance of man, whether it be to the king as SUPREME, or
to governors," &c. 1 Pet. ii. 13. But the Pope not only denies obedience to any earthly sovereign, but even in this enlightened age, *His Holiness still claims the right of depriv-
ing princes of their rule, and liberating their subjects from
the oath of fidelity!* Whilst the ridiculous claim of universal temporal supremacy is avowedly repudiated, the Romish
Priests are still taught by their theology, " *When the Spiritual power cannot be freely exercised, nor his (i. e., the
Pope's) object be attained by Spiritual, that he may have
recourse to temporal means, according to St. Thomas, who
teaches that princes may sometimes be deprived of their
rule, and their subjects be liberated from the oath of fidelity; and thus it has been done by Pontiffs more than
once!!*" (Sec. 98.)

Thus Pope Zachary deposed Childeric, King of France,
and set up Pepin in his stead! Thus Pope Alexander III.,
planting his foot upon the neck of the Emperor Frederic I.,
profanely quoted the Scripture. Ps. xci. 13. "Thou shalt
tread upon the lion and the adder," &c. Thus Pius V., in
the insolent Bull, which he issued as a declaration of Queen
Elizabeth's deposition, and by which her subjects were *absolved*, forsooth! from their allegiance, applied to himself
the words, "See, I have this day set thee over the nations, and
over the kingdoms, to root out, and to pull down, and to de-

stroy, and to throw down, to build and to plant." Jer. i. **10.** This is " submitting to every ordinance of man," with a vengeance !

Now I desire to call attention to the fact, that the Pope still claims, BY DIVINE RIGHT, *indirect* power over all the kingdoms and nations of the earth. His priests are his sworn subjects, and must promote the interests of their Lord God, the Pope, or they are perjured men ! From their own principles, therefore, we prove the system of Popery to be nothing more nor less than a politico-religious power, which must aim at supremacy, because it claims it as its due !

But to return to the consideration of the Pope's claim to universal supremacy. Let us hear the story of his succession as Romish authors relate it. Platina, the Secretary of Pope Sixtus IV., who wrote the lives of the Popes, tells us that Peter, some time before his death, consecrated Clement, and commended him to the chair of the Church of God, in these very words : " The same power of binding and loosing I deliver to thee, which Christ left me : do thou, contemning and despising all outward things, promote by prayer and preaching the salvation of men, as becomes a good pastor." Certain it is, that the successors of Peter have, in late ages, grievously neglected and forgotten the latter part of this charge. But how is it, after this formal story, related no doubt with the utmost gravity, that the same author mentions one Linus as Peter's immediate successor, and tells us that he occupied the chair eleven years, three months, and twelve days exactly ; and after him a certain Cletus was Pope for just twelve years, one month, and eleven days ; and then, after this lapse of nearly twenty-four years, honest Father Clement begins to occupy the seat of Peter, and holds it nine years, two months, and ten days. Now this story twists the line of succession into a knot at the very outset ; for if Peter ordained Clement as his successor, Linus and Cletus had no right to interfere with his claim. But without pressing this point, if Peter did ordain either Clement or Linus, or any other man as Head of the Church, then he either divested himself of that authority, and became subject to the new Head, or else from that time to his death the Church had two visible heads.

Moreover, if Clement, Linus, or any one else succeeded Peter in the primacy, then James and John, and the other apostles, who survived Peter, became subject to Clement or Linus, or whoever the new Head might be. For the historians, upon whose authority Papists mainly rely, tell us that Peter suffered under Nero, but John long after under Domitian. But is it reasonable to suppose that the men, who were called by Christ himself to the *apostolic* office, and who are represented as at least equal with Peter, should become inferior and subject to an ordinary pastor, who was called by man and not by Christ to the primacy? How then are we to account for the fact, that the writings of James and John are owned by the Church as pertaining to the canon of Scripture, whereas the writings of Clement are rejected as apocryphal?

But even supposing that Christ ordained Peter, and Peter ordained Linus or some one else, what has this to do with the Popes of the last ages, who are elected by the Cardinals? From whom do the Cardinals receive their power? If from God, let them produce a "thus saith the Lord;" if from men, let them show by what authority. The name of Cardinal was never heard of in the church till the 8th Century, and it was not till the 11th Century that they were formed into a regular order under John XVIII., if ecclesiastical history is to be credited. Besides, Platina, the Romish historian, calls this John " a robber and a thief in his pontificate," and thinks him unworthy to be " placed in the number of the Popes," having assumed the pontifical authority while Gregory V. was alive. This is a hopeful origin indeed of the blessed order of Cardinals! But their subsequent history is

21

not unworthy of their parentage; for he is very ignorant, who does not know that ambition and bribery, and the influence and interests of temporal princes, have ruled the conclave, instead of the blessed Spirit of the living God!

And then, look for a moment at the *uninterrupted* succession of the "Series of 258 Popes!" Is it not notorious, that for several years there was no Pope at all? Do we not know that at other times there were two or three Popes at once; that one anathematized another, and that infallible Popes and Councils have condemned several of the occupants of Peter's chair as heretical and illegitimate? Through which of these channels must the pure stream of uninterrupted succession flow? Some of these Popes must be spurious, and amidst this endless variety of contradictory decrees, who can determine which were the true successors of St. Peter, or whether the present Pope is lawfully descended from him?

But since Papists will insist upon their succession, let us see if Peter Dens is authorized to say, "that it could never yet be proved, concerning any Pope, that he was a formal heretic!" The 97th section, in which the question is discussed, "Whether the Pope, at least as a private person, may be a heretic," is a model of Jesuitical cunning. When evidence as clear as the sun is brought forward to controvert a doctrine, which Papists must maintain at all hazards, there are distinguos enough at hand to foil every objection. But if we admit, for argument's sake, that Marcellinus, Liberius, &c., were not heretics, and that the apology offered for them, lame as it is, is sufficient, what are we to think of John XXII., who denied the immortality of the soul? What say our Romish friends to John XXIII., Gregory XII., and Benedict XIII., who were all Popes at once, and were all cashiered by the Council of Constance as illegitimate? Did not the Council of Basil convict Pope Eugenius both of schism and heresy? Was not Pope Anastasius excommunicated by the Roman clergy as a heretic? Is it not matter of historical record, that Pope Sylvester sacrificed to the devil, that Pope Formosus obtained the chair by perjury, that *his holiness*, Sergius III., caused another Pope's body to be digged up out of his grave, the head to be cut off and thrown into the Tiber, and that Pope Boniface imprisoned his infallible predecessor and plucked out his eyes?

These are but a few samples of the immaculate orthodoxy of the successors of St. Peter! Atheists and blasphemers, rebels and murderers, conjurors and adulterers supply not a few of the links of this apostolical chain! No wonder that not a man who has ever occupied the papal throne has ever presumed to bear the name of Peter *after his inauguration;* even when they had formerly been known by that name, they changed it at their accession to the chair! Thus Peter de Tarantasia became Innocent IV.; Peter Carafa changed his name to Paul V.; and Sergius III. was once a Peter too. This fact would seem to imply that these men must have been conscious of the vast disparity between Peter the Pope, and Peter the apostle! It is not without reason, certainly, that the anecdote is related of the famous painter, Raphael Urbin, who, when reproved by the Pope for putting too much colour on the faces of Peter and Paul, replied, that he did it on purpose to represent them as blushing in heaven to see what successors they had on the earth!

CHAPTER XXV.

THE Treatises on the virtue of hope and the virtue of charity, which constitute the 2d and 3d parts of the second volume, although marked by a few peculiarities, contain nothing which would be specially interesting to the general reader, and I therefore omit them. The Treatise concerning Right and Justice, which occupies a large portion of the third volume, presents amongst other things sound practical casuistry in a variety of cases in which restitution should be made, about which, however, there could be very little debate among men of common honesty. The 88th, and the following sections of this treatise may speak for themselves.

Concerning the grievousness of the sin of theft and rapine. (88.)

" How great a sin are theft and rapine?

" *Ans.* They are from their very nature mortal sins. It is proved from 1 Cor. vi. 10., where it is said : ' nor thieves, nor extortioners shall possess the kingdom of God :' besides they are grievously repugnant to the love and justice of our neighbour, and tend to overturn the common peace.

" *Obj.* Prov. vi. 30. It is said, ' The fault is not so great, when a man hath stolen : for he stealeth to fill his hungry soul.'

" St. Thomas replies to this : I. ' It must be said that theft is declared to be not a great fault for a twofold reason. First, indeed, on account of the necessity inducing to theft, which diminishes or totally removes the fault. And hence, it is added : *for he stealeth to fill his hungry soul.* Theft is said in another mode not to be a great fault by comparison with the guilt of adultery, which is punished with death. And hence it is added, concerning the thief, that if he be taken he shall restore sevenfold : but he that is an adulterer shall destroy his own soul.'

" In how many ways may theft be venial?

" Principally in two ways : namely, from the *imperfect deliberation of the act ;* and from the *trifling value of the matter.*

" The former mode is not easily imagined in the external removal of the property of another, but it may more readily be done by inflicting injury, and by internal acts. The theft, for instance, of a single farthing is venial by reason of the small value of the thing.

" Some add two other modes, 1. From *ignorance slightly culpable*, that the thing was the property of another.

" 2. That the owner in an *important* matter is not *much*

opposed, but is unwilling only *as to the mode of taking it.* But these two ways may be absolutely reduced to the trifling value of the thing; because, although a thing may be important in itself, yet in the degree of this theft, it may be said to be of little moment.

" The theft of a trifling thing may become mortal in various ways, as will be shown hereafter.

" What quantity is requisite before a theft can be mortal in regard to its matter?

" *Ans.* Certain authors refer the quantity respectively to the persons, upon whom the loss is inflicted : so that a thing may be a mortal matter if it is taken from a poor person, which would not be mortal if it were taken from a rich man : but this in our day appears antiquated, and the absolute quantity is now usually determined not by considering whether the person from whom it may be taken is rich or poor : the reason is that the richer has not a less right over his property than the poorer person ; and, therefore, when an equal quantity is taken from both sides, injury is in so far inflicted, not less on the richer than on the poorer.

" With these remarks the fact agrees that the penitent in confession ought to declare, whether he has taken the thing from a poor or from a rich man : but this is not in regard o the theft, but on account of the inconvenience and the consequences, which usually proceed from a theft committed on a poor man ; as, his earnings being suspended, loss accruing, hunger, grief, &c. : but all these things are apart from the theft.

" If you say that a rich man is not so unwilling as to the theft of, for instance, 24 farthings : I reply that he must be presumed to be unwilling in proportion to the amount. That if it is admitted that the owner is not much opposed, then indeed it may become venial, as was said above : but independently of the question, whether the owner is rich or poor.

" What quantity appears absolutely sufficient for mortal theft in regard to amount?

" The more common and plausible opinion reckons that the hire or daily wages of a man labouring in some honourable trade is sufficient; that is three or four shillings for this time and for this country ; because, in proportion as daily labour is accounted severe, the pay is correspondent.

21 *

" It is said, *three* or *four* shillings ; because this quantity cannot be physically or mathematically determined, but only morally ; ' and perhaps it is concealed for this reason,' says St. August. (Bk. xxi. de Civ. Dei. last chap.,) ' lest the desire might abate of improving so as to avoid all sins.' And 17th chap. of Enchirid. he says : ' there are certain things, which it is more useful not to know than to know.'

" It is said, also, *for this time and for this country;* because, where money is more plenty or more scarce, a greater or less quantity is requisite, and in the time in which money was more scarce here, a less quantity was sufficient ; as in accordance with these things, the daily pay of a labourer is usually increased or diminished."

Concerning the palliations or Excuses of thefts. (89.)

" There are two principal claims, under which thefts are wont to be covered ; namely, the claims of *necessity*, and of *just compensation.*   Hence it is asked :

" Whether it is lawful to steal in a case of necessity : or rather, whether it is lawful to take another's property on account of necessity ?

" *I. Observe.* It is important to distinguish a threefold necessity : *extreme*, in which life is in danger : *urgent*, in which health, or station is endangered ; and *common*, which the poor suffer everywhere.

" *II. Ans.* It is lawful to take another man's property, either secretly or openly, in so far as there is necessity for supplying extreme want: the reason is, because then all things are common.

" If this was lawful in order to supply my own extreme necessity, the same will be lawful for the necessity of my neighbour ; unless I can succour him from my own means.

" This case alone is excepted, namely, when by taking another man's property, the owner would be also brought into similar necessity.

" Is he thought to be in extreme necessity, who by asking or begging can relieve his extreme necessity ?

" *Ans.* No : for no one is thought to be in extreme necessity, who may relieve it by lawful means, nor should this means be called unbecoming for an honourable man : for nothing is dishonourable for necessity.   Besides such a pretext would open the door for many thefts and for disturbance of the state.

" Should those things which are taken away through necessity be restored?

" If the thing taken away still remains after the necessity is over, it is doubtless to be restored: because extreme necessity does not confer a right to another man's property except in so far as is necessary for its relief: and hence if, in order to escape death, you have made use of another man's horse, you ought to restore it when the exigency is over.

" If the thing be consumed,—for instance, wine, bread, &c., he ought to restore nothing, even if after suffering want he should come into better fortune. Except unless he has goods elsewhere, and thus may be supposed rather to take another's property by way of borrowing; for then it should be restored: nor is such a one properly in extreme necessity, but only in respect to some thing.

" What must be said concerning common and urgent necessity?

" It is agreed among all that it is not lawful to take another's property on account of common necessity.

" Nor is it lawful to take what is another's on account of any pressing necessity whatsoever, distinct from extreme; because goods do not become common on account of such a necessity; the reason is, because as cases of urgent necessity are very common, disturbance of the state would easily ensue if then it were lawful to steal the property of another.

" Hence this 36th proposition was condemned by Innocent XI.: ' It is permitted to steal not only in extreme but also in urgent necessity.'

" Yet authors agree that the sin of him who steals from urgent necessity is diminished so much the more as the necessity is greater.

" *Obj.* St. Thomas does not distinguish between extreme and urgent necessity, therefore, &c.

" *Ans.* I deny the antecedent. It is plain from Art. 7, in corp., &c.

" *Obj. II.* The things which some persons have superabundantly, are due by natural law to the support of the poor, says St. Thomas: but this is true, not only in extreme, but also in urgent necessity; therefore poor people may take those things as due to themselves in urgent necessity.

"*Ans.* From this argument it would follow that this might be lawful not only in urgent but also in common necessity; which no one would say. Besides, when any one is obliged to give something to another, the other may not on that account steal it; and especially here, when it is not a debt of justice, but only of charity and mercy," &c. &c.

Concerning Recovery or Compensation.   (90.)

"What is compensation?

"*Ans.* It is called in law, *a mutual settling of debt and credit.* It may be done in two ways, either by retaining so much, or by privately taking so much from the property of a debtor as the debtor owes.

"How manifold is compensation?

"*Ans.* Twofold; namely, *manifest* and *secret.*

"What is manifest compensation?

"*Ans. It is a mutual settling of debt and credit with a knowledge of the debtor:* for instance, John owes Peter 100 for clothing, and Peter owes John 100 for wine; debt and credit are compensated, and satisfaction is made to both.

"Is manifest compensation always lawful?

"*Ans.* If the question is asked concerning retaining property due to another, because another owes me an equal amount, such compensation is lawful.

"It is also lawful to recover one's property in revenge of an act of theft, or when it is not yet put away in a safe place; because this has the plea of just defence: and what is more, many authors say, that this is lawfully done with moderate force, if the thing to be recovered is plainly in sight, and cannot otherwise be recovered; only let there be no scandal and other improprieties.

"But if a thing owned by another is manifestly taken, because the other owes that thing or an equivalent, such compensation is ordinarily unlawful; because it is contrary to the order of justice, and calculated to disturb the public peace.

"What compensation is called secret?

"*Ans. That which is made without the knowledge of*

the debtor.   But it may be done in a threefold manner : 1st.
By recovering one's property in the whole, unjustly kept
back by another.   2d. By privately stealing from the debtor
an equivalent to the amount due, if he will not pay or make
restitution.   3d. By secretly retaining from the goods of the
debtor so much as he owes me.

"Is secret compensation lawful ?

"*Ans.* St. Thomas, Art. 5. ad. 3., says : ' But he who by
stealth takes his own property, unjustly kept back by another, sins indeed, not because he wrongs him who detains
it, (and therefore he is not obliged to make any restitution or
recompense,) but he sins against common justice, when he
usurps to himself the judgment of his own case, passing by the
established order of law.   And therefore he is bound to make
satisfaction to God, and to take care that the scandal among
his neighbours, if any should thence arise, may be allayed.'

"Hence Steyaert maintains that it is always unlawful, in
Appendix, Controv. 4, &c.

"Besides, although the offence against the common law
might sometimes be only a venial sin, yet other serious dis-
orders are liable to follow, as scandal, infamy, risk of double payment, danger of frequent abuse against the common
good, &c. ; hence most authors, even those who defend it as
lawful, say that it is dangerous in practice ; and therefore,
generally, the contrary is to be recommended.

"Yet Sylvius, Wiggers, de Cocq, Billuart, Collet, &c.,
teach that it may be lawful through circumstances, the following conditions being laid down :

"1. That the debt is certain and apparent, or that it is
certainly agreed that the property is yours.   Also, that it is
due from justice, not from charity or any other virtue.

"2. That it cannot be recovered by any other method ;
for instance, by way of the law, except with great difficulty
and inconvenience.

"3. That there is no danger of scandal and infamy : lest,
for instance, he may be regarded as a thief by recovering in
this way.

"4. That care must be taken lest the debtor in this way,
should pay or restore twice.

"5. That a thing is taken the same in kind if it can be

done, and that no injury is done to a third person by taking his property ; for instance, if lent to the debtor.

" 6. That compensation be not made from the property of a debtor deposited with a creditor, or from something lent : for this the laws forbid (Chap. Good faith respecting Deposit) : nor can this compensation be made from property due to the state or governor : v. g., from tolls ; thus also, he who has been condemned to give money or anything else, cannot use compensation.

" 7. In order to avoid the difficulty of objections, Billuart adds, that it is requisite that all these things are ascertained, not by the private judgment of the person taking compensation, but in the opinion of some prudent man : lest iniquity should lie to itself.

" But so many conditions and cautions, which can scarcely ever all be afforded, justly argue the weakness of this opinion : besides, the reason of St. Thomas always militates against it, that the person compensating himself sins against common justice, when he usurps to himself the judgment of his own case, neglecting the established order of the law.

" Whatever this may be, it is certain, however, that servants, although in fact they might receive less pay than the labour which they undergo is worth, yet may not on that account avail themselves of secret compensation ; as is plain from this 37th proposition, condemned by Innocent XI. ; ' servants and house-girls may secretly steal from their masters for the compensation of their labour, which they deem greater than the salary which they receive ;' and authors extend this even to the case in which a servant has been compelled by poverty, &c., to serve for too little wages."

Concerning Small Thefts. (91.)

" It has been said, No. 88, that theft from its very nature is a mortal sin : yet it may be venial from the imperfect deliberation of the act, and the trifling value of the matter.

" Is theft always venial, when the matter which is taken away is trifling ?

" *Ans.* No : for it may become mortal in seven ways, just as any sin whatever, venial on account of the smallness of the matter, can become mortal ; as may be seen, from No. 165, &c.

" Yet a theft, trifling as to matter, becomes mortal, principally in the three following ways :

" 1. He sins mortally, who takes away a trifling matter, having the will, desire, or intention of taking away a valuable article, if opportunity were afforded.

" 2. Any one sins mortally as often as he takes away a thing of little value, intending by many small thefts to reach a considerable sum, thus, v. g. he who from an intention of stealing 5 florins should have taken away at each time one farthing, would have committed up to that time 100 mortal sins : the reason is, because each theft proceeds from a bad intention.

" Daelman with some others maintains that many such thefts continually committed constitute one mortal theft, because they flow from one and the same prevailing, uninterrupted intention ; but practically the thing amounts to the same, because this one is equivalent to many.

" 3. Although any one should not have the intention either of taking away anything valuable, nor yet intend by small amounts to reach a considerable sum, yet he who often steals small amounts from one or even from different persons, sins mortally from the very circumstance that he makes up the same, perceiving, or being able and in duty bound to perceive, that it would reach a considerable amount.   And hence the previous acts will be venial sins from the trifling value of the matter ; but the act by which the amount is completed, sufficient for a mortal sin, will be mortal : because this last act is regarded as pertaining to an important amount, for the reason that the previous amounts coalesce with the last ; and thus by willing the last, he by inference wills the former amounts.

" For the same reason, it must be said, that if, v. g. a person by the ninth trifling theft shall have completed an important amount, he will have sinned mortally, and he again sins mortally by adding the tenth trifling theft, and so of the rest, &c.

" In relation to this subject, this 38th proposition has been condemned by Innocent XI. ' A person is not bound under pain of mortal sin to restore what has been taken away by small thefts, however great the sum may be.'

" From what has been said, you will infer, that innkeepers, merchants, or those who keep a shop, who defraud in number, weight, or measure, even if at each time, they may intend to steal only something trifling, yet at each time sin mortally, because their intention is by such frauds to reach a considerable sum. Even if from the beginning they may not have had this intention, they still sin mortally every time after they have completed an important amount.

" Many authors say that a greater quantity of matter is requisite in order to be mortal, when things are taken away by small thefts from different persons, or from the same person at different times : but Braunman rejects this as pernicious in practice : because, in order to be mortal, a considerable absolute quantity of loss, or of another's property which is unjustly detained, is sufficient.

" When each one of several persons causes a loss to the same person, which, when taken together, is serious, do the amounts coalesce ?

" *Ans.* No : unless they mutually co-operate. See Daelman, &c.

" Is he who takes a considerable sum by small thefts, bound under mortal sin to restore the whole ?

" *Ans.* No : BUT IN ORDER TO BE FREE FROM THE MORTAL SIN OF UNJUST DETENTION, IT IS SUFFICIENT TO MAKE RESTITUTION SO FAR THAT WHAT HE RETAINS MAY NO LONGER BE A SERIOUS AMOUNT.

" Yet authors remark that this is dangerous in practice : and hence confessors, in regard to all thieves, should be inexorable, and oblige the penitents to the restitution of all, even the minutest thefts ; in order that thus they may more efficaciously be deterred from greater.

" How to proceed practically with him, who confesses that he has stolen, may be seen in Schema 7, in the volume concerning Penance."

Concerning the thefts of certain persons in particular.
(92.)

" What is to be thought concerning thefts of children from the property of their parents ?

" If the son steals a considerable amount from parents who are seriously unwilling, it is certain that he sins mortally.

" It is said, a *considerable amount :* because all admit that the quantity of the matter should be greater in this case to constitute a mortal sin, that when something is taken away from strangers : the reason of which is, that children have a certain remote right to the property of parents, which after death ought to devolve to themselves : also, because parents are usually not so unwilling.

" It is said, *from parents who are seriously unwilling :* with respect to which it must be observed, that they either are unwilling only as to the manner of stealing it, or that they are unwilling also as to the amount taken away.

" If they are unwilling only as to the manner, it is usually admitted that a greater quantity is required in order to the commission of mortal sin in respect to the amount, than when they are unwilling as to the value : it is also admitted that if the manner only is displeasing, not the act itself, there arises no necessity for restitution.

" But when parents are at the same time unwilling as regards the value, and the quantity is pretty considerable, children are not to be excused from mortal sin, nor from the obligation of making restitution.

" With respect to such cases, the condition of the parents should be considered, whether they are wealthy, or whether they are in straitened circumstances, &c. : also, the age of the children, and the purpose for which they consume what they have stolen : the custom of the place is also to be regarded, or what parents of such a condition may be accustomed to concede to their children in such a place.

" The method which a child takes in stealing, is also to be principally considered : whether, v. g., by breaking open chests, by collecting debts in the name of parents under a false seal, for instance, by receiving the returns of revenues due to parents, &c.

" Practically, for the most part, they ought to be obliged to make some restitution, or to ask pardon, although the parents might be unwilling only as to the mode : because this is the best remedy against a relapse.

" If a son is under obligation to restore something considerable to his parents, and is not able, then he is to be compelled to permit so much to be subtracted from his portion in

22

the division of the inheritance : unless the parents should in a valid manner remit the restitution.

" May a husband commit theft upon a wife, and vice versa, a wife upon a husband ?

" *Ans.* Yes : he, if against the consent of his wife, he squanders property, the controk of which belongs to her : such as dowry, &c. : but the wife, in more instances commits theft, by taking, secretly, and without the consent of her husband, their common property. Yet it ought to be understood what things are permitted to wives, according to the custom of the place ; for instance, in order to give alms, to help poor relations, for decent ornament, &c.

" Even parents themselves sometimes commit theft upon their children, by stealing from the military property, whose control and administration belongs to the children.

" Servants and maids, very often sin by theft, when, for instance, they avail themselves of secret compensation, as was said No. 90 : also, if they do not perform the work which is due ; which ought also to be taken into consideration with regard to other labourers.

" Besides, they sin by theft, in proportion to the value of the thing, when they convert to their own use, costly articles of food and drink, or things which are usually denied to them : unless the consent of the master can be presumed, at least as regards the amount taken away ; for instance, if the master, knowing it, does not say anything to the contrary, or readily grants permission, when asked, &c.

" However, masters are usually extremely unwilling that servants should steal such things in order to give or sell to strangers : authors likewise are of opinion that they sin grievously, if, without the consent of their masters, they give to the poor, goods to a considerable amount.

" An aggravating circumstance in this matter is, if servants carry off a thing committed to their care.

" What is to be thought concerning thefts, which servants commit in feeding cattle ; for instance, by giving them more than the master wished, or those things, which he has forbidden them to give ?

" *Ans.* These are sins and common enough : and if from this cause a considerable loss should accrue in the household affairs, it is a mortal sin, and restitution is a duty.

" But if the cattle are so much improved, that the loss is as it were compensated, they will not be obliged to make restitution, nor will they so easily sin mortally.

" Persons attached to religious orders, in this respect are nearly similar to the children of a family, so that they commit theft if they dispose of anything against the consent of the superiors : but besides they sin by the offence of sacrilege against the vow of poverty.

" The universal admonition of authors is that in such thefts there should be no dissembling, lest they should be multiplied ; although it might be evident that the owners were unwilling only as to the mode of taking ; but that some restitution is always to be enjoined, or asking pardon, or that they make amends for what has been done amiss by more diligent care and labour."

It need scarcely be said that the preceding sections contain principles, which must inevitably lead to licentiousness and dishonesty. The *theology* of the Romish Church teaches that the theft of an article of small value is a venial offence ; and farther, that if the person who is robbed is not very unwilling to be defrauded, the sin is but a little one. Is this the morality of the Bible? Does Jesus Christ teach such doctrine as this? No ; but he says, " *He that is unjust in the least, is unjust also in much.*" It stands to reason that the man who will violate the dictates of his conscience for a small inducement will feel very little scruple about transgressing the law of God when the incentive is greater. If he pleads in extenuation of his guilt that he has yielded to a small temptation, and that he has stolen an article of but little value, who that is possessed of common sense would trust him in a matter which presents *strong* inducements to dishonesty? If he could not resist the former, how is he to overcome the latter? The very weakness of the temptation aggravates his guilt. The Romish Church weighs guilt not by the balance of the gospel, but in scales of her own invention, and her false weights are an abomination to

the Lord! What can be more execrable than the principle
that the guilt of an offender is to be ascertained from the
feelings, with which the injured person resents the trespass
committed against him? If the individual defrauded is a
benevolent and merciful man, and is grieved more on account of the manner than the amount of the injury, then
the offence is venial! But if he is a churlish Nabal, a very
son of Belial, whose God is his belly, then the guilt of the
offender is greatly aggravated! Was there ever a more preposterous doctrine palmed upon the simplicity of foolish men
by the arch-deceiver of souls?

Every instance of theft, no matter how small soever the
amount may be, is an offence committed, not only, nor even
principally against man, but against that God who has said,
"Thou shalt not steal." The claims of God's law are almost entirely overlooked in Peter Dens' casuistry; the guilt
of the transgressor is enhanced or mitigated by considerations drawn almost exclusively from human conceptions of
justice; and every honest man must admit that our author's
deductions are not very honourable either to himself or to
the pious fraternity, who are trained under his tuition!

But I must call the attention of my reader to the translation furnished in the Doway Bible of Prov. vi. 30. "The
fault is not so great, when a man hath stolen, for he stealeth
to fill his hungry soul." The translation in the Protestant
Bible reads thus: "Men do not despise a thief, if he steal
to satisfy his soul, when he is hungry." In the Greek
Septuagint it is Ου θαυμαζον εαν αλω τις κλεπτων, κλεπτει
γαρ ινα εμπλησῃ την ψυχην πεινων; literally, "It is not wonderful if one is caught stealing, for he steals in order that he
may fill his soul being hungry." This differs somewhat
from the Doway text, "*The fault is not so great* when a
man hath stolen; for he stealeth to fill his hungry soul." In
the original, the degree of the guilt of theft is not the question, but the strength of the peculiar temptation; and hence

the Doway text is rather objectionable ; and as for the comment of the *divine* St. Thomas " that the necessity inducing to theft *diminishes*, or TOTALLY REMOVES THE FAULT," it is altogether *Romish*.   Solomon is comparing the temptation to which the starving man is exposed with that to which he yields who commits adultery.   Even when the theft is committed in order to satisfy the cravings of hunger, the guilt remains ; hence it is said in the very next verse that the offender shall restore seven-fold ; he shall give all the substance of his house, (ver. 31.) Solomon seems to have been ignorant of the doctrine that in extreme necessity ALL THINGS ARE COMMON.   Though a man is starving, he has no right to steal—he had better die than disobey the law of God. Let him use the lawful means, which God has put within his reach ; and he who feeds the ravens, and hunts for the young lion, will never suffer the righteous to perish with hunger. " Seek ye FIRST the kingdom of God and his righteousness, and all these things shall be added unto you."   The object of insisting upon the above translation, probably is to glean a little more argument for the propriety of the Romish distinction between mortal and venial sin.

The attempt to establish the amount necessary to constitute theft a mortal offence, and all the reasoning in relation to that point, are ineffably ridiculous ! " The daily wages of a man labouring in some honourable trade is sufficient." Supposing then that three or four *shillings*, the amount specified by this discriminating divine, are equivalent to one dollar of our money, then the thief who purloins 99¾ cents commits a venial offence ; but he who takes a quarter of a cent more, and thus completes the dollar, is guilty of mortal sin ! !   Oh ! tempora ! oh ! mores !

Then, too, the cases in which restitution is to be made are peculiar.   If a man in extreme necessity has stolen " wine, bread, &c., he ought to restore nothing, even if, after suffering want, he should come into better fortune !" The old law was,

22 *

that when a man stole, even "to satisfy his hungry soul," "he shall restore seven-fold; he shall give all the substance of his house;" but of course the law of the Bible has nothing to do with the Popish code of morals.

Again: He who takes a considerable sum by small thefts is bound to restore only so much, that the amount which he retains may no longer be serious!! And although a kind of *caveat* is inserted that this is dangerous in practice, according to some authors, and that penitents should be obliged to make restitution, even of the smallest thefts; yet this is enjoined only on the ground of *expediency*, not because it is an absolute obligation!

The sum and substance of the whole chapter is briefly this, that if Protestant parents wish to have their children effectually trained up as candidates for the penitentiary, we recommend to them the schools in which the morals of Peter Dens are inculcated.

CHAPTER XXVI.

THE sections which treat of injuries committed against the good name of another, and of the restitution which is due in such cases, I shall omit. The 119th sect. treats

Of injuries against the body of a neighbour.

OF SUICIDE.

"There are various means by which injury is inflicted on the body of a neighbour; namely, suicide, homicide, mutilation, adultery, incest, fornication, rape, and the things which are included in these, as duelling, abortion, whipping, imprisonment, &c., which are forbidden respectively by the fifth (i. e., the *sixth*) commandment of the Decalogue: 'Thou shalt not kill;' or by the sixth, (*seventh*,) 'Thou shalt not commit adultery.'

" What is suicide?

" Suicide is, *when any one without the command or per-mission of the divine authority inflicts death upon himself.*

" Is it lawful to kill one's self?

" *Ans.* To kill one's self directly and intentionally, without divine authority, is a most grievous sin.

" It is proved, 1. from the command, ' Thou shalt not kill ;' for if it is not permitted by the force of this commandment to kill a neighbour, much less one's self; as every one is nearest to himself.

" 2. To kill one's self is contrary to the inclination of nature ; because every thing preserves and guards itself against harm ; but no exception against this inclination ought to be admitted, unless it is clear that it has been made by the author of nature.

" The suicide therefore sins against God, who has reserved to himself the power of life and death ; he sins also against the state, a member of which he takes away without her consent : and against himself by violating the law of preserving his own life, which was granted to him by God never to be abrogated ; also, by offending against charity, by which every one is bound to love himself.

" St. Jerome, writing on Jonas, ch. i., seems to teach that it is lawful to kill one's self for the preservation of chastity : but in this point we must, with St. Augustine and St. Thomas, differ from him, &c.

" As for the Holy Virgins, who are said to have killed themselves lest they should be violated, it must be said, with St. Augustine, THAT THEY DID IT BY THE DIRECTION OF THE HOLY SPIRIT. Some excuse them by reason of ignorance, which, in regard to them, could be at least not very criminal.

" As to the direction of the Holy Spirit, or divine authority to kill one's self or others, Peter Marchantius correctly admonishes that it cannot be presumed, but ought to be most clearly evident ; because, in such cases, fraud and illusion of the devil may easily intervene.

" From these remarks it is plain, that acts in themselves fatal, are never lawful against one's self, those which in themselves and their own nature tend to death : as cutting the throat, strangling, taking poison, &c.

" Can a judge who is guilty of death lawfully kill himself, as he can kill others ?

" *Ans.* No ; because that judge is not a judge of himself, but must be judged by others.

" Can a judge condemn any criminal to kill himself?

" *Ans.* The negative answer seems proper : because such power is not necessary to the state, as other modes of punishing criminals are supplied : nor is it clear that God has granted this power to the state.

" Hence authors teach that a person condemned to die of hunger, cannot abstain from food secretly offered, nor take the poison which he might be condemned to take.

" Is it lawful to leap into a river, in which a man must certainly be drowned, in order to baptize an infant, which would otherwise die without baptism ?

" *Ans.* No : because the immediate effect of such a leap would be his own death ; and the baptism of the child by no means follows from this, but only from the application of the matter and form.   We are indeed bound, in order to succour such a child to expose ourselves to risk of death ; but it is one thing to expose one's self to the danger of death, and another to kill one's self.

" Is it lawful to leap from a tower on fire, in order to avoid the severer pains of burning, when in either case there is no hope of escaping death ?

" *Ans.* Yes, probably : at least then, if by leaping from the tower he does not accelerate his death ; the reason is, because that leap is immediately an escape of a greater evil, namely, a more painful death ; and hence it seems that permissively he may have recourse to the less painful death which follows from it."

Whenever any of the traditions or doctrines of Holy Church are contradicted by the moral law, or are plainly at variance with opinions now generally received, an explanation is always at hand.   If the saintship of any of the gods or goddesses of Rome is rendered problematical by the manner of their lives or their death, some Father is prepared with a pious suggestion, and this is at once received as perfectly satisfactory ; v. g., the Holy Virgins who committed suicide, and who are invoked with great fervour by their admirers, killed themselves BY THE DIRECTION OF THE HOLY SPIRIT. Thus God is made to suspend the operation even of his moral law in order to preserve the idols of Rome from suspicion! If this is not blasphemous presumption, what crime is there which deserves the name?

Of all the cases of conscience that ever tormented a casuist, surely there are few so perplexing as that which is proposed towards the close of the last section, relative to the immersion of an infant which is in danger of dying without baptism!

Of Indirect Suicide. (120.)

" Is it lawful to kill one's self indirectly, or to do or neglect any thing from which, though not intended, death may follow?

" *Ans.* In itself considered, no: because death would thus certainly be voluntary in the cause, or might be so construed; and therefore it is sinful, unless a sufficient reason for so doing is afforded.

" Therefore, they are guilty of suicide, 1. who, for trifling reasons, expose themselves to danger of death: as, for instance, fool-hardy rope-dancers, or such as take poisons for the sake of vain-glory, unless they know how to meet the danger by means of an antidote, so that it may be morally removed.

" 2. They who accelerate death by surfeit, drunkenness, drinking heated wine, immoderate passions, &c.

" 3. Sick persons refusing ordinary remedies, which would probably be an advantage, and would not do any harm, if there is danger of death from their neglect.

" It is to be observed that the abovementioned persons sin so much the more as they accelerate death, and so long as they are in this state of grievously injuring themselves, so long are they in constant mortal sin, and unworthy of absolution.

" Do they sin, who shorten their days through austerities?

" *Ans.* It is a rare thing that days are shortened by moderate austerity of life, but life is rather prolonged. Be-

sides, although certain austerities might abbreviate life somewhat, yet if they are moderate they are lawful : because the
subjection of the flesh, and the manifold spiritual advantage,
which immediately accrue from it, overcome this bad effect :
this, also, the common experience of the Saints proves.

" Yet immoderate austerities are unlawful as fatal to a
person.   Nor is there ever any need of them for primary
purposes.   But those are regarded as immoderate under
which nature cannot be sustained, or a person is rendered
unable properly to perform his duties : and so far are they
from producing the effect that by them the body is subjected
to the Spirit, that it is rather hindered from obeying the Spirit
on account of languor.

" It is to be observed, 1st. from the Saints, Philip Nerius,
and Francis Sales, that they are to be more highly esteemed,
who, mortifying the flesh with the moderation of reason, are
wholly devoted to correcting the understanding, and subject-
ing and conforming their own will to the divine, than they,
who neglecting the care of the mind wish to afflict the body
alone.

" 2d.   That in undergoing austerities, every one depends
upon the suggestion and direction of his own confessor, notwithstanding any private imagination and will.

" It was said at the commencement of this number, *unless
a sufficient reason for so doing is afforded ;* and hence a
pastor administering the Sacraments to persons infected with
the plague with the risk of contagion, the soldier continuing
in his station at the peril of his life for the common good,
&c., are not to be blamed, but very greatly commended.

" For a similar reason, the soldier does not sin, who first
ascends the wall, and sets fire to a train of powder in order
to overthrow a tower, although he sees that he will certainly
be killed in consequence.

" He also appears probably excusable, who being placed
on an enemy's ship sets fire to a train of powder in order
that the ship and the enemy may perish, even with his own
certain destruction, if the liberty of his country may accrue
from it ; the case is otherwise, if it would not ensue, for this
reason, for instance, that many other ships of the enemy
might still remain.

" Yet that soldier would be culpable, who should do the

same remaining in his own ship, in order that he himself with the ship may not come into the power of the enemy, &c.

"May or ought a person about to be condemned, or already condemned, flee from prison if he can do it without violence ?

"If he should be innocent, he would properly be bound to make his escape : unless the good of the state or of religion should otherwise advise : thus many martyrs, although they could escape, remained in prison.

"But if he is guilty, it is commonly taught, that such a one may flee, but yet that he is not obliged to escape : that he is not obliged to flee, is proved from this, that death would not ensue from his failing to escape, but from the crime which he has committed : yea, more, it is believed that a criminal may, of his own accord, give himself up to the judge, that he may make satisfaction to God and the republic.

"That he may escape, is proved from this, that flight is the means of preserving life : but he would too much repugn his natural inclination, if it were not lawful to avail himself of such means : and hence some believe that to this end, he may even break from jail and confinement.

"He is not considered a suicide who permits himself to be killed, because he cannot preserve his life, except by extraordinary means; for instance, by the most costly medicines, the severest pains, &c. : thus, also, a monk is not obliged to go out of the cloister, that he may get a change of air, for the sake of obtaining health.

"Whether a Carthusian is obliged, at the risk of life, to abstain from eating meats, see resolved, No. 46, concerning the Laws, &c."

I will here insert the chapter to which allusion is made in the last paragraph.

Concerning the obligation of the constitution of the Carthusians. (No. 46, Vol. II., p. 82.)

"Is the constitution of the Carthusians, by which all eating of meats is forbidden, under mortal sin, obligatory when life is in extreme danger ?

"*Ans.* If other articles of food are not at hand, they

eat meats lawfully; indeed they are obliged to eat them, lest they may perish of hunger: because their constitution cannot include this case, as it cannot oblige them to perish with hunger. The case would be the same, if there were no other except poisoned articles of food at hand; because these are not naturally adapted to sustain life.

" But if other articles of food may be supplied, it is not lawful for them to eat meats, even if in the judgment of physicians the eating of them would be necessary for the preservation of life. The reason is, because their constitutions, approved by the church, most strictly forbid the eating of meat: and the ancient custom of this order teaches that this prohibition holds good even in this case.

" Besides, this rigour is necessary for the preservation of the strength and honour of this institution, which would easily decline, if a dispensation should be granted even in a single instance, as the event has frequently shown in other religious orders, and also sometimes in this itself: which Vasquey records that he had himself heard from the strictest fathers of this order.

" *Obj.* A Carthusian who has no food except meats, is obliged to feed on meats, as was said above: but when he cannot preserve life without meats, it is the same to him as if he could have no other food: therefore, he then lawfully eats meat.

" *Ans.* I deny the minor: for although other articles of food might be thought not advantageous, yet certainly they are sufficient in themselves, and serve to sustain life: and hence, although the sick man may perhaps die from the disease, yet he cannot be said to die of hunger: and therefore it is not the same as if no food was at hand: therefore, the eating of meats in this case can only be regarded as medicine; but just as a sick man is not obliged to procure the most costly medicines, although others may seem of no advantage, so neither is the Carthusian obliged to eat meats, which would be very injurious to his order, by relaxing discipline, &c."

To most of the preceding chapters, I have thought it advisable to subjoin short refutations of the erroneous and unscriptural principles, which are inculcated in the theology of the Romish Church; but it will not be necessary to offer one word of comment, when the poison is so rank, that no sane man would touch it, and my readers will therefore understand why it is that in subsequent chapters, I shall often refrain entirely from commenting upon the text, which Peter Dens offers. Whenever there is anything so specious that an honest man might be deceived, I shall feel it my duty, for the sake of those who may not always be prepared to separate the precious from the vile, to furnish suggestions, which will perhaps not be altogether unprofitable.

Not a few of the subjects upon which we are about to enter are of a somewhat delicate nature, and in many instances I shall therefore be obliged to condense and give a mere outline, in order that details, offensive to modesty, may be avoided. I wish to present a fair and full exposition of the principles, which are inculcated in Romish Seminaries, in so far as I can accomplish it without defiling my pages with anything indecent or obscene; at the same time, however, I shall not suffer myself to be hampered by prudery, or false modesty; I shall spread before Protestants and Papists, so much of the *theology* (!) of Romish priests, that it will be an easy matter for an ordinary imagination to supply as much of the suppressed matter as a decent person would choose to know. But whilst endeavouring to present my reader with a correct idea of Peter Dens' theology, I shall not designedly pander to the depraved curiosity of any vicious mind.

23

CHAPTER XXVII.

OF HOMICIDE.   (No. 122.)

" WHAT is homicide ?

" *It is the voluntary and unjust killing of a person.*   It is forbidden both by natural and by positive and divine law, ' Thou shalt not kill.'

" Is the killing of irrational animals also forbidden by the command, ' Thou shalt not kill ?'

" No. For God, Gen. ix. 3., has expressly permitted this : ' Every thing that moveth and liveth shall be meat for you.'

" St. Thomas observes that by killing animals in a cruel manner a certain impropriety may be committed ; for animals have been left not for our cruelty but for our use. This cruelty Sacred Scripture also condemns ; Prov. xii. 10. ' The just regardeth the lives of his beasts ; but the bowels of the wicked are cruel.'

" Whether the eating of meats was permitted before the deluge, is disputed : Sylvius thinks that it was permitted, but THAT THE MORE RELIGIOUS ABSTAINED FROM IT.

" Explain the command, ' Thou shalt not kill.'

" By this command, not only homicide is forbidden, but also mutilation, wounding, whipping, &c., and whatever tends to the injury of a neighbour's person.

" Indirectly, gentleness, patience, peace, love, beneficence, &c., are enjoined, as the Roman catechism explains, part 3., concerning the fifth precept of the decalogue.

" Is every killing of a person, under all circumstances, forbidden by this precept ?

" No : but that which is committed by private authority, without either the command or permission of God : hence, in the definition of homicide, it was said that it is the unjust killing of a person.

" What killing of a person is not forbidden by this precept ?

" That which is done by divine authority : Thus, 1. Abraham did not sin, who, at the command of God, was willing to kill his own son Isaac, Gen. ch. xxii. ver. 10.

" 2. Nor does the state, which puts malefactors to death : as God has likewise given this power to the state for the common good, as will be proved in the following number.

" 3. Nor they who wage war justly by slaying the enemies : for Sacred Scripture, the fathers, and the practice of the most conscientious rulers abundantly prove that this power has been divinely given.   The conditions of a just war, see briefly in the Analogy of Becanus, ch. xviii., quest. 1."

" *Is it lawful to kill malefactors by public authority?*
(No. 122.)

" It is not only lawful, but it is also commanded by public authority and due process of law to put to death criminals who are hurtful to the state : such as robbers, incendiaries, sacrilegious persons, thieves, &c.   This was enacted in the Third Lateran Council against the Waldenses.

" It is proved from the divine permission granted, Exod. xxii. 18. ' Wizards thou shalt not suffer to live.' And Rom. xiii. 4. ' If thou do that which is evil, fear : for he beareth not the sword in vain, for he is the minister of God, an avenger to execute wrath upon him that doeth evil.'

" Add to this also natural reason, which dictates that a limb must be amputated, when by it the destruction of the whole body is threatened : but from these pernicious malefactors there is danger of the corruption and disturbance of the state ; therefore, &c.

" May the state at its option put to death any malefactors whatever ?

" No : but only such as are very injurious to the state : and hence, in this case, the grievousness or malice of the sin, in itself considered, is not to be regarded, but the injury which it occasions to the republic.

" Hence the military laws are just, which decree the penalty of death for faults in themselves slight, for trifling disobedience, neglecting trust, petty theft, &c. ; because from faults of this kind, although they are in themselves trifling, be most grievous evils might arise to the state, unless they were most strictly forbidden.

" Is it lawful to put a man to death for mere theft?

" Yes: when this is seriously pernicious to the state: and this the practice of tribunals approves.

" Nor is it any matter that the punishment seems disproportioned to the offence, when any one is deprived of life on account of the loss of temporal property; for from what has been said before, it may be observed that the punishment is not inflicted for the theft of another man's property, in itself considered, but for the sake of the injury which is inflicted on the peace and tranquillity of the state.

" *Obj.* St. Thomas says, &c.: ' For a theft which does not inflict an irreparable loss, the penalty of death is not inflicted according to present judgment, except the theft is aggravated by some important circumstance.'

" *Ans.* St. Thomas only says that in his time, according to the old imperial laws, mere thefts were not punished with death.

" Many authors accuse Scotus in 4 dest. 15, quest. 3, as though he had taught that it is not lawful to put thieves to death, nor any others than those expressed in the old law. But Herinx, Henno, and other Scotists, endeavour to offer an explanation for him, and reply to the passage quoted as we reply to St. Thomas.

" Is it lawful, by public authority, to put to death an innocent person?

" *Ans.* In no case is it directly lawful to put to death an innocent person, unless God has expressly commanded it. Hence, on account of the expressed command of God alone are the Israelites excused for killing all whom they found in the city of Jericho, from the infant to the old man, Jos. vi. 21. Thus also David is excused when, 2 Kings xxi. 9, (2 Sam.,) he gave up the seven sons of Saul, that they might be crucified by the Gibeonites for the sins of Saul when deceased. A similar command also God gave to Saul with respect to the Amalekites, 1 Kings xv. 3, (1 Sam.)

" Is it not certainly lawful for a state indirectly to put innocent persons to death?

" It is lawful for the state for a just cause to do or omit any thing from which the death of an innocent person follows not intending it, which is as it were indirectly to put to death. Thus, a commander justly besieging a city lawfully explodes and overthrows a tower in which are innocent persons, if otherwise he cannot storm the city : because that general avails himself of his right ; and thus an effect cannot be imputed to him which has followed beyond his intention.

" In the same way, if a king besieging a city threatens totally to overthrow it, unless some innocent person be sent to him, the authors commonly resolve that the state may send the innocent man himself, and even deliver him to the king, not with the intention that he may be killed by him, but with the intention that the country may be freed. In this way, St. Thomas excuses Simon, who sent the two sons of Jonathan to Tripho, 1 Mach. ch. xiii.

" In this case, indeed, that innocent person seems obliged to expose his own life for the common good ; and, according to Daelman, he would become guilty of a grievous offence against the state, if he should refuse to go to the king, and as such he might be given up.

" The case would be different if that innocent person were in no way a subject of that place : because a stranger is not bound to undergo death for the sake of a foreign state ; yet the state might compel such a stranger lurking within her jurisdiction to depart with danger of death.

" *Obj. I.* From this mission the death of an innocent person follows, and the freedom of the state only from the changed will of the king ; therefore, &c.

" I answer, that from this mission the death of an innocent person does not follow immediately, but from the depraved will of the king : but when a bad effect follows only mediately, a good one should follow only mediately.

" *Obj. II.* It would not be lawful in any case to give up an innocent person to wild beasts, nor the sacred books to be profaned by a king ; therefore, &c.

" *Ans.* I deny the inference : as to the first, there is this difference : that wild beasts naturally are savage and devour ; and thus they who cast a person to wild beasts, put him directly to death ; but the king acts freely, and thus he himself, who does not send directly, puts to death.

" As for the second, there is this difference, that by the profanation of the sacred books, an injury is done to God himself, and to religion, which is much more serious than

23 *

any injury inflicted on the commonwealth; besides, the sacred manuscripts are of a higher order, and are not ordained for the preservation of the state, but for the salvation of souls; but the members of a community are ordained for the preservation of the community.

" Various examples of the Holy Martyrs add to the confirmation of this opinion, who chose rather to die than give up the sacred manuscripts into the hands of kings, as is to be seen in the Roman martyrology, on the second day of January, and on the eleventh of February.

" For the same reason it is thought that it is not lawful to send a virgin to a king to be defiled : because the chastity of a virgin is not so ordained for the preservation of the state as the life of an innocent subject. Besides, in the case of a virgin, there is the proximate danger lest she may consent to his lust ; and such danger there is not in case of putting to death an innocent person : so that, on this account, the state might maintain itself permissively in the case of the innocent person, rather than in the case of the virgin."

In the following sections, cases are proposed in which it is asked whether homicide may be lawfully committed. By private authority it is never lawful to put a man to death. Banditti, who are outlawed, and may therefore be killed by any one, are considered as being put to death by public authority. A husband is not at liberty to put a wife to death, when taken in the act of adultery. It is the more common opinion of the doctors that it is lawful to take lives in self-defence. The following proposition has been condemned by Alexander VII. " It is lawful to kill a false accuser, false witnesses, and even the judge by whom an unjust sentence is certainly threatened, if the innocent person can in no other way escape injury." But when the moderation of a blameless defence is preserved, homicide is lawful. The conditions are the following (No. 125).

" *First*, that the defence be not made in order to take revenge, but in order to repel injury. Against this condition he sins, who defends himself through anger, hatred, or revenge.

" *Second* : that the attacked person does not use greater defensive force than may be necessary to avert the threatened death ; hence, if the attacked person may escape by fleeing, crying out, thrusting aside the weapons of the assailant, wounding, &c., he defends himself unlawfully by the death of the assailant.

" *Third* : that real violence is offered ; otherwise it would not be defence but aggression ; and that the defendant repels the offered violence, by violence of a similar nature.

" Hence, you may not anticipate and kill him who threatens you with death only by menaces ; nor a robber who meets you, and attempts nothing against you by any action ; nor even him who, by deceit, treachery, or calumny, endeavours to inflict death upon you, say a false accuser, a false witness, &c. ; as is plain from the condemned proposition above quoted.

" But do not understand these remarks, as if the assailed person ought to wait until the assailant shall have given the first stroke ; but it is sufficient that he does something, by which he may be morally regarded as attacking ; for instance, if he already draws a sword, &c.

" *Fourth* : that the good effect of the defence may exceed or at least equal the bad effect : otherwise a just cause would be wanting. See this at large in De Cocq and Daelman.

" *Fifth* : that a bad effect do not immediately and directly ensue, and the good effect only mediately and indirectly : because this would be to do evil that good may result. Hence it is not lawful to throw an infant into a well, that it may be baptized.

" *Sixth* : that the death of the assailant be not intended, neither as end, nor as means, nor as the effect of defence : because, as it is unlawful by private authority to kill a person, it is also unlawful that an attacked person should intend to kill the assailant.

" These conditions being supplied, it is no sin, not even against charity, (as the common opinion teaches,) to defend one's own life by killing an unjust assailant : unless the person should perhaps be necessary, or very useful to the state, or some other circumstance should be in the way, which might dictate, that the life of the assailant should be preferred to the life of the assailed."

After adducing as proofs, a sentence from Augustine and the Roman Catechism, and Clement, the last authority quoted is St. Thomas, as follows.

" It is proved 4th, from the reasons of St. Thomas, q. 64, art. 7, of which the first is that according to justice it is lawful to repel force by force; second, because in itself considered, and other things being equal, a man is bound to provide more for his own life than for that of another : the third and principal reason, is, that the killing of an assailant in this case is not voluntary, because it is beyond intention ; for, as from such a defence one's own preservation immediately follows, as well as the death of the assailant, it is lawful thus to defend one's self by intending a good effect, and by permitting a bad effect.

" Here several justly remark, that these and similar things ought not to be preached to the people, lest it should too much extend the license ; these things are to be very rarely advised, because it is seldom that another means of escape is wanting."

The 128th section discusses the question, *whether it is lawful, in defence of chastity, to kill the assailant ?*

" The negative opinion, as it is in our day the more common, seems also more correct, and to be practically observed."

" It is proved, 1. Because chastity is taken either for a virtue of the mind ; and this cannot be taken from those who withhold their consent : and hence Saint Lucia said to the tyrant : ' If you command me to be violated against my will, my chastity will be doubled to a crown ;' or it is taken for the integrity of the body ; and this is of inferior value to the life of a man, and therefore cannot be preferred to the life of an assailant : therefore, a person defending chastity thus understood, by killing the assailant, would not preserve the moderation of blameless defence.

" It is proved 2, from St. Aug., Book I., concerning free will, chap. 5, where he says : ' I do not indeed find fault with the law, (it was the civil law, by which assailers of chastity were slain with impunity,) which permits such persons to be killed with impunity ; but on what condition I shall defend those who kill, I cannot discover.'

" Add to this, that among the Saints, whom the church worships, we read of none who made use of this defence, although doubtless, sometimes opportunity would have been afforded. Nor is this case also found excepted from the general law, ' *Thou shalt not kill.*'

"In the loss of chastity, there is danger of consenting to the lust of another, unless the assailant is slain ; therefore, he is lawfully killed.

*　　*　　*　　*　　*　　*

" *Ans.* Admitting also that the danger of consenting is very probable, it would not therefore be lawful thus to defend one's self : because it is not lawful to commit the certain sin of killing a person, in order that an uncertain one may be avoided. 'For who can be so foolish,' (says St. Augustine,) 'as to say, Let us sin now, lest perhaps, we may sin afterwards : let us commit homicide now, lest perchance we may afterwards fall into adultery.'

*　　*　　*　　*　　*　　*

" *Obj. IV.* S. Aug., book against lying, says that it is less wicked to lie in order to preserve chastity than to preserve life : but life may be defended by killing the assailant ; therefore chastity also.

" *Ans.* The text of St. Aug., in which our opponents wonderfully rejoice, treats evidently concerning chastity as it is a virtue of the mind.

" It is to be observed, that, although a person, whose chastity is invaded, may not kill the assailant, yet she is bound in every possible way to resist by fleeing, crying out, struggling with hands and feet, &c., &c.

" Concerning kisses and immodest embraces, &c., it must be said, that even afterwards, the person who has suffered violence, may defend herself, for instance, by giving the fugitive a box on the ear ; not indeed for revenge, but as an evidence of indignation ; that thus for the future the immodest aggressor may be deterred." (!!)

Concerning Duelling. (132.)

" What is a duel ?

" It is a contest between two or more by agreement, at an appointed time and place without public authority, undertaken with deliberate intention with the risk of killing.

" Hence, if two persons without any agreement, or without a determination of time and place, flying into a passion take up weapons and fight, it will not be properly called a duel.

" It is considered a duel properly so called, if two persons beginning to quarrel, v. g. in church, say mutually one to another, This is not a fit place to settle our disputes : let us go out of doors, or let us go into the next street ; and thus begin a fight.   Also, if they say, Let us fight with swords, in the first place which shall occur for battle more convenient than this : because in these instances, place, time, &c., are sufficiently determined.   Collet adds that it is a duel, if they resolve to fight with swords, whenever the one may meet the other alone.

" It is not a duel, if the battle is commenced without danger of killing : yet a moral danger is sufficient : such as, if the fight be commenced under this condition ; let us stand until the first effusion of blood.

" The weapons, also, with which they fight, should in these circumstances be morally deadly : such as a sword, knife, stones, heavy clubs, &c.   But if it be done with hands only, it is not thought that such a danger is incurred.

" How is duelling divided?

" Into *simple*, and *ceremonial ;* also, into *public*, and *secret*.

" A *ceremonial* one is that in which certain ceremonies are used ; as the designation of weapons, election of seconds, assumption of witnesses, &c.   A simple one is that which takes place without these ceremonies.

" By what law is duelling prohibited?

" By the natural, positive divine, and human law, as well civil as ecclesiastical.

" In what consists the wickedness of duelling?

" In this, that each of the duellists throws himself into the peril of eternal damnation, squanders his own life and that of another, and attempts to kill by private authority : the person challenging is besides guilty of gross scandal against the person challenged, the seconds and witnesses.

" Is duelling always unlawful?

" A duel commenced by private authority under any pretext whatever, or for the sake of displaying strength, or of defending honour, or reputation, is always unlawful : the reason is that for these causes, it is never lawful to kill. But when undertaken in order to settle some obscure question, or to ascertain justice, or truth ; it is, moreover, superstition, or tempting God.

" *Obj*. If a noble or military man does not accept a duel he will be regarded as infamous; therefore, &c.

" Be it so that he might be so considered, it would not therefore be lawful to engage in a duel; as according to No. 129, it is unlawful to kill an unjust assailant of reputation, or honour: but how utterly false it is too, that any thing truly disgraceful can be found in the refusal of a duel: and hence our rulers resolved on the 27th of Feb. A. D. 1610, to this effect, art. 4. 'Since most duels have their origin in a wrong opinion, as if they were hindered by unmanly fear, who do not avenge insults or revenge with their own hand: the rulers declare that this opinion is false; they take under their protection the honour of those who have suffered insults; and they forbid any one to upbraid under the arbitrary penalty of their indignation.' The same was renewed in the year 1660, Aug. 19, art. 5.

" St. Lewis, Henry IV., and Lewis XIV., decreed as to France, that they who fought in a duel should be regarded as guilty of an offence against divine and human majesty, and that their bodies should be cast to wild beasts.

" Hence, also, Alexander VII. justly condemned this proposition. 'A knight challenged to a duel may accept it, lest he should incur the mark of infamy amongst others.'

" May a duel entered upon by public authority be lawful?

" Yes; princes may certainly agree about a fixed time and place, in order that one or more, chosen on both sides, may fight in order to terminate a just war, the event of which is uncertain, in order that thus a multitude may be spared: nor is this properly called a duel, but a certain kind of just war in behalf of the state. An example is afforded in David meeting with Goliath.

" Is he who kills or mutilates another in a duel, obliged to make restitution?

" If the person killed or mutilated, has accepted the duel freely, induced by no force, fraud, or treachery, and could in a valid manner waive the right of restitution, the person who has killed or mutilated him, does not appear to be obliged to make restitution: because they are believed mutually to remit restitution to one another; it must be determined otherwise, if he has been induced by force or fraud, or has not been able to waive his right in a valid manner."

Concerning the punishments of Duellists. (133.)

" What are the punishments of duellists?

" They are various, as well ecclesiastical as civil, and those very severe.

" 1. *First :* by virtue of Council of Trent, sess. 25. concerning the Reformation, ch. 19., temporal lords are excommunicated, who grant room in their territories for a duel between Christians.

" They, also, are excommunicated, who have fought the battle, and their seconds : and these all incur the penalty of perpetual infamy, and the confiscation of all their property.

" They also are excommunicated, who have given counsel in the case of a duel as well in right as in fact ; also spectators, viz., such as are present by appointment and intentionally, &c. &c.

" The *second* penalty appointed by the Council of Trent is, that if they die in the very act of conflict, they must for ever be without ecclesiastical burial, even if (says the Mechlin Manual), before death, they have given signs of penitence ; indeed, even if they have been sacramentally absolved by the priest.

" Authors have commonly resolved, that he who, having received a wound in the duel, does not die immediately, should not be deprived of ecclesiastical burial ; because such a one cannot be said to have died in the very conflict ; but Benedict, XIV., in his Bull, DETESTABILEM, of the year 1752, decreed, 1. that every one, whatsoever, dying from a wound received in a duel, whether he died on the battle-ground or elsewhere, is to be deprived of ecclesiastical burial ; and he takes away from the Bishops the power of dispensing upon this penalty. Yet if the duel is secret, they should not be deprived of ecclesiastical burial : because secret crimes ought not to be punished by a public penalty. In a doubtful case, recourse must be had to the ordinary.

" The *third* penalty is that by which a person killing a man in a duel, incurs an irregularity reserved to the Supreme Pontiff.

"According to the edict of the Archduke Albert and Duchess Isabella, of the year 1610, renewed Oct. 26, 1626, duellists are punished with death, as well those who accept, as those who give a challenge, also with the confiscation of their property.

"Art. 2. Challengers are declared infamous, are deprived of all rank, honour, and pension, and the half of their property is forfeited.

"Finally, they who carry messages or letters containing a challenge, or who have assisted duellists in any manner whatsoever, or have accompanied them, are punished with death and the confiscation of their property.

"In what way shall a common confessor treat a duellist, who from a wound inflicted on him is in the article of death, and begs to be absolved?

"As regards reservation or excommunication, nothing hinders from absolving him; because, in the article of death, there is no reservation; but he is to be induced as effectually as possible to lay aside all rancour of mind, and the spirit of revenge; looking at the example of Christ: besides when time permits the delay, it should be imposed on him that he take care, or even an oath that if he recovers he will abide by the commands of the church, and absolutely make amends for all losses inflicted on the injured party, if he owes any.

"But generally the confessor ought to inquire of the penitent confessing a duel: 1st, whether he was the challenged party or the challenger: 2d, what is the quality of each person: 3d, whether he had cherished hatred, and for what time: 4th, whether he has killed the other in the duel, &c.

"It is to be observed, that soldiers, noble officers, &c., who in the preparation of mind are always ready to engage in a duel, whenever it is offered them, can not be absolved; yet if they seem disposed, they are not to be interrogated in particular, whether they might have done the same when an occasion offered, but they are rather to be severely rebuked, by placing before their eyes the enormity of the sin, and the danger of ruining body and soul, to which they have exposed themselves; and they are to be strongly warned not to dare attempt it in future."

24

The following sections are offered to the reader as a specimen of the puerile and filthy casuistry, which constitutes so large a portion of the *divinity*, which Roman doctors teach, *and which Roman priests are taught.*

Concerning Abortion. (134.)

*   *   *   *   *   *

"That the fœtus is alive long before birth is certain from daily experience; as many who have been cut out of the womb of the mother have survived a long time : and hence, Innocent XI. justly condemned this 35th proposition : 'It seems probable that every fœtus, so long as it is in the womb, is without a rational soul ; and that it then first begins to have it, when it is born; and consequently it must be said, that in no abortion is homicide committed.'

"As regards the incurring of punishments, in order that some thing certain in practice may be afforded, authors commonly suppose that they are incurred by procuring abortion after the fortieth day of the conception, if it is a male, and after the eightieth day if it is a female ; and when it is doubtful whether it is a male or female, it is presumed in the court of conscience to be a male ; that this was the practice of the Holy Penitentiary, Narsarrus attests, who had long and much experience in it. (De Hom. leg. 5. cons. 46.)

"Is it sometimes lawful to procure abortion ?

"It is a most grievous sin, directly and intentionally to procure abortion, whether the fœtus is alive or not.

*   *   *   *   *   *   *   *

"Hence, Innocent XI. justly condemned this proposition, (No. 34.) 'It is lawful to procure abortion before the quickening of the fœtus, lest a girl found pregnant may be put to death, or rendered infamous.'

"Is the procuring of abortion properly called homicide?

"*Ans.* If the fœtus is alive, it is undoubtedly homicide, properly so called, and indeed so much the more severe, because it is destined in addition eternally to destroy the soul of the infant. Therefore, the person procuring such an abortion becomes obnoxious to irregularity, and the other penalties of homicide."

" If the fœtus is not alive, (which is always uncertain,) it is not homicide, properly so called, but only by way of inference, in so far as Tertullian says in apolog. ch. 3, ' to hinder from being born, is an anticipation of homicide.' Hence, the person procuring such an abortion, would indeed commit a sin similar in wickedness to homicide, yet he would not incur the penalties of homicide.

" Is it not lawful to cause abortion, at least indirectly ?

" Ordinarily, he sins grievously, who does that from which he may and ought foresee that abortion will follow, although he may not formally intend it," &c. A mother is not at liberty to take medicine to procure abortion, even if the death of the child as well as of herself appears certain unless the remedy is applied.

" But what if, unless a medicine be taken, the mother will certainly die, together with the fœtus, and without baptism ?

" In this speculative case, Steyaert thinks that it is not unjust, if she be saved who can be, and he be left to perish, who would have perished at all events.

" But practically, it must be said with Daelman, that this supposition can scarcely ever be true : for it will not be clear, whether even if the mother were dead, the fœtus could not be cut out alive : nor can it certainly be known, whether the mother might not have survived without such a remedy, as in similar cases the most expert physicians may often be deceived. Besides, if this supposition were once practically admitted, a risk and a certainty would be supposed, which do not in reality exist, and thus frequently a pretext might be given for expelling the fœtus.

" Authors agree, however, that if the danger to the fœtus is equal, whether the remedy be taken or not, then it is proper for the mother to take it : because, from this, greater danger is not brought upon the fœtus, and care is taken for the life of the mother.

" If it can be ascertained that the fœtus is not alive, and the mother will die unless she take the remedy, then it is admitted that the mother may use a medicine which is directly curative of the mother, and in itself does not tend to abortion, although there may be danger that abortion may follow from .t, provided that the mother cannot be saved by another remedy : because then abortion would be only permitted, not procured.   Yet if danger of death does not threaten the mother from the natural disease, but from another source, as for instance, because it is foreseen that she must be killed, or that she will die in labour, then she may not by any means use such a remedy.

" More about abortions, and the mode of preventing, especially voluntary ones, may be seen in the celebrated Cangiamila, in his SACRED EMBRYOLOGY." (!!)

Concerning the punishments of those who procure abortion. (135.)

" It is to be premised, that to procure abortion, is, by design and intention, to effect by one's self, or by another, that the fœtus be prematurely expelled from the womb : and hence it is not called simply a procuring of abortion, if it is casual or only indirectly voluntary in the remote cause, to which the effect is joined by accident ; but it is requisite that abortion be intended, either as the means, or as the end, at least as much as it is from the nature of the action.

*   *   *   *   *   *

" What punishments do they incur, who procure abortion ?

" Those who cause abortion only indirectly, by not formally intending it, do not seem to incur the penalties appointed for those who procure abortion, because to *procure*, as was said above, means studiously and intentionally to effect that the fœtus be prematurely expelled.

" Sixtus V., in the Bull EFFRENATAM, Oct. 29, 1588, decrees that all who procure the abortion of a *fœtus*, whether living or dead, this effect having followed, also those who drink potions to produce sterility, or who have afforded any hindrance to the conception of the fœtus, or in any way have given advice or aid to them, incur all the penalties, provided in every law against voluntary homicides ; and besides, subjects the same, from the very fact, to irregularity and excommunication, reserved to the Supreme Pontiff, excepting the article of death : he also deprives them of offices and benefices, and disqualifies them from holding them ever afterwards.

" This Bull of Sixtus V., Gregory XIV. modified, in the Bull, SEDES APOSTOLICA, given May 31, 1591, and restricted the said penalties of irregularity, excommunication, and the others passed by Sixtus, to those only, who procure the abortion of a living fœtus, or in any way whatever have given assistance or advice to them : besides, he declares that the bishop, and any confessor whatsoever, deputed by the bishop for this special case, may absolve from this case and the annexed censure, &c.

" Authors remark, that as in the Bull of Sixtus V., it is said, *the effect having followed*, he does not incur said penalties, who has endeavoured to procure abortion, or to induce to abortion, if that effect has not followed.

" The civil laws appoint for abortion before the quickening of the fœtus, the punishment of exile for the woman, after quickening, the punishment of death, &c.

" What things are to be observed relative to the confession and absolution of one who has procured abortion ?

" *Ans.* 1st. The quality of the person is to be asked, who has procured abortion in herself or in another.

" 2. The quality and number of the persons by whom the abortion has been procured : because perhaps they are implicated in the nefarious scandal.

" 3. For how long a time they have intended the abortion, because such crimes are not usually committed, except through a long course of time, during which very many crimes are performed, on account of different and intervening intentions of the same crime, on account of repeated attempts, &c.

" Concerning absolution, it must be ascertained, 1st. Whether excommunication has been incurred.

" 2. Whether proximate occasions of sins, which are almost connected with this sin, have been afforded, as incest, sacrilege, concubinage, &c. ; for those who procure abortion are generally obnoxious to these crimes.

" 3. Whether he has made satisfaction, or is at least prepared to make satisfaction for the losses which have followed by reason of the abortion : for instance, that an inheritance must on this account pass over to another family.

" Akin to abortion is the *overlaying of children*, (a reserved case in various dioceses,) which is a species of homicide or parricide by which some one suffocates children, or in any way kills them, either altogether voluntarily and directly, or casually and in consequence of smothering, as is usually done, v. g., when they place infants of a very ten-

24 *

der age with them in the same bed ; such persons cannot regularly be excused from mortal sin on account of the danger of smothering, &c. &c.

" Is it lawful to cut open a living mother, in order that offspring may be baptized, which would otherwise die without baptism ?

" If this operation cannot be done with a well-founded hope of preserving the mother alive, (which hope is sometimes believed to exist, as may be seen in Cangiamila above cited,) it is unlawful, whatever might be hoped concerning the preservation of the offspring ; for although the mother ought to expose her own life for the preservation of her child, her life may not for this reason be taken from her, nor should she therefore herself consent that it should be taken away.

" BUT IF A PREGNANT MOTHER DIES, THIS OPERATION NOT ONLY MAY, BUT OUGHT TO BE PERFORMED, AND INDEED BY THE PRIEST, IN THE ABSENCE OF A SURGEON AND OTHER SKILFUL PERSONS, IN ORDER THAT THE CHILD MAY BE BAPTIZED.

" Is it lawful to throw a boy into the river that he may be baptized, if he cannot otherwise be baptized ?

" No : because this throwing, as is supposed, is in itself destructive of the child, and the good effect, namely, the baptism of the child, follows only mediately from it, if the form and intention of baptism are doubtless present, whereas the bad effect, namely, the killing, follows immediately.

" Besides, it is disputed whether such baptism is valid ; which question, see No. 8, concerning the Sacrament of Baptism."

Concerning Whipping and Imprisonment. (137.)

" Is it lawful to whip any one ?

" *Ans.* St. Thomas, art. 2. in corp., replies, ' It is not lawful, except by way of punishment, on account of justice ; but no one justly punishes another, unless he is subject to his jurisdiction ; and therefore it is not lawful to whip any one, except for him who has some authority over him whom he whips.'

" Thus, for the sake of reproof and discipline, a father can lawfully whip a child ; the same is the case with a master and a tutor, and with others who sustain the place of a father, or any one else having similar authority.

" Is it lawful for a husband to whip his wife?

" The Germans and the rougher sort of our own country gladly embrace and practise the affirmative. AS FOR MODE-RATE WHIPPING IT MAY BE PERMITTED, IF THE WIFE IS MUCH IN FAULT, AND THERE IS NO HOPE THAT SHE MAY BE CORRECTED IN ANY OTHER WAY : but this case is very rare ; and hence the French and the more polished of our own country regard it as barbarous to whip a wife ; but the remark of a letter among the works of St. Bernard pleases them better ; ' You will chastise a bad wife with ridicule more effectually than with a stick ;' the reason is, because the wife is not the slave of the man, but his companion, and one flesh with him.

" Is it lawful to imprison any one?

" St. Thomas, art. 3. in corp., replies : 'To imprison, or in any way whatever detain any one is unlawful, unless it be done according to the order of justice, or as a punishment, or as a caution for avoiding some harm.'

"Although parents may not justly imprison children, they may yet, for a time, shut them up at home, for the sake of discipline," &c.

Concerning the Confessor of a Homicide. (141.)

" How must the confessor treat a homicide in the tribunal of penance?

" *Ans. 1.* Let him ask him, for what cause or end the homicide has been committed ; whether on account of the just defence of life, by preserving the moderation of blameless defence, or by not preserving it, &c.

" 2. Whether he killed the person from sudden passion, or from inveterate hatred, at the same time questioning about the time during which this hatred has lasted, how often it has been renewed, &c.

" 3. Whether no blasphemies, reproaches, or curses have preceded ; also, whether he has perpetrated cruelty or pollution on the body of the slain person.

" 4. Whether it was directly voluntary ; in which event it is at the same time a reserved case.

" 5. What means he employed, whether he has killed by treachery and stratagem, by a quick or slow poison ; which chiefly takes place with female homicides : whether he has employed associates ; for he has besides committed just so many sins of scandal as he has employed associates.

" 6. The quality of the person slain is to be asked : v. g. if he is a near relation, allied by the same blood, it is parricide ; if a clergyman, it is sacrilege ; and it has the annexed greater excommunication reserved to the Supreme Pontiff.

" Finally, let the confessor inquire the injuries caused, &c., that he may enjoin due restitution.

" These things having been duly examined, let the confessor of the homicide set before him the grievousness of his crime : also, the penalties, both civil and ecclesiastical, to which he has made himself obnoxious, and induce him to conceive contrition worthy of such a crime, and having imposed a salutary penance (especially one, which may last long, &c.) HE MAY ABSOLVE HIM WHEN RIGHTLY DISPOSED, *if he has authority to absolve from this crime,*" &c.

The sections from 142–150, treat of seduction, fornication, and adultery, and the restitution which is due in the different aspects which such cases may present. I must be excused from translating them all in detail. The following are a few of the principles, which are inculcated.

Concerning restitution for seduction, if the virgin has freely consented. (143.)

" If the virgin and her parents freely give their consent, &c., the seducer is under no obligation to make restitution to them : because, on the supposition even that they cannot waive their right, they can certainly waive their right to restitution ; and this they are regarded as yielding by affording their consent.

" If the virgin consents, but the parents are unwilling, or ignorant ; then if the intercourse remains secret, the seducer is again under no obligation to make restitution.

" If it becomes known to the parents only, he is bound to make satisfaction for the sorrow he has unjustly occasioned them by ASKING PARDON, by the EXHIBITION OF RESPECT, &c.

" But if it is widely divulged, he is besides obliged to bear and put a stop to the infamy in the best way he can.

" Observe, parents are to be regarded as unwilling, not only when they positively resist, but also when they are ignorant of the fact, unless, indeed, they knowingly neglect the proximate danger of the seduction being effected ; for instance, when they permit their daughter to engage in familiar conversation with an immodest young man.

" In case that the parents do not consent, is the seducer bound to an increase of the dowry, which the parents are now obliged to make greater, in order that their daughter may contract a suitable marriage?

" Authors are divided : those who maintain the affirmative, say that, not only has the daughter a right to contract a suitable marriage, but the parents also : those who maintain the negative, say that parents have no such right, except dependently upon the right and will of the daughter, who, if she chooses, may, without injury to her parents, remain unmarried, or unite herself with one, who is her inferior in rank.

" Practically on account of the probability of both opinions, the seducer appears obliged to some augmentation of the dowry, according to the arbitration of a prudent man ; especially if he is rich, and she is poorer ; and this certainly by the law of charity, if the seduced, on account of the loss of her virginity, and the want of dowry, is in danger of prostituting herself : for as the seducer is also to blame, he is bound to guard against these evils : and this confessors should observe, as Wiggers admonishes ; otherwise seducers may not readily be absolved, say De Cocq and Braunman."

What restitution is he obliged to make, who has seduced by force or fraud ? (144.)

* * * * * *

" He is bound to repair all losses and evils that have followed ; as he is the true and unjust cause of them all.

" He is under obligation to repair the personal injury, &c. if the virgin requires it, &c.

" 3. He is obliged to make honorary satisfaction, both to the parents and the virgin, by asking pardon, &c.

"4. If the injuries cannot be repaired except by marrying the seduced, the corrupter is bound to marry her even before the sentence of the judge : but if she refuses marriage, the seducer is under obligation to compensate all injuries in so far as it can be done.

"5. If the seduced marries another, who treats her badly, dismisses her, &c., on account of her lost virginity, the seducer is again bound to compensate those losses and evils according to the judgment of a prudent man.

"Precisely, the same things are to be said of him, who, indeed, does not seduce a virgin, but has done such things from which she is believed to be seduced ; even if the girl was not a virgin, but was only considered such before," &c., &c.

If the seduction has been effected through a real promise of marriage, or through feigned marriage, he is obliged promptly to fulfil his engagement, and is forbidden to enter any religious order, which would require celibacy, unless the injured party is willing.

The case is different, 1. If the seduced commits sin against chastity with another. 2. If she has pretended to be a virgin, or noble, &c. 3. If the promise of marriage was made in such a way that she might know it was only feigned ; for instance, from threats, exaggerations, inconstancy, ambiguity of language, or great disparity of rank : because in such circumstances, the girl is regarded not as being deceived, but as having deceived herself. 4. If the girl will not marry him, or her parents are unwilling to give her up to the seducer. 5. If greater evils may prudently be apprehended from the marriage, as serious quarrels between families, disinheritings, grievous scandal, &c. 6. If a hindrance from which no dispensation can be obtained supervenes ; as, if the seducer has contracted with another, has solemnly made profession, &c. The seducer is bound to remove every impediment which is morally removable. In all these cases, the seducer is not only obliged to marry the girl, but in the first three, he is ordinarily not obliged to repair the injury done to her, " nor as it seems in the fourth," &c.

Concerning the Confessor of a Seducer or Fornicator.
(No. 147.)

The confessor is directed to inquire, after hearing of the illicit intercourse:

" 1. Whether offspring has followed or will follow; if it be said that it neither has followed nor will follow, then let it be prudently and circumspectly asked, whence he knows it; in order that if perchance abortion has been procured, the penitent may tell it; and if it has not been procured, that he may not learn to do it.

" But if it be ascertained that offspring has followed or will follow; let the penitent be instructed concerning the obligation of maintaining it when it has followed; but concerning that which is likely to follow, he must be prudently and strongly admonished, to take care that no injury may happen to the fœtus, but that it may be brought safe to light, and that provision may be seasonably made for its baptism. He is also to be admonished that the child, when born, be not exposed or otherwise neglected; also that it be legitimated, if it can be done, and greater evils are not in the way.

" 2. Let the confessor inquire whether he has induced the woman by force, or fraud, or importunities equivalent to force; whether under promise of marriage: let him also show the obligations with regard to the seduced, as it has been explained in preceding numbers.

" Let the confessor also reflect that it often happens that offspring does not ensue, because conception is hindered by the sin of Onan, &c.

" Concerning dissolute young men, it is also to be considered whether they do not belong to those abandoned characters, who, when they have secretly seduced a girl, openly boast of the fact among their associates, and thus deprive the deceived of all honour and reputation by their nefarious detraction.

" Likewise concerning immodest women, it should be observed that they sometimes abuse young men of a tender age, and often ignorant, for purposes of lust, by force, deceit, or fraud; and these, without doubt, are guilty of seduction, the most grievous scandal, &c.

"3. Generally, in all sins of licentiousness, the circumstances are to be asked both of the person confessing, and of the person with whom, or about whom the sin has been committed; whether she is single, married, bound by a vow, a relative, &c.

"4. As for external sins of licentiousness between two persons, the confessor ought to ask, whether those persons live together in the same house: because when once the sense of shame is taken away, such dwelling together is most dangerous; and therefore, ordinarily, they should, without dissimulation, be separated. Farther, it should then be asked, how long they have thus lived together, what sacraments they have frequented, &c.; as is taught more at large in the Treatise concerning Penance."

The chapters which treat of the injury and restitution due in case of adultery, and the manner of making such restitution, I decline translating.

The Treatise concerning Contracts, which constitutes the remainder of the 3d volume, contains nothing of special interest to the general reader.

CHAPTER XXVIII.

Vol. IV. commences with a Treatise on the Virtue of Religion.

"Religion is defined as a *virtue exhibiting the worship due to God, as the first principle of all things.* It is also rightly defined by others, *a virtue inclining the will to pay the worship of latria due to God.* Religion is a supernatural virtue connected with charity," &c.

At the close of No. 3. the following question is asked.

"How can all the worship of religion be said to be due to God, when there are works of supererogation, by which God is worshipped; suppose the vow of chastity?

"I answer with Wiggers, that all our works are rightly

said to be due to God; because we are in every way the servants of God; yet as God does not exact all these works, as to the exercise of the act, as though due by a special precept, in this sense, some are called works of supererogation; for there are no works of pure liberality in man with respect to God. Besides, this worship is said to be due to God, because it is due, or can be paid to no other."

No. 12 treats of the necessity of prayer to salvation.

No. 13. *Of the precept of prayer.*

" Is there a command to pray?

" St. Thomas teaches the affirmative answer, q. 83. art. 2., &c., saying,—' To ask (or pray) falls under a precept of religion, which precept is plainly enjoined,' John xvi. 24, where it is said, *Ask and ye shall receive.* The catechism of the Council of Trent teaches the same. But this precept is divine and natural.

" When is the precept of praying obligatory?

" *Ans.* Wiggers, Sylvius, Layman, and other scholastics enumerate many occasions in which the precept of prayer is obligatory, either in itself or by some circumstance according to the ordinary laws of God; namely,

" 1. About the beginning of the use of reason. Thus Wiggers, Boudart, &c., teach.

" 2. In danger of death. Sylv., Boud., Laym., Bec.

" 3. In grievous temptation. Wigg., Boud., Van Roy.

" 4. When it is necessary to begin some arduous work. Sylv.

" 5. When the sinner is obliged to prepare himself for a state of grace; or when some sacrament is to be received or administered. Wigg.

" 6. In any necessity of the church, state, or community. Wigg., Laym.

" 7. Also in our own necessity or danger, or in that of our neighbour, especially in spiritual, according to the rule by which charity obliges; when, indeed, prayer will appear to be a very convenient means of obviating the necessity. Less., Laym., and St. Thom., &c.

" 8. That the precept of prayer is obligatory on festival days, St. Thomas indicates in the passage already cited, saying: ' The appointed time of prayer seems determined by the church for all people; as by the statute of the canons

25

they are obliged on festival days to be present in the divine services, especially in the sacrifice of the mass, that they may conform their intention to the ministers praying for the people. * * * * * *

" It ought to be observed that not every defect of prayer induces mortal sin, &c."

From No. 16 to No. 24, the Lord's prayer is explained and discussed.

No. 25. *Concerning the angelic salutation.*

" Hail Mary, full of grace, &c.

" The pious devotion of the faithful from the most ancient custom of the church in its infancy, observes, that after the Lord's prayer, the angelic salutation be recited, that through the intercession of the Blessed Virgin Mary, we may obtain what we ask from God : for she, next to Christ, is our hope.

" The angelic salutation consists of three parts : the first part contains the salutation of the archangel Gabriel ; the second, the words of St. Elizabeth to Mary, spoken by the inspiration of the Holy Spirit ; the third part contains the prayer of the church, invoking the patronage of the Virgin Mother of God : but this part is believed to have been added in the 5th cent., against the heresy of Nestorius, who denied that Mary was to be called Deipara, or the Mother of God.

" Marchantius, in the Hortus Pastorum, book 2, de Spe., Tract. 4, furnishes a more ample explanation of the angelic salutation, for the use of preachers."

No. 26. *Concerning the Rosary.*

" From the Lord's prayer and the angelic salutation, is framed the celebrated form of prayer, approved by the church, which is called the Rosary, containing fifteen decades of angelic salutations, fifteen Lord's prayers intervening, in which are called to mind the principal mysteries of the life, death, and resurrection of our Lord Jesus Christ.

" In this Rosary, the fifteen mysteries are disposed in this order : that first, the five joyful mysteries may be remembered, viz : 1. The annunciation of the Blessed Vir. Mary; 2, the visitation ; 3, the nativity of Christ ; 4, Jesus pre-

sented in the temple at the feast of the purification of the B.
M. V., (i. e., the Blessed Virgin Mary,); 5, Jesus found in
the temple.

" Five dolorous mysteries follow : 1. The sorrow of Christ
in the garden ; 2, his scourging ; 3, his crowning with
thorns ; 4, the bearing of the cross ; 5, the crucifixion.

" Five glorious mysteries are added : 1. The resurrection
of the Lord ; 2, his ascension ; 3, the advent of the Holy
Spirit ; 4, the ASSUMPTION of B. M. V. ; 5, the CORONATION
of the Blessed Virgin Mary, in heaven.

" It is proper, in catechisms and sermons, to teach the
faithful these mysteries of the Rosary, because they contain
an idea of the life of Christ.

" The practice of reciting the Rosary, is that the person
praying in the recitation of each decade represents to himself one of these mysteries, and bows his head at the names
of Mary and Jesus, and salutes the same as though represented and formerly constituted in such mystery."

No. 27. *Concerning Litanies.*

" St. Gregory encouraged the use of the litanies of all
saints : which form of praying had been practised in the
church long before him, &c.

" The litanies of the B. M. V. of Loretto, were approved
in subsequent periods, by the custom of the church, and the
authority of the Popes, in which the B. Virgin Mary is called
by various peculiar and metaphorical names, in order that
prayer to her at any time may be protracted without weari-
ness.

" Observe, that these two litanies alone have been approved by the church as public prayers : and hence these
two only may be publicly sung in the divine service, according to the decree of Clement VIII., and the declaration of the
S. Congreg. Rit. in Alexand., May 15, 1608.

" Yet in this general prohibition, the litanies approved by
the Apostolic See do not seem to be included, such as it is
commonly affirmed the litanies of the holy name of Jesus
are, from the circumstance that Sixtus V. Const. *Reddituri*
has conceded 300 days of indulgence to those who recite
them, as Luc. Ferrarje remarks after others in, &c., &c.

"It would appear that litanies, which are everywhere found in prayer-books, approved by the censor, may be recited by private persons."*

---

* The following is the litany of the Blessed Virgin, as furnished on p. 128 of the Catholic Companion, published with the approbation of the Right Rev. Dr. Kenrick.

THE LITANY OF THE BLESSED VIRGIN.

ANTHEM.

We fly to thy patronage, O holy mother of God! despise not our petitions in our necessities, but deliver us from all dangers, O ever glorious and blessed Virgin!

Lord have mercy on us,
Christ have mercy on us,
Lord have mercy on us,
Christ hear us,
Christ graciously hear us,
God the Father of Heaven, have mercy on us,
God the Son, Redeemer of the world, have mercy on us,
God the Holy Ghost, have mercy on us,
Holy Trinity, one God, have mercy on us.

Holy Mary,
Holy Mother of God,
Holy Virgin of Virgins,
Mother of Christ,
Mother of divine grace,
Mother most pure,
Mother most chaste,
Mother undefiled,
Mother unviolated,
Mother most amiable,
Mother most admirable,
Mother of our Creator,
Mother of our Redeemer,
Virgin most prudent,
Virgin most venerable,
Virgin most renowned,
Virgin most powerful,
Virgin most merciful,
Virgin most faithful,
Mirror of justice,
Seat of wisdom,
Cause of our joy,
Spiritual vessel,
Vessel of honour,
Vessel of singular devotion,
Mystical rose,
Tower of David,

Pray for us.

No. 28. *Concerning canonical hours.*

" What are canonical hours ?

" *Ans.* They are vocal prayers, ordained and prescribed by the church, to be spoken or sung daily, at certain hours.

" They are called *prayers,* in a wide sense, because the greater part consists of prayers : they are called *hours,* because they are to be recited at certain hours of the day : also, *canonical,* because most have been prescribed by canons : they are called also, *divine* or *ecclesiastical service,* because they have been instituted for the worship of God, and are performed in the name of the church.

" This service is composed of psalms, lessons, hymns, &c., in pleasant variety ; all which are ordained for the worship of God ; thus, therefore, the recitation of the hours is an act of the virtue of religion ; but it contains various acts of religion, prayers, the praises of God, returning of thanks, &c., as also various acts of other virtues, faith, hope, charity, obedience, penitence, *dulia,* (i. e., worship of saints, &c.), &c.

" How many canonical hours are there ?

" Seven are commonly enumerated, conformably to that saying of David, Ps. 118, 164. ' Seven times a day, I have given praise to thee ;' the names of which are derived from the hours in which they are usually recited, namely, the matin with praises, first, third, sixth, ninth, vespers and the

Tower of ivory,
House of gold,
Ark of the covenant,
Gate of heaven,
Morning star,
Health of the weak,
Refuge of sinners,
Comforter of the afflicted,
Help of Christians,
Queen of Angels,
Queen of Patriarchs,
Queen of Prophets,
Queen of Apostles,
Queen of Martyrs,
Queen of Confessors,
Queen of Virgins,
Queen of All Saints, &c., &c.
} Pray for us.

25*

completorium.   But they are adapted to the mysteries of the
passion of Christ, according to these verses :

Matutina ligat Christum, qui crimina solvit :
Prima replet sputis, causam dat Tertia mortis ;
Sexta cruci nectit ; latus egus nona bipertit ;
Vespera deponit ; tumulo Completa reponit.

The matin binds Christ, who absolves from sins.
The first covers him with spittle ; the third gives the cause of his
death.
The sixth binds him to the cross ; the ninth pierces his side.
The vesper takes him down ; the completa lays him in the tomb.

" That certain hours of prayers were observed from the
time of the Apostles, the Sacred Writings show, Acts iii. 1.
' Now Peter and John went up to the temple, at the ninth
hour of prayer ;' and x. 9. ' And on the next day Peter
went up to the higher parts of the house to pray about the
sixth hour.' "

From the 29th No. we learn that they who are initiated
in Sacred Orders are obliged to recite the Canonical hours.

" The Clergy of the first Tonsure, or of the lower orders
are in our day not under obligation : but whoever contends
with Huygens that they were formerly bound by this obligation, ought certainly to admit that it has ceased through contrary custom, so that they are not even obliged to recite the
office of the B. M. V. nor the penitential psalms, if we regard positive, ecclesiastical law."

Concerning the obligation of Religious orders to observe the Canonical hours. (30.)

" The Religious of both sexes, who have by profession
attached themselves to the choir are obliged to observe the
Canonical hours, so that if they have been absent from the
choir, they are bound to recite them privately.   This obligation is founded more upon the generally received custom of
the church than on the decrees of Canons.   Neither the
Novitii, nor the Conversi, nor Brethren, as they are called,
are under this obligation ; nor the Religious of the Society
of Jesus (Jesuits), nor the Hospitalarii, nor the Militares, &c.
because they have never by profession attached themselves
to a choir.

The obligation whenever incurred " begins from the time of making the profession, or joining the order, so that if any one should be ordained or make profession about noon, he is obliged after assuming the order, or publishing his profession, to begin on that day, from the ninth of the hours, or at least from the vespers ; because that is the ordinary time of reciting the aforesaid hours : he is not obliged to read the matin, which is accustomed to be recited early ; because the obligation which now begins is not retrospective to past time.

" What if some one, who has been ordained, or has professed about noon, had already before recited the ninth and vespers ?

" He seems bound to repeat those hours ; because he has not satisfied the precept ; as he has not recited in the name of the church, inasmuch as he was not as yet assumed or deputed by the church," &c.

Those who hold a benefice sufficient for the decent support of a clergyman of common condition are obliged daily to recite the Canonical hours. (No. 31.)

If the benefice is unproductive, they are bound to recite them sometimes, but not daily. (No. 32.)

" But it is to be observed that the preceding conclusions are to be understood concerning a benefice, which constantly, and in itself produces no fruit at all, or but little : for he who has a benefice in itself productive, although he may for some years lose the returns through the devastation of wars, or of the seasons, or on account of particular statutes, by which he is compelled to fast for one or two years, as is said, he is not freed for that time from the recitation of the Canonical hours ; because this benefice is in itself productive : but the benefice, which is a perpetual right, and the obligation of the benefice, have nothing to do with the division of the proceeds of one or another year.

" Is he, who is absent for the purpose of study, or by dispensation, or for other reasons, on account of which he derives no returns from his benefice, delivered from the burden of reading the Canonical hours ?

" *Ans.* No : because the defect is not owing to the benefice ; indeed the beneficiate is not exonerated, although he should substitute in his place an alternate, who frequents the

choir and recites the hours, and bears the other burdens of
the benefice, &c.

"Hence, observe that the obligation of the beneficiate to
recite the Canonical hours is personal, and therefore requires
the beneficiate's own agency," &c. (No. 33.)

What a wretched perversion of the sacred privilege of
prayer is this! The very Priests are taught to regard their
devotions as a grievous task! Is it any wonder then that
the Scriptural adage "Like Priest, like people," should be
verified? These *holy* men speak of being "delivered from
the burden of reading the Canonical hours!!" Bless God,
Christian, that you have not received the Spirit of bondage,
but the Spirit of adoption, whereby you cry, Abba, Father!

No. 36. treats "Of Restitution for the omission of the
Canonical hours." The amount which the negligent beneficiate is obliged to pay has been determined by a Bull of
Leo X., A. D. 1514, which decree Pius V., A. D. 1571,
renewed and amplified; the substance of which is the following:

"We being desirous to provide more evidently and expressly for this thing, resolve, that he who has intermitted
the Canonical hours for one or more days, shall lose all the
proceeds of his benefice or benefices, which correspond to
that day, or to those days, if they should be daily divided;
but he who omits the matin only, shall lose the half; he
who omits all the other hours, the other half; he who omits
single ones of these, loses the sixth part of the proceeds of
the same day," &c., &c.

In No. 37, the following question is asked:

"Is a parish priest, who omits the Canonical hours on
one day, obliged to restore all the proceeds of that day according to the proportion above explained, if on the same
day, he has discharged many pastoral functions; when the
Priest receives the same proceeds also on account of pastoral duty?

"We answer that he is obliged to restore all the proceeds
according to the positive law of the constitution of Pius V.:
and it may be said that this law, by way of punishment, de-

prives the Priest also of the control of that part of the proceeds, which appertains to the pastoral service.

"Yet, by divine or natural law, he is not deprived of this part of the proceeds, and therefore if we regard natural right, not all the proceeds must be restored in the case laid down : because some are due to him on account of pastoral duty : and this division may take place in the first six months from the time of obtaining a parochial or otherwise onerous benefice.

"Hence, observe it would seem that this axiom—' Benefice is waived for the sake of duty,' should be understood not only concerning the office of the canonical hours, but concerning all other functions and burdens annexed to the benefice. Thus, Suarez and Billuart, &c., say that it is more plausible that a priest omitting an office may retain part of the proceeds for the pastoral duty which he has performed."

No. 39. A CASE IN POINT.

"A beneficiate throws away his breviary, that he may not read the canonical hours this week ; but being sorry for this deed, cannot get any other breviary : it is asked,

"Whether this inability of reciting the canonical hours excuses from the restitution of the proceeds ?

"*Ans.* It does not excuse : because this inability proceeds from open fraud ; but the fraud ought not to be excused in him.

"*Obj. I.* Fraud is not excused in him, but inability.

"*Ans.* As this inability proceeds from fraud, thus the excuse proceeds originally from fraud.

"*Obj. II.* The omission of the hours after penitence is involuntary in him ; therefore it excuses from restitution.

"*Ans.* The omission is involuntary in him in regard to the will then present, so that he does not sin more. I admit the omission is involuntary in regard to the will by which he occasioned it, but I deny the antecedent ; for that omission was voluntary and directly intended, in throwing away the breviary, which is sufficient to occasion the obligation of restitution ; just as unjust injuries, which have been voluntary in the cause, ought to be repaired."

ANOTHER CASE.

" A beneficiate, through drunkenness, or through a serious fault, has contracted a sickness by which he is rendered unable to recite the canonical hours ; it is asked, whether he may be excused from restitution of the proceeds ?

" *Ans.* Casuists solve this case by a distinction : if he has done it for the sake of fraud, or with the intention that he may not recite the hours, he is not excused from restitution, for reasons alleged in the former case. — La Croix, lib. 4, v. 1, 210.

" But if it happens without fraud they excuse him from restitution on the plea of impotence ; indeed, they adjudge to the same the daily distributions and residence. The reason assigned is, ' that sickness is from God, and the superiors ought not to make inquiry concerning him, but leave him to the judgment of God, lest affliction be added to the scourged ;" &c.

Concerning the Sin of the Omission of the Canonical Hours. (No. 40.)

" What kind of sin is it to omit the canonical hours, with respect to him who, by the precept of the Church, is bound to recite them ?

" *Ans.* It is a sin against the virtue of religion ; because the law enjoining the canonical hours has been introduced and passed formally for the purpose of religion : for the recitation of the canonical hours is commanded as an act of religion.

" Moreover, a rather probable opinion teaches, that the beneficiate sins in addition against commutative justice, and therefore that by omitting the canonical hours he sins with a twofold offence ; and hence, he is obliged to declare that condition of the benefice in confession, and is bound to make restitution, &c.

" What meaning, therefore, has this axiom : ' Benefice is waived for the sake of duty.'

" *Ans.* This meaning, that the right of receiving the proceeds is given as a just stipend of support for the recitation of the divine office, or the annexed spiritual functions. By no means does it suffer that meaning, that the proceeds of the benefice are given as the hire of spiritual duty, which sounds like simony," &c.

Concerning the Grievousness of the Sin of the Omission of the Canonical Hours. (No. 41.)

" How great a sin is the omission of the canonical hours?

" It is a sin, from its very nature, mortal : but the common opinion declares, that the omission of one little canonical hour, v. g., of the third, is sufficient matter for mortal sin.

" This is proved more from the common opinion and practice of the faithful, than from any law or reason.

" Huygens indeed, otherwise rigid, here liberal, attempts to prove with many arguments that the omission of a little canonical hour does not constitute a serious matter : but in a thing of such moment we ought not to recede from the common opinion ; and from him we also learn that the omission of one of the shorter psalms is not a serious matter. Suarez adds : if any one should omit nearly the half of the Completorium, I should not dare affirm that he sins mortally.

" He who should omit vespers on the Holy Sabbbath should be judged to have sinned mortally, if not from the seriousness of the matter, certainly from contempt.

" Small quantities omitted in distinct hours of the same day, coalesce, and if together they amount to the quantity of one little canonical hour, they will again constitute a matter sufficient for deadly sin. The quantities of distinct days do not coalesce, because they have not respect to the same singular precept.

" Does the omission of all the seven hours of one day contain seven sins or a single one?

" *Ans.* It is more correctly said to be one external sin, equivalent to seven ; and therefore to contain a circumstance to be explained in confession ; because several hours are as it were integral parts of the enjoined office, just as the theft of seven *patacones* is one sin ; internal sins, however, may be multiplied."

Concerning the causes which excuse from the recitation of the Canonical Hours. (No. 42.)

These three are specified.

" 1. *Inability, physical or moral ; 2. Necessity, or a duty of justice or charity ; 3. The dispensation of the Pope.*

" To inability are referred natural inadvertence, blameless forgetfulness, also infirmity, in which, without serious difficulty or inconvenience, the hours could not be recited. A slight infirmity, which does not hinder the ordinary actions of the head or tongue, such as a moderate pain of the head or stomach is, does not excuse.

" The danger itself, or the fear of a grievous evil, of death, relapse into sickness or debilities, &c., can afford a rational ground of excuse ; as the laws of the church ordinarily are not obligatory in such a danger. In a doubtful case, we must abide by the decision of a physician or a prudent man.

" A duty of charity excuses from the reading of the hours, v. g., if, in an unforeseen case, the whole remaining part of the day must be spent in administering the last sacraments to a dying person.

" The employment of preparing a sermon, or a similar function, does not excuse from the recitation of a divine office.

" Observe, that the above-mentioned causes may at one time excuse from the recitation of one canonical hour, yet so that they do not excuse from the recitation of the others ; because the office of the hours is not prescribed as an indivisible whole ; for a part may present the consideration of a notable prayer. This is confirmed from this 54th prop., condemned by Innoc. XI. ' He who cannot recite the matin and the praises, but can recite the remaining hours, is under no obligation, because the greater part draws to itself the less.'

" Hence, if any blind person, or one who is without a breviary, knows from memory how to recite some hours, or a considerable part, he is obliged to recite them ; the case would be different if he could only recite very small disconnected parts ; for then neither the end nor the substantial form of the precept could be preserved : yet, if with a companion he is able to recite it entire, he is bound to do so."

If about noon a fever is expected, the time of reciting the hours must be anticipated; and so if any other obstacle is likely to intervene. Excommunication, suspension, degradation, or any other spiritual punishment, not even imprisonment, nor condemnation to the galleys can excuse from the duty of reciting the canonical hours. A dispensation or commutation which shall validly excuse from this act of devotion must come from the *Pope.*

As to the manner of reciting the hours, it must be devout and studious. "The office is studiously recited, when it is performed, entirely and distinctly, without abridgment, mutilation, or interruption.

"It is devoutly recited, when it is recited with religious intention and attention. The intention is the act of the will; but attention is the act of the intellect," &c.

As to the place, the prayer which is offered in the temple is more profitable. (No. 43.)

Concerning the requisite intention in the recitation of the Canonical Hours. (No. 44.)

"This intention is the will or purpose of reciting the divine office as such.

"Is this intention absolutely necessary?

"Yes: because the church enjoins the recitation of the office as an exercise of certain religious acts; but without this intention, the recitation would not contain that exercise; therefore, this intention is necessary. Hence, he who reads the office merely materially from the intention only to study or commit it to memory, or to know the histories, does not satisfy the obligation of the precept of the church, because the intention of worshipping God, of praise, of prayer, &c., is wanting. Thus Suarez, Wiggers, Antoine, and La Croix teach," &c. &c.

The following sections treat of the attention requisite in prayer; of distraction; of distraction indirectly voluntary; of the sin of distraction. In No. 50, which treats "Of other defects occurring in the recitation of the canonical hours," we find this question:

"Ought the person reciting the office to hear himself, as many scholastics crudely declare?

26

" *Ans.* This is wont to be the torment of the scrupulous : it may be said with Benac., &c., that it is not necessary that he should perceive his voice with his own ears as, v. g., happens, when the organs of sound are acted upon ; but that is enough, if the words, by the allision of the air against the teeth and lips, are so formed that the reciter pronounces sensibly in his mouth all the words, and perceives it by an internal hearing as it were ; and this is sufficient for vocal prayer, although the external voice may not be heard : because the hearing is not noticed ; nor do I practically see any, except, perhaps, the scrupulous, tormented, and distressed in this matter ; for thus the deaf, and those who shut their ears, may afford satisfaction."

The faithful are then cautioned against too great celerity and anxious slowness, in reciting the canonical hours, &c., &c.

" What advantage does this prayer, *Sacrosanctæ, &c.,* afford with a *Pater* and *Ave,* when it is said after the recitation of the office ?

" *Ans.* Leo X. remitted, by way of indulgence, to him who says it, the defects and faults contracted in the recitation of the office, namely, the venial ones, adds Billuart ; so that he may relieve from the task of repeating the things thus recited.

" Do not, therefore, these defects, v. g., committed in the recitation of the matin, if after the matin, some one should say *Sacrosanctæ, &c.,* coalesce with the defects which one commits afterwards on the same day, in the recitation of the first, third, &c. ?

" *Ans.* According to the above-mentioned explanation, it must be said, that they would not coalesce : because a person thus reciting has been freed from all the preceding burden, just as if he had recited all correctly. But it ought to be said with a contrite heart : for an indulgence supposes that the fault is remitted."

Concerning the time of reciting the canonical hours.
(No. 58.)

" The time of reciting the canonical hours, runs from midnight, that is, from the twelfth hour of one night, to the twelfth hour of the following night ; after twelve, the obligation of the precept ceases : for this burden passes with the day, because the time is determined for finishing the obligation, and the obligation of the precept is distributed through single days.

"By legitimate custom, the permission has been introduced to recite the matin and the praises of the office of the following day, on the preceding evening, and thus from the time at which the sun is nearer to setting, than to midday, as is plain from the table concerning the time of beginning the matin, published A. D. 1706, at Rome, with the type of the apostolic chamber. According to this calculation, it is permitted in Belgium, in midsummer, to begin in the seventh minute after the fourth hour, in the afternoon, because the sun then sets with us at twelve minutes past eight; in the midst of winter, at five minutes before the second hour; and in each equinox, after the third hour.

"Here, beware of the 35 Prop. among those condemned by Alex. VII.: 'Any one may by a single office satisfy a double precept for the present day and for to-morrow.'

"*Obj.* This liberty does not seem reasonable, because the person reciting the matin in the evening, at the second feria will be obliged to say a falsehood in the hymn, 'With limbs refreshed with sleep, we rise from the spurned bed;' therefore, &c.

"*Ans.* I deny the antecedent and the proof: for such words are referred figuratively to the legitimate time, and thus are not false.

"Moreover, in the choir, certain times are assigned for the separate offices of the hours, which it is necessary to observe under grievous sin, according to the custom of the same church: not so out of the choir, in private recitation: but yet out of the choir, it will be considered a venial offence if the office, as far as the first, is not said before noon: because custom and the propriety of the office require this: therefore, the accurate time of reciting the matin is about night; very early it is proper to recite the praises and the first: in the subsequent time, the other little hours; vespers are said after noon, Lent excepted. To anticipate this time, or defer till after it, is nothing objectionable; as is mentioned ch. 2, concerning the celebration of the mass," &c.

CHAPTER XXIX.

CONCERNING THE SIGN OF THE CROSS.

" THE sign of the cross is called by our catechism, lesson 2, by way of distinction, the sign of a Christian man : for in every age, Christians have distinguished themselves from infidels, by making the sign of the cross.

" The same catechism denotes 2d, a two-fold manner of marking one's self with the cross.

" The first is that by which a person touches himself on the forehead with the right hand, the fingers being extended and joined, and the palm being turned towards him, saying : *In the name of the Father ;* then he lets his hand down below the breast, saying : *and of the Son ;* from there he moves his hand to the left side of his breast, and immediately transfers it to the right side, saying at the same time : *and of the Holy Ghost ;* whilst he adds Amen, he joins his hands before the breast.

" The second mode is that by which one describes a cross with the thumb on the forehead, saying : *In the name of the Father ;* and over the mouth, saying : *and of the Son ;* and over the breast, saying : *and of the Holy Ghost.*

" This mode we use at the reading of the gospel, by which we profess that we bear the faith and the gospel in the mind, in the mouth, and in the heart, or affections.

" The catechism above-mentioned observes 3d, that in forming the sign of the cross, we profess the principal mysteries of our faith, viz. The mysteries of the most holy Trinity, the incarnation, and the passion of Jesus Christ, and our redemption.

" Show in what way we profess the mystery of the most holy Trinity.

" *Ans.* By saying : *Of the Father, and of the Son, and of the Holy Ghost,* we profess three divine persons, and that they are distinct among themselves, by the interjection *and :* by saying in the *name* in the singular, and not in the *names,* we profess one and the same nature, or the divine essence of those persons, and therefore that they are one God : for the *name* does not denote any word, but signifies the divine virtue, power, and essence, as if it were said, In the virtue, in the power, in the majesty of the Father, &c.

" Moreover, when we draw the hand from the forehead below the breast, we profess that the Father through intellect generates the Son from eternity : and when in drawing the hand from the left side to the right, we join the lines of the cross, we profess that the Holy Spirit is the bond and love of the Father and the Son, and proceeds from them.

" We profess the mystery of the incarnation of Jesus Christ : viz., by placing the hand from the forehead below the breast, we profess that the Son of God descended from the bosom of the Father into the womb of the Virgin, and assumed human nature ; thus, both Christ's generations are here signified, either his eternal nativity from the Father, or the temporal from his mother.

" We profess the mystery of our redemption, and of the passion of the Lord Christ, when we draw forward the hand from the left side to the right side, and at the same time make the cross : for in this is signified that the Lord Christ, by his cross and passion, has brought us from a state of damnation to a state of salvation.

" For what causes, and to what purposes do we use the sign of the cross ?

" With the Mechlin Catechism we reply, we use it for the exercise of virtues ; for it contains, 1. an act of faith and of profession of the faith of the principal mysteries, as has been shown above.

2. It contains an act of religion ; for it is a short and most efficacious prayer to God through the merits of the passion of Christ, by which we invoke the help of God in all cases : it contains also a reference to God of the works to which it is prefixed.

" We use the sign of the cross against all temptations, and molestations of evil spirits ; for the devil greatly fears and flees from the cross, by which he has been overcome. Thus St. Antonius.

" We exhibit the sign of the cross about temporal things in blessing them, or averting evils from them ; thus we bless food, clothes, houses, &c. St. Benedict with the sign of the

26 *

CROSS BROKE IN PIECES A POISONED CUP; St. Rochus, by a little sign of the cross CURED THOSE INFECTED WITH THE PLAGUE. Examples of the virtue and efficacy of the sign of the cross, you will find in Hazart, Turlot, Marchant, &c., &c.

"From these remarks, it is plain to what salutary effect we may use this sign of the holy cross, frequently through the day, and before all business.

"From what time has the sign of the cross been in vogue?

"*Ans.* From the time of the apostles and of Christ himself, says the Mechlinian Catechism.

"Tertullian, à most ancient writer towards the close of the second century, has these words, lib. de Corona Militis, c. 3. 'At every progress and moving forward, at every going in and going out, in clothing ourselves and putting on our shoes, at the bath, at table, at the lights, at the bedchambers, at the seats, wherever business engages us, we rub the forehead with the little sign of the cross.'

"St. Jerome to Eustochius: 'At every action, at every step, let the hand describe the cross.'

"Many similar testimonies from the Holy Fathers, Augustine, Chrysostom, Gregory, &c., you will find produced by Hazart, Catech. less. 4., Turlot, Catech. l. 4 and 5; so that the temerity of the Calvinists, who abrogate the use of the sign of the cross, is insane.

"In the Old Testament, the figure of the little sign of the holy cross is found Ezek. ix., where they are forbidden to be slain whose foreheads were marked by the sign Thau, or T, which designates the cross.

"*Obj.* The cross brought shame and sorrow to Christ: therefore, the sign of the cross is rather to be held in abhorrence than to be venerated or honoured: because the son does not honour the gibbet on which his father has been hanged.

"*Ans.* I deny the inference: because the cross and its sign are not honoured by us in so far as the cross was employed for ignominy by the crucifiers, but inasmuch as the cross was voluntarily assumed by Christ as the instrument of our redemption, and the sign of his triumph and victory over sin and the devil.

"For proof, I say, that there is a disparity, because the gibbet affords to the father, neither triumph, nor victory, nor honour.

"Why do we venerate all figures of the cross, of whatever material prepared, but not all nails?

"Because the sign of the cross everywhere presents the passion and victory of the Lord Christ; but this all nails do not."

If Christ and his apostles authorized the use of the sign of the cross, and were in the habit of employing it, as we learn from the foregoing remarks, it is very strange that the sacred writers are utterly silent on this subject. We do not read that they ever undertook to cast out devils, or heal diseases by this potent charm; much less that they blessed their raiment or their food by making the sign of the cross. That St. Benedict broke in pieces a poisoned cup, and St. Rochus cured those who were afflicted with the plague, by making the sign of the cross, are facts which of course are not to be questioned by any but infidels. We may perhaps, however, be permitted to say, that if there is any priest or saint, in these ends of the earth, who believes that there is such potency in the use of this sign, we shall be glad to afford him a public opportunity of testing its virtue on any sound piece of poisoned crockery, just so soon as he is prepared to make the experiment. How their reverences can reconcile it to their consciences to suffer so many cases of small pox and yellow fever to terminate fatally, when they have such a remedy at hand, and have free access to the hospitals, is strange, very strange, indeed! The man who boasted that he had leaped fifty feet at Rhodes, was told, "make the same leap here, and we will believe you"— when we see a priest or a saint break a cup by the sign of the cross, we shall be ready to believe that it has been done. Till then, "credat Judæus Apella!"

CHAPTER XXX.

CONCERNING MAGIC. (No. 190.)

" THE word Magi, among the Greeks, formerly signified wise men ; in which way it is understood, Mal. ii. ver. 1 : ' Wise men (Magi) came from the east :' hence, magic is divided into natural and superstitious.

" What is superstitious magic ?

" *Ans.* It is the art of effecting wonderful results by signs through the aid of the devil. Suarez places the observance of cures under the head of magic.

" But the devil, the rival of God, has instituted certain magical signs in imitation of Christ's instituting the sacraments.

" Observe again, that the fundamental reason of all that is to be said depends on this, that magical signs do not produce those effects, either from the nature of the thing, or from the appointment of God or the church ; therefore, by the influence of the devil.

" Superstitious magic is divided into magic, properly so called, or *not hurtful,* and into *hurtful* or *witchcraft,* which therefore has a twofold malice, both against religion and against justice.

" *Witchcraft* is subdivided into *amatory,* by which carnal love or hatred is excited : and into *sorcery,* for inflicting diseases or other injuries upon men, animals, fruits, &c. ; but the devil can do very many things which relate to local motion.

Concerning Magical Signs, and the remedies against Magic. (No. 191.)

" What do you call a magical sign ?

" That which they exhibit or lay down according to an agreement, at least implicit with the devil, which being produced, the devil procures the effect.

" This sign sometimes consists in words, and is called *incantation ;* sometimes in a permanent thing, as straw, pots, strings, bars, &c., v. g., straw plaited in a certain way is hidden in the earth in order to kill animals; so long as that appointed sign of straw continues, the devil does injury to the cattle, unless he be hindered by exorcisms, or in some other way.

"May evil spirits, therefore, injure certain people?

"*Ans.* No: unless God permits it to them, as is plain from the history of Job. Yet, when the devil has the aid of some person, who co-operates, then God frequently permits this to the devil; because then the human race is thought to injure itself.

"Are those things which sometimes appear through magic art really such; or are they legerdemain and fantastic?

"I reply with St. Thomas, that these things sometimes appear truly, and sometimes by means of trick: in the former mode, the sorcerers, Exod. viii., brought real frogs upon the earth; in the latter way, the transmutations of men into cats or beasts appear; because these cannot be effected by the power of the devil, but they are done through the illusions of the senses, or through forms portrayed in the air.

"Likewise the apparitions of the dead through incantations are false; so that if any one appears, he is a devil, and not the soul of a deceased person. We admit, indeed, that Samuel, 1 Kgs. xxviii., truly appeared, according to Eccli. xlvi.; but by the special appointment of God for the reproof of Saul.

"What are the remedies against magic?

"*Ans.* A lively faith, and great confidence in God. Ps. xc.

"2. The frequent use of the Sacraments.

"3. Prayer and fasting, the sign of the cross, the invocation of the name of Jesus and the Saints.

"4. The exorcisms of the church, the use of blessed water, the exhibition of holy relics, &c.

"5. The use of natural medicines against diseases or evils of this kind.

"6. The lawful destruction of the magical sign: v. g. by burning the straw or papers, by breaking the pots," &c.

"Is it lawful to destroy the magical signs of witchcraft, and in what way? (192.)

"Certainly it is unlawful to destroy them by any other

witchcraft, or by any other superstitious act : because it is
not lawful to do evil that good may come.

" It is certainly lawful to destroy magical signs with the
intention and aim that sins may be diminished, and for the
detestation and hatred of magical iniquity, in the same way
as it is lawful to destroy idols.- But the question is mooted,

" Whether it is lawful to destroy these magical signs for
the sole purpose that the injury may cease?

" This question is more speculative than practical ; because by destroying, the purpose of detesting the diabolical
art may easily be intended : however,

" Delrio, Suarez, Wiggers, Boudart, and others, maintain
the affirmative answer, because the object is honourable and
proportionate, against Hesselius, Estius, and Sylvius. Delrio
also observes that Hesselius was the first who contradicted
this opinion : but the principal argument of Hesselius upon
which the others depend is this following :

" *Obj.* He who destroys a magical sign that the injury
may cease, does not expect the effect of cessation from God,
nor from any cause, natural or human : therefore he ex-
pects it from the agreement of the devil.

" *Ans.* I deny the antecedent ; for the sign being destroyed, the effect is expected from God, not by a miracle, but
from his ordinary providence, by which he does not usually
permit that the devil should inflict injury upon men, after the
magical sign is destroyed. But this destructive action is
honourable from its object and end : for it is just to destroy
the works of the devil, 1 John iii. 8. ' For this purpose the
Son of God appeared, that he might destroy the works of
the devil.' And because he who destroys the magical sign
does not fulfil the compact of the devil, but rather destroys
it ; and for this reason we think the same is lawful, although
the magical sign should consist in something negative or
privative.

" Is it lawful to ask a sorcerer to take away the spell?

" It is lawful, on condition that he takes it away in a lawful manner.

" If it is foreseen that he will do it by magic art, it is not
permitted to ask : indeed, if any magician should of his own
accord, offer to destroy the spell by magical or superstitious
art, it is lawful neither to accept nor to permit it.

" The reason is, because it is not lawful to accept a benefit from the devil : because this involves a certain fellowship with the devil, and a recognition of his excellence as a benefactor through his own compact.

" *Obj.* It is lawful simply to ask a loan from an usurer, and an oath from one who will swear by false gods ; therefore it is lawful to seek the destruction of witchcraft from a wizard, at least when he can destroy it in a lawful manner.

" *Ans.* I deny the inference : there is a reason of disparity, because it is lawful to receive benefits even from sinful men, but not from the devil, for the above-mentioned reason : hence St. Leo : 'The benefits of devils are more injurious than wounds.' "

Rules for discerning Witchcraft. (No. 193.)

" From what things can it be discerned, whether an evil proceeds from witchcraft, or from some other cause ?

" *Ans.* This discrimination is sometimes difficult : however, these marks of witchcraft are usually assigned.

" 1. If the evil exceeds the natural or ordinary causality of things ; v. g., if hair, bones, needles, bits of iron, &c., are found in the stomach.

" 2. If the afflicted person suffers violence, by intervals, as it were.

" 3. If skilful physicians are confidently of opinion that the evil does not proceed from a natural cause : if medicines, and other natural means, produce no effect.

" 4. If spiritual means and exorcisms are seen to be specially advantageous ; or, on the other hand, if when they are employed, the evil appears to be increased on their account ; in which case we are not to cease, but more boldly to persevere with all spiritual means.

" You will find more on these subjects in Malderus, Tract. 10. dub. 15, and Neesen, Tract 9. *De Dæmoniacis.*"

This chapter presents a specimen of the present fanaticism and foolery of the Church of Rome. Exorcisms are constantly performed by their priests, and evil spirits are made to flee before the sign of the cross, the sprinkling of holy water, the exhibition of sacred relics, &c. &c. ! ! We certainly believe that evil spirits exist, and that the prince of darkness exerts a fearful power over the children of disobedience, and we should be rejoiced if the exorcisms of Romish priests possessed infinitely more virtue than the credulous faithful believe, for then there would be strong evidence that the kingdom of Satan would speedily be overthrown; as a house divided against itself cannot stand! As matters are at present, we apprehend, the Devil never feels greater satisfaction than when the priests aim at him a quantum suff. of holy water, and exhibit the musty rags, dry bones, &c., which are facetiously called " *sacred* relics !"

CHAPTER XXXI.

Concerning Lying and its division. (No. 242.)

" THE vice opposed to the virtue of truth, is *the habit of lying ;* yet *lying* is used more frequently for the act of this vice, and is thus defined : ' Speaking contrary to the mind of the speaker.'

" Under speaking is comprehended every external sign whatsoever ; and thus we can lie by writing, by gestures, nods, or other actions.

" May any one lie, whilst speaking a thing that is true ?

" *Ans.* Yes : if he supposes in his mind that it is false : on the other hand, one who speaks a falsehood does not lie, if he prudently believes it to be true : the reason is that he does not speak against his mind : yet any one may be guilty of the fault of lying, if through defect of due investigation, through precipitancy or much speaking, he exposes himself to the danger of saying what is false.

" How is falsehood divided ?

" It is divided, by reason of the fault and of the object, into *officious, jocose,* and *pernicious.*

" Lying is called *officious,* which is committed only on account of one's own advantage or that of another : v. g., some

one says that he has no money, that he may not be robbed
of it by soldiers.

"*Jocose* is that which is committed only for the sake of
sport : v. g., some one lies that he is a Mechlinian, that he
may provoke to laughter.

"Lying is called *pernicious*, which, besides the wickedness of lying, has some injury or evil adjoined, from which
it contracts other wickedness : therefore, all pernicious lies
are not of the same kind, but they assume an appearance of
wickedness from the injury or evil from which they are
called pernicious : thus a pernicious falsehood, by which detraction from the reputation of a neighbour through the imputation of something false is occasioned, has the wickedness
of injustice ; lying against the faith is pernicious, and assumes
malice against the faith."

Pernicious lying is from its nature, a mortal sin ; officious and jocose lying, are from their nature, venial sins.

May Lying be lawful in any case ? (No. 243.)

"Plato, Origen, and some ancients, thought so ; but the
negative answer is certain ; the reason is because all lying
is intrinsically evil, and forbidden by the natural law ; for
words are naturally the signs of the understanding, says St.
Thomas. The same is proved from the Holy Fathers, Ambrose, Augustine, &c. ; and it is said, Eccl. vii. 14, 'Be not
willing to make any manner of lie.'

"*Obj.* Out of two evils the less is to be chosen ; therefore,
it is lawful to lie, v. g., to avoid homicide.

"*Ans.* I deny the inference : because to lie is a formal
sin : and thus to lie is a greater evil than to permit homicide
merely permissively. And, according to the apostle, Rom.
iii. 8, it is not lawful to do evil that good may come.

"Therefore, it is not lawful to lie in order to avert death
or the ruin of the state or any other evils : in perplexities of
this kind, men should betake themselves to the help of God,
of their guardian angel, &c."

Concerning mental Restriction. (No 244.)

"Mental restriction is twofold : *purely* mental, and *not
purely* mental, or *real*.

"Real restriction occurs, when the declaration is false ; if
27

we regard the words alone : but circumstances concur which signify that something is to be secretly understood, which the speaker keeps in his mind, and which being secretly understood, the declaration is true: v. g., John, desiring forthwith in the market to speak to Peter, asks of Paul: ' *Have you seen Peter ?*' Paul replies, '*I have not seen him,*' although he has seen him yesterday, or four hours ago.

" This reply or real restriction does not contain a lie, because by the circumstance of John's asking forthwith to speak to Peter, he is restricted to the immediate time; but now not the words alone make the declaration true, but also external circumstances, or concomitant signs, custom, &c., are likewise significant.

" Hence infer, how it is that metaphors, hyperbole, and other rhetorical figures, do not involve falsehoods.

" A purely mental restriction is committed, when a declaration is made, which, considering all the external circumstances and signs, is false, but to which in the mind of the speaker something is internally added or secretly understood, by which it would become true, which internal thing is yet manifested or made known by no sign; v. g., John being asked, whether he has seen Peter to-day, whom he had in reality seen, replies, I have not seen him to-day, by secretly understanding, *in Spain*, &c.

" Does purely mental restriction excuse from falsehood ?

" *Ans.* No : because this internal restriction is manifested by no external sign ; and therefore is not signified with the other ; and thus the external declaration remains simply false.

" Moreover, by restriction purely mental, human society would be disturbed in the same way as by falsehoods.

" It is proved also by the condemnation of this 26th proposition of Innocent XI., ' If any, either alone or before others, whether asked, or of his own accord, or for the purpose of sport, or for any other object, swears that he has not done something which in reality he has done, by understanding within himself something else, which he has not done, or a different way from that in which he has done it, or any other truth that is added, he does not really lie, nor is he perjured.'

" La Croix, indeed, prudently admonishes, lib. 3. p. 1, n.

295, refuting restriction purely mental, that since the condemnation of the aforesaid proposition, certain authors, who wrote before the condemnation, are to be read cautiously: meanwhile, however, I do not clearly see how he himself, No. 228, sufficiently differs from them, when he says that it is lawful for a homicide, who is asked whether he has killed that man, to reply, I have not killed him, by secretly understanding in his mind, so. that I ought to confess it to you ; in the same way that it is lawful to reply to one who asks whether a robber has passed this way : he has not passed this way, if he at the same time puts his hand into his glove, meaning that he has not passed through the glove ; for this sign is supposed to be secret, or not perceptible, so as to be signified together with the rest ; just as the motion of the eyes in speaking would not be a sufficient consignificant sign to be secretly understood externally, *he has not passed through my eyes*.

"However, if this thrusting of the hand into the glove should be sufficiently manifest, and perceptibly or intelligibly connected with words, then Boudart himself excuses the reply from falsehood," &c. &c.

Concerning Ambiguity and Equivocation. (No. 245.)

"Is it proper to speak with ambiguity and equivocation?

"The case is this : a proposition or a word admits of two senses or meanings : v. g., this proposition, ' Dico latronem Petrum occidisse.' *I say a robber killed Peter*, may signify that the robber has killed Peter ; and on the other hand, that Peter has killed the robber. In the same way, the word *mundus* may signify the globe, and cleanliness ; hence this declaration is equivocal : ' Mundus non est mundus ;' (which may signify either, *the world is not a world*, or *the world is not clean*.')

"An equivocation of this kind does not contain a lie, in whatever sense it may be received ; because the external words truly signify that sense, which the speaker has in his mind ; and thus differs from a purely mental reservation, in which the external words do not contain the mental sense.

"Therefore, it is proper for just reasons to use this in either sense ; thus the angel, Tob. v. 18, said metaphorically ;

' I am Azarias, the son of the great Ananias, that is, I am the aid of the Lord, the adopted Son of God,' &c.

" *Obj.* The person using such an equivocation intends to cheat and deceive another : but this is contrary to the sincerity of human society ; therefore, it is not lawful.

" *Ans.* I deny the assertion : but he intends to speak the truth which he has in his mind : he permits the deception of the other from his wrong understanding.; and because a jus. cause is required that he may be excused from all sin.

" An opportune mode of getting rid of the importunate questions of inquisitive men, is reciprocally to propose a question : v. g., if they ask, whether you know this? whether you have done this? you may reply, whence should I know this? why should I do this? &c. In a similar way, Christ, Luke xxiv. 19, to the question of the disciples going to Emmaus, replied, saying : *What things ?*"

The closing remarks of this section plainly show that *equivocation* is no sin, in the estimation of a disciple of Peter Dens. This is no new discovery, and it is therefore not becoming that we should speak of it as something strange or unexpected. A very little acquaintance with the practice of the veracious pupils and admirers of Peter Dens, is sufficient to teach us that they understand the art of equivocation to perfection. But the horrid attempt to make the blessed Saviour, whose title is, FAITHFUL AND TRUE WITNESS, encourage the practice of this detestable vice, is blasphemy for which we were not prepared. The very attempt at refutation would be irreverent. Let the reader turn to Luke xxiv. 19, and he will see that nothing could have been farther from the Saviour's mind than the intention of furnishing a precedent for the deceitful equivocations, which are the glory of the Church of Rome !

CHAPTER XXXII.

Concerning Fasting, and its division. (No. 254.)

POLMAN explains several meanings of the word *fasting*, and thus he divides fasting into the *philosophical, medicinal, penitential, moral, spiritual, natural,* and *ecclesiastical.*

" *Spiritual* or *metaphorical* fasting is to abstain from sins. S. Aug. Treat. 17, on John.

" *Moral* fasting is abstinence from food and drink, according to the dictate of natural reason, for a moral end, v. g., to restrain concupiscence. This fasting may, by natural right in itself, be obligatory upon every one, even an infidel, by the force of the precept of temperance; or through some circumstance, by reason of another virtue : for natural reason dictates that every one ought to use a proper remedy for avoiding sin : but this obvious remedy frequently is fasting : for this reason, St. Thomas says, a. 3., that fasting in general falls under the precept of natural right.

" Theologians here treat principally of the fasting which falls under the precept of the church ; and they divide it into *natural* and *ecclesiastical* fasting.

" What is natural fasting ?

" It is abstinence from all food and drink transmitted to the stomach, or from every thing that is taken by way of food, or drink, or medicine, from midnight.

" Observe that this natural fast which is enjoined before taking the Eucharist, is not properly an act of the virtue of abstinence or temperance, but an act of the virtue of religion : because it is enjoined by the church for the purpose of reverence to the sacrament : but an ecclesiastical fast is an act of the virtue of abstinence."

Concerning Ecclesiastical Fasting. (No. 255.)

" What is an ecclesiastical fast ?

" It is on certain days, according to the custom and prescription of the church, to abstain from meats under a single

27 *

refreshment in the day, not to be taken before the proper hour.

" Therefore an ecclesiastical fast contains three parts, viz. 1. Abstinence from meats, under which are understood, eggs, and milk diet, which derive their origin from flesh ; 2, abstinence from more refreshments except a single one from other food ; 3, that the appointed hour be not anticipated ; and thus in this time, refreshment may not be taken before noon.

" Hence, it is plain that this fast may be violated in a threefold way, and thus mortal sin may be committed in a threefold manner ; 1, by eating forbidden food ; 2, by taking several refreshments ; 3, by anticipating the hour of refreshment.   For this reason, he who confesses that he has broken his fast, must be asked, which of the three parts of the fast he has violated.

" Observe, that some fasts do not oblige to the observance of these three parts : thus fasts on holidays and Sabbaths, throughout the year, oblige to the mere abstinence from meats, according to the custom of the place ; and fasts of the days of Rogation do not forbid a second refreshment after noon : but these fasts are called imperfect fasts."

Concerning the Quadragesimal Fast. (No. 256.)

" The quadragesimal fast is the most solemn throughout the whole church, because it derives its origin from the Apostles, in imitation of Christ ; although it has since then undergone various changes : for formerly, until the times of S. Bernard, the fast was observed until evening ; in the thirteenth century, in the time of S. Thomas, until the third hour in the afternoon : a little after, from the time of Durandus ; and in these times, it is permitted through custom to take a single refreshment about noon, and a little collation in the evening. The vestige of the ancient custom, is, however, still preserved in the church, when, in Lent, vespers are sung before noon, or before the refreshment.

" During the time of Lent, abstinence must be observed also on the Lord's days occurring in it, not only from meats, but also from eggs and milk diet, namely, butter, milk, cheese, &c., which derive their origin from flesh ; by custom, however, in this country, in our day, the eating of milk diet is permitted, except on a few days designated by the Bishop ;

only this, indulgence is compensated by certain prayers or alms. Steyaert admits the real obligation of this, &c.

"On Lord's days in Lent, although abstinence from meats must be observed, yet abstinence from several refreshments is not obligatory; nor is a certain hour of refreshment to be observed. Generally, on the other Lord's days, no fast is kept on account of joy for the resurrection of Christ; although this is proper on that day. Formerly, indeed, some Holy Fathers prohibited fasting on the Lord's day, but in order to avoid the errors of heretics, suppose the Manichæans. Hence it is observed, that when a vigil in which a fast is to be observed, falls on a Lord's day, the fast is kept on the preceding Sabbath: but yet a festival, except the Lord's day, does not alter the fast, unless it is the feast of Corpus Christi, or the solemnity of the Patron of the State, says Sylvius.

"Is the obligation of abstaining from eggs and milk diet serious?

"*Ans.* It appears so; because in them a serious matter may be afforded: yet it is often light. Hear, prop. 32, condemned by Alexand. VII.; 'It is not evident that the custom of not eating eggs and milk diet in Lent is obligatory.'

"Heretics object that there are no testimonies extant concerning the fast of Lent in the epistles of the apostles.

"This fast has been propagated by apostolic tradition. For the proof of this, that golden rule of St. Augustine, bk. 4, against the Donatists, ch. xxiv., is sufficient: 'What the universal Church holds, and which is not appointed by Councils, but has always been retained, is most justly believed to be handed down by nothing else than apostolic authority.'

"Whoever wishes more particularly to learn the rise, progress, and changes of the aforesaid fasts, let him consult the work, R. P. Cozza, 'Concerning fasting.'

"*Obj.* Mark ii. 19, Christ says, that the sons of the Bridegroom can not fast; but Christians are the sons of the Bridegroom; therefore, &c.

"*Ans.* The saying is parabolical: by the sons of the Bridegroom are meant the disciples of Christ, and it is signified that it is not proper that Christ, whilst he tarried with them on earth, should make them fast or mourn, as Matthew expresses it, ch. ix. v. 15; but after the death of Christ they fasted; as Paul testifies concerning himself, 2 Cor. vi. 5, and xj. 27.   St. Thomas offers two other replies, q. 147, art. 4, ad. 5.

Concerning Abstinence from Meats.   (No. 257.)

" Why is the eating of meat on a fast day forbidden ?

" Because fasting has been instituted for the mortification of the flesh, or for restraining the lust of taste and concupiscence, &c.

" Under meats are included the broth of meats, and those things which derive their origin from flesh, as eggs, &c.

" The meats of the animals which are considered as forbidden, are better ascertained from common custom : the flesh of turtles, frogs, and the like, which are nourished in the water, are not included, &c.

" Why is not wine forbidden, in which there is luxury ? Prov. xx.

" Because wine elsewhere is an ordinary and necessary drink.

" St. Thomas, art. 8, ad. 1. Because wine excites lust only by reason of heat, which quickly passes away ; but meats promote it by reason of the humour, which remains long," &c. &c.

" How great a sin is it to eat flesh on a day of fasting or abstinence ?

" It is, from its very nature, a mortal sin ; because, in it a serious matter is afforded, and the object of the law likewise is important ; and because the opinion of the faithful so has it.

" May it become venial from the trifling amount of the matter ?

" Yes : because a single mouthful of meat, v. g., is not in itself an important amount of food or nourishment ; nor does it become serious on account of the object of the law ; therefore, &c.

" Yet this eating will everywhere be a mortal sin on account of erroneous conscience and scandal, and on account of acting against the profession of faith ; for the people apprehend the eating of meat on a fast-day as a proof and sign of heresy ; and for this reason Tannerus does not admit it as a light matter.

" Observe, that any one sins just so often as he eats meat on a fast-day ; for the precept of not eating meats is nega- tive.

" *Why does the Church permit only one refreshment on a fast-day ?*

" St. Thomas, art. 6, &c. : because, by a single refresh- ment human nature is saved from perishing, and at the same time something is taken away from lust.

" A natural day is meant from the twelfth hour of the night to the twelfth of the following night.

" Observe 1. In what way each taking of food without cause on a day of fasting, besides the refreshment and col- lation, occasions sin, either mortal, if the matter be respec- tively considerable, or venial, if the matter is trifling.

" Observe 2. That several small quantities taken on the same fast-day coalesce among themselves by reason of the effect of nutrition, and thus may constitute matter serious enough for mortal sin ; just as several small thefts coalesce : hence this prop. 29, was condemned by Alex. VII. ' He who frequently eats a little on a fast-day, although he may in the end have eaten a considerable quantity, does not break his fast,' " &c.

Of sins respecting the single refreshment. (No. 259.)

" Sin may be committed in a threefold way, in the case of the single refreshment : 1. By taking several refresh- ments, or several parts of a refreshment : 2. By dividing the refreshment, or interrupting it through a considerable time : 3. By protracting the refreshment to too long a time : for thus the refreshment is virtually multiplied.

" To how long a time may the refreshment be protracted ?

" It is said reasonably, that IT MAY NOT BE PROTRACTED BEYOND TWO HOURS. Henno adds that THEN THE GUESTS ARE TO BE ADMONISHED TO ABSTAIN FROM EATING.

" May any one, who hastily finishes his refreshment in the time of half an hour, eat again after the space of one hour, on the ground that the two hours of refreshment are not yet elapsed ?

" No ; because he is supposed in intention and fact to have entirely finished his refreshment ; so that the latter eating is not a part of the former meal, which was finished, but is rather a part of a second refreshment.

"Does he sin, who divides his meal into two parts by a considerable space of time, when these two parts are equivalent in regard to the food, to only a single entire refreshment?

"Yes: the reason is because the unity of the refreshment is not preserved. Besides not only are several entire meals forbidden, but also several semi-refreshments, or parts of a meal.

"How great a space of time is thought in this case, to make a considerable interruption?

"According to Cozza, the space of half an hour does it; especially if there is no just reason, or if any one has ceased without the intention of afterwards continuing the refreshment he had commenced: Cozza indeed supposes, that he who rises from table with no intention and desire of resuming the meal, or, which is equivalent, who has said the prayer of thanks with the intention of finishing the refreshment, cannot resume the meal, although but a short time after: yet others think, that it is proper if he has changed his mind. See La Croix, lib. 3. p. 2, &c.

"For a just reason, it will be lawful without any sin to interrupt the refreshment for a short time, for a quarter or half hour, says Cozza: and thus, if any one has commenced a meal, and is called away for a purpose of necessity or business, he may on his return finish the single refreshment which was commenced before.

"On the same ground Diana excuses those who wait at table, and those who read during the time of the meal, who take some food immediately before the meal: because these persons intend to begin the refreshment with those who are eating, and after performing their duty, immediately to finish it, &c.

"What quantity of food taken above the refreshment and the little collation, is regarded as a serious or sufficient matter for mortal sin: but what quantity is a trifling matter?

"As regards an ecclesiastical fast, it is agreed that there is an amount which may be considered trifling; and thus one or two mouthsful of bread is a small matter; or as Cozza and Antoine say, one or two ounces, v. g. a cake of a single quarter which weighs an ounce and a half is a small matter : but here I think again that there should be some respective consideration.

" A man's breakfast by which he is sufficiently nourished until noon, is certainly a serious matter, &c.

" Apples, pears, nuts, grapes, and other fruits, are also included among articles of food ; but yet, as they are commonly rather light diet, a greater quantity is requisite in order to constitute a serious matter : it follows, that it is not permitted even for the purpose of allaying thirst, to eat apples, grapes, &c., just as it is not lawful on account of thirst to drink milk, when necessity does not require it. See Cozza more at length, p. 3. a. 1. dub. 5., who, in the same place, num. 59, disapproves of the mode of chewing apples and grapes, by which only the juice seems to be taken : must, however, is regarded as simple drink."

Of the Sins of the Third and Fourth Refreshment. (260.)

" Does he, who has violated the fast by a second refreshment, sin by taking the third and fourth on the same day ?

" *Ans.* Yes : indeed he sins as often as he eats afterwards, or at least increases his sin : because the ecclesiastical precept of the fast includes the negative : you shall not take several refreshments, which equally prohibits the third and second : any one sins just so often as he eats meat on a fast-day. Thus, Sylvius, &c., Antoine, &c.

" Busenbaum thinks, that this person, although he has sinned mortally in the second refreshment, sins only venially in the third and the rest : but he does not give the reason of his peculiar remark : nor can a solid one be given, when the quantity of the third and of the other meals is serious : as Sylvius teaches with the passages cited from La Croix, lib. 3. p. 2. n. 1265. The opinion of Busenbaum may perhaps be admitted when the quantity of the other meals is so trifling that it does not occasion a considerable increase and amount of the first transgression.

" Does he break the fast, who on the fast-day, or the day before, eats more than usual in the refreshment, that he may more easily sustain the burden of fasting ?

" *Ans.* He does not seem directly to violate the precept of the fast, because the quantity of food in the refreshment, according to S. Thom., is not rated by the law of fasting. Bonac. &c., Abul., &c., and the modern Cozza prove this answer by this reason: because this person observes everything which is commanded, the single refreshment, the hour, and abstinence from meat.

" Nor is it any objection that he sins against temperance: because he certainly observes the precept as to substance: it is not obligatory that the fast be an act supernatural in substance.

" Some, among whom is Billuart, teach that he acts contrary to the law of the fast," &c.

Divers objections are then refuted; and at the close of his answers, Peter Dens remarks:

" This, however, is readily granted, that he acts in some measure against the object of the law and against temperance, and in so far he may sin. Indeed, a repletion of this kind renders fasting more onerous, when the food too much oppresses the body and mind, generates bad humours and phlegm, whilst a moderate refreshment recruits and fortifies the body and mind."

Concerning the Hour of the Single Refreshment.
(No. 261.)

" At what hour of the day, in time of fasting, is it proper to take refreshment?

" According to present custom, about the twelfth hour, at noon: it is permitted to wait longer, and anciently it was commanded to wait until evening, afterwards till the third hour, as was said above, (No. 256.) It is not lawful to anticipate the hour, &c.

" How great a sin is it to anticipate the hour?

" Sylvius replies, quest. 147, &c., that the anticipation of half an hour is a light offence, but of two hours, it is grievous; because it is a considerable anticipation; in case some one should take refreshment about the ninth or tenth hour in the morning · So Lessing also, &c., with some others.

" Cozza, however, is not so indulgent, for he says, that to anticipate the hour of eating, appointed by custom, by one hour, is a considerable time and a mortal sin.

"The single refreshment may be anticipated for a just cause, for instance, for the sake of beginning a journey, which will not admit of a refreshment at the proper time, and for similar matters and necessities. Sylvius, Cozza, Regin.

"Therefore observe, how any one refreshing himself with meat early on a fast-day, without cause, with the intention of taking a second refreshment, commits a threefold mortal sin, or one equivalent to three.

"For which reason, he who confesses that he has broken his fast, must be asked, which, or what parts of the fast he has violated, whether without any just reason, whether he has caused scandal, or an occasion of sin to others."

Concerning the Little Collation at evening. (No. 262.)

"The little collation at evening, which is also called the little refreshment, the little supper, and the collation, anciently unknown, because the refreshment was taken about evening, commenced from the time at which the refreshment began to be taken about noon : the name has been derived from the collations or conferences and spiritual lectures in the evening, when the faithful assembled ; where they then first took a little drink ; afterwards, lest this drink should be injurious to an empty stomach, they took a little food ; by degrees this custom increased to such an extent, that this little collation is at present taken so as to afford some nourishment, the church in so far relaxing her own law. No decree of the church has indeed been promulgated concerning this relaxation ; but the law has been modified by custom, with the connivance of the church ; and this indulgence of the church we learn from the unanimous interpretation of theologians, and the practice of the faithful.

"The little collation, therefore, may be described as the taking of a little food, in order that drink may not injure the body, and that the body may at the same time be moderately refreshed.

"It is to be observed, that whilst the little collation has indeed been introduced by custom, it is only in so far lawful, as the legitimate custom of the scrupulous faithful approves it.

"How much food may be taken for the little collation ?

28

" Some have appointed a certain quantity for all, or a fixed number of ounces of bread. S. Car. Borr. has determined an ounce and a half of bread, Cozza eight ounces, Concina three or four; but, as it seems, not with sufficient propriety; because, what would be very little for one man, v. g., a German, would be too much for another, say, an Italian: therefore the constitutions of persons should be regarded, the kinds of food, &c. For this reason, the quantity of the little collation is more properly determined by respect and proportion to the quantity which this person needs for a moderate supper or refreshment; according to this mode, Van-den Bosch restricts the quantity of the little collation to the seventh or sixth part of a refreshment: Layman, Filliuc, Busenbaum and others extend it to the fifth or fourth part of a whole supper; and none are found, even the most liberal, who indulge regularly beyond the fourth part of an entire refreshment. Therefore, according to this more liberal computation, if I need for a meal sixteen ounces of food, I may take four ounces of bread for a collation.

" The custom has prevailed in monasteries that a cake of two quarters is distributed to each one at the collation, although all do not eat it up.

" May he who has been sufficiently strengthened by the refreshment of dinner, or who is not hungry in the evening, take the little evening collation?

" Cozza replies affirmatively, on account of custom; and on account of continual anxieties which will occur, says Azorius.

" What kinds of food is it lawful to take in the little collation?

" The custom from which the little collation has its origin teaches this; therefore it is permitted to take fruits, herbs, bread, or cake; bread and butter, with cheese in this country, says Sylvius; and he teaches that it is not lawful to take fish, and therefore still less eggs, because they are solid food, and proper for a perfect meal; the moderns, Antoine, Cozza, Concina follow Sylvius.

" Diana, although the prince of the liberals, earnestly defends the aforesaid opinion of Sylvius, and adduces in its favour an army of doctors.

" It is indeed true, that in this country, the custom of many prevails that they take a little fish, with the bread and butter ; but whether this habit shall prescribe to the law, would be a matter for inquiry : certainly, this custom has not yet invaded the refectories of the religious, or of monks, nor even every table of all the scrupulous : but because it is a small quantity in food not forbidden on that day, it is little cared for, and thus is used by many.

" For the same reason, hot articles of food which have been boiled are not permitted : therefore, the furnishing of the table with food of different kinds, and hot meats for the little collation, is an abuse, nor is it either the practice of the scrupulous, nor is it custom.

" May not any one, therefore, who has been in the habit of taking a cake and drinking a pint of ale, mix them, and boil a little broth from them, and take it in the same quantity as a little collation ?

" No ; because the form of the collation or the quality of the food is not observed ; for such a boiled mess is the ordinary food of a meal (the same rule seems to hold good in relation to minced meats) ; but for the little collation custom permits only cold things, which are usually taken out of the refreshment ; for hot articles of food that have been boiled are more pleasant, and more nutritious. — La Croix, Antoine, &c.

" Some, however, consent in so far that if the quantity of the collation does not exceed (this amount,) he does not sin mortally : because, they say, the collation respects more the quantity than the quality of the food.—Wiggers, Bonac., &c.

" In this country, certainly, the common opinion of all regards the obligation of observing the quality of the food in the collation as not serious ; whilst indeed the usual or not forbidden articles of food are taken in the small quantity of the collation."

Concerning the time of taking the Little Collation.
(No. 263.)

The proper time is about evening. Though it is not lawful to invert the order of the meals on a fast day, so as to take the collation at noon, and the regular refreshment in the evening, yet it is not a mortal sin, because the quantity and quality of the food, and the times are observed. It is no sin at all, if there is sufficient reason for it, v. g., if it is done on account of a journey, or of attending to business at noon, say on a market day.   Also, if any one should be unable to sleep at night, unless he has a refreshment in the evening, he may then take a regular supper and a collation at noon, but not two full meals.   To take the collation early in the morning is not orthodox, because it is anticipating the appointed hour.   In case any one on a fast day, whether through ignorance or not, should take a breakfast equivalent to a full meal, he must restrict himself to the little collation ; but if the breakfast was equivalent only to a collation, he may take a full meal in the evening, or even at noon, if some reason requires it.   If the breakfast was equivalent to only half a meal, he must confine himself to the collation ; unless, perchance, this unwonted abstinence should occasion too much inconvenience or weakness.   These things are conformable to the doctrine of Sylvius, Billuart, &c.

" The insane distinction of certain casuists, by which they liberate him from the observance of the fast who has maliciously violated it, but not him who has done it without any fault, and altogether inadvertently, merits indignation ; for if the ulterior observance is useful and reasonable for one, it will be also for another.   Oh, blindness in morality !"

" If any one after dinner, before the time of the collation, takes some food, he sins ; but let him abstain from the collation: but if he takes only a little something, La Croix concedes that he may take a collation so much less in the evening.

" A little excess in the collation can be only a venial fault."

Much has been said about the abstemiousness enjoined upon the faithful, but it is no very serious matter after all. A dinner, which may lawfully be protracted for two hours, is certainly sufficient for a stomach of ordinary capacity, even if there were no additional license of a " little supper." Besides, the pious man may gorge himself on the previous day, so as to fortify himself against the siege of the first half of the fast day ; and it is not likely that he will be famished, when he has two full hours by the watch in which to make amends for his painful abstinence.   There is not much danger that either priests or laymen will injure their health by abstemiousness, if they follow the rules prescribed by Doctor Dens. Now, we are not finding fault;—we certainly commend them all for their good sense in this particular; only we think they have rather a roundabout way of getting at the thing. They might take their tea without all this stratagem. We suspect the truth of the matter is, that fasting does not agree with their reverences; and that there is no sensitive plant so perfect a "noli me tangere," as a holy priest's stomach.

One or two more highly important sections on fasting, and we will vary the subject.

Concerning the taking of Chocolate. (No. 265.)

"Does the taking of chocolate break an ecclesiastical fast?

"It is certain, with the consent of all, that to eat chocolate undiluted breaks the fast; because it is food, and is taken by way of food.

"The question is concerning the drinking of chocolate; to wit, when chocolate, mixed with water and diluted and boiled, is drunk, or rather, is sucked.

"Cozza and La Croix propose this as a question controverted by their patrons on both sides, whom they cite.

"Benedict XIV., the Supreme Pontiff, has published a lucid dissertation upon this question, who, however, resolves that it is more safe to abstain from chocolate on a fast day; and to him we adhere with Billuart.

"The reason is, because such a potion in itself, and more especially serves for nourishment, and not properly for cooling, or for quenching thirst; for it is a kind of hot concoction. This is confirmed from the fact that by this potion weak persons are nourished, &c.

"Obj. I. A drink or a liquid does not break a fast; therefore, &c.

"Ans. The drinking of chocolate is not a mere drink, according to what has been said above.

"Observe that this axiom, 'a liquid does not break the fast,' is not universally true: for milk, honey, and similar liquid things when taken break the fast.

28 *

" *Obj. II.* A single ounce of chocolate, as it is ordinarily taken, affords very little nourishment.

" *Ans.* We do not dispute that the smallness of the matter may excuse from mortal sin: for this reason, Cozza, although a patron of the opposite opinion, cautions that the drink of chocolate be not taken oftener than once on a fast-day.

" Finally, Antonius de Leone, in Cozza, says that chocolate is very nutritious.

" *Obj. III.* Strong beer is also a concoction from water and the flour of grain: but this drink does not break the fast: therefore, neither a concoction of chocolate.

" *Ans.* I deny the assertion: for beer is only an extract from grain: for in clarified ale, there is no gross matter of the grain, but only the spirit of the grain: and hence, it is a mere drink, which by accident nourishes but little; which is plain from the fact that they who drink freely without food injure their constitution. Indeed, he who makes this objection does not understand the art of brewing; gruel is concocted of meal and a liquid, but not beer.

" *Obj. IV.* At Rome, under the eyes of the Supreme Pontiff, the use of chocolate is permitted; therefore, &c.

" *Ans.* A learned man has told me that when he was himself at Rome, he made diligent inquiry concerning this practice: and he has assured me, that there, some use it, but others do not.

" The Supreme Pontiffs perhaps permit it for just reasons; perhaps in due course of time they will forbid it: and in this way the custom obtained at Rome, and almost everywhere, that when a dispensation was given for eating meat in Lent, they mixed the eating of fish in the refreshment with the eating of meat; and yet the Supreme Pontiff, Benedict XIV., declared, that this custom was and always had been an abuse.

" Hence, Concina lays down this rule: a probable opinion permitted and tolerated by the Pope is not considered implicitly approved: for many propositions have been condemned only after a long time: so too, the husbandman has permitted tares to grow."

Of Causes which excuse from Fasting. (No. 266.)

" These three or four causes are usually assigned :

" 1. Inability, v. g., bodily infirmity. 2. Necessity, as heavy labour. 3. Piety, or a greater good, such as troublesome waiting on a sick person, performed without sleep. 4. The dispensation of a superior. Some reduce all these causes to one, inability or impossibility.

" It is to be well observed, that as fasting contains three parts, some causes may excuse from the observance of one part, yet not from the observance of the other parts ; v. g., one who has a dispensation to eat meat, may not, therefore, take several refreshments, or anticipate the hour ; thus the cause of labour which permits several refreshments, does not permit the eating of meat ; likewise, some reason for anticipating the hour does not permit the eating of meat, nor always several refreshments, &c.

" Observe, moreover, that the cause ought to be reasonable and proportionate : so that a greater cause be required for the eating of meat, than for the anticipation of the refreshment.

" Politeness does not excuse from fasting in order that you may eat with a friend.

" The multiplicity of excuses from fasting, which casuists and probabilists fabricate, so that there is scarcely a man living, who may not apply some one to himself, merits indignation rather than theological refutation. For Concina on fasting, quotes from Hurtadus, how Pasqualigus enumerates about fifty conditions or orders of men, whom he declares to be free from the command of fasting.

" Who then are held under obligation by the ecclesiastical law of fasting ?

" All baptized persons who have attained to the use of reason, unless they should be excused from some claim, or be free from the whole or from a part.

" Heretics also ?

" *Ans.* YES, IF THEY ARE BAPTIZED ; BECAUSE THEY ARE SUBJECT TO THE CHURCH, which does not seem to relax her law in their favour.

" Unbaptized infidels are not under obligation, because they are not subject to the Church.''

The following sections on this subject, treat of particular cases, when the excuse from fasting is valid, and when the contrary.

A journey undertaken from a proper motive, not for the purpose of eluding the precept of the Church, excuses from the single refreshment and from the hour, but not from abstinence from meat. The journey must be not a mere excursion of pleasure—riding on horseback, or in a carriage, does not ordinarily excuse from fasting—but when the journey is laborious, difficult, and very fatiguing, especially for one who is not used to ride on horseback, then he is not obliged to fast. Pedestrians need not fast.

The age at which the obligation of the ecclesiastical fast begins, is fixed at about seven : but parents, who deprive their children of meat at an earlier age, in order that they may from infancy learn to be subject to the rulers of the Church, are commended.

" The perfect ecclesiastical fast, according to the three parts explained above, No. 255, obliges those who have completed their twenty-first year.

"Observe 1 : that young men of this kind, before the age of twenty-one, may be obliged, by the natural law, to some fasts, as proper and ordinary means against the lusts and sins of the flesh : hence, the custom of the pious observes that, at the discretion of the confessor, they assume certain fasts in Lent.

"Observe 2 : that this junior age does not excuse from a fast that is due from some other cause, v. g., from a vow, or from some sacramental satisfaction which has been imposed, or for enjoying a jubilee, &c." (No. 270)

No age has been fixed at which the law of ecclesiastical fasting ceases to be obligatory : but when people are believed to be so infirm or weak as to be disqualified from fasting, they are excused.

Pregnant and nursing women are excused from fasting, but are not at liberty to eat meat on a fast day.

Beggars may eat whenever they have a chance, provided they cannot procure enough at once to make a full meal ; but if they can, they are not excused from fasting, unless the dry bread and vegetables, which they have, should not sufficiently recruit them when debilitated by hunger.

Works of mercy, corporeal and spiritual, which are incompatible with fasting, absolve from the obligation. (No. 271.)

The power of granting a dispensation from the ecclesiastical law of fasting, belongs primarily to the Pope; but bishops, regular superiors, abbots, priors, but neither the subprior, nor the lady abbess, says Cozza, if the prior is present, may afford dispensation.

It is customary for parish priests to grant this license; at least when the Bishop is not present. Confessors or physicians have no such authority; they can only declare that a just cause subsists.

" May those who have a dispensation to eat meat on the same day eat fish also ?"

This weighty question is controverted. On the one hand, Sylvius says, that, regarding the nature of the thing, they may; but Pope Benedict XIV., the erudite author of the brilliant treatise on the lawfulness of drinking chocolate on a fast day, says that it is not lawful to eat fish and meat at the same feast, when a dispensation has been granted only with reference to meat; and his Holiness in divers Briefs has laid down the following conclusions in this momentous question, equalled only by the awful controversy, which convulsed the Lilliputian empire in the days of Gulliver, when the Emperor and Nobles were divided on the question of the orthodox mode of breaking eggs.

" 1.- One who has a dispensation to eat meat on a day of fasting, may not at the same feasts eat meat and fish; and this under grievous sin, not even on Lord's days in Lent. Put oysters and crabs, even delicate ones, under the same rule with fish, to which add shell-fish.

" 2. Neither may he eat meat in the evening collation, not even in that small quantity which is allowed in other food.

" 3. Neither may this dispensed person on this account anticipate the hour nor take several meals, &c.

" 4. One who has a dispensation to eat eggs, may also eat fish.

" By these aforesaid rules they are not bound, who are grievously sick or disqualified by a similar necessity," &c., &c., No. 273.

No. 275, treats of the sins of others in the cause of fasting.

It is not proper to give food on a fast-day to a person, if you know that he will violate the fast; you may not offer such a one a breakfast or a supper. In the same way, it follows that tavern-keepers may not, in a Catholic country, offer meat to heretics on a forbidden day; and if they ask for it, they are to be told that the laws of the country forbid it, and that as they are bound to obey the other laws of the land, they must obey the law concerning fasting too. But in case of war, when the armies of the heretics occupy the country, then the laws of the church yield to fear and necessity; so too when the country is ruled by heretics. Reginald excuses servants who prepare forbidden dishes for their masters, on a fast-day, because they do it in obedience to orders, but Peter Dens advises them in this case to leave such families and seek employment elsewhere, unless other just reasons should be in the way.

The following question and answer closes the chapter on fasting:

"What is to be done, when you see any one through ignorance or inadvertence eating something on a fast-day, contrary to the precept of the fast?

"You are bound by a debt of legal justice to remind him of his obligation, or to hinder him, &c.

"Sylvius wishes to excuse from mortal sin, those who, by an imaginary claim, suppose themselves to be excused from fasting, when gross ignorance does not concur: but La Croix is more rigid in this case."

One of the marks by which Paul designates the great apostasy, which was to afflict the church in the latter times, is ABSTINENCE FROM MEATS. Be it remembered, the apostle does not condemn fasting, nor does he say that fasting would be a peculiarity of the man of sin. It certainly is abundantly evident from the doctrines inculcated in the above sections that a fast in the Romish Church is a perfect farce; on the most solemn day of ecclesiastical fasting, the faithful have full license to eat one hearty meal, which may be protracted to the length of two hours; and they, who

cannot appease the cravings of hunger in that time must
certainly be tormented with ravenous appetites! Besides
this,. they may have a "little supper," so that there is very
little danger that the "good *Catholic*" will spend a sleepless
night, on account of the gnawings of hunger! But, whilst
it is only a venial sin if he offends against Temperance on
a fast-day, by glutting himself with lawful food, if he EATS
MEAT on that day, he commits mortal sin; i. e. an offence,
which entails damnation upon his soul, unless confession be
made, penance duly performed, and absolution from a Holy
Priest received! So exactly does the mark of the beast,
ABSTINENCE FROM MEATS, designate the Church of Rome
as the Man of Sin. It is not an uncommon thing, for Papists to endeavour to raise a smile at the application of such
terms as the above to Holy Mother; but where will they
find another to answer the description which the Bible gives?
Observe, this apostasy is to grow out of the CHURCH OF
CHRIST; it is to be literally an *apostasy;* where then we
ask again, can another church professing to be Christian, be
found, that shall answer this description of the Apostle,
"forbidding to marry and commanding to ABSTAIN FROM
MEATS?"

————————

The remainder of Vol. IV., treats of sins of licentiousness. It would not be decent to translate even the least
offensive of these chapters. The most outrageous forms of
bestiality which it is possible for iniquity to assume are
gravely discussed, and held up with most revolting particu-
larity before students of *divinity*, who are under a vow of
chastity and perpetual celibacy. The filthiness of this slimy

puddle of Romish casuistry is so offensive, that I must be excused from stirring the scum ; I cannot permit its effluvia even from a distance to annoy the mental olfactories of my reader by a translation, but in order to furnish evidence of the vileness of this *theology* / I will present a few extracts from the original Latin.

DE MODO CONTRA NATURAM. (No. 295.)

" I. Quinta species luxuriæ contra naturam committitur *quando quidem copula masculi fit in vase feminæ naturali, sed indebito modo,* v. g. stando, aut dum vir succumbit, vel a retro feminam cognoscit, sicut equi congrediuntur, quamvis in vase femineo.

" II. Possunt autem hi modi inducere peccatum mortale juxtà periculum perdendi semen, eò quòd scilicet semen viri communiter non possit apte effundi usque in matricem feminæ.

" III. Et quamvis fortè conjuges dicant quòd periculum diligenter præcaveant, illi interim lascivi modi á gravi veniali excusari non debent, nisi forté propter impotentiam, v. g. ob curvitatem uxoris, nequeat servari naturalis situs et modus, qui est ut mulier succumbat viro."

DE POLLUTIONE. (No. 296.)

*   *   *   *   *   *

" *Quid agere debet is, qui sub pollutione in somno inchoata evigilat ?*

" Evigilans non potest ei ullum consensum præbere, sed potius dissensum seu displicentiam voluntatis formare debet.

" *An tenetur illam pollutionem in somno inceptam, mox ut evigilat, vi cohibere, suumque corpus comprimere, ne continuetur in vigilia ?*

" R. cum Antoine : tenetur, saltem ut pollutio non continuetur per effusionem seminis necdùm è lumbis vel ex testiculis extravasati. Sanchez, Billuart, aliique videntur permittere continuationem ob periculum infirmitatis ; sed omnino puto, eos id dicere solummodò de semine jam extravasato, nimirum ut exterius effluat : alioquin non licet promovere formalem pollutionem, nequidem ad evadendam mortem.

" Notat Neesen difficilem esse correctionem eorum, qui dediti sunt huic vitio pollutiones."

.The atrocity of these and similar passages can be appreciated only, when we bear in mind that the most revolting questions concerning these subjects are put to penitents of every age and sex at the confessional, whenever the Priest deems it expedient.

." Confessarius prudens omnem evadet invidiam hâc methodo : dum puella confitetur se esse fornicatam, confessarius petat, an prima vice, quâ simile peccatum commisit, exposuerit circumstantiam amissæ virginitatis.

" Si respondeat categoricè, ita, vel non, cessat difficultas ; et quidem si jam sint primæ vices statim reponet, jam fuisse primas vices, adeòque solùm ei dici debet, ut conteratur de illa circumstantia, et eam confiteatur : si taceat, instruatur, illam circumstantiam tutiùs semel exprimendam, adeòque si id nunquam fecerit, jam desuper doleat et se accuset," (No. 287.)

In No. 293, De Bestialitate, the following passage occurs:

" Ad hoc crimen reducitur congressus carnalis cum dæmone in corpore assumpto : quod scelus aggravatur per circumstantiam contra religionem, quatenus includit societatem cum dæmone ; ideòque gravis est et gravissimum peccatum contra naturam : consideranda est etiam forma corporis vel hominis, vel bestiæ, in qua apparet dæmon ; item repræsentatio personæ virginis, monialis, &c. Verùm plerumque præsumendum est, talia solum fieri per fortem imaginationem, quâ decipiuntur homines," &c.

29

CHAPTER XXXIII.

Vol. V. commences with a Treatise on the Incarnation of Christ. The 24th No. treats

OF THE WORSHIP AND INVOCATION OF THE SAINTS.

" Prove that the Saints in heaven are to be worshipped and honoured with the veneration of dulia.

" *Ans.* It is proved from this that they have supernatural excellence and are the friends of God : and therefore a reason for their worship truly subsists.

" The same is proved from this that the church has instituted festivals of the Saints ; and THEREFORE, the worship of the Saints may be said to be a commanded duty.

" Finally, it is proved from the Old Testament ; for Abraham, Jacob, Samson, and others, exhibited reverence or honour to angels : therefore, as men are blessed as the angels of God, (as is said, Matt. xxii. v. 30.), it follows also, that their worship is lawful.

" Is this worship of the Saints absolute or respective?

" It is absolute : because it is exhibited on account of the excellence, intrinsic, and peculiar to themselves : yet it may also be called respective, inasmuch as God is honoured in the Saints.

" *Obj. I.* 1 Tim. i. 17, it is said, *to the only God be honour and glory*, therefore, not to the Saints.

" *Ans.* The worship of *latria* not of *dulia* is spoken of in the text ; otherwise, the apostle would contradict himself, writing to the Romans ; ii. v. 10 ; *but glory and honour to every one that worketh good.*

" *Obj. II.* Mardochæus, Esther xiii. 14., gives as a reason why he would not rise up before Aman : *I feared lest I might transfer the honour of my God to a man ;* therefore, &c.

" *Ans.* Aman had required honour as though he were in himself somewhat of a divinity : for when the Gentiles were promoted, they supposed that divinity was communicated to themselves ; and thus we see that the Cæsars after their death were reckoned among the number of the gods.

" *Obj. III.* Apoc. xix. 10.   The angel refused to be wor-shipped by John, saying, *See thou do it not ;* therefore, &c.

" *Ans.* The angel refused this ON ACCOUNT OF THE GREAT HOLINESS OF JOHN.

" Are the Saints to be invoked by us ?

" I answer, with Council of Trent, sess. 25. *Concerning the Invocation of the Saints :* ' that it is good and useful to supplicate them, and to fly to their prayers, power, and aid : but that they who deny that the Saints are to be invoked, or who assert that they do not pray for men, or that their invocation of them is idolatry, hold an impious opinion.'

" It is proved also from Gen. xlviii. 16., where Jacob in-vokes his own angel : besides that angels have conferred many benefits is plain from various passages, and especially from the history of Tobias : but there is the same reason for the invocation of beatified men as of angels : and thus, also, 2 Macc. xv. 14., it is plain that the Saints which are still in limbus pray for men : for it is there said concerning Jere-miah : *this is he that prayeth much for the people :* final-ly, according to sectarians themselves, it is proper to call upon Saints whilst they are still upon earth to pray for us, (thus God, Exod. xxxii. 14., was appeased by the prayer of Moses for the people) ; therefore, it is more proper to pray to the Saints who are reigning with Christ, as to those who are more closely connected with God in heaven."

The objections against the Invocation of Saints are solved.
(No. 25.)

" *Obj. I.* 1 Tim. ch. ii. 5., it is said : *one mediator of God and men, the man Christ Jesus ;* therefore the Saints are not our mediators.

" *Ans.* I make a distinction in the inference : I entirely agree, that, therefore, the Saints are not the principal media-tors ; for Christ alone is the one who asks in his own name, as he who by his own proper merit renders God propitious to men : I deny the inference, that, therefore, the Saints are not secondary mediators, and *participatively,* who relying on the merits of Christ beseech God for us ; and thus, in-deed, Gal. iii. 19., the name of mediator is given to Moses, and in this sense, also, the Divine Virgin is called *our life and hope :* but when we ask of her, *give salvation to thy servants,* it is meant that she give it by obtaining it ; and thus, the apostle, 1 Cor. ix. 22. ventures to say of himself: *that I might save all.*

" Nor does this diminish the dignity and power of Christ : because the Saints are invoked as mediators with the media- tor and God, says St. Thomas : so that they themselves by their intercession may supply that which is wanting to the weakness of our prayers.

" *Obj. II.* The Saints have no knowledge of our pray- ers ; therefore, they are invoked in vain.

" *Ans.* I deny the antecedent : because the Saints know all things which pertain to their state in the Word ; and, therefore, they see our prayers directed to themselves in the Word or in God, as in a mirror containing all things, just as the angels have knowledge of our prayers.

" You may urge ; Eccl. ix. 5., it is said, *the dead know nothing more ;* therefore, the Saints do not know our prayers.

" The best solution is that THESE ARE THE WORDS OF THE FOOLISH AND OF THOSE WHO SAY THAT THE SOUL PERISHES WITH THE BODY.*

" *Obj. III.* All benefits come forth from God to us, who is prepared to give them ; therefore we ask these things of the Saints improperly.

" *Ans.* I deny the inference : because we do not ask any- thing of the Saints in excluding God, but rather that through the Saints, as through intercessors, we may receive them from God.

" But that we implore the clemency of God through the Saints, is not through the defect of the power or mercy of God : but because God is willing to grant certain blessings only through the Saints : that thus the Saints may be hon- oured and God in them ; or, also, that thus subordination and order in second causes may be preserved, says St. Thomas.

" Generally as to these and other objections you will con- vince sectarians that all these things do not hinder us from

---

* Not a word is said in the context, which affords the least ground for such a supposition. My reader can refer to the passage.

imploring the prayers of the living : therefore, neither can they be any objection to our seeking the suffrages of the Saints in heaven.

" Is the invocation of the Saints a commanded duty ?

" Some reply that it is neither necessary to salvation, nor is it enjoined upon every one : yet Sylvius, Billuart, &c., think more probably that it is a commanded duty : concerning the Blessed Virgin, at least this seems to be sufficiently inferred from the Holy Fathers and the common opinion of the faithful."

CONCERNING THE WORSHIP OF IMAGES. (No. 26.)

" What is meant by an image ?

" *A similitude or representation of some existing thing, expressed for that thing as a copy :* for it is called an image from imitating : because it represents the thing which it imitates.

" How does it differ from an idol ?

" Because an idol is a likeness representing that, which either simply does not exist, or certainly is not such as that which is worshipped : but an image is the similitude of a thing which really exists, v. g. of a man : hence the apostle says concerning an idol, 1 Cor. viii. 4 ; *because we know that an idol is nothing in the world ;* nothing certainly in its representation : because it is no divinity in itself or in its own prototype.

" Prove that the images of Christ and the Saints are to be worshipped.

" *Ans.* It is PROVED in the first place from the COUNCIL OF TRENT, (!!) sess. above cited, where it will say against sectarians, ' that the images of Christ and of the Virgin Mother of God and of the other Saints, are to be kept and retained especially in temples, and that due honour and veneration are to be paid to them.'

" The seventh general Synod or the II. Nicene, under Adrian I., had decreed the same against the Iconoclast heretics, saying, that salutation and honorary adoration were to be exhibited to the images of Christ and the Saints.

" It is proved further : because proper veneration was due and was given to the ark of the covenant in the old law ; because it bore the image of heavenly things ; although the

29 *

ark in itself was something inanimate and destitute of intrinsic holiness : hence, concerning it, it is said literally, Ps. xcviii. 5., *adore his footstool, for it is holy ;* therefore, &c.

"Finally, it is proved also from reason : because the honour of an image in itself redounds to the prototype ; just as on the contrary, an insult offered to a royal statue redounds to the king, as S. Amb. remarks, Serm. x. on Ps. cxviii.

"ARE IMAGES OF GOD AND OF THE MOST HOLY TRINITY PROPER ?

"YES : although this is not so certain as concerning the images of Christ and the Saints ; as this was determined at a later period.

"But it is to be observed that the divinity cannot be depicted, but those forms are depicted under which God has sometimes appeared, or to which divine attributes are paid in some similitude : thus GOD THE FATHER is represented under the form of an old man :·because Dan. vii. 9. we read that he appeared thus : *and the ancient of days sat ;* and the Holy Ghost under the form of a dove ; because he appeared thus, Matt. iii. 16 : *He saw the Spirit of God descending like a dove ;* or under the form of cloven tongues, such as he appeared on the day of Pentecost, Acts ii. 3. *And there appeared unto them cloven tongues as it were of fire.*

"Therefore, images of this kind are not to be painted according to any one's will, but only under these forms in which they have sometimes appeared.

"It is proved by an equal reason : for just as it is proper to describe these histories and apparitions with words, thus also with colours : for pictures as well as words are signs of things.

"With this also agrees the condemnation of prop. 26, by Alexander VIII., A. D. 1690 : 'It is a sin to place a likeness of God the Father in a Christian temple.'

"*Obj.* Exod. xx. 4., God commanded : *thou shalt not make to thyself a graven thing, nor the likeness of anything that is in heaven·above, or in the earth beneath ;* therefore God himself has forbidden images.

"*Ans.* 1. Some who think that under the old law it was for-

bidden to make images on account of the proneness of the
Jews to idolatry, say that this precept is partly moral, inasmuch as it forbids idolatry; partly ceremonial in so far as it
forbids every image : and in this respect it ceases in the new
law so much the more, because its cause now no longer
exists.

"*Ans.* 2. That idols are only forbidden to be made such
as the Gentiles made, to which they paid divine honour :
hence it is added: *that thou mayest adore them ;* viz., as
gods.

"But that all images are not forbidden is plain from the
fact that by the command of God the images of two Cherubim were made about the ark.

"Finally, you will generally CONFOUND HERETICS FROM
NATURAL REASON, which dictates that it is proper to make
pictures of parents, kings, &c., and to honour them with
civil worship ; therefore, much more is it right to make and
to honour the images of the Saints."

N. B. When *heretics* make pictures of kings and presi-
dents and parents to bow down before them, and pay them
the worship of dulia, they will deserve to be confounded ;
according to the Scripture, "confounded be all they that
serve graven images !"

Of the quality of the worship of Images. (No. 27.)

"With what worship are the images of Christ and the
Saints to be worshipped?

"It is to be premised with St. Thom. in corp. that images
may be regarded in a twofold manner.

"I. In so far as they are anything or certain matter, say
gold or sculptured or painted wood ; and in this respect they
cannot be honoured.

"II. In so much as they are images or representations of
Christ or the Saints : and in this respect they may be honoured with relative or respective worship ; so doubtless that
they may not be honoured for the sake of a dignity intrinsic
in themselves, but on account of the dignity of the prototype
or pattern : and consequently the honour shown to an image
redounds to the prototype as to the formal reason of the

worship; although the object which the representing image itself is, is not the reason why it is worshipped.

"III. Therefore, St. Thomas replies to the question, that images may be honoured with the same worship, with which their prototype is honoured, but only with a relative or respective worship: therefore, the images of the Saints are worshipped with the respective veneration of dulia; of the Divine Virgin with the relative worship of *hyperdulia*; of Christ and of God with the respective worship of *latria*: almost just as if by the same virtue we love God and our neighbour on account of the goodness of God in himself.

"Many, however, maintain that this respective worship paid to images ought to be less than the worship shown to the prototype itself: and hence they infer that the worship of latria is due to no image. They rely upon the Seventh Synod, which says that latria is not to be shown to images, because it belongs only to the divine nature.

"But others explain the Seventh Synod concerning absolute latria, which is not due to the images of Christ, although the respective worship of latria is due to them; and, therefore, they may be adored with less honour than the prototype; which are not repugnant to one another.

"However this may be, it is sufficient for us against sectarians, that all Catholics teach and prove that the images of the Saints are to be worshipped.

"*Obj.* It seems superstitious to worship and distinguish certain images as though miraculous.

"*Ans.* I deny the antecedent, with St. Aug. Epist. cxxxvii.: for this distinction is to be sought from the gratuitous will of God whom it pleases to confer special benefits upon persons who worship one image rather than another; just as God restored those to health, who looked at the brazen Serpent erected by Moses, (Num. xxi. 9.) not so to those who looked at any other: Christ restored sight to the man who had been born blind, when he washed himself in the pool of Siloam, John ix. 7., and Naaman the Syrian was cleansed from leprosy in the Jordan, 4 Kgs. v. 10., rather than elsewhere.

"In the same way, a solution is given when the objection is made against the invocation of Saints, that it is superstitious to invoke one Saint for such a disease, another for another.

"However, the Council of Trent, sess. xxv. admonishes concerning the invocation of the Saints, that the faithful be instructed that they do not believe that there is any inherent divinity or virtue in images, on account of which they are to be worshipped, or anything to be asked of them, or confidence to be placed in them, as was formerly done by the Gentiles. Besides, it admonishes that all superstition and filthy lucre be guarded against: now if certain abuses are, perhaps, committed by some idiots, the church neither teaches nor approves them; although the simplicity and good intention even of these idiots often extenuate if they do not excuse."

OF THE WORSHIP OF RELICS. (No. 28.)

"What is understood by the relics of the Saints?

"The bodies of the Saints, bones, or other parts of the body, or other things made holy by touching those bodies, as garments, chains, or other instruments of suffering.

"Prove that they are to be honoured and venerated.

"It is proved from the passage from the Council of Trent, already often cited.

"It is confirmed by various examples of Sacred Scripture: thus, Gen. l. and Exod. xiii., the bones of Jacob and Joseph were preserved with great honour and carried over from Egypt, 4 Kgs. xiii., a dead body touching the bones of Elisha revived: see, also, ch. xxiii. 18. Matt. ix. 20; a woman afflicted with an issue of blood touches with the greatest veneration the hem of Christ's garment and is healed. Acts v. 15., they expose believing sick persons in the streets in order that at least the shadow of Peter might cover them, and they might be healed: and ch. xix. 12., the handkerchiefs and girdles of St. Paul were laid upon the sick, and their maladies left them.

"To these are added the miracles done at the presence or at the contact of the Sacred Cross and the relics of the Saints. See St. Aug. S. xxii. *de Civ. Dei.*, c. 8. it. Serm. cccxxii. al. 31. *de diversis.*

"Finally, it is proved by reason, founded on the words of St. Aug. 'Whoever has affection for a person, venerates

all those things which are left of him after death ;' therefore, as we venerate the Saints as members of Christ and
our intercessors, we consequently ought, also, to venerate
their relics with proper honour in memory of them.

" With what worship are relics honoured ?

" In a similar way and worship in which the images of
Christ and of the Saints, according to what has been said,
No. 27 ; and, therefore, with the same worship with which
the person is honoured, whose relics they are, but relative
and respective : for just as images are honoured, because
they represent the prototype or person ; so, also, relics in so
much as they are or have been connected with him.

" *Obj. I.* Christ, Matt. xxiii. 29, says, *Woe to you Scribes
and Pharisees, hypocrites who build the sepulchres of the
prophets, and adorn the monuments of the just ;* therefore,
he forbids the worship of relics.

" *Ans.* I deny the inference : because Christ does not
blame the deed itself, but the hypocrisy in the deed : for if
any one could have seen their hatred of heart against Christ,
whose heralds the prophets had been, he would have judged
that the Jews did this not with a religious intention in honour
of the Prophets, but rather for the triumph of their own
murderous parents.

" *Obj. II.* A dutiful son does not honour the instruments
of disgrace by which his father was put to death ; therefore,
the Christian ought not to venerate the cross, or the other
instruments of the death of Christ or the Martyrs.

" *Ans.* I deny the inference : there is a disparity, because
the disgraceful instruments of the father, v. g., the scourge,
or the block, would be considered by the son only as the disgrace or misfortune of the father ; for if they had been the
cause of exaltation to the father, and of liberation from
bitter tyranny to the son, he would have held them in
esteem. We therefore venerate the cross, &c., not in so
far as they were the instruments of the wicked action of
torture, but inasmuch as they were instruments of the vic-
torious passion and exaltation, which also were made holy
by contact with the body of Christ or the Saints."

Corollaries concerning the worship of relics. (No. 29.)

" Would it therefore be proper to honour the lips of Judas, the hands of the crucifiers, &c., on account of their touching the body of Christ?

" *Ans.* By no means : because they were animate instruments of iniquity, not made holy through contact with the body of Christ, but rather dishonoured by the wickedness of those, whose members they were.

" Is the Divine Virgin to be honoured with the respective worship of latria on account of contact with Christ, just as the cross of Christ is adored?

" *Ans.* St. Thom. art. 5. no ; there is a disparity, because the cross is an inanimate thing, the worship of which is in itself only respective; but as the B. Virgin is a person capable of absolute worship with respect to herself, thus the honour paid to her is considered absolute, and not respective : but the Divine Virgin cannot be adored with the absolute worship of latria ; therefore, neither with the respective.

" Observe, that the true cross of Christ has both the claim of an image, inasmuch as it represents the figure of the crucified Lord ; and the claim of a relic on account of contact with the sacred body and blood : but other crosses made after the likeness of the real cross have only the claim of an image.

" *Obj.* Therefore, not only the real nails and the real spears, but also, all nails and all spears have the claim of an image of Christ crucified, and thus may be honoured.

" *Ans.* I deny the inference : for any kind of similitude is not sufficient for an image, (and thus an egg is not said to be the image of another egg ;) but it is requisite that one be expressed by the other for its similitude : just as crosses are now made only to express the first on which Christ was crucified ; as they now have no other use amongst us since the edict of Constantine the Great, prohibiting criminals to be crucified : but not all nails or spears are made for the representation of those which were the instruments of Christ's passion, but they are made for other purposes : yet if they should be made as a representation of the former, they would not be unworthy of proper veneration ; as when they are painted in a picture together with a cross.

" From these things, it is plain, how justly the Emperor Theodosius has forbidden that crosses should be painted or sculptured on the ground, v. g., on the stones of monuments, on account of the danger of trampling them with the feet.

" In what sense does the church sing: *O cross! Hail only hope?*

" I answer with Sylvius, because by a personification the cross is introduced for him who hangs on the cross: and thus the sense is: *O Christ crucified! Hail our only hope.*

" Observe finally, that, although true relics may be privately worshipped, yet they may not be exposed for public veneration in the temple, unless they have been approved by the Ordinary or Bishop.   Thus the Council of Trent, sess. xxv."

For a detailed refutation of the Romish reasons in favour of the worship of Saints, Images, and Relics, my reader must permit me to refer him to my Lectures on Romanism. My limits will not permit me to repeat the argument in this connection, and he will there find as satisfactory an answer as I am able to give.   The words of Paul to Elymas may aptly be addressed to Anti-christ, who with all deceivableness of unrighteousness endeavours to destroy the souls of men.   " O full of all subtilty and all mischief, thou child of the devil, thou enemy of all righteousness, wilt thou not cease to pervert the right ways of the Lord?"

OF THE VIRGINITY OF THE BLESSED VIRGIN MARY.

" Prove that Mary always remained a Virgin.

" It is proved, because she was a Virgin before the birth and in the birth (of Christ), from the prophecy of Isaiah, ch. vii. v. 14.   *Behold a Virgin shall conceive and bear a son:* where it is not only signified that she who was before a Virgin should conceive and bear ; for what sign or prodigy would it be, that she who was a Virgin should conceive and bear having lost her virginity ? where the prophet still foretells it as a great and extraordinary sign that she shall conceive and bear.

" The same is PROVED by the APOSTLES' CREED : *Born of the Virgin Mary.*

" That she remained a Virgin also after the birth is proved

by divine tradition against the heretics, Jovinian, and Helvidius; and this has been settled in various councils; signally in general ones, &c.

"*Obj. I.* It is said, Matt. i. 25. of Joseph: *he knew her not until she brought forth her first born son;* therefore, he knew her after the birth, and the Divine Virgin brought forth a second born.

"*Ans.* I deny the inference: because the particle *until* implies that this was not done before the birth, in order that it may be signified that the virginity was unimpaired until the birth, the contrary of which seemed to proceed from the birth itself: but concerning the following time nothing is affirmed: indeed, it is clearly supposed, that it had been much less lost after the birth: thus, when it is said, Gen. viii. 7: *the raven did not return until the waters were dried up;* it is not signified that it afterwards returned, but rather that it never returned. To the second part of the inference, it is replied that in Scripture, every one is called the first born, before whom no one has been born, although he may be the only son.

"*Obj. II.* Matt. xii. Christ is said to have had brethren, therefore, &c.

"I answer, they were not Christ's own brothers, neither by the Virgin Mary, nor by St. Joseph: but in Scripture phrase relations or cousins are called so, even beyond the first degree.

"The Holy Fathers commonly suppose that the Blessed Virgin Mary had a vow of preserving her virginity; and hence, St. Aug. lib. de virginit. ch. iv. says, 'Mary replied to the angel when he announced, *How shall this be, since I know not a man!* Which she certainly would not have said, unless she had devoted herself as a Virgin to God.' See more at length, St. Thom. art. 4."

The perpetual virginity of Mary is a point which must be maintained at all hazards, for great is Diana of the Ephesians! We venerate the memory of the humble and holy Mary, and sure we are that if the spirits of the just in glory could take cognizance of all that transpires on earth, her heart would be pained by the idolatrous worship that is paid

30

to her. The Church of Rome makes a goddess of the Virgin Mary; she is the Diana of the Romans! The Priests must sustain her claim to perpetual virginity, or their craft is in danger to be set at nought, the magnificence of Holy Mother would be destroyed at once, if this key-stone of the arch of idolatry were knocked out. But after all that has been said, the utmost that can be alleged in favour of the question is that it is a doubtful case; probability is greatly against it. Certainly, if the Lord had intended that the virginity of Mary should be an article of faith, to be always held and cherished by believers to the end of time, he would have clearly revealed it in the Scriptures, " which are able to make wise unto salvation." We need not say that there is no such declaration. The Evangelists seldom mention the name of Mary after the history of the Saviour's birth and childhood, and the Apostles NEVER speak of her at all. The virginity of Mary before the birth of Christ, is plainly a doctrine of revelation, which can be disputed only by the most reckless infidels; but the passage cited in the preceding section appears to my mind conclusive evidence against the doctrine of the Church of Rome, especially as it is distinctly affirmed by the Holy Spirit, that marriage is honourable in all. As for tradition and St. Augustine, they may both be very good in their way, but as proof they are very indifferent.

The chapter which treats of the nativity of Christ, closes with the following paragraph, which I prefer offering in the original Latin.

" Peperit autem B. Virgo absque dolore vel infirmitate, ut dicitur Can. 79. Concilii Trullani; egressus est enim Christus ex utero clauso matris : quia decebat, ut, quæ sine libidine conceperat, sine dolore pareret; neque tantum sine dolore, sed cum ingenti jucunditate et lætitia B. Virgo peperit, juxta illud Isaiæ cap. xxxv. 2 : *Germinans germinabit, et exultabit lætabunda et laudans.*"

In the following section, the question is asked:
" Where and by whom was Christ circumcised?
" Very likely in the same stable in which he was born and very probably by St. Joseph : because no place was determined for this, nor was that office sacred."

In No. 30, we are told that " it is disputed whether Joseph was a blacksmith or a carpenter : yet from the opinion of the ancient Christians and common tradition, the latter appears the more probable."

The question is also asked: " Had Christ several garments? *Ans.* Yes," &c.   And it is also stated that " he did not walk barefoot, but with sandals, as is gathered from Mark vi. 9 : *but shod with sandals ;* but he did not use shoes, because he seems to have forbidden that, Matt. x. 9, 10," &c.

To No. 41, the following *N. B.* is appended :
" Observe against the heretics that Christ rose from the sepulchre when closed : for the glorious body penetrated the stone, just as he afterwards came to his disciples when the doors were shut : but the stone was rolled away from the monument by the angel only at the approach of the women to the sepulchre : therefore, certain painters erroneously depict Christ as rising from the open sepulchre."

At the close of No. 42, which treats of the apparitions of Christ after his resurrection, we find the following remarks :
" Did not Christ appear to his mother?
" I answer according to common opinion, yes ; and that on the first day of the resurrection : for so says the Holy Father, Bk. iii. de virginibus : ' therefore, Mary saw the resurrection of the Lord, and saw it first and believed ;' and this the affection of Christ for his dearly beloved mother appears to suggest.
" *Obj.* Mark xvi. 9., it is said : *he appeared* FIRST *to* MARY MAGDALEN ; therefore, not to his own mother.
" *Ans.* I deny the inference : for Mark seems to be speaking of those persons whose duty it would be to be witnesses and proclaimers of the resurrection of Christ, or who should confirm those who were doubtful concerning it : but these things do not relate to the Divine Virgin," &c.

CHAPTER XXXIV.

CONCERNING THE SACRAMENTS.

PREFACE.

Decree of the Council of Florence.

"There are seven Sacraments of the New Law: viz., Baptism, Confirmation, the Eucharist, Penance, Extreme Unction, Orders, and Marriage; which differ greatly from the Sacraments of the ancient law. For they did not cause grace, but prefigured that it was to be given alone through the passion of Christ: but these our Sacraments both contain grace and confer it upon such as worthily receive them. Of these, the first five have been ordained for the spiritual perfection of every man in himself: the last two for the government and increase of the whole church. For by Baptism we are spiritually born again; through Confirmation we are increased in grace and strengthened in the faith: but being born again and strengthened we are nourished by the divine aliment of the Eucharist. If through sin we contract a malady of the soul, through Penance we are spiritually healed: spiritually, also, and corporeally, according as it is expedient for the soul through Extreme Unction: but by Orders the church is governed and spiritually increased: by Marriage it is increased corporeally. All these Sacraments are performed in three things, viz., in things as to matter, in words as to form, and in the person of the minister conferring the Sacraments with the intention of doing what the church does: if anything of these be wanting, the Sacrament is not performed. Among these Sacraments there are three, Baptism, Confirmation and Orders, which impress character that is a certain indelible spiritual sign distinct from the rest. And hence, they are not repeated in the same person. But the other four do not impress character, and admit of repetition."

Canons of the Council of Trent concerning Sacraments in general.

" I. If any one shall say that the Sacraments of the new law have not all been instituted by Jesus Christ our Lord; or that they are more or less than seven; viz., Baptism, Confirmation, the Eucharist, Penance, Extreme Unction, Orders, and Marriage : or, also, that any one of these seven is not truly a Sacrament, let him be anathema! (i. e. cursed in this world and damned in the next.)

" II. If any one shall say that the Sacraments themselves of the new law, do not differ from the Sacraments of the old law, except, because the ceremonies are different, and the external rites different : let him be anathema !

" III. If any one shall say that these seven Sacraments are so equal among themselves, that for no reason can one be more worthy than another; let him be anathema !

" IV. If any one shall say that the Sacraments of the new law are not necessary for salvation, but superfluous, and that without them, or the desire of them, men may through faith alone obtain from God the grace of justification; although all are not necessary for every person; let him be anathema !

" V. If any one shall say that these Sacraments have been instituted merely for the sake of nourishing faith; let him be accursed !

" VI. If any one shall say that the Sacraments of the new law do not contain the grace which they signify : or that they do not confer the grace itself on those who put no obstacle in the way, as if they were only the external signs of grace or righteousness received by faith, and certain marks of Christian profession, by which among men believers are discerned from infidels; let him be anathema !

" VII. If any one shall say that grace is not conferred by Sacraments of this kind, always, and upon all, as far as respects God, even if they rightly receive them; let him be anathema !

" VIII. If any one shall say that grace is not conferred by the Sacraments of the new law themselves by their own power, but that mere belief of the divine promise is sufficient to obtain grace; let him be anathema !

30 *

"IX. If any one shall say that by the three Sacraments, Baptism, Confirmation, and Orders, character is not impressed on the soul, that is, a certain spiritual and indelible sign, on which account they may not be repeated; let him be anathema!

"X. If any one shall say that all Christians have power to preach the word and administer all the Sacraments; let him be anathema!

"XI. If any one shall say that the intention at least of doing what the church does, is not requisite in ministers, when they perform and confer Sacraments; let him be anathema!

"XII. If any one shall say that a minister living in mortal sin, does not perform or confer a Sacrament, although he may have preserved all essential things which pertain to performing or conferring a Sacrament; let him be anathema!

"XIII. If any one shall say that the received and approved rites of the Catholic Church, commonly used in the solemn administration of the Sacraments, may be either omitted by ministers at their option, without sin, or that they may be changed for other new ones by any pastor of the churches; let him be anathema!"

Concerning the Matter and Form of the Sacraments.
(No. 5.)

"A Sacrament which is a certain moral entity consists of two things as essential and intrinsic parts of which it is composed: to wit, of things, as matter, and of words as form; yet the Eucharist is excepted according to what has just been said.

"What is here understood by matter?

"*That sensible thing, which less methodically signifies grace:* whether that be a certain thing subsisting by itself, or a substance as water in baptism, or whether it be a certain action concerning those things, as ablution, &c.

"What is here meant by form?

"*Ans.* The words are meant by which the minister more accurately and clearly restricts the sensible thing in the Sacrament to signify the grace and spiritual effect; as in baptism, *I baptize thee*, &c.

" For what reason are the parts of Sacraments called by the name of matter and form?

" *Ans.* We use these philosophical terms for the sake of explanation, &c.

" It is to be observed, therefore, that in Sacraments properly there are no matter and form, but as it were the matter and form as St. Thom. adds : yet for the sake of brevity it has become customary to say simply the matter and form."

Of various modes of changing the form. (No. 11.)

* * * * * *

" The form is changed if in the same idiom synonymous words are taken for those which the church employs ; and it will be only an *accidental* change, if by common consent they signify the same not only as to the thing, but also explicitly and distinctly, or if they signify the same in the same manner. Hence, baptism would be valid if in place of *I baptize*, should be said, *I wash,* or *I sprinkle ;* but not if it should be said, *I cleanse* or *purge :* because the cleansing of sins by way of washing ought to be signified in baptism. Nor would it even be valid, if any one should say : *I baptize thee in the name of the Most Holy Trinity :* because the word *Trinity* does not signify the same thing in the same manner. For it does not expressly signify the Father, the Son, and the Holy Ghost.

" The form is changed by the transposition of the words, concerning which the decision would be the same as above. Hence, it would be no obstacle to the validity of baptism, if any one should say : *In the name of the Father, and of the Son, and of the Holy Ghost, I baptize thee,* &c. So too, it would not invalidate the Eucharist according to Wiggers, if the Priest should say, *this body is mine,* instead of *this is my body,* &c., &c.

" The form may be changed by interruption in pronouncing the form of the words. But whether a substantial or accidental change is induced, depends upon this, whether the delay of the interruption according to common opinion separates, or whether it leaves morally one speech and one sense ; and hence it would be only an *accidental* change, if some one between the words of the form, should sneeze or cough once : so, also, after the minister has said, *I baptize thee*, if he should say to some who are chatting, *be still*, and should immediately subjoin *in the name of the Father*, &c., the Sacrament would subsist, &c.

" The form is changed by an addition, concerning which the reason is the same as above ; and hence, if any one with the Arians should baptize *in the name of the Father*, *the greater*, *and of the Son*, *the less*, &c., he would not perform the Sacrament.

" By the subtraction of a word or syllable : which change will be substantial or accidental, according as the word omitted concerns the essence of the form or not.

" A change of form may be made by the corruption of the words : concerning which St. Thomas speaks thus : If the corruption is such that it entirely destroys the sense of the phrase, the Sacrament appears not to be performed : and this principally happens, when a corruption is made which concerns the principle of the sentence : suppose if instead of that, which is *in the name of the Father*, he should say *in the name of the Mother*. But if the sense of the discourse is not entirely destroyed, the Sacrament is performed notwithstanding : and this principally happens when a corruption is made with respect to the end : suppose if any one should say : *In nomine Patrias et Filias*, &c. &c.

" Thus also all are of opinion that a stutterer performs the Sacrament, although he may separate the first syllable : v. g. *E ego te te bap baptizo*, &c. I, I bap baptize thee thee, &c., also *ho hoc est co corpus me meum*. The this is me my bo body : also if instead of *corpus*, *copus* should be said, in place of *calix*, *calis*, &c. And hence says Billuart, let the scrupulous observe these things, who frequently repeat the words irreverently and for the purpose of ridicule, &c."

Concerning the intention of the Minister relative to the change of Form. (No. 12.)

" May the intention of the minister effect that the change of the form is substantial or accidental ?

" If the form is ambiguous or equivocal on account of the change, so that according to the common mode of speaking it receives a twofold sense, viz. the legitimate sense of the form, and a false one ; then it depends on the intention of the minister, whether the change is substantial, or accidental : or he intends the true and legitimate sense, and it will be only accidental : but otherwise substantial.

"Therefore if it be asked, what is to be said concerning this form : I baptize thee in the name of the Father, and of the Son, and of the Holy Ghost, and of the Blessed Virgin Mary ?

"I answer by making a distinction with St. Thomas, art. 8. in corp.   'The change will be substantial if it be so meant that the person is to be baptized in the name of the Virgin Mary, just as in the name of the Trinity : for such a sense would destroy the verity of the Sacrament : but if it be so understood, that (and in the name of the Blessed Virgin) is added not as if the name of the Blessed Virgin can effect anything in baptism, but that her intercession may be of advantage to the baptized person in order to preserve the baptismal grace, the perfection of the Sacrament is not destroyed.'

"Tournely rejects this distinction, saying that such a baptism is entirely invalid.

"If the form is essentially invalid, the minister cannot supply the defect by his own intention : for the form consists in the settled sense of the words, but words have their signification from common application and custom, and not from the application of any private person whatsoever.

"If the form when changed retains altogether the same sense with the essential form, then whatever may be the private intention of the minister with respect to the signification of the words, the change will be only accidental, and the Sacrament is performed, so far as the form is concerned.

"It is said : *In so far as the form is concerned ;* because the intention is required in the minister, of doing whatever the Church does and Christ has appointed : and hence he who knowingly introduces an accidental change, which he erroneously supposes to be essential, regularly does not perform the Sacrament: not indeed through defect of the matter or form, but through defect of the intention of doing what the Church does," &c.

It is not lawful except in case of absolute necessity, to make use of a doubtful form or matter in the administration of the Sacraments.   (No. 13.)

To make a substantial change is a mortal sin : it is a sin of sacrilege against religion, because it contains grievous irreverence towards the Sacrament, and towards Christ himself, the author of the Sacraments.   It is also a sin against love to our neighbour, and against justice.—An accidental change for a just reason is no sin at all ; but if done from contempt, &c. it is a mortal sin, though the change be trifling.

"Authors observe, that although ignorance may excuse certain laymen from mortal sin, who baptize in a case of necessity with a form essentially or accidentally changed, yet it does not excuse midwives, who ought to know the ceremony of baptism by heart, before they are admitted to the office of a midwife, as the Roman ritual and the IId provincial Synod of Mechlin prescribe.   In like manner ignorance will not excuse a minister ex officio, as he ought to know what things belong to his own office."

If the form is so changed as to invalidate the Sacrament, the Sacrament must be repeated.

If there is a reasonable doubt whether it has been legitimately pronounced, then it is lawful to repeat it.   If there is no reasonable doubt, it is improper. (No. 14.)

Do the Sacraments of the New Law confer grace by their own power (ex opere operato ?)   (No. 18.)

" It is a Catholic doctrine that the Sacraments of the new law contain grace, and that they confer it by their own power was decreed in the Council of Trent, sess. 7. can. 8. Concerning Sacraments, &c.   ' Whoever shall say that by the Sacraments themselves of the new law, grace is not conferred by their simple administration, let him be accursed.'

" In what sense does the Council there say, canon 6., that the Sacraments of the New Law contain grace ?

" Not as if grace were in the Sacraments, as the accident in the subject, a thing in a place, or liquor in a vessel, (as Calvin basely calumniates ;) but that they contain grace by way of cause and instrumentally ; or as Steyaert says, inasmuch as they are not only signs of grace, like those of the old law, but also instrumental causes, from which it is proper to derive it."

This theory is then sustained as follows.

" John, iii. 5.   It is said, ' unless a man be born again of water and of the Holy Ghost, he cannot enter into the kingdom of God ;' where the power of regeneration is attributed not less to the water than to the Holy Ghost ; to the water doubtless as the instrument, and to the Holy Ghost as the principal cause.

" In a similar way, Eph. v. 26, the apostle says, ' cleansing it by the laver of water in the word of life ;' therefore the baptism of water truly cleanses. See more texts in authors.

" It is proved, 2. If Sacraments could not confer grace by their due administration, but could only excite faith in the divine promises (as sectarians profess,) it would follow, 1. that baptism conferred on a child would be of no efficacy : 2. that a Sacrament conferred in the Latin or Greek language would effect nothing for him, who does not understand this idiom : 3. that a Sacrament sometimes may afford grace to the spectators, in whom it might excite faith, and not to the receiver himself, in whom perhaps faith might not be excited.

" Calvin objects, 1 Pet. iii. 20 and 21, it is said : ' eight souls were saved by water ; whereunto baptism being of the like form now saveth you also : not the putting away of the filth of the flesh, but the examination of a good conscience towards God :' therefore baptism does not confer grace, but faith, which is called the *examination* of a good conscience.

" *Ans.* I deny the inference : for the sense of this passage is that baptism does not save us precisely through external washing, by which the filth of the body is washed off, as the baptism or purification of the Jews did : but by internally cleansing the soul from sins through the proper deposition of the internal conscience. See a more extended explanation in authors.

" *Obj. II.* If Sacraments confer grace by their due administration, a proper disposition is not required in the recipient, nor does it contribute to a greater or less conferring of grace : but these things are false ; therefore, &c.

" *Ans.* I deny the maj., for it is certain that in order to a profitable reception of a Sacrament, a proper disposition is required in adults ; and according as this is greater or less, so much the greater or less will be the grace to be conferred, as the Council of Trent teaches, sess. 6. ch. 7.

" But this disposition is only an indispensable requisite :

because Sacraments act in the manner of natural agents, which effect is more or less according to the greater or less capacity or disposition of the subject: which disposition still has no efficiency; as is plain in fire, which burns dry wood more effectually than green, although the dryness is merely the remover of a hindrance, or an indispensable requisite and not the efficient cause of combustion.

Something similar is found in those whom Christ miraculously cured; of whom although it was required that they should believe, yet the cure was not effected by their own faith, but by the virtue of Christ."

Section 19. discusses the question whether the Sacraments cause grace physically or morally. The opinion that they cause it physically is the more probable.

In No. 22., which treats of the grace peculiar to each Sacrament, this passage occurs:

" Mention briefly the graces which are peculiar to each Sacrament.

" *Ans.* In baptism, is habitual grace, in so far as it is regenerative, and as it gives to a person his first spiritual existence, destroying every fault and punishment.

" Actual grace is the assistance which is afterwards given in its own time in order to preserve the purity of the soul, to live in a Christian manner, and to receive the other Sacraments worthily.

" In the Sacrament of confirmation, habitual grace or its increase is corroborative and augmentative of regeneration.

" The aids of actual grace are in order to keep and profess the faith constantly, and to overcome contrary temptations.

" In the Eucharist sanctifying grace tends to nourish spiritual life, and to unite the person with God by more fervent performance of virtues, &c.

" The habitual grace of the Sacrament of penance tends to make reparation by way of spiritual healing and resuscitation, &c.

" The habitual grace of Extreme Unction tends more fully to heal the soul, &c.

" The habitual grace of the Sacrament of Orders is ministrative, or in order to the due performance of the sacred functions of the office, &c.

"Finally the habitual grace of the Sacrament of matrimony tends to unite the minds, and to restrain the lusts of the flesh, &c. &c."

No. 26. treats of the Sacramental character. This is a spiritual and indelible sign impressed on the soul. It is called spiritual not only because the soul on which it is impressed is spiritual, but also because it is the cause of spirituality. "It is indelible so that it never can be destroyed either in this world or in the world to come, but it will remain in the good for their glory, and in the bad to their disgrace. Hence if a priest should arise from the dead, he would not have to be again baptized, confirmed or ordained. It would be another thing if one of a married couple should be raised from the dead; for then they would have to be united: because the bond of marriage is dissolved by death." Baptism, confirmation and orders confer this character. (No. 27.)

In No. 34. which treats of the faith and probity of the minister, we are informed,

"Neither the probity nor the faith of the minister is necessary to the validity or effect of the Sacrament: so that all who are out of a state of grace, as well infidels and heretics as believers, whether excommunicated, suspended, degraded persons, &c. may confer Sacraments in a valid and profitable manner, if only the other requisites to the validity and effect of the Sacraments are afforded."

"The reason is, because the Sacraments do not take effect from the virtue of the merits or faith of the minister, but from a divine virtue and from the merits of Christ, which cannot be hindered by the wickedness of others," &c.

"To administer the Sacraments unworthily or in a state of mortal sin, is in itself a mortal sin of sacrilege: but any one is regarded as administering thus unworthily, when he is conscious to himself of mortal sin, and ventures to do it without sincere repentance." (No. 35.)

In a case of this kind it is not sufficient that the Priest is sorry for the sin, but he must confess sacramentally. (No. 37.)

It is not lawful to ask or receive Sacraments from a minister who is not tolerated, that is who has been denounced as one whom the faithful must avoid, except in cases of extreme necessity: if there is danger of some one's dying without Baptism, &c.

31

CONCERNING THE INTENTION NECESSARY ON THE PART OF
THE MINISTER. (No. 39.)

" Is intention in the minister requisite to the valid performance of a Sacrament ?

" YES ; to wit, the intention of doing what the Church
does : so that a Sacrament conferred through mimicry and
for ridicule, or by a crazy, drunken man, or in any other
way devoid of reason, is no Sacrament at all.

" This doctrine the Council of Florence delivers, and likewise the Council of Trent, sess. 7. can. 11. of the Sacraments : ' If any one shall say that the intention is not required in ministers, when they perform and confer Sacraments, at least of doing what the Church does, let him be
accursed.'

" The primary reason of this is sought from the institution
of Christ, which is clear, especially from tradition.

" Besides it may also be inferred from the words and the
manner in which Christ instituted the Sacraments : v. g.
when he said : *Whose sins ye remit—and whose ye retain,*
&c. ; which words suppose that the minister confers the Sacraments with full purpose and deliberation."

" It is to be observed that the intention is an act of the will
tending towards the object : and hence the necessary intention
in the minister consists in the act of his will, by which he
wills the external performance of the Sacraments, with the
intention of doing what the Church does." This intention is
distinguished as *actual, virtual, habitual,* and *interpretative.*

" Actual intention is the present and actual application of
the mind to that which is deliberately done.

" Does this require that any one must formally say in his
heart or by his lips—I intend, I wish to do this, &c., v. g. I
intend to baptize, to consecrate, &c. ?

" No : but it is enough that any one when called to the
administration of the Sacraments, and girding himself for this
purpose, begins reverently to handle the matter, &c.

" Indeed those scrupulous reflections upon the intention
itself are to be disapproved, inasmuch as they hinder devotion and diminish attention relative to the very object of the
act."

" Virtual intention is that by which some person by the

influence of the actual intention previously entertained and still morally persevering, with self-possession applies himself to the duty and proceeds in its performance, although on account of some mental distraction, he does not notice the object of his intention or what he is doing."

" Habitual intention is that which consists only in a certain habitual disposition : such is a past wish that has been interrupted, also a disposition of the will, which neither actually exists, nor ever has existed, but which would be elicited if this or that should occur to the mind."

" Interpretative intention is that which does not proceed from the will as the eliciting principle, but only as the voluntary effect in the cause according to moral interpretation ; such is v. g. in a drunken person, who knows that he has been accustomed to perform sacramental actions."

Habitual and interpretative intentions are not sufficient ; but actual and virtual ones are.

" Therefore he, who advertently has gone to the baptistry, confessional, altar, &c. in order to perform some ministerial duty, baptizes, absolves, consecrates, &c. in a valid manner, although at the time of the ministration he should be distracted."

"Say the same of a priest, who, being roused at midnight in order immediately to administer the Sacrament of baptism, penance, Extreme Unction, &c., hastens thus half-asleep to the baptistry, &c., and whilst still thus confused administers the Sacrament."

In No. 41, the following cases are solved.

" Is a right intention in the minister requisite to the perfection of the Sacrament?

" If only a right intention with regard to the Sacrament, or at least an implicit intention of performing a Sacrament is entertained, the Sacrament will be valid, although the ulterior intention may not be right : and hence St. Thomas teaches, 9, 64. art. 10. in c. : ' If a priest intends to baptize some woman that he may abuse her, or if he intends to prepare the body of Christ that he may use it for poisoning : and because the former does not depend upon the latter, hence it is that such perversity of intention does not destroy the verity of the Sacrament, but the minister himself sins grievously by such an intention.'

"Ought the intention of the minister to be fixed as to a certain person or matter?

"Yes, as is plain from the very forms of the Sacraments: thus by *I baptize thee, I absolve thee,* a certain and determined person is designated; and in the form of the Eucharist, the pronoun *hoc* designates the determined matter to be consecrated.

"Hence in the Roman missal, where, concerning defects of the mass, 87, we read thus : ' If any one has before him eleven hosts, and intends to consecrate only ten : not determining which ten he intends : in these cases he does not consecrate, because the intention is required.' For a reason cannot be given, why in this case one should be consecrated rather than another.

"What if any should think that there were only ten hosts, and there should be eleven, or that he holds a single one whilst he holds two?

"They will all be regularly consecrated : because he has the intention of consecrating that which was placed before him ; or his intention is directed simply to the matter before him," &c.

An intention which is based on certain conditions renders the Sacrament invalid, unless the conditions are verified. (No. 42.)

Of the number of the Sacraments.   (No. 46.)

The Sacraments of the New Law are seven ; to wit, Baptism, Confirmation, the Eucharist, Penance, Extreme Unction, Orders and Matrimony.

The primary reason of this is the will of Christ as made known by divine tradition.   " This number of seven is also insinuated in various passages of Scripture.   Thus Prov. ix. 1. it is said, *Wisdom,* which is Christ, *has built a house for herself,* that is the Church, *and she hath hewn out* SEVEN *pillars,* doubtless the seven Sacraments, which like so many pillars sustain the church.

" So in like manner, Exod. xxv. by the seven lamps which were on one candlestick, this is implied : for there are seven Sacraments, just so many as there are lamps, which illumine the church," &c. (! !)

This peculiar exegesis is further sustained by an argument

based upon reason, thus. " These seven things seem necessary for a man in order to live and preserve his life, &c. &c. —viz. that he should be ushered into the light, increased, nourished ; healed, if he falls into sickness : that the weakness of his strength be recruited ; farther as regards the state, that magistrates may never be wanting by whose authority and rule, government may be exercised : and lastly that by the legitimate propagation of offspring it may preserve itself and the human race."

" From all which things, since it appears that they sufficiently correspond to that life by which the soul lives in God, the number of the Sacraments may easily be inferred : for thus by baptism a man is born again in Christ, &c."

CHAPTER XXXV.

Treatise concerning the Sacrament of Baptism.

PREFACE.

Decree of the Council of Florence for the instruction of the Armenians.

" Holy Baptism, which is the gate of spiritual life, occupies the first place of all the sacraments ; for by it we are made members of Christ and of the body of the Church. And as through the first man, death has passed upon all ; unless we are born again, of water and the Holy Spirit, we cannot (as the Truth declares) enter into the kingdom of heaven. The matter of this sacrament is true and natural water : nor is it of importance whether it be cold or hot. But the form is : *I baptize thee in the name of the Father, and of the Son, and of the Holy Ghost.* Yet we do not deny but that also by these words, *Let this servant of Christ be baptized in the name of the Father, and of the Son, and of the Holy Ghost ;* or, *such a one is baptized by my hands, in the name of the Father, and of the Son, and of the Holy Ghost,* a true baptism may be performed : because as the principal source from which baptism derives its virtue is the Most Holy Trinity, and the instrumental one is the minister, if the act is expressed, which is exercised by the minister himself, with the invocation of the Most Holy Trinity,

31 *

the sacrament is performed.   The minister of this sacrament is the priest, on whom it is ex officio incumbent to baptize.   But in case of necessity, not only a priest, or deacon, but also a layman, or woman, indeed even a pagan and a heretic may baptize, provided only he observes the form of the Church, and intends to do what the Church does. The effect of this sacrament is the remission of all original and actual guilt; also of all punishment, which is due for that guilt.   On this account no satisfaction is to be enjoined upon baptized persons for past sins; but if they die before they commit any fault, they immediately arrive at the kingdom of heaven, and the vision of God."

Canons of the Council of Trent concerning Baptism.

" 1. Whoever shall say that the baptism of John had the same virtue as the baptism of Christ; let him be accursed!

" 2. Whoever shall say that true and natural water is not absolutely necessary for baptism, and therefore wrests those words of our Lord Jesus Christ, as though they had been a kind of metaphor: ' Except a man be born of water, and the Holy Spirit;' let him be accursed!

" 3. Whoever shall say that in the Roman Church, which is the mother and mistress of all churches, the doctrine concerning the sacrament of baptism is not true; let him be accursed!

" 4. Whoever shall say that the baptism which is also given by heretics, in the name of the Father, and of the Son, and of the Holy Ghost, with the intention of doing what the Church does, is not true baptism; let him be accursed!

" 5. Whoever shall say that baptism is optional, that is, not necessary to salvation; let him be accursed!

" 6. Whoever shall say that a baptized person cannot, even if he would, lose grace, how much soever he may sin, unless he is unwilling to believe; let him be accursed!

" 7. Whoever shall say that baptized persons, by baptism itself, become debtors to preserve faith alone, and not the whole law of Christ; let him be accursed!

" 8. Whoever shall say that baptized persons are free from all precepts of Holy Church, which are either written or traditional, so that they are not bound to observe them, unless they choose to submit themselves to them of their own accord; let him be accursed!

" 9. Whoever shall say that men are so to be recalled to the memory of the baptism which they have received, that they may regard all the vows which are made after baptism as null and void, by virtue of the promise already made in baptism itself, as if by it they detract from the faith which they have professed, and from the baptism itself; let him be accursed!

" 10. Whoever shall say that all the sins which are committed after baptism, by the mere remembrance and faith of the baptism received, are either dismissed or become venial; let him be accursed!

" 11. Whoever shall say that a baptism, truly and with due ceremony conferred, is to be repeated on him who has denied the faith of Christ among infidels, when he is converted to repentance; let him be accursed!

" 12. Whoever shall say that no one is to be baptized, except at that age at which Christ was baptized, or in the article of death; let him be accursed!

" 13. Whoever shall say that infants, because they have not the act of faith, are not to be reckoned among believers after having received baptism, and on this account are to be re-baptized when they arrive at years of discretion; or that it is better that their baptism be omitted, than that they should be baptized in the faith only of the Church, when they do not believe by their own act; let him be accursed!

" 14. Whoever shall say that baptized children of this kind, when they have grown up, are to be asked whether they wish to have that ratified which their sponsors promised in their name when they were baptized; and that when they reply that they are unwilling, they are to be left to their own choice; and that they are not in the mean time to be compelled by any other punishment to a Christian life, except that they be prohibited the enjoyment of the Eucharist, and the other sacraments, until they repent; let him be accursed!"

CONCERNING THE SACRAMENT OF BAPTISM.

The sacrament of baptism is defined as " *the external washing of the body, performed with the prescribed form of words;* and by the Roman Catechism : *the sacrament of regeneration through water in the word.* But it is commonly defined, *A sacrament instituted by Christ the Lord, in which through the external ablution of the body with the invocation of the Most Holy Trinity, a person is spiritually regenerated.*"

" Did Christ himself baptize no one?

" Although it is said, John iv. 2, ' Although Jesus did not baptize, but his disciples;' it is still on the whole probable, that he at least baptized some one of the Apostles, lest the Apostles, when unbaptized, should have baptized others : and therefore Nicephorus quotes from Eurodius Antiochanus, that Christ himself with his own hands baptized Peter. Others say, that Christ did this in the case of his mother and John the Baptist." (No. 2.)

The remote matter of Baptism is all natural or elementary water, and that only.

" Mention some kinds of natural water which are sufficient for the matter of baptism.

" Such are the water of the sea, rain-water, water from a spring, or river, mineral water ; whether it is muddy or clear ; cold or hot ; whether it has been blessed or not.

" The same is maintained with S. Thom. concerning lye and the waters of sulphur baths. So also of waters, dissolved from hail, snow, or ice, before the ablution. Henno and Billuart say the same of the moisture of a pavement, or of walls, in damp weather ; also of water strained out of clay.

" On the other hand, baptism is invalid when performed with clay, wine, thick beer, milk, oil, spittle, sweat, tears, urine ; also with ice, snow or hail not yet dissolved ; also most probably with rose water, or any other distilled from trees, herbs, or flowers.

" Yet they maintain plausibly that it is valid with beer, gruel, tea, and similar weak and light decoctions : but it would certainly not be valid if the solution of the distilled substances is made so strong that the liquor has more of the foreign substance than of the water. It is more doubtful in the case of water dissolved out of salt." (No. 3.)

" From the preceding remarks, infer

" 1. That every one who administers baptism is bound to use the proper matter under mortal sin, properly speaking.

" 2. If the proper matter is not at hand, and necessity is urgent, he may and should apply doubtful matter, always preferring the less doubtful.

" 3. If the child thus baptized in doubtful matter afterwards survives, it must be re-baptized on this condition in proper matter.

" 4. But to use matter which is positively insufficient, (as wine, oil, &c.) whatever necessity may urge, is useless and unlawful."

In order that baptism may be performed in a proper as well as in a valid manner, observe

"1. Water from the baptismal font should be applied, and this obligation is certainly important for a solemn baptism.

"2. Braunman maintains the same concerning baptism, privately administered: and hence the minister called for such an emergency, must take with him a little flask of water from the sacred font, or order it to be obtained.

"3. Yet urgent necessity is excepted, or in case baptism must be administered by a midwife, &c.

"4. The water of the sacred font should be kept clean: and therefore too much chrism ought not to be mixed, nor should it be spoiled in any other way: and hence a child infected with a contagious disease ought not to be baptized over the font, but away from the font, with water taken from the font.

"5. If the water in the font is frozen, or too cold, it may be warmed with the hands, or mixed (but in a greater quantity,) with common warm water.

"6. If the water of the sacred font has been so much diminished that a failure may be apprehended, other common water may be mixed with it, yet in a smaller quantity.   If it has been corrupted, or in some other way become defective, let fresh water be poured into the font when properly cleansed, and let it be blessed, &c." (No. 4.)

The proximate matter of baptism is the application of the remote matter, viz., natural water, or the corporeal ablution itself.   This ablution may be performed in a threefold manner; 1, by immersion; 2, by sprinkling; and 3, by pouring out, or pouring in, or pouring on.   Any one of these three modes is sufficient to constitute the sacrament valid.   A threefold immersion, or sprinkling, &c., is not essential to the validity of the sacrament; but the latter is enjoined, and any one baptizing in any other manner would commit a grievous offence in not observing the rite of the Church in an important thing.   (No. 5.)

In order necessarily to constitute a sacrament, the ablution should be "generally such that the minister may be truly said to wash the person to be baptized; so that he may be morally regarded as washed or cleansed: concerning which the following things are requisite:

" 1. That the ablution be performed by a minister, or by the intervention of his agency ; for otherwise he could not truly say, *I baptize thee;* and hence if upon seeing some one falling, or thrown by another person into a river, or washed with water in some other way, he pronounces the words of the form, it will be no sacrament.

" The same seems rather probable if he is baptized with snow or ice, applied indeed by the minister, but dissolved only after the application through the heat of the body of the person to be baptized. Yet it is not necessary that the minister should immediately touch the water, or the person to be baptized : and hence in some places water is poured on the head of the candidate for baptism, by means of a shell ; in such a manner also the minister may consult his own safety against a contagious disease, v. g., in time of pestilence.

" 2. It is requisite that the ablution be successive, so that it be performed with some motion of the successive contact of the water around the body : whether this successive contact arises from the application of water to the body, (as is done in baptism by effusion,) or from the application of the body to the water, as in baptism by immersion.

" Hence the baptism would be invalid if the person to be baptized should be held motionless in water that is not agitated : also if only a few drops of water that has not been stirred remain on his forehead without any local motion.

" 3. It must be the ablution of the body itself by the immediate or physical contact of the water with the body : yet it is not necessary that it wash off the filth. Hence the baptism is not valid, if the water touches only the clothes : as may easily happen in baptism by sprinkling.

" If the water touches only the hair, nails, the pelles secundinæ or the galea nativitatis, the baptism is very uncertain ; hence they admonish that care must sedulously be taken, that when persons who have much hair are brought forward for baptism, that the skin be rubbed with the water, lest the ablution be performed only on the hair. It should likewise be enjoined upon midwives, that when they baptize in a case of necessity, they first break the secondary skin, in order that the water may immediately touch the body.

" 4. The ablution should be performed on so considerable a part of the body, and with such a quantity of water, that the man may in consequence be morally denomınated washed or cleansed.   Hence it is rather probable that one or two drops of water are not sufficient for baptism : yet because some teach that it is enough if it only flows, in case of necessity this may serve : it would be however on condition that if he survives he must be rebaptized.   For greater security, that quantity of water should always be applied (if it is at hand) which is certainly sufficient for baptism : and hence it is better to exceed a little in the quantity than to be deficient." (No. 6.)

As for the part of the body in which the ablution should take place, according to the practice of the church, the head is to be washed as the principal abode of the soul, and the part in which all the senses are strongest ; but it is not necessary that the whole head should be washed, but a considerable part of it, or according to the practice of the church, the top.   The Roman ritual has decided in certain cases as follows.

" If an infant has put forth its head from the womb of the mother, and the danger of death is imminent, let it be baptized on the head ; neither must it afterwards be baptized a second time, if it comes forth alive.   But if it has put forth another member which gives indication of vital motion, it may be baptized on it, if danger threatens ; and then if it survives when born, it must on that condition be rebaptized : but if thus baptized it afterwards comes forth from the womb dead, it ought to be buried in consecrated ground.

" What if the infant baptized in this case of necessity, v. g., in the hand, afterwards puts forth its head?

" *Ans.* Without delay it must on this condition be rebaptized on the head, if the danger continues : but otherwise its entire egression from the womb must be waited for.   The same is to be observed, if in a danger of this kind the baptism may be rendered considerably more certain : v. g. an infant before baptized only on the toes, ought now if the danger is still urgent, to be conditionally baptized on the feet themselves.

" But what if there appears no sign of life in the part protruding from the womb?

" *Ans.* It may be baptized on that part on the condition, *if thou art alive ;* for it has been found in the experience of midwives, that, although no sign of life may appear in the part thus protruding, yet it may afterwards be found to be alive. If, however, says our manual, no sign of life has afterwards appeared, it may not be buried in consecrated ground." (No. 7.)

"*Is baptism validly conferred by a fatal ablution?*

"*Ans.* It may be fatal in a twofold manner : one by reason of the matter, as when an infant is baptized in boiling or in poisoned water : and such ablution is sufficient for the validity of baptism ; because it certainly remains a true moral ablution, &c. The one is called fatal in itself, or by reason of the action, as when any one throws a boy into a well or a river without hope of emerging. This action is certainly unlawful, &c. But it is controverted whether it is sufficient to constitute valid baptism, if the form is pronounced together with the intention of baptizing." The case is then argued pro and con at considerable length. Suarez, Wiggers, Neesen, Pauwels, Van Roy, Boudart, &c., maintain the affirmative ; and Scotus and the Scotists, Daelman, Peringuè, &c., the negative. (No. 8.)

"*What is the legitimate form of baptism?*

"Among the Latins it is this : *I baptize thee in the name of the Father, and of the Son, and of the Holy Ghost.* That this is the legitimate one is plain from the Council of Florence in the decree for the instruction of the Armenians ; from the Council of Trent, sess. 7. can. 4 ; from the Roman ritual, &c., and from the most certain practice of the whole Western or Latin Church. But this form is gathered from Matt. xxviii. : *baptizing them in the name,* &c.

"Among the Greeks the form is this : *Let this servant,* or (as others now say,) *this servant of Christ is baptized in the name,* &c. This also is legitimate and sufficient as is plain from Eugenius, iv. in the same decree of the Council of Florence : for each expresses the action of baptizing (the Latins' in the act signified, the Greeks' in the act exercised,) and the explicit invocation of the most holy Trinity. It is evident also from the practice of the Church in not baptizing Greeks, although some Greek schismatics have dared to baptize those who had been baptized by Latins. The Greeks use this form, in order to avoid and refute among their own people, the error of the ancients, who attributed the virtue of baptism to the persons baptizing as the principal cause, and said with the Corinthian schismatics : *I am of Paul, I am of Cephas,* &c.

"Which of these two forms is to be preferred?

"*Ans.* Each is to be observed respectively in its own Church, and this under grievous sin, as Pauwels observes. Further, both are to be approved as respectively proper, and absolutely sufficient. The form of the Latins, however, is more perspicuous, and corresponds better with the words of Christ: *Baptizing them in the name of the Father,* &c. (No. 9.) *As for the essentials of the form of Baptism* it is necessary that in it the person to be baptized is expressed, either by the particle *thee,* or by his proper name, or in some other way. The act of baptizing must also be expressed ; and although the baptism would be valid in saying, *I wash, I sprinkle,* &c., yet the words *I baptize* are to be retained. If the particle *in* is omitted, according to Daelman the Sacrament becomes null and void, so also if the minister should say *in the names,* instead of *in the name ;* but if the minister should say *in the name of the Father, and in the name of the Son,* &c., Sylvius, Van Roy, and Billuart think that it is valid, because this multiplication does not imply a diversity of virtue and essence: however, Boudart, Pauwels, Neesen and Daelman more properly say the contrary : because although a diversity may not then be implied, identity is certainly not signified. Baptism conferred under these forms is not valid: *I baptize thee in the name of the most Holy Trinity,* or *in the name of the three divine Persons,* or *in the name of the one and triune God,* or *in the name of the first, and of the second, and of the third Person,* or *in the name of the Omnipotent, of the Wise and of the Good.*"

"Does the conjunction *and* belong to the essential form?

"*Ans.* Some say it does : because, if it be taken away, the distinction of the Persons is not sufficiently expressed. The contrary, however, seems more probable to many ; because it is sufficiently understood. The case would be different, however, if it should be omitted in the sense of Sabellius, in signifying that these three names designate the same Person, endowed with three faculties," &c., (No. 10.)

Baptism in the name of Christ only is never valid, (No. 11.)

32

" Although any one may baptize in a case of necessity, yet if several persons are present, the order of dignity is to be preserved, of which the Roman ritual treats in these words : ' If a Priest is present, let him be preferred to a Deacon, the Deacon to a sub-Deacon, a Clergyman to a layman, and a man to a woman, unless for the sake of modesty it may be more proper for a woman rather than a man (understand, also, a Priest and Pastor) to baptize an infant not entirely brought forth, or unless the woman should know the form and mode of baptizing better.' The latter exception often takes place in midwives, who are usually better instructed concerning the mode of baptizing than others of the laity. But in the former case of exception, the Pastor, if he is at hand, should remain present in some place where he may observe that the form is not corrupted."

It is a mortal sin to invert this order of procedure in the case of a Priest, even if he consents. In case of a Deacon, it is not certain ; but in respect to others inferior to a Deacon, it is not a serious offence.

" Midwives are moreover to be instructed that in a dangerous parturition they have water at hand, and that with self-possession without consternation, attentively and fully, and with a voice truly audible, they pronounce the words of the form ; together with a proper ablution by natural water on a proper part of the body of the person to be baptized, according to what was said, (No. 7.)

" And hence, baptism (even supposing that the proper ablution has taken place) is at least very much endangered, when certain midwives in baptizing a child not entirely brought forth, lest they should deject the mind of the mother, pronounce in a very low and modest tone : *I baptize*, and after a little delay, *thee*, and again after a short pause, *in the name of the Father, &c.*

Midwives are further admonished that they never venture to baptize except in a case of real necessity ; if they do, they commit a heinous sin. No Clergyman inferior to a Deacon, and no layman may perform the peculiar ceremonies of giving the name, presenting the godfather, &c. (No. 13.)

One person may baptize several at the same time, and in a valid manner by a sufficient ablution with this form, *I baptize you :* but this is not proper except in a case of necessity, when life is in danger, and there is no room for delay.

No one may in a valid manner baptize himself. (No. 14.)

Baptism is necessary to salvation in every case except martyrdom, according to the Scripture, John iii. 5 : 'Except a man be born of water and the spirit, he cannot enter into the kingdom of God." (No. 18.)

"*Is baptism or a baptismal character necessarily a prerequisite for other sacraments ?*

"*Ans.* 1. It is necessarily a pre-requisite to the lawful reception of the others : for as the Council of Florence says : ' Holy Baptism holds the first place, because it is the gate of spiritual life : for by it we are made members of Christ, and of the body of the Church.'

" 2. It is indubitable that the sacrament of penance necessarily requires previous baptism for its validity ; &c."

" In the practice of Christian life any other sacraments whatever received before baptism, are to be considered as null and void, and conferred in vain, although a person may have received them in good faith, believing himself to be baptized : because the validity of these sacraments is at least uncertain : therefore sacraments of this kind after baptism are at least to be repeated conditionally, if the baptized person has hitherto been without them." (No. 19.)

Every person not yet baptized in a valid manner is a fit subject of baptism, and is bound to receive this sacrament. Even those who are born without original sin, as John the Baptist, who was sanctified from his mother's womb. Infants are also fit subjects of baptism. (No. 20, 21.)

" *May infants be baptized in the womb of the mother ?*

" *Ans.* 1. If any part of the infant has already been brought forth to light, it may and should be baptized on that part, in case of necessity, according to what has been said. (No. 7.)

" 2. An infant living in the womb can in no manner be said to be baptized by the baptism of the mother, if it perchance happens that she is then baptized : because the infant is distinct from the mother, both as to soul and body.

" 3. And hence if it is so shut up in the womb of the mother that it cannot be touched and washed with water, baptism is attempted uselessly and in vain : because ablution is a necessary part of the sacrament.

" *But the question is, whether a child, being as yet entirely in the womb, may be baptized in a valid manner, if after the labour has commenced it can be sprinkled with water either by the hand or by some other instrument : as is sufficiently plain from the testimony of physicians and midwives may be done ?*

" The ancient and many more recent authors hold the negative opinion, and prove it by the following arguments :

" 1. Because by baptism a person is born again, according to that passage, John iii. 3, ' *Except a man be born again,*' &c., also v. 7 ; but no one can be said to be born again, or to be re-born, unless he was born before : but in this case the child has not been born, therefore, &c.

" 2. By the authority of S. Augustine, whom S. Thomas cites, &c.

" 3. By the Roman ritual, which under the caption, *Concerning children to be baptized*, says : ' No one who is shut up in the womb of the mother ought to be baptized.' And our pastoral under the same head : ' No one shut up in the womb of the mother can be baptized.'

" Many of the more recent authors, however, maintain the affirmative side, which they also attempt to prove in various ways.

" 1. The infant in this case is born in a true sense, according to Matt. i. 20, which was spoken by the angel to Joseph, *that which is conceived in her is of the Holy Ghost.*

" 2. Such a one is so far born as to contract original sin ; therefore also that the remedy for it be applied.

" 3. An infant putting forth any part of the body may be baptized, although it is not perfectly born : therefore likewise if it can be washed in the womb.

" 4. A child is baptized in a valid manner which has by no means been brought to light by birth, but has been cut out of the womb of the dead mother, (as S. Raymund, on this account called unborn,) ; therefore likewise one that is confined in the womb.

" 5. Daelman replies to the authorities of the other opinion, that the rituals, &c., proceeded from a false hypothesis, as if such children could not really be washed ; the contrary of which is certain at present.

"However this diversity of opinion may be, the latter is certainly probable : and hence in a case of necessity, (in which extremes must be tried,) it takes place, baptizing to be sure under the condition : *if thou art a capable subject;* but if afterwards such a child is brought forth to the light alive, it will have to be conditionably re-baptized.   In this case, however, it must then be observed, that warm water be applied, as cold water would greatly injure the mother : farther, that the person thus baptizing break the secondary skin in which the child is enclosed, in order that the water may immediately wash the body itself, (and, if it may be, the head) : but if he cannot break the secondary skin, the baptism is not therefore to be omitted ; because according to some, this skin is a part of the infant in this state."   (No. 23.)

CONCERNING THE CÆSAREAN SECTION. (No. 24.)

"*Is it lawful to kill a pregnant mother that the fœtus may be extracted alive, and be baptized ?*

"*Ans.* No : although she may be despaired of by the physicians : because it is never proper to put any one to death in order that assistance may be given to another.   Some except the case, when the mother is condemned to death : but it is better to defer the execution, even the notification of condemnation, until she is delivered.   Some also say that the section of a living mother is lawful, if a person is so skilful that he can cut open the mother with a well-grounded hope of her recovery, and then extract the child, which would otherwise die without baptism ; especially in those cases, in which this section is the only means, not only for saving the child, but also for preserving the mother.   But if a pregnant woman is certainly dead, she ought immediately to be cut open, that the fœtus may then be extracted, according to the prescription of the Roman ritual, and the instructions of St. Carolus Borr., &c. ; in order that if it is living, it may be immediately baptized ; but if it is found to be certainly dead, it may neither be baptized, nor buried in consecrated ground ; unless it had not yet been extracted from the womb ; in which case it may be left there, and be buried with the mother as a part of her.   Among the signs from which the death of the

32 *

mother is inferred, the following are most generally assigned : if the flame of a candle placed near the mouth is not at all moved, or if no breath is perceptible on a mirror placed near the mouth : but these frequently are deceptive. More certain ones, are : 1. If the eyes become altogether flaccid, and lose their brightness ; 2. Stiffness and inflexibility of the limbs, so that it is only with difficulty that another position can be imparted to them ; and when once it has been imparted they do not restore themselves any more to their former condition, unless perhaps slowly, but never entirely ; but if the members restore themselves to their former condition with force, it is a sign that the subject is still alive. As the want of perceptible motion in the mother is not a certain sign of death, much less is it so in her fœtus : whose death should be considered nearly doubtful, so long as manifest putrefaction or disruption of members is not observed : and therefore the operation may not be omitted, because no motion can be perceived in the womb. It is advised, that a tube be inserted in the mouth of the mother, when dead, and in a similar way patula uteri vagina servetur, in order that heat may be maintained in the womb, until the operation is commenced. The said operation, however, (which is commonly called the Cæsarean,) is most conveniently performed by a surgeon, or some other person skilled in this thing ; in the absence of whom it is incumbent on the priest to perform the same operation ; for this reason the pastors of villages in which there is a want of surgeons, &c., ought to be acquainted with the mode of opening the womb of a dead mother without injuring the fœtus.

" The mode of opening a dead pregnant mother at present practised by physicians, and according to them the more easy and expeditious one, is the following : with a knife or scalpel let a transverse scissure be made in the upper part of the abdomen, (or a little below the thorax, in the middle of the body,) so broad and deep that he may easily introduce his finger into the cavity of the abdomen : then introducing the finger, &c., &c., &c.

" *When ought the Cæsarean section to be instituted ?*

" As the opinion is probable which says, that the fœtus is alive not only on the 40th or 80th day, but immediately upon the conception, or at least in the first days after the conception : hence it is proper that it be instituted as often as a probable suspicion is entertained that the deceased has conceived : but whether any one can be obliged to do this before the fortieth day, I will not venture to affirm.

" These things and very many more most worthy to be observed may be seen in Cangiamila, in the excellent work on SACRED EMBRYOLOGY, or in the compendium of it which Dinouart has published in the French tongue."

OF BAPTIZING AN ABORTIVE FŒTUS. (No. 25.)

" By an abortive fœtus is meant one which is prematurely brought forth to light. *Ought such a one to be baptized ?* It should absolutely be baptized, if it is certain that it is alive : conditionally, if it is doubtful whether it lives : by no means can it be baptized if it is admitted that it is dead. *When is a fœtus animated with a rational soul ?* It is certain that the fœtus is alive long before the birth, as experience proves in the case of infants cut out of the mother's womb ; and hence Innocent XI. justly condemned this 35 proposition : ' It seems probable that every fœtus, so long as it is in the womb, is without a rational soul, and then first begins to have the same, when it is born.' However, it remains uncertain at what time precisely the fœtus is alive. Many, among whom is Neesen, contend that a soul is never infused into any except a well-organized body. Yet very many physicians, and more recent theologians maintain that this takes place immediately after the conception, or at most, on the third or seventh day from the conception ; as may be seen in the dissertation, *On baptizing Abortions.*

" Therefore, abortions, whether they have all the members developed, or have not yet obtained that perfection : the former if they give evidence of life by motion, are absolutely baptized : conditionally, however, if they manifest no motion, but are nevertheless not putrid or lacerated, although they may appear livid, and without pulse, respiration, motion, and feeling. The latter, if they but appear to be human embryos, even on the first days of pregnancy, are baptized conditionally ; although being very small and most imperfectly formed, they may be without perceptible motion : but they are first baptized whilst enclosed in the film, in order that time may not elapse, at the risk of their death, when they are exposed to the air : afterwards the skin is cautiously opened, and when it is unclosed, the fœtus is again baptized, on the condition, *If thou art capable, &c.*"

Directions are then given in order to ascertain whether the premature birth is a fœtus or not.

Of baptizing Monsters and Idiots. (No. 26.)

" ' A monster,' says our pastoral, conformably to the Roman ritual, ' which has not a human appearance, ought not to be baptized : but the decision of a thing of this kind is most properly to be derived from the head, (which is the seat of reason and the senses,) ; therefore, if the head be human, or nearly human, it may be baptized : if it is doubtful, it may be baptized on the condition, *If thou art a human being :*' and thus if the head were that of a wild beast, and the other limbs human, it ought to be baptized conditionally."

But the decision of the Roman ritual is called in question, because the form of the human fœtus, in the womb of the mother, is so soft and flexible, that it may be deformed or changed by the violent imagination or fright of the mother, and thus the fœtus, when born, may exhibit the form of a brute ; and yet there is no sufficient proof to show that the rational soul, by which the fœtus was probably animated before the deformity was occasioned, has subsequently left the body.   We are then referred to the *Sacred Embryology*, for information relative to the proper course to be pursued with monsters which are the fruit of bestial intercourse ! Directions are then offered by which it may be determined whether the monster is single or double.

" If it has one head and one breast, it is certain that it is only a single human being, although it may have, v. g., three hands, feet, &c., and then it may be simply baptized.   Or it is plain that there are two human beings, when it has two heads, and distinct breasts, although the other members may not be double ; and then they may be baptized separately : but if the danger of death is imminent, they may be washed at once, by saying, *I baptize you, &c.* Suppose it is doubtful whether there are one or more human beings, as when it has two heads and breasts not well defined : then one may be baptized absolutely, and the other under the condition

If thou art not baptized. It is the same whether it has two heads and one breast, or the contrary."

My apology for offering the preceding Nos. to the English reader is, that no adequate conception of the imbecile and filthy fanaticism of the Church of Rome, can be afforded, unless these features are exhibited without the Latin veil.

Infants are to be baptized as soon as possible after birth. The degree of delay necessary to constitute mortal sin, is to be determined by circumstances. Adults, if in danger of death, must be baptized without delay ; and if no such danger exists, they must not defer long. (No. 28.)

The effects of the sacrament of baptism, are *grace* and *character.* Original sin is remitted in baptism, unless some obstacle is in the way, besides all personal sins committed before baptism, whether mortal or venial. All temporal and eternal punishment, due on account of past sins, are also remitted through baptism. (No. 29.)

Baptism, when once conferred in a valid manner, is not to be repeated, for the following reasons :

" 1. Because baptism is spiritual regeneration : and hence as there is but one carnal birth in the case of one and the same person, so too there is but one spiritual birth.

" 2. Because baptism is a figure of the death, burial, and resurrection of Christ. But Christ died, &c., but once ; therefore, &c. And hence, Heb. ch. vi., the repetition of baptism is compared to the renewed crucifixion of Christ.

" 3. Because it impresses an indelible character with a kind of consecration of the person.

" 4. Because it has been instituted as the remedy of original sin, which is single in every person, and once remitted, never returns." (No. 32.)

The repetition of baptism with the knowledge that it has once been conferred in a valid manner, is a grievous sin of sacrilege, both in the minister and in the recipient. The penalty of this crime is in the cival law CAPITAL, both with respect to the person rebaptizing, and the person rebaptized. (No. 33.)

Whether persons baptized by midwives are to be rebaptized, depends upon the knowledge, prudence, and mode of applying the matter and form : if there is reason to believe that owing to the trepidation or ignorance of the operator, something essential in matter or form has been omitted, they must be rebaptized ; but in other cases all that is necessary is to supply the usual ceremonies. (No. 36.)

" *Are those who have been baptized by heretics to be re-baptized ?*

" In the first place they are not to be rebaptized, precisely for the reason that they have been baptized by heretics : because it is a settled point in the faith, that a heretic who observes all the essentials, baptizes in a valid manner.   Yet, because there is just reason for doubting whether sectarian heretics rightly apply all the essentials, as it has been learned from experience that these heretics either apply rose-water for the sake of honour, or that one pours the water, and another pronounces the form, or that they are frequently negligent about essentials in some other way, v. g., the ablution ; hence our pastorale has decided, as well the modern as the ancient, that persons baptized by those heretics, (say Lutherans, Calvinists, Anabaptists, and other sectarians of this kind,) are to be rebaptized conditionally when they are converted from heresy to the faith, &c.   But as there is no reason for doubting that all the essentials are duly observed by Jansenist ministers, hence persons baptized by them ought by no means to be rebaptized.   Neither would a person baptized by any heretic whatsoever have to be rebaptized, if a Catholic eye-witness, and one skilled in the point, should testify that all the essentials had been observed ; unless perhaps there should be some doubt remaining concerning the intention of the one who conferred the baptism : but as this is very rare, Benedict XIV. observes that baptism is not to be considered doubtful on this ground, only that the heretic (as he does not believe that sins are remitted through baptism,) does not confer it for the remission of sins, and thus his intention might appear doubtful : for St. Pius V. decreed that for such a reason persons baptized by Calvinists, were by no means to be rebaptized.   Braunman rightly observes, that the priest should attempt nothing in relation to persons baptized by heretics, until the opinion of the bishop has been ascertained." (No. 37.)

In case of necessity, baptism may be administered anywhere; but when there is no necessity, it is not proper to baptize anywhere but in a church which has a baptismal font. The children of kings and princes are excepted; these may be baptized in their private chapels. By princes are meant those nobles who have the supreme power of the state, and are not under the jurisdiction of any king or prince; whether they are called princes, or dukes, or marquises, &c. Inferior nobles may not enjoy this privilege, and consequently the priest may not acquiesce in their request, if they ask that their children may be solemnly baptized at home, but he must send them to the bishop or archpresbyter, to bring a written license. (No, 38.)

The Ceremonies of baptism must be duly observed in its solemn administration, and are always to be performed, except in a case of necessity. The omission of the ceremonies in an ordinary case is a grievous offence? These ceremonies are divided, for the sake of distinction, into *general* and *particular*. The latter may be divided into ceremonies *antecedent, concomitant,* and *subsequent.*

"The *general* ceremonies are five, to wit, *the solemn benediction of the font,* as it is prescribed in the missal; the *place;* the *time;* the *godfather*, and the *giving of the name.* Concerning this conferring of the name, the 2d provincial Synod of Mechlin resolved, 'that the priests take care as much as possible that the names of Gentiles, or others that are profane, be not given to children.' And our pastorale: 'But the priest will take care that the name of some saint be always given to the person to be baptized, by whose example he may be excited to live piously, and by whose patronage he may be assisted.' Authors observe that the name of some saint of the New Testament is more properly given than of the Old; also rather one than many.

"The *particular* ceremonies preceding baptism, which are performed before the entrance of the baptismal font, among various others, are principally four: viz., *exorcism, the sign of the cross, the tasting of salt,* and *the anointing of spittle.* The *concomitant,* which are performed after entering the baptistry, are also principally four: viz., *renunciation, the anointing of the candidate for baptism with oil of catechumens, the catechism, and the inquiry of the desire of receiving baptism.* The *subsequent,* which are performed after the sacrament has been finished, are chiefly these three : the *anointing of the baptized person with chrism*, the *donation of a white garment*, and *the delivery of a burning wax candle*. There were formerly certain *special*- ceremonies, which concerned the state of the catechumens, &c." (No. 40.)

Sponsors are to be employed only in a solemn baptism, and then the obligation is imperative and important. The Council of Trent has fixed the number at two, one a man, and the other a woman. The first effect is a spiritual relationship ; the second effect is a serious obligation of providing that the baptized person be duly instructed and educated in the Christian faith and life. The qualifications of a sponsor, are the following. He must be baptized ; he must not be an idiot ; he must be designated by the parents or others on whom the care devolves of having the infant baptized ; or in defect of these, by the pastor, to whom it pertains to admit the designated sponsor, or for a just cause to reject him, &c. The priest commits a grievous sin if he admits more than two sponsors. (No. 41.)

Whether a Catholic may be a sponsor for a child that is to be baptized among heretics, is a controverted point. " But it is certain that in the baptism of Catholics, the priest ought rather to baptize solemnly without sponsor than with a heretic, because of two evils the less is to be chosen." (No. 42.)

Every priest must keep a baptismal register, in which the names and surnames of persons baptized, of the parents, and of the godfathers and godmothers, and the day of the baptism, are carefully written down. It is a grievous sin to neglect this duty. (No. 43.)

CHAPTER XXXVI.

TREATISE CONCERNING THE SACRAMENT OF CONFIRMATION.

PREFACE.

Decree of the Council of Florence for the instruction of the Armenians.

"THE second sacrament is Confirmation, the matter of which is chrism prepared from oil, which signifies clearness of conscience, and from balsam, blessed by the bishop, which signifies the odour of a good reputation. But the form is : *I sign thee with the sign of the cross, and I confirm thee with the chrism of salvation, in the name of the Father, and of the Son, and of the Holy Ghost.*

"The ordinary minister is the bishop. And whilst a mere priest has power to apply other unctions, none but the bishop ought to confer this ; because we read of the apostles only, whose room the bishops hold, that by the imposition of hands they gave the Holy Spirit, as the reading of Acts viii. 14, manifests. But in place of this imposition of hands, confirmation is given in the church. It is recorded, however, that sometimes by the dispensation of the Apostolic See, from a reasonable and urgent cause, even a simple priest has administered the sacrament of confirmation, with chrism prepared by the bishop. But the effect of this sacrament is the increase of strength, because in it the Holy Spirit is given, just as it was imparted to the apostles on the day of Pentecost, to wit, in order that a Christian may boldly confess the name of Christ. And therefore the person to be confirmed is anointed on the forehead, where the seat of bashfulness is, that he may not blush to confess the name of Christ, and especially his cross, which to the Jews indeed is a stumbling-block, and to the Gentiles, foolishness, according to the apostle, 1 Cor. i., for which reason he is signed with the sign of the cross."

Canons of the Council of Trent concerning Confirmation.

"1. Whoever shall say that the confirmation of baptized persons is a needless ceremony, and not rather a true and proper sacrament ; or that anciently it was nothing else than a kind of catechising, by which

33

the youth expressed the reason of their faith before the Church; let him be accursed!

"2. Whoever shall say that they do despite to the Holy Spirit, who attribute any virtue to the holy chrism of confirmation; let him be accursed!

"3. Whoever shall say that the ordinary minister of holy confirmation is not the bishop alone, but any mere priest whatsoever; let him be accursed!

This sacrament is called *confirmation* from its effect, inasmuch as by it spiritual strength is conferred. It was anciently called the *sacrament of chrism*, or the *sacrament of unction*, "also, *the seal*, or the *little sign*, both because when the chrism is applied we are sealed on the forehead by the sign of the cross, and because through the character a seal is impressed on the soul." It is also termed *perfection*, *consummation*, and *plenitude of grace*, because in it is specially conferred the Holy Spirit, or the copious grace of the Holy Spirit. For the special benefit and edification of heretics, it is defined: *A sacrament instituted by Christ the Lord, by which the Holy Spirit is given to baptized persons, in order that they may steadfastly and boldly profess the faith of Christ.* (No. 1.)

It is a matter of faith that confirmation is a sacrament. "It is proved 1. from sacred scripture, Acts viii. 14, &c. 'When the apostles had heard—that Samaria had received the word of God, they sent to them Peter and John. Then they laid hands upon them, and they received the Holy Ghost.' The same is maintained ch. xix. 6, 'And when Paul had imposed his hands on them, the Holy Ghost came upon them, and they spoke tongues, and prophesied.'"

Tradition and the practice of the Church also prove it. A reference is also made to Matt. xix. 15, and 2 Cor. i. 21, 22; but these latter proof texts are not insisted upon as positive. The *remote matter* of this sacrament is chrism, prepared from oil and balsam, blessed by the bishop. Whether this mixture is essential to the validity of the sacrament is a controverted point; and so is the question whether the blessing or consecration of the chrism is requisite in order to its validity. It is also a disputed point whether the priest ought not to be permitted to consecrate the chrism, as well as the bishop. The *proximate matter* is the *total and adequate* application of the chrism, or the anointing of chrism, and the imposition of hands. This application must be made on the *forehead* and *in the form of a cross.* The sacrament is valid " whether this anointing be performed with the thumb of the right hand, (as the pontifical manual prescribes,) or with another finger of the right or left hand :" but it is essential that it be made with the hand, and not with a rod, or any other instrument, as it ought to be done by imposition of hands. (No. 5.)

The form is among the Latins, *I sign thee with the sign of the cross, and I confirm thee with the chrism of salvation, in the name of the Father, and of the Son, and of the Holy Ghost.* (No. 6.)

The proper minister is the bishop. (No. 7.)

According to modern usage, the age at which confirmation is regularly conferred, is not less than seven years ; there are exceptions in which it may be performed even earlier. Idiots are to be confirmed, " because they are capable of character, and of sanctifying, and even of sacramental grace, &c." (No. 8.)

As for the dispositions requisite for a person who is to be confirmed, a state of grace is necessary in an adult. Children, although not seven years old, should be previously disposed to confession ; instruction, reverence, and devotion suited to their age, are also required. As for the corporeal preparation, observe, 1. When it can conveniently be done, it is more proper that it be given and received fasting. 2. That the persons to be confirmed have the forehead open and clean. 3. That the dress, especially of the girls, be decent and modest. 4. That each one of the persons to be confirmed have a ribbon, or a linen band, clean, and of proper size, with which the forehead, when anointed with the chrism, may be covered, and may remain bound, out of reverence to the sacred chrism : if however any one at a more advanced age is confirmed, the band may soon be laid aside by the priest, before the confirmed person goes out of the church. (No. 9.)

The effects of this sacrament are, 1. Sanctifying grace, by which the person is strengthened, having annexed the abundance of the virtues and of the seven gifts of the Holy Spirit, of which Is. xi. 2, 3 ; the virtues of faith and boldness are specially augmented. 2. Sacramental grace, or actual grace dispensed whenever opportunity is afforded of strenuously and boldly professing the faith with heart and mouth. 3. The third effect is character, by reason of which this sacrament can never be repeated. (No. 10.)

Whether confirmation is necessary to salvation is a disputed point, but the more probable opinion is the affirmative. (No. 11.)

A sponsor is to be employed in confirmation. " Just as a sponsor in baptism contracts the obligation of instructing the baptized person in the faith and in Christian morals ; so the person holding the confirmand in confirmation like a veteran soldier, should instruct the confirmed person, as yet a novice, more perfectly in the Christian warfare." (No. 12.)

The principal ceremonies of confirmation are the following :

" So soon as the bishop has pronounced the form of the sacrament, he inflicts a slight blow on the jaw of the confirmed person : ' in order that he may remember that it behoves him as a brave combatant to be always ready to bear with an indomitable spirit, all adversity for the name of Christ,' says the Roman Catechism, num. 20, on confirmation.

" At the same time the bishop prays for peace, saying : *Peace be with thee* (Pax tecum) : ' in order that (says the Roman Catechism,) by this peace the confirmed may understand that he has obtained the plenitude of celestial grace, and the peace which passes all understanding.'

" These things having been performed by the bishop, the forehead of the confirmed is bound with a band or linen ribbon, both out of reverence for the sacred chrism, and in order to designate, that the grace of the Holy Spirit just obtained is to be diligently preserved, and also, (says the Mechlinian pastorale,) as the symbol of a mind prepared for all reproach and adversity for the name of Christ, whose face was veiled and smitten with blows.

" Anciently the ribbon was kept tied for seven days ; afterwards, in some churches, for only three days ; but now it is usually laid aside on the following day, and the forehead is wiped off on the same day : concerning which the Mechlinian pastorale thus directs : ' Let the ribbon be laid aside by the priest, and preserved in the sacristy or some other proper place, to be burned to sacred ashes on the day of ashes in Lent.'

"All being now confirmed, the bishop prays over all at once, that God would confirm the grace received, by perfecting it in them.   Finally, he bestows upon them the benediction, before which no one of the confirmed may depart, &c. And likewise, all are to be present, at all the ceremonies, from the commencement," &c.

CHAPTER XXXVII.

TREATISE CONCERNING THE ADORABLE SACRAMENT OF THE EUCHARIST.

PREFACE.

Decree of the Council of Florence for the instruction of the Armenians.

"THE third is the Sacrament of the Eucharist, the matter of which is wheaten bread, and wine from the vine, with which, before the consecration, a very small quantity of water should be mixed.   But water is thus mixed, since it is believed that the Lord himself instituted this sacrament in wine mixed with water ; besides because this agrees with the representation of our Lord's passion : because it is recorded that blood and water flowed forth from the side of Christ : and also because this is proper to signify the effect of this sacrament, which is the union of Christian people with Christ : for water signifies the people, according to Revel. xvii. 15. *And he said to me, the waters which thou sawest, where the harlot sitteth, are peoples, and nations, and tongues.*

" The form of this sacrament are the words of the Saviour, by which this sacrament is performed : for the priest, speaking in the person of Christ, performs this sacrament : for by virtue of the words themselves, the substance of the bread is converted into the body, and the substance of the wine into the blood, of Christ ; yet so that Christ is contained entire under the form of bread, and entire under the form of wine :

33 *

Christ is entire also under every part of the consecrated host, and of the consecrated wine, after a separation has been made. The effect of this sacrament which it produces in the soul of a worthy partaker, is the union of the person to Christ," &c.

Canons of the Council of Trent concerning the Most Holy Sacrament of the Eucharist.

" 1. Whoever shall deny that in the sacrament of the Most Holy Eucharist are contained truly, really, and substantially the body and blood, together with the soul and divinity of our Lord Jesus Christ, and therefore the entire Christ; but shall say that he is in it only as in a sign, or figure, or virtue; let him be accursed!

" 2. Whoever shall say that in the most holy sacrament of the Eucharist, the substance of bread and wine remains together with the body and blood of our Lord Jesus Christ; and shall deny that wonderful and singular conversion of the whole substance of the bread into the body, and of the whole substance of the wine into the blood, only the forms of bread and wine remaining: which conversion indeed, the Catholic Church most aptly calls transubstantiation; let him be accursed!

" 3. Whoever shall deny that in the adorable sacrament of the Eucharist, the entire Christ is contained under each kind and under the single parts of each kind, when a separation is made; let him be accursed!

" 4. Whoever shall say that the body and blood of our Lord Jesus Christ are not present in the admirable Eucharist so soon as the consecration is performed, but only in the use when it is received, and neither before nor after; and that the true body of our Lord does not remain in the hosts, or consecrated morsels, which are reserved or left after the communion; let him be accursed!

" 5. Whoever shall say either that remission of sins is the principal fruit of the most holy Eucharist, or that no other effects proceed from it; let him be accursed!

" 6. Whoever shall affirm that in the holy sacrament of the Eucharist, Christ the only-begotten Son of God, is not to be adored even with the external worship of latria; and therefore that the Eucharist is to be honoured neither with peculiar festive celebration, nor to be solemnly carried about in processions according to the laudable and universal rite and custom of the Church; or that it is not to be held up publicly before the people that it may be adored, and that its worshippers are idolaters; let him be accursed!

" 7. Whoever shall say that it is not lawful that the holy Eucharist be reserved in the sacristy, but that it must necessarily be distributed to those who are present immediately after the consecration ; or that it is not proper that it be carried in procession to the sick ; let him be accursed !

" 8. Whoever shall say that Christ as exhibited in the Eucharist, is eaten only spiritually, and not also sacramentally and really ; let him be accursed !

" 9. Whoever shall deny that each and every one of Christ's faithful of both sexes, when they have attained to years of discretion, are obliged at least once every year, at Easter, to commune according to the precept of holy mother Church ; let him be accursed !

" 10. Whoever shall say that it is not lawful for the officiating priest to administer the communion to himself; let him be accursed !

" 11. Whoever shall affirm that faith alone is a sufficient preparation for taking the sacrament of the most holy Eucharist ; let him be accursed ! And lest so great a sacrament be taken unworthily, and therefore to death and condemnation, the said holy synod doth decree and declare, that sacramental confession must necessarily precede in the case of those whom conscience accuses of mortal sin, if a confessor is at hand, however contrite they may suppose themselves to be. But if any one shall presume to teach, preach, or pertinaciously assert, or in publicly disputing, to defend the contrary, let him by this very act be excommunicated."

Canons of the same Council concerning the communion of children, and in both kinds.

" 1. Whoever shall say that each and every one of Christ's faithful ought to take both kinds of the most holy sacrament of the Eucharist, by the command of God, or because necessary to salvation ; let him be accursed !

" 2. Whoever shall say that the holy Catholic Church has not been induced by just causes and reasons, to administer the communion to the laity, and also to the clergy not officiating, only under the form of bread ; or that she has erred in this ; let him be accursed !

" 3. Whoever shall deny that the whole and entire Christ, the fountain and author of all graces, is received under the one form of bread, because as some falsely assert, he is not received under both kinds, according to the institution of Christ ; let him be accursed !

" 4. Whoever shall say that the communion of the Eucharist is necessary for little children before they have attained to years of discretion ; let him be accursed !" &c.

As this Sacrament has reference to the present, past, and future, its names are applied with reference to these relations. In respect to the past, inasmuch as it is commemorative of the Lord's passion, it is called a *sacrifice*, also the *host*. As it signifies something *present*, or is a *demonstrative sign* of the ecclesiastical unity by which we are specially united to Christ, it is called the *communion*. Inasmuch as it designates something future, or is a *prognostic* sign of the enjoyment of God in the heavenly country, it is called the *viaticum*; because here he affords us a way of arriving there: and so also it is called the *eucharist*, that is good grace: or because it really contains Christ, who is the fountain of grace: or also according to others, because Christ in the institution of this sacrament gave thanks and is still daily offered in giving thanks to God. It is also called *bread*, generally with the addition *of eternal life, of angels, &c.*; or *the body of Christ, the body of the Lord ;* also, *the sacred feast, the table of the Lord:* "*the supper*; because it was instituted in the last supper: but because the heretics abuse this name that they may persuade that the sacrament consists in the use or the act of supping, and that fasting may not be enjoined at its reception, therefore, this name is to be seldom used." (No. 1.)

The sacrament of the Eucharist is usually defined ; "*a sacrament instituted by Christ the Lord, which under the consecrated forms of bread and wine, contains the body and blood of Christ, for the spiritual refreshment of man.*" It differs from the other sacraments, principally in two respects :

" 1. Because it consists in a permanent thing, the other sacraments being only a transient action.

" 2. Because the Eucharist contains Christ himself, the author of all holiness, and the fountain of all grace, truly, really, and substantially ; but the other sacraments have only a certain instrumental virtue imparted by Christ. And hence this sacrament is far more important than the rest, is called by more distinguished names, and is termed antonomastically *the sacrament*." (No. 3.)

The matter to be consecrated should be morally so present that it may be perceptibly designated by the pronoun *hoc* and *hic :* and this is requisite for the validity of the consecration, the demonstrative words of which would otherwise not be verified. Hence we may infer that matter placed behind the priest's back, a host lying under a napkin, under the bottom of the cup, is not consecrated in a valid manner. It is not necessary, however, that the matter be seen or touched, or that it should be, as it were, struck by the sound of the words, but it is sufficient that it is demonstrable by the pronoun *hoc* and *hic*, (*this*,) either in itself or in something else which contains it. Thus, hosts lying in a heap one on top of the other are duly consecrated, or if they are shut up in a case or pixis; according to the rubrics however, the pixis containing the hosts to be consecrated, ought to be open when the ceremony is performed. The practice of some unmannerly priests, who put their mouth too near, and as it were breathe upon the cup and the bread, is reproved; the rubrics prescribe merely that in the consecration, the priest stand with his head bowed, and that he pronounce the words distinctly, secretly, and reverently.

"Should any priest having before him eleven hosts intend to consecrate only ten, not determining which ten were meant, the consecration is invalid. Not so, however, if thinking there were but ten, he wished to consecrate all which he had before him:—and therefore, every priest ought always to have the intention of consecrating all the hosts which he has before him. On account of this intention, if the priest without knowing it has in his hands two greater hosts, they are both consecrated, and in such a case the Roman missal prescribes that both must be taken. Hosts placed upon the altar altogether without the knowledge of the priest are not consecrated: for the will is not exercised on any thing unknown. The case is different however if the priest himself, or any one else by his direction, or with his observation, has brought them to the altar to be consecrated: although at the time of consecration he may not have thought of them: because the virtual intention remains: only at the time of consecration the hosts should be placed in such a way and place as that in which hosts are usually deposited, which are to be consecrated. When the cup has been consecrated, the drops of wine adhering to the outside of the cup, are not consecrated, supposing that the ordinary intention has been afforded: and hence such drops may without scruple be wiped off even after the consecration. Opinions vary, however, concerning the drops adhering to the cup inside, or within the vessel, and separated from the whole : and therefore let the priest be careful to wipe them off before the oblation or consecration : after the consecration, they may not be wiped off because they have then perhaps been consecrated," &c. (No. 11.)

The kind of bread proper for consecration is wheat bread only, truly and properly so called. And the water used in kneading the flour should be natural ; the Roman missal considers it doubtful whether the sacrament is performed when the bread is made of rose-water or any other distillation. (No. 13.)

Whether the bread is leavened or unleavened does not affect the essence or validity of the sacrament. The Greek church uses leavened bread, the Roman unleavened. But each must scrupulously observe the custom peculiar to it.

The kind of wine is the fruit of the vine and that only which is properly wine, and is simply so called ; whether white or red, French or Spanish ; or the wine miraculously produced, such as that was in Cana of-Galilee. Insufficient matter are artificial wines made out of grain, apples, pears, or other fruits ; also vinegar prepared from wine and *verjuice* or the liquor prepared out of unripe grapes, &c. *Must*, or wine recently pressed out of grapes, is indeed matter sufficient, but it is not lawful to perform the celebration with it on account of its impurity, except in a case of necessity. Whether congealed wine may be used or not is a disputed point ; the probable opinion is that it may be. The respect due to so great a mystery requires that the priests and others whose business it is should be very careful with respect to the adulterations of the wine, and also of the bread. The custom of some, who contract with the merchant, who will furnish the wine for the Eucharist at the lowest rate, is severely reprimanded, for the obvious reason that in order to make profit or at least not lose on his contract, he will be apt to furnish the vilest wines. (No. 15.)

Water is to be mixed with the wine, but it is not essential to the validity of the sacrament. But now the question arises, what becomes of this water in the consecration ? There are three opinions mentioned by Innocent III. The first is that this water is turned into the water, which flowed from the side of Christ ; but this is rejected as improbable. The second is that the water is *not* changed into the blood of Christ, and this opinion also is scarcely probable. The third is that it *is* changed into the blood of Christ ; and this may be held as certain. But there is a greater controversy whether this water is immediately converted into the blood of Christ ; or whether it is first converted into wine, and thus mediately into the blood of Christ. The latter is evidently the orthodox view. (No. 16.)

The form of administering the Eucharist in general, is, *Take, and eat, this is my body.* Observe that it is not sufficient to pronounce the words of consecration in a narrative style, but it is necessary to pronounce them by way of assertion : for the priest does not merely narrate that Christ by these words changed the bread and wine into his body and blood, but he himself also as a secondary minister effects this change. According to St. Thomas, the words of consecration take effect at the end of the sentence of consecration, or in the last instant of pronouncing the words, *hoc est corpus meum,* " this is my body," which is the usual form of consecrating the bread. Daelman affirms that the consecration would not be valid, if in place of *hoc, illud,* or *istud* should be used. (Both these words mean *this.*) Sylvius and some others admit the fact with respect to *illud,* but not to *istud.* If *hic, here,* should be said instead of *hoc,* the consecration would unquestionably be invalid. But if a priest through ignorance or carelessness should say *hic* in the masculine instead of *hoc,* the consecration would be valid, because though he would sin against latinity, yet he would not imply a sense substantially different from that, which the words have when properly pronounced.

" The word *corpus* is taken properly and strictly, as it is distinguished from blood, comprehending flesh, bones, nerves, &c., and hence if instead of the word *corpus,* (body) *caro,* (flesh) should be said, the consecration would not be valid ; so also if the priest should say *this is the body of Christ,* hoc est corpus Christi. (Nos. 17, and 18.)

The usual form of consecrating the cup is this :

" For this is the cup of my blood of the new and eternal testament, the mystery of faith, which shall be shed for you and for many for the remission of sins." The only essential words in this form are "this is the cup of my blood." (No. 19.)

The real presence of Christ in the Eucharist.

"The Catholic dogma concerning the real presence of Christ in the Eucharist, up to this time, steadfast and undoubted among the faithful, Berengarius, the Archdeacon &c., in the XI. cent., first openly denied, asserting that the Eucharist is the mere sign of the body of Christ. This heresy, however, was assailed by most learned men and condemned in various councils: and although Berengarius several times relapsed, yet many attest that he still died, penitent and a catholic. The Albigenses and Wiclif followed Berengarius, and Wiclif taught that the substance of the material wine and of the material bread remain in the sacrament of the altar.

"In the XVI. cent., Carlostadt, Zuinglius, Bucer, Calvin, and after him the Calvinists likewise taught that the Eucharist is the mere and naked figure of Christ's body. Against whom the Council of Trent thus defined, Sess. 13., Can. 1. (See preface to this chap.)

"*Luther would gladly* have denied this truth, but in his letter to the Argentines, he confesses himself convinced by the most evident testimonies of Scripture. Declaring war however, upon the Roman Church, he maintained the impanation or that the substance of the bread and wine remains with the body and blood of Christ. Another error of Luther is, that Christ is not present in the Eucharist except in the act of receiving it, &c."

"From which it is moreover inferred that Christ must be adored in this sacrament with the worship which is due to God, as the council of Trent teaches. This Calvin and the Calvinists simply deny. The adoration to Luther, however, appeared at first a thing indifferent; afterwards also useful and necessary: but of the modern Lutherans some admit the adoration in receiving; others do not admit it, even in the reception." (No. 20.)

The real presence is proved from John chap. vi. "It is to be premised, that three parts are distinguished in the chapter above cited. In the first as far as v. 25, the question is concerning *material* food, or the multiplication of the five loaves, with which Christ fed the five thousand people.   In the second, the question is as far as v. 52, concerning food *purely spiritual*, namely *faith in the incarnate Messiah.* But in the third part from v. 52, to the end of the chapter, the question is concerning *the real and sacramental eating of the flesh of Christ.*   Having premised these things, this last is proved.

"Because Christ promising this sacrament says, v. 52 : *the bread which I will give is my flesh for the life of the world ;* signifying that his own flesh was truly to be given by way of food, not only in the sign and figure : because v. 59, he places it in opposition to the manna, which was the figure of this sacrament.   He designates also that his flesh was to be really given, and not only by faith : because he is speaking of a thing not yet done, but future : but the spiritual eating through faith both existed then, and also had existed under the old law : nor otherwise, v. 56, ought he to have distinguished between spiritual meat and drink.   Likewise he does not signify that his own flesh was to be given only by its virtue and energy, but substantially, as is gathered from the circumstance that the Jews disputing about these words said v. 53 : *How can this man give us his own flesh to eat ?*   To whom Christ said, v. 54 : *Unless you eat the flesh of the Son of man, &c. :* and on this account still more offended, they said, v. 61, *This saying is hard,* &c., which however, he still confirmed, v. 63, by the testimony of the future ascension of his body : and when, v. 67 : *many of his disciples went back,* he did not correct their interpretation ; which the infinite goodness of the excellent master, seemed in accordance with his custom to require, if he had meant those words concerning the spiritual eating alone : and what is more he asked his apostles, whether they too would go away, unless he should remit something from the severity of the truth.

" *Obj.* Christ himself explains his promise as referring to a spiritual eating, saying, v. 64, *It is the Spirit that quickneth : the flesh profiteth nothing.   The words that I have spoken to you are spirit and life.*

" *Ans.* Christ does not correct their interpretation concerning his real presence in the Eucharist, but only the

34

carnal mode of interpretation, according to that remark of St. Aug. Treatise 27, upon John. 'The flesh profiteth nothing': but how did they interpret? They understood such as is cut up in a carcase, or is sold in the shambles. See authors more at large." (No. 21.)

The argument contained in this chapter is certainly conclusive. Of course the disciples *must* have understood our Lord to be speaking of the Eucharist, although it was an institution of which they had previously known absolutely nothing, and the nature of which they could not possibly understand, because they were not prepared even to receive the doctrine of his death. The passage from Augustine explanatory of the words, which at first sight do seem to favour the *spiritual* interpretation somewhat, gives the *coup de grace* to the heretical argument, and decides this vexatious controversy.

But the vindication is not yet complete, as the following remarks will show ; though we do think it is ungenerous to press the point so strenuously, after the unanswerable argument already advanced.

The same doctrine is proved from the words of the institution.

" 1. For the words : *This is my body : this is my blood ;* related by the three evangelists, Matthew, Mark and Luke, and by the Apostles, 1 Cor. xi., are most plain, and understood in their proper, natural and obvious sense, import the real presence of the body and blood under the forms of bread and wine : but the words ought to be thus understood, and not improperly and figuratively.

" This is proved, 1. From the most correct rule of interpreting Sacred Scripture, which St. Aug. gives, Bk. 3, de Doct. Christ. ch. 10, to wit, that the words of Scripture are to be understood in their proper and natural sense so often as they contain nothing which may not be referred to propriety of morals, or to the truth of faith, or so often as there is no obstacle to the contrary ; therefore, &c.

" 2. From the circumstances, which all conspire towards the proper and natural sense : for Christ framed a testament, instituted a sacrament, sanctioned a law according to that passage in Luke : *Do this in remembrance of me ;* he delivered a peculiar doctrine, and addressed his friends when death was immediately at hand : but all these things are done usually by the proper, natural and obvious mode of speech, not in a metaphorical or figurative style; therefore, &c.

" 3. These words were spoken to those, to whom (as it is said, Luke viii. 10,) *it is given to know the mystery of the kingdom of God, but to the rest in parables :* which Christ was accustomed privately to explain to the disciples : but that this was done in this instance is no where recorded.

" 4. The things which the Apostle adds concerning one who receives the sacrament unworthily, necessarily evinces more than the figure of Christ's body and blood : *He shall be guilty of the body and blood of the Lord :* also : *He who eats and drinks unworthy, eats and drinks judgment to himself, not discerning the Lord's body.*

" The heretics object that in the words of the form, the word *is* may be taken improperly for *signifies :* just in the same way as Luke viii. 11, *the seed is the word of God ;* John xv. 1, *I am the true vine ;* 1 Cor. x. 4, *But this rock was Christ ;* Gen. xli. 26, *The seven fat oxen, and the seven full ears are seven years of plenty.*

" *Ans.* It is true that in many passages of Scripture, the word *is* may be understood improperly and figuratively : but then this is evidently gathered from the circumstance for instance of a dream, a parable, &c. ; as may be seen among interpreters and others in respect to this : but in this case no circumstances denote the same, but all imply rather the contrary, as is plain from the remarks already made. Some heretics place the metaphor on the words *body* and *blood ;* but this may easily be refuted from the fact that the Apostle, 1 Cor. xi. 24, subjoins to those words : *This is my body :* *which shall be delivered for you ;* and Matthew and Mark to the words, *This is my blood,* add : *which shall be shed for many.* (No. 22.)

" *The same doctrine is proved by tradition.* This Bellarmine, amongst others, clearly proves from the testimony of fathers and councils, which he deduces from the time of the apostles, through every age of the Church. The same is moreover incontrovertibly proved, from prescription or continual possession in this way: it is certain that in the XI. cent., in the time of Berengarius, the whole Catholic Church acknowledged the real presence of Christ in the Eucharist: as is plain from the very confession of Berengarius, and from his condemnation: but no time can be assigned in which this faith was introduced into the Church; which, however, could be shown, if it had not been introduced by the apostles themselves, and by Christ; because if introduced subsequently, it must have been done either simultaneously or successively: if the former, (which is altogether inconceivable), historians would at least mention it as extremely wonderful; if the latter, this could not be done without perturbation and contradiction, which we should again know from historians; therefore this is the faith left to the Church by Christ and the apostles, and therefore true. By a similar argument, the other truths of the faith may be demonstrated against the heretics. The Calvinists object chiefly against this last, that such a faith might be successively introduced without opposition or contradiction, just as new discipline has frequently been introduced in the Church, v. g. about the time of breaking the fast, &c.

"The reason of faith is one thing, that of discipline is another: the one is immovable, but the other is mutable through change of times and circumstances. Besides new discipline may be introduced, without the old being condemned; but a new doctrine of faith implies the falsity of the contrary opinion. At all events, the changes of discipline are not so obscure but that they have been designated by historians; and nearly all have occurred not universally, but in certain places.

"To the arguments already mentioned, must be added that God has confirmed the truth of the real presence, by open and frequent miracles performed at various places and times. These, the heretics indeed are in the habit of vilifying, but with no greater right than all credit may be denied to history; the Jews too explore the miracles of Christ, by ascribing them to the devil, for the most distinguished fathers mention them, as may be seen in Bellarmine, Wiggers, &c.; indeed from the apostle himself, 1 Cor. ii. 30, &c. It would be too tedious to refute all the things which the heterodox have heaped together from the holy fathers; however, for the understanding of those things which are opposed from the fathers, it is of assistance to note the following rules.

" *First :* When some holy fathers call the Eucharist, the figure, image, type, sign, &c., of the body of Christ, these are understood in a manifold and true sense, without detriment to the real presence : 1. By reason of the forms of bread and wine, which by the institution of Christ, are a sign, figure, &c., of the body of Christ not absent, but present : 2. Inasmuch as the body of Christ, veiled under the forms, is the sign of himself existing in his proper form, v. g. hanging on the cross, or of his glorified body in heaven : 3. Because the Eucharist is sometimes called the sign, &c., of the mystical body, which is the Church.

" *Second* : This sacrament, as well in scripture as in the fathers, is often called *bread :* 1. By reason of the forms which remain : 2. On account of the matter converted into the body of Christ, just as the rod of Aaron, when turned into a serpent, is still called a rod. Ex. vii. 12. Because it is the spiritual bread of the soul.

" *Third :* When some say that in the Eucharist there is not the same body, which the Son of God assumed from the Virgin, in which he suffered death, &c., they only mean that it is not the same body as to condition and affections, &c., although it is the same as to the substance.

" *Fourth :* When some fathers so extol the spiritual eating that they seem not to admit the other ; they only intend that the external and real does not profit without the spiritual.

" *Fifth :* If some fathers, who wrote before these heresies arose, occasionally spoke without sufficient accuracy, this was because they knew that they were understood in a good sense by the faithful, who were afflicted with no doubt. Some also spoke sparingly and somewhat obscurely, because in the first centuries, the more sacred mysteries of religion were hidden from Pagans, Jews and Catechumens ; both because these were incompetent to understand those things, and lest they should deride and profane them. By these rules, all things which heretics propose from the holy fathers, may be answered." (No. 23.)

" *Objections from scripture and reason are solved.*

34 *

" *Obj*. 1. Christ commanded the Eucharist to be performed in remembrance of him (Luke xxii. 19.); but memory is only concerning a thing that is absent, not present; therefore, &c.

" *Ans*. The meaning of the words of Christ, is : Do this in remembrance of my suffering and death : as is plain from the apostle, 1 Cor. xi. 26 ; but the suffering of Christ neither then was, nor is now present. Besides the minor is false in its generality : because the memory of a present thing is possible, especially if it is not visible or sensible.

" *Obj*. 2. According to various passages of scripture, Christ is no longer in this world, but has ascended into heaven, as Matt. xxvi. 11 ; John xvi. 16 ; and Acts iii. 21.

" *Ans*. In these the question is only concerning the visible presence of Christ, but not the invisible or sacramental, which he has in the Eucharist.

" Heretics object from reason, that our dogma is an impossible thing, and involving a contradiction, because Christ must be supposed to be bodily present in many places under a little host.

" *Ans*. Besides the solution of such objections in detail, (which see in Tournely), the general reply is given, that the prejudice of heretics must be corrected by showing, that the understanding must be captive to the obedience of faith; for which the following will afford assistance :

" 1. To remember that it is a mystery of faith, and faith is the evidence of things not seen. 2. To allege that there are other mysteries impervious to reason; as that of the most holy Trinity, and the incarnation. To reason from the less to the greater in this way : there are very many things in nature which are rather to be admired than explained ; therefore a fortiori in the mysteries of faith. 4. To allege some similar things : v. g. according to theologians, the whole soul is in the whole body, and the whole soul is in each part of the body. Christ came forth from the sepulchre and the womb when closed, changed water into wine, &c., which faith teaches and reason does not explain. 5. To declare that the fathers of the church have always acknowledged, that in the Eucharist, there are stupendous miracles and mysteries of inscrutable truth ; and therefore, by such arguments of the heretics, the truth of the Catholic

doctrine is not impaired, but is on the contrary, confirmed."
(No. 24.)   In No. 25, transubstantiation is defined in accordance with the council of Trent, sess. 13. can. 2. "That
wonderful and singular conversion of the whole substance
of the bread into the body, and of the whole substance of
the wine into the blood of Christ, only the forms of bread
and wine remaining."

"This word *transubstantiation*, although it is not found
in scripture, is yet rightly consecrated by the church, and
employed to the explanation of those truths, which are found
in the scriptures and in tradition, and to the exclusion of the
heresies opposed to them; just as the church has rightly
adopted the names, *consubstantiality, Trinity, mother of
God*, &c., because what those words signify, is truly derived from tradition and scripture, &c."

"That when the consecration has been performed, all the
accidents of the bread and wine, (or their form) remain,
both faith and the senses teach : for the same size, the same
colour, the same taste, &c., remain.   Thus, however,
Christ chose to give his body and his blood in the Eucharist, both with regard to the rite and reverence of the mystery, and the merit of faith, and to the convenient use of
the sacrament."

"St. Thomas teaches 'that these accidents subsist in
the sacrament without any subject, by a divine virtue.'
(No. 26.)

"*How long does Christ remain in this sacrament?*"
Just so long as the forms remain preserved, or so long as
they are not corrupted, or until the substance of the bread
and wine no longer exists.   But how long the forms remain
preserved in the stomach or otherwise, is uncertain.   "It is
very probable, according to Pauwels, that this sacrament
confers its effects not only in eating and swallowing, but
also so LONG AS THE PRESENCE OF CHRIST CONTINUES IN
THE STOMACH : and consequently, that it is highly praiseworthy to tarry in the temple at least a quarter of an hour,
and to stir up one's self in the spirit of devotion and medi-
tation, that thus a continual increase of grace may be acquired."

The box in which the hosts are kept, should be cleaned

from time to time, that the older particles may not adhere
to the pixis and spoil.   (No. 28.)

As it belongs to the power of the sacerdotal order to consecrate, which continues with a character never to be lost;
hence any priest consecrates in a valid manner, although
he may be a wicked man, a heretic, suspended, excommunicated, degraded, &c.: but every one who is not a priest,
does not consecrate in a valid manner.   (No. 29.)

The proper minister for dispensing the Eucharist, is the
priest alone, "and indeed by divine right; and it is inferred
from these words of Christ: *Do this*, &c. That is, consecrate, take, and distribute to others, as ye see me do." The
extraordinary minister is the deacon, with the permission,
however, of the bishop or priest; but this office is not to be
entrusted to the sub-deacon, or the other inferior clergy, or
to the laity.   (No. 30.)

For the due reception of the Eucharist, baptismal character and the wish of receiving this sacrament are required;
also a state of grace, when it is a sacrament of the living.
Whoever is conscious of mortal sin is under obligation first
to make confession.   Sufficient instruction and discernment
are required, so that the communicant may be able to discern this table from a profane one, this celestial bread from
common.   Also, a right intention, and devotion befitting this
sacrament; acts of faith, hope, charity, humiliation, and
contrition. He must come fasting, and with decent and
clean apparel. (No. 31.)   In No. 36, the following grave
question is discussed.

WHETHER THE TAKING OF TOBACCO BREAKS THE NA-TURAL FAST.?

"*Ans.* 1. If the question is concerning snuff, it seems
sufficiently clear that by it a natural fast is not broken; because it neither is food or drink, nor is it taken as such;
and although it might be supposed that casually some of it
might be passed into the stomach, this is supposed to be done
by way of respiration or saliva.   2. By smoking, some say
that the fast is broken, from the circumstance that something
of the oil is swallowed with the smoke; but more hold the
contrary opinion, because all the smoke is usually admitted
through the mouth and nostrils by the smoker (especially if

he is expert); and if a small quantity is transmitted, it may be as before.   However, if this takes place in a great quantity, then, according to others, the fast is broken.   3. The difficulty as to chewing is greater; however, Pontas and Billuart maintain against Van Roy and others, that by this the fast is not impaired: because it is not designed to be taken inwardly: nor are very many of the more succulent particles of the tobacco taken inwardly, as chewers avoid this very carefully, on account of the acrid and unpleasant taste; yet if this latter should take place, a natural fast would be broken.   Benedict XIV." (my reader has not forgotten the lucid dissertation of his Holiness on the chocolate question,) "thinks that the fast is not broken by taking snuff, or by smoking, but he determines nothing with respect to chewing.   But as it is very indecent that any one should approach the sacred table with his mouth or nostrils smeared with tobacco, and redolent with its stench: therefore, it is proper to abstain from its use, and indeed entirely from smoking and chewing." (No. 36.) AMEN!

In No. 47, the question is discussed, "*When does the Eucharist confer the increase of Grace ?*   At what instant is the grace conferred?   Steyaert and Daelman reply that it is conferred immediately from the commencement of eating; Suarez and Billuart, when the host is passing down through the throat; but Gonet, when the forms first touch the stomach; Sylvius, however, replies, that no one can know this, save he who effects it."

Three things hinder the effect of this sacrament, viz.: want of baptism, want of intention in an adult, and mortal sin. (No. 49.)   There is a threefold mode of communing, viz.: merely sacramentally, merely spiritually, and sacramentally and spiritually at the same time.   He receives the Eucharist *sacramentally*, who, with the intention of receiving it, really takes it, but without spiritual profit: such a case is, when a person communes who is conscious of mortal sin, &c.   If a mouse or a dog eats the sacramental forms, it does not receive them sacramentally, though the body of Christ does not cease to be under those forms.   They commune *spiritually*, who, desiring it, eat that heavenly bread by a living faith, which operates through delight, and feel its profit and advantage.   And they commune sacramentally and spiritually who receive the Eucharist really and worthily, and obtain its effects, as the righteous do. (No. 50.)

No. 63 *treats of the punishment for not communing at Easter.* A dispensation may be obtained on account of indisposition, or a peculiar case of conscience; but "He who without the leave now mentioned, or some other legitimate excuse, shall omit the Easter communion, &c., incurs the punishment that, living, he be driven from the threshold of the church, and dying, be denied Christian burial. This punishment, according to Steyaert, is not the same as excommunication, but as it were only a part of it, as is evident from the other effects of excommunication." (No. 63.)

The 65th No. treats of the communion of the sick, and, among the rest, the question is asked, "*What if the sick man vomits up the sacred host?* *Ans.* Conformably to the Roman Missal, if the forms appear whole, they may be reverently gathered up, and afterwards taken; but if nausea forbids this, then they must be carefully separated from the filth, and thus they must be laid aside in some sacred place, and after they have become corrupt, they may be put away into the sacristy, or some sacred sink; for so long as they are entire, they cannot be burned without a kind of sacrilege. The same course must be pursued if, by any means whatsoever, whether through negligence or for some other cause, the forms should be found to be spoiled." But if the forms have not become corrupt on account of the brief space that has intervened, then the matter thus vomited may be burned, and the ashes put away into some sacred place, v. g. the cemetery.

"*What if the sick person dies immediately after having taken the viaticum?*

Ans. If the sacred host does not appear in his mouth, then the dead man is to be left thus, although it may not be known whether he has swallowed it; but if it appear in his mouth, let it be modestly extracted, and reverently kept until the forms are corrupted: and then proceed as has just been said with regard to the vomited host."

I have refrained from comments on many of the last chapters, because in most instances they effectually refute themselves, or are so puerile as to be beneath sober refutation; but some of the assertions of Peter Dens, on the subject of the Eucharist, are so outrageously false, that a few historical reminiscences appear to be a necessary appendage to this chapter.

In the first place then, in the face of the impudent assertion of the Romish theologian, that transubstantiation always has been a doctrine of the Church of Christ, we distinctly affirm that it never was regularly acknowledged as an article of faith, imposed as absolutely necessary to be believed by all the faithful, even in the *Church of Rome*, until the Lateran Council, held at Rome, A. D. 1215. That the notion had existed for some centuries before, we admit; it had either originated or been harboured in the brain of a monk, at the beginning of the seventh century, and received some countenance from the second Council of Nice, which first sanctioned the worship of images. It was afterwards introduced into the Latin Church, towards the close of the ninth century. Paschasius Rathbertus first reduced this novel doctrine into something like its present shape, and proposed it in the Western Church, where it was most vigorously opposed by Rabanus Maurus, Archbishop of Mentz, who in his Epistle to Heribald, ch. 33, denounces it as an alarming innovation. The contest in which Berengarius was conspicuous, and to which allusion is made by the Romish theologian, occasioned the convention of two synods. For upwards of 300 years, this strange doctrine was opposed by a host of the most learned and pious men of those times; and as already remarked, was not foisted by ecclesiastical authors upon human credulity, until the 4th Lateran Council, in 1215, and then it was effected in an imperious manner, more by the decision of Pope Innocent III. ex cathedra, than by the general concurrence even of that ignorant and besotted council. The Council of Trent, A. D. 1545, gave it its full and final institution, as an article of faith.

That this is the true state of the case, can be abundantly sustained. The learned Erasmus says in his annotations on 1 Cor. vii. " It was late ere the Church defined Transubstantiation." And Tonstal de Euch. Lib. 1. " Touching the manner of the real presence how it might be, it had perhaps been better to leave every man that would be curious to his own conjecture, AS BEFORE THE LATERAN COUNCIL IT WAS LEFT FREE."

Scotus, whom the Papists call *Doctor Subtilis*, for the pungency and discrimination of his wit and learning, and who lived about the year 1300, says, 4th Bk. of Sentences, Dist. ii. 2, 3. " That which chiefly sways me, is, that we must maintain touching the sacraments, as the holy Church of Rome maintains. But she *now* holds that the bread is transubstantiated into the body, and the wine into the blood: as manifestly appears in the creed of the Lateran Council, under Innocent III., which begins with these words: *We firmly believe, &c.* And if you ask, why should the Church make choice of so difficult a sense of this article, when the words of the Scripture, *this is my body,* might be explained in a sense more easy, and in appearance more true: I answer, the Scriptures are expounded by the same Spirit that made them; and so it is to be supposed that the Catholic Church expounded them by the same Spirit whereby she delivered the faith unto us: namely, being taught by the spirit of truth, and therefore she chose this sense, because it was true."

Surely no one will be disposed, after reading this cunning argument, to question the right of Scotus to the title of *Doctor Subtilis!* However, it is nothing new for the most subtle Papist to *beg the question;* in fact he can scarcely argue without doing it.

A singular statute, enacted by Henry VIII., appeared in 1540; it was to this effect:

" That if any person or persons, within the king's dominions, should after the 12th day of July next, by word, writing, imprinting, cyphering, or any otherwise, publish, preach, teach, say, affirm, declare, dispute, argue, or hold any opinion, that in the blessed sacrament of the Altar, under the form of bread and wine, after the consecration thereof, there is not present really, the natural body and blood of our Saviour Jesus Christ, conceived of the Virgin Mary: or that after the said consecration, there remaineth any substance of the bread or wine, or any other substance than of Christ, God and man: or that in the flesh, under the form of bread, is not the very blood of Christ: or that with the blood of Christ, under the form of wine, is not the very flesh of Christ, as well apart, as though they were both together: or shall affirm the said sacrament to be of other substance than is above said: that then every such person so offending, their aiders, comforters, counsellors, consenters, and abettors therein, shall be deemed and adjudged heretics, and every such offence shall be judged manifest heresy: and that every such offender and offenders shall therefore have and suffer judgment, execution, pain, and pains of death, by way of burning, without any abjuration, benefit of the clergy, or sanctuary to be allowed: and also to forfeit to the king, his heirs, and successors, all his or their honours, lands, tenements, goods, chattels, and estates whatsoever."

Streams of innocent Protestant blood have flowed, because men were not prepared to deny the evidence of their own senses, of reason, and of scripture, by acknowledging the truth of the horrible doctrine of the real presence, than which a more daring and outrageous blasphemy has never been invented by the Prince of hell!

The following suggestions may perhaps lead the mind of an honest inquirer, who may be in doubt, to the truth.

1. We cannot admit the doctrine of transubstantiation to be true, because it overthrows the very nature of a sacrament, which requires a sign, and a thing signified. According to transubstantiation, the bread ceases to be a sign, because it becomes the thing signified, viz., the body of Christ.

2. From 1 Cor. xi. 25, and elsewhere, it is manifest that the bread and wine remain such *after* the consecration.

3. To say that the glorified body of Christ, which is in heaven, and shall there remain to the end of time, is daily created in ten thousand different places upon earth, by the hocus pocus of a priest, is the first born of absurdities.

4. If the substance of the bread and wine does not remain after the consecration, then when poison is mixed in the sacrament, either it is mixed with the mere accidents, (i. e. with the taste, smell, colour, &c.) or with the body of Christ; both of which are absurd. Now poison has been mixed with the consecrated host, and with the wine, and it has been but too manifest that the substance of the bread and wine has been affected by it. Witness the case of Pope Victor III., who was poisoned by the cup, and that of the Emperor Henry VII., who died in consequence of receiving a poisoned host.

5. If the bread entirely loses its substance, then it must cease to exist; for that which has been, but has ceased to be, is of course annihilated. Hence it is absurd to speak of the bread and wine being *converted* into the body and blood of Christ, for in every change the matter must remain, otherwise it becomes an *exchange*, or a *substitution*, or *succession*. And therefore, as the substance of the forms does not remain, the body and blood of Christ must be substituted, or must succeed in their place; and hence it would be far more rational to speak of day being transubstantiated into night, than to maintain the doctrine of the Church of Rome even with her own premises.

8. Christ says, *Do this in remembrance of me.* We remember the absent, not the present. Christ instituted the Eucharist as a memorial of himself *until* he should come.

9. The Saviour says, John xii. 26, *Where I am, there shall also my servants be;* that is they shall be with him in his glory. Christ is now in his glory, and therefore his saints and servants, who have de-

35

parted this life, are with him. Now when Christ is in the sacrament, or rather when the sacrament becomes Christ, is he in his glory, or is he not? If he is, then the saints must be there present to see, and be partakers of his glory, *For they are ever with him*, 1 Thess. iv. 17, *And follow the Lamb whithersoever he goeth*, Rev. xiv. 4. But if Christ be *not* in his glory in the Romish Eucharist, then it is sacrilege to deprive him of it, by thus CRUCIFYING THE LORD AFRESH, AND PUTTING HIM TO AN OPEN SHAME!

CHAPTER XXXVIII.

TREATISE CONCERNING THE SACRIFICE OF THE MASS.

PREFACE.

" Hitherto we have treated of the Eucharist, inasmuch as it is a sacrament, or is ordained to the sanctification of man; now we must discuss the subject in so far as it is a sacrifice, or as it relates to the worship of God.

Canons of the Council of Trent concerning the sacrifice of the Mass.

" 1. Whoever shall say that in the mass there is not offered to God a true and proper sacrifice, or that Christ's being offered is nothing else than his being given to us to be eaten; let him be accursed!

" 2. Whoever shall say that by these words, Do this in remembrance of me, Christ did not appoint the apostles as priests; or that he did not ordain, that they and other priests should offer his body and blood; let him be accursed!

" 3. Whoever shall say that the sacrifice of the mass is merely an offering of praise and thanks, or a simple commemoration of the sacrifice performed on the cross, and not propitiatory; or that it is of benefit only to the recipient; and that it ought not to be offered for the living and the dead, for sins, penances, satisfactions, and other necessities; let him be accursed!

" 4. Whoever shall say that by the mass the most holy sacrifice of Christ, finished upon the cross, is blasphemed, or that the mass is derogatory to it; let him be accursed!

" 5. Whoever shall say that it is an imposture to celebrate masses in honour of the saints, and for the purpose of obtaining their intercession with God, as the Church intends ; let him be accursed !

" 6. Whoever shall say that the canon of the mass contains errors, and therefore ought to be abrogated ; let him be accursed !

" 7. Whoever shall say that the ceremonies, robes, and external signs which the Catholic Church uses in the celebration of masses are impious vanities rather than offices of piety ; let him be accursed !

" 8. Whoever shall say that the masses, in which the priest alone communes sacramentally, are unlawful, and therefore should be abrogated ; let him be accursed !

" 9. Whoever shall say that the rite of the Roman Church, by which a part of the canon and the words of consecration are pronounced in a low voice, ought to be condemned ; or that the mass should be celebrated only in a vernacular tongue ; or that water should not be mixed with the wine in the cup that is to be offered, because it is contrary to the institution of Christ ; let him be accursed !"

" Sacrifice properly and strictly taken, for the sacrificial action of which we here treat, is thus defined : *An external oblation, by which any sensible and permanent thing is consecrated, slain, or changed by a legitimate minister, as a protestation of the dominion of the Supreme God, over all created things, and of our subjection to him.*"   (No. 1.)

" Sacrifice is divided according to the different state of the world, into the sacrifice of the law of *nature*, of the *Mosaical* law, and of the *new* law."

" By reason of the *matter*, it is divided into hosts, or victims, when an animal was offered ; into immolations, when the fruits of the earth were offered ; and into libations, when any liquor was offered.   On account of the *form*, or of the *various action* by which the thing was wont to be changed, it is divided into the *holocaust*, in which the thing offered was burned entire, so that nothing of it could be employed for human use, and it was the most perfect sacrifice ; into the *sin-offering*, which was partly burned, and went partly to the use of the priests, who eat of it in the court of the temple ; and the *peace-offering*, which was offered either for returning thanks for benefits received, or for obtaining new ones : this sacrifice was divided into three parts, one of which was burned in honour of God, another was appropriated to the use of the priests, and the third to the use of the offerers.   On account of its *object*, it is divided into a *reve-*

rential, propitiatory, or *expiatory,* a *Eucharistical* and *impetratorial* sacrifice. This division differs but little from the preceding. It is called *reverential,* because it is directed only to the worship of God, by solemnly declaring his supremacy and our subjection; and this is best done in the *holocaust.* The *propitiatory* is offered for sins and for averting the penalties and scourges of sins; and is the same as the sin-offering. The *Eucharistical* is performed as a return of thanks for benefits received; and the *impetratorial* for benefits to be received: but both in the old law were called a *peace-offering.* On account of the *time,* it is divided into the *perpetual sacrifice,* which was offered daily; into the sacrifice of the *paschal lamb,* which was offered at Easter; and into sacrifices, which were offered in other solemnities. By reason of the *mode,* it is divided into *bloody* and *unbloody.*"

"Observe that these manifold sacrifices both of the law of nature and of the law of Moses, all prefigured the sacrifice of the new law; and therefore they cease under the new law.

"*Is the sacrifice of the new law, single or twofold ?*

"*Ans.* The sacrifice of the cross is altogether the same as to substance with the sacrifice of the mass; because the priest in both instances is the same, and the victim, Christ the Lord, is the same; and by thus regarding it the sacrifice of the new law is single. If the *mode* and *ceremony* of offering be regarded, it is twofold: to wit, *bloody,* by which Christ offered himself on the cross for the salvation of all: and *unbloody,* by which the same Christ, under the forms of bread and wine, is daily offered in the mass in memory of the bloody. Hence the Council of Trent, sess. 22, ch. 2, Of the Sacrifice of the Mass, teaches: 'For the victim is one and the same, the same who then offered himself on the cross, now offering by the ministry of the priests, with only a different manner of offering.' The sacrifice of the new law might be called twofold in another sense: the one *of redemption on the cross,* by which he has merited for us a full remission of sins: the other *of religion in the Eucharist,* by which the same remission is applied to us." (No. 2.)

"Formerly a twofold mass was distinguished, the one *of the catechumens and penitents,* whom the deacon dismissed after the gospel and sermon; and hence from the commencement to the offertory it was called the *mass of the catechumens:* the other of the *faithful*, and that lasted from the commencement to the end, at which time the deacon dismissed the people with these words: Ite missa est, *Depart, the mass is over:* which second dismission even now remains, and therefore the sacrifice which is daily offered in the temples by the ministry of the priests, is called the *mass*. Further, the mass is taken for that whole sacred action, by which, in the Catholic Church, the unbloody sacrifice of the new law is offered with the various prayers and ceremonies; all these, however, do not in the same way regard the sacrifice of the mass: but some pertain to the *essence* of the sacrifice, others to its *integrity*, others to *greater reverence*, the *explanation of the mystery*, and *the edification of the faithful*, as will appear afterwards."

" *What is the sacrifice of the mass? Ans. It is the external oblation of the body and blood of Christ, through the forms of bread and wine, sensibly exhibited by a legitimate minister, offered to God in recognition of his supreme dominion, with the use of certain prayers and ceremonies, prescribed by the Church for the better worship of God and edification of the people.* The Zuinglians and Calvinists, and as many as deny the real presence of Christ in the Eucharist, consequently deny that in the mass there is offered a true sacrifice, properly so called. The Lutherans, although they admit the real presence, yet also reject the sacrifice of the mass, so that Luther, Bk. concerning *private mass*, was not ashamed to write that it had been suggested to him, and that he had at length been persuaded by the devil, that the sacrifice of the mass was to be abrogated. Therefore the innovators pretend, that in the new law there is only the spiritual sacrifice of good works; that the mass or Eucharist, is a mere commemoration of the sacrifice of Christ on the cross, and that Christ has given to us a table at which we may feast, but not an altar upon which we may sacrifice: against which errors, the council of Trent, sess. 22, can. 1., has decreed in these words: ' Whoever shall say that in the mass there is not offered to God, a true and proper sacrifice, or that Christ's being

35 *

offered, is nothing else than his being given to us to be eaten : let him be accursed !'

" *Prove that in the mass there is offered a true sacrifice, properly so called ? Ans.* 1. It is proved from the prophecy of Malachi i. 10. *I have no pleasure in you, saith the Lord of hosts ; and I will not receive a gift of your hand.* And v. 11 : *For from the rising of the sun, even to the going down, my name is great among the Gentiles, and in every place there is sacrifice, and there is offered to my name a clean oblation,"* &c.

" 2. It is proved, because Christ, Ps. 109., is called *a priest for ever, after the order of Melchisedech ;* which words according to the apostle, Heb. vii. 8 and 9, so apply to Christ, that he cannot be called *a priest after the order of Aaron :* but Melchisedech offered sacrifice in bread and wine, as is plain from Gen. xiv. 18 ; therefore Christ also, who was a priest according to the ceremony of offering of Melchisedech, ought to offer sacrifice in bread and wine : but now unless he has done this in the Eucharist, he has nowhere done it : certainly not *upon the cross,* where he offered his own body and blood in the proper forms ; therefore in *the last supper :* and not only there, but daily unto this time, as the principal minister, he offers himself by the ministry of the priests, and in this way *he has also a perpetual priesthood, ever living to make intercession for us,* as the apostle says, Hebrews vii." &c.

" 3. That the Eucharist is a sacrifice is proved from the words of the institution, related, Matt. xxvi. Mark xiv. Luke xxii., and 1 Cor. xi., from which we thus argue : in order that the Eucharist may be a sacrifice it is sufficient that in it there be an oblation with the shedding of blood : but as is inferred from the passages cited, this predicted oblation is found in the Eucharist ; because the question is concerning the oblation and the effusion, which were done in act, when Christ spoke, as the words of the present tense insinuate : thus Luke xxii. 19, it is said of the body ; *which is given for you :* according to the Apostle, 1 Cor. xi. 24, in the Greek text : *Which is broken for you :* the Greek text of the three evangelists has concerning the blood, *is shed.* Nor is it any objection that we read in the evangelists, and in the canon of the mass, *shall be shed* in the future, because both readings are true, whether in the present, *is shed*, that is, now in the supper ; or in the future, *shall be shed*, that is a little while after on the cross, and afterwards to the end of the world in a sacrifice to be celebrated by the priests.

" 4. It is proved from those passages of Scripture in which the practice of the sacrifice of the mass is implied : thus Acts xiii. 2, *As they were ministering to the Lord*, in Greek, λει τουργούντων δε αυτῶν τῷ Κυρίω, that is as they were offering sacrifice ; and hence Erasmus renders it, *as they were sacrificing to the Lord.* Likewise 1 Cor. x. 21, *Ye cannot be partakers of the table of the Lord, and of the table of devils ;* where the Apostle implies that there is an altar and a sacrifice of the Lord, just as there was an altar and sacrifice of devils.

" 5. It is proved from tradition and the perpetual doctrine and practice of the church, as is plain from the most ancient Liturgies and from the Holy Fathers, who speaking of the Eucharist call it a sacrifice, a host, a victim, &c.

" 6. It is proved from the circumstance that the definition of a sacrifice properly so called pertains to the mass : for in the consecration of both forms (in which alone the essence of the sacrifice consists) an *oblation* is held at least in the act performed ; *external* as it is performed with words ; of *a sensible and permanent thing*, viz., of the body and blood of Christ, through the forms of sensible bread and wine : a consecration is also afforded through the dedication to the divine worship : also a change inasmuch as by the power of the words the blood is separated from the body, and the body from the blood : a legitimate object is also given, to wit, the worship of God : for no more honorable worship can be exhibited to God, than that by which the God-man is offered to God, the Father : finally the primary minister, namely Christ ; and the secondary, the priest, concur." (No. 3.)

The host or the thing offered in the sacrifice of the mass is *the body and blood of Christ*, not indeed *simply*, but under the forms of bread and wine : " *What is the action in the mass in which the essence of the sacrifice consists?* It is to be observed ; 1. That in the mass several actions concur, as v. g. the *elevation of the host*, without which the sacrifice subsists essentially ; because it imparts no change except locally to the host which is still requisite for the essence of the sacrifice.) 2. The *breaking of the host*, which does indeed change the forms, but not the body of Christ, &c.   3. The communion of the priest is not an essential part of the sacrifice: the reason is, 1. Because St. Thomas says: 'This sacrament has the nature of a sacrifice inasmuch as it is offered, but the nature of a sacrament inasmuch as it is taken.' 2. The *taking* is a participation of the benefit of the sacrifice: and therefore presupposes a slain victim through the consecration.   3. It is a settled point in the faith that Christ offered sacrifice at the last supper; and yet it is not a point of the faith that Christ did take the Eucharist: which, however, according to the faith ought to have taken place, if the eating of the host by the priest belonged to the essence of the sacrifice.

"Notwithstanding, however, it is rather probable that Christ did take his own body and blood in the last supper: because Christ, Luke xxii. 15, says, *With desire I have desired to eat this passover with you before I suffer*, &c. Besides if he himself had not taken his own body and blood, there was danger, lest his disciples might be scandalized," &c.

"Moreover, the communion of the priest is an integral part of the sacrifice: because the Eucharist is not only a sacrifice, but also, a sacrament, and in so far has the nature of food and drink, &c. And this is the reason why the solicitude of the church is so great that she requires if the priest overcome with sudden sickness should not be able to take both kinds, that another priest be substituted even if he should not be fasting, should another not be at hand to take both forms, in order, says St. Thomas, that the sacrament may be performed.   From which it seems to follow, that the communion of the person celebrating is not only of divine right but also pertains to the integrity of the sacrifice.   These things being premised, the opinion is the more probable which teaches that the essence of the sacrifice consists *in the mere consecration of both forms*."   (No. 4.)

" Next to Christ every priest legitimately ordained is the true and proper minister of this sacrifice, because they only can perform this sacrifice, who have received supernatural power for this purpose: but the priests alone have received this power, as is evident from their consecration.   To its validity the wickedness of the priest is no impediment, if he only applies the proper matter and form with the intention of consecrating : for the power of orders is indelible in him : but in order to celebrate it piously and properly, amongst other things which relate to the disposition of the mind, purity of life, rectitude of intention, devotion and reverence are required." (No. 5.)

The object of the sacrifice of the mass is *reverential*, inasmuch as it pertains to the honour of God, and the recognition of his sovereign power, and of our subjection, &c. It is *Eucharistical*, inasmuch as it is an expression of thanks for benefits received whether of natural or supernatural order, and signally for our redemption, &c. It is *propitiatory ;* because according to the Apostle, Heb. v. it is the principal duty of priests for sins : but the Church certainly has her own priests : therefore they are appointed to offer sacrifices for sins : now that a sacrifice is offered for sin and that it is *propitiatory* are synonymous : and hence the sacrifice of the mass is offered in order to obtain the remission of sins, to appease an offended God, for the remission of punishment still due to sins, remitted as respects their guilt : and thus in the mass it is said ' For innumerable sins and offences,' &c.

" It is also *impetratorial :** because by it we obtain both spiritual benefits, as it applies the merits of the cross of Christ, on which Christ has merited for us every kind of spiritual blessings and temporal benefits : because these are useful to us, and may be the means by which we are brought to God. Hence it is offered for peace, for the weather, for averting rain, &c." See canon 3. of council of Trent, at the commencement of this chapter. (No. 6.)

The effects of the sacrifice of the mass, are said to be the following : 1. The most excellent worship of latria ; both on account of the principal priest, who is Christ, and on account of the victim, which also is Christ. 2. An expression of thanks for favours received. 3. The mediate remission of sins, as well mortal as venial. 4. The pacifying of the divine anger, &c. 5. The remission of punishment still due from a sin remitted as to its guilt, and to be expiated in this life or in purgatory, unless its remission

---

* I claim the same right to coin an *English* word, that Peter Dens has to make a *Latin* one ; *impetratorial* for " impetratorium ;" *obtaining by entreaty.*

be obtained through this sacrifice, indulgences, &c. 6. The obtaining of all spiritual and temporal blessings, in so far as they conduce to salvation. (No. 7.)

The mass is infallibly efficacious, in so far as it is an act of worship and eucharistical; so also, inasmuch as it makes satisfaction for just persons, whether living or dead, who are obnoxious to the debt of temporal punishments, which remains after the penalty has been remitted. As for the dead, it is probable that God either has regard to the degree of the pious disposition in which they departed, or that the punishments are moderated, according to the secret judgments of his justice. It is not to be supposed that the rich, who can have many masses offered for them, will fare better in the other world than the poor, for whom scarcely any mass is offered; because the poor usually have less to answer for than the rich; besides, their suffering souls receive benefit from the masses put into the treasury of the Church, according to the rate of the holiness of every man.

The remission of sins is not infallibly secured by the mass, for many persevere in sin, for whom the sacrifice of the mass is frequently offered, yet more plentiful actual grace is infallibly imparted, in order to elicit acts of contrition, unless some obstacle should be in the way, such as the desire of actual sin might be.

" *Is the mass of a bad priest worth less than that of a good one?*" In so far as the validity of the sacrifice is concerned, there can be no difference; nor can the mass of a bad priest be less profitable than that of a good one, inasmuch as he is a minister of the Church.

In so far as the prayers which are said in the mass, are considered as the work of the priest himself, as a private person, a preference should be given to the prayers of a good priest. (No. 8.)

There is a triple portion of fruits resulting from the sacrifice of the mass: *general*, *special*, and *most special*. The *general* portion is that which falls to the whole church, according to that passage of the Roman Missal, " But also for all believing Christians, living and dead," &c. " Henno teaches that a priest excluding even a single member of the church in his application, whether from hatred or from enmity, or from any other pretext, sins grievously against

charity, and the obedience due to Christ and the church."
The *special* portion belongs to those for whom the priest intends specially to sacrifice; he may, however, apply it to
himself, when he celebrates mass for no one: "But this is
indeed very convenient," says Daelman, "that every priest
may sometimes apply to himself a special portion of the
sacrifice, as he himself often needs it." The *most special*
portion belongs to the priest, even when he is celebrating
for another, although for pay: and indeed, according to
Suarez, Collet, Steyaert, Daelman, and Pauwels, against
Henno, this portion belongs properly to the priest thus celebrating, so that he cannot even relinquish it to the other
when applying for it; because the priest, according to the
apostle to Heb. vii. 27, ought "*first to offer for his own sins,
and then for those of the people.*" (No. 9.)

The *special* portion is left to the free application and
disposition of the person celebrating; but if it is not applied
to any person either explicitly or implicitly, it then reverts
to the treasury of the church. (No. 10.)

A distinction is to be made between the *value* of the mass
and its *effect;* its value is infinite, "considered as to the
substance and sufficiency of the thing offered, and of the
principal offerer, Christ; because this sacrifice, as to its substance, is the same with the sacrifice of the cross, whose
value, as to its sufficiency, is infinite: therefore, also the
value of this sacrifice. And hence, there are no benefits,
however great, but may be obtained by this sacrifice; nor so
many, but more may be obtained; nor for so many, but that
it may avail for more: and likewise, no punishment is so
great for which it is not sufficient to make satisfaction; neither in so many subjects, but that it may avail in more."
As to its actual application and efficiency, the value of the
sacrifice of the mass is finite, both with respect to its ability
to make satisfaction, and procure blessings; this is plain
from the practice of the church, and the common opinion of
the faithful; as in order to obtain one and the same thing
for one and the same soul, the sacrifice of the mass may be
repeated. This limitation of the advantage "proceeds from
the disposition and devotion of him for whom the sacrifice is
offered;" and according to this opinion, the sacrifice of the
mass offered for many is just as profitable to each individual,

other things being equal, as if it were offered only for one because as the value is infinite, and the sacrifice benefits every one according to the quantity of his own devotion, as St. Thomas teaches, nothing is taken away from the advantage due to the devotion of him for whom it is offered, by the circumstance that it is offered for others : for that which is infinite is inexhaustible." Yet it would be wrong to receive several payments for one mass. (No. 11.)

" *For whom may the sacrifice of the mass be offered ?* Generally speaking, for the living and the dead." Under the former head are included all Christ's faithful, as these words of the canon of the mass show : " We offer to thee for all the orthodox, and the worshippers of the Catholic and apostolic faith." For catechumens and unbelievers, the mass may not only be offered indirectly but also directly, for the good of unbelievers themselves, whether temporal or spiritual. It is proper also to offer mass indirectly for baptized heretics, but whether it may be done directly is a controverted point ; and the more probable opinion is, that baptized heretics are entirely excluded from all the direct benefits of the sacrifice of the mass. (Alas! Alas!) Mass can not and ought not to be offered for the lost, who are suffering in hell, because it can not help them, for in hell there is no redemption. The sacrifice of the mass is not offered to the Saints, as it is a worship of latria, which is due to God alone. Nor is it offered for the Saints, because as they enjoy the vision of God, there is no more guilt remaining for which they must atone. It is piously and usefully offered only for the souls in purgatory ; and it is certain that the sacrifice of the Mass is infallibly of advantage to them for the remission of the punishments remaining from guilt, at least as to a part. (No. 12.)

Concerning the Payment of Masses. (No. 14.)

" It is to be observed that in the primitive church every one of the faithful as often as they assembled for the solemnities of the mass offered according to his own means bread and wine, of which a small portion was consecrated and the remaining portion fell to the priests and the clergy. Afterwards the custom was introduced of offering money at the altar, in place of bread : and to this succeeded the practice of giving pay to the priest, in order that advantage might be derived from the sacrifice either for themselves or for others. It is proper to receive pay for the celebration of the mass; not indeed as the price of the mass, but on the ground of support. "The labourer is worthy of his hire," and "they who serve at the altar," &c. 1Cor. ix. 13. It is not simony according to Daelman if a priest refuses to offer mass unless he is paid for it. The amount of pay depends upon custom, which will be varied by time, place and circumstances; and priests are properly admonished by Steyaert, not to ask more than the amount thus authorized, as this would be to sin both against the church and against justice. Yet they may accept more if it is given gratis from liberality. It would not be proper for one, who has received a larger amount than the ordinary stipend for a mass, to give the usual sum to another on condition of his performing the sacrifice, and retain the balance; unless he should be a beneficiate, or unless it is done as an act of kindness to another because he is poor, or a relative, &c.

"*May a priest, who is only obliged to celebrate in a certain place for the convenience of the people, with a free intention, as they say, receive another payment besides ?*

"*Ans.* Yes: because in such a case the priest imposes on himself two obligations, for which he may receive distinct payments : the one as the price of the extrinsic labour by which he is bound to be prepared for the celebration in such an hour, in such a place, &c.: the other as support, which he justly claims from him who desires the mass." Whether a priest omitting to celebrate a mass for which he has been paid, sins mortally or not, is not altogether settled as yet. In case a priest receives money for masses, and transfers the obligation of saying them to another, for merchandize, v. g., books, he does nothing wrong, provided it is morally certain that the masses will be duly celebrated, that he does not receive more than the pay he has taken, and that the goods are just as acceptable to the buyer as the money. It is also perfectly right for a priest, who has received a florin for 100 Sacra, to say to another, "help me in reading, afterwards I will help you," though the latter has received only 8 stivers' worth of Sacra, and the former gives him nothing more. It is not proper for a priest to collect several payments for

36

masses, which he foresees he will not be able to celebrate for a long time to come; and indeed he sins mortally who defers the masses longer than is just, and is bound to make restitution. According to some, one or two months is a moderate delay; but this will depend on circumstances; if, v. g., a mass is offered for a woman in travail, for one in the agony of death, &c., it is a mortal sin to defer it for one day. (No. 14.)

Pastors or others who have a parochial charge are bound, by virtue of the pastoral office, to apply a mass occasionally, specially for the benefit of their parishioners, without pay. (No. 15.)

As for the *time* of celebrating mass, the rubrics of the Roman missal affirm that "a private mass may be said at least after the matin and lauds, at any hour from daybreak to noon." And if public exigency requires, the time may be anticipated, or for the benefit of a sick person, who would otherwise die without the viaticum, it is proper to celebrate immediately after midnight. As to the *place* in which the mass is to be offered, according to common right, it ought to be in a church consecrated by the bishop, or blessed either by the same, or by a priest by his permission, or in an oratory, appointed to this use by those who have the authority. "But there is this difference between the consecration and benediction, that the consecration by far more laborious, concerns the walls, which are anointed with chrism : but the benediction may be done with holy water and a few prayers, and has respect to the floor or pavement of the church." The church is violated by voluntary homicide, or by any considerable effusion of human blood. "The church is violated by the voluntary effusion humani seminis." Whether the effusion be according to nature or against nature ; "sive per copulam fornicariam, sive conjugalem !" "Authors commonly decide that the church is not violated by pollution which occurs in sleep, although it might perhaps have been culpable in the cause." The burial in the church of an excommunicated person, particularly of one denounced, or a notorious persecutor of the clergy, also, of a Gentile or infidel, desecrates the church ; so too, the burial of an unbaptized child. In the same modes a cemetery that has been blessed is violated ; indeed if the cemetery is attached to the

church, the desecration of the church violates it, but not vice
versâ. It will not be lawful to bury in it until it has been
reconciled. In order to render an immediate reconcilation
of a church necessary, the causes must be public; if they
are private, the ordinances may be administered until a suitable opportunity of effecting the reconciliation is afforded.
(No. 16.)

Certain things respecting the celebration of the mass, worthy to be observed. (No. 17.)

" To touch the sacred vessels whilst they actually contain
the body and blood of Christ the Lord, is by common opinion, not permitted to any one under pain of mortal sin, excepting the priest or deacon. It is permitted to the sub-
deacons alone to touch the empty vessels; it is unlawful for
others, except in case of necessity or special leave; but
according to common opinion only, under venial sin. The
case is the same with the purifications applied for cleansing
the cup; which, however, after they have been washed by
the sub-deacon with the first ablution, which ought to be
cast into the Church sink, may be touched and repaired by
the laity, and so long as they are not considerably broken,
they do not need a fresh benediction after the washing.
When does a cup lose its consecration? When it is so
broken that it does not remain fit for a convenient sacred
use; v. g., if the cup be separated from the foot, (unless the
foot should be turned), or a hole has been made in the bottom of the cup, or the cup is otherwise very much broken.
The consecration is not lost, although the gilding of the cup
should fall off a little. However, the opinion is the more
common, that the cup needs a new consecration, if the internal surface of the bowl be newly gilded. Steyaert says,
that the custom of giving to boys, labouring under a cough
peculiar and most distressing to them, wine to drink out of
a consecrated cup, as a medicine, is not to be accused of
any superstition, or any other vice. *Is it lawful sometimes
to celebrate without the sacred robes?* He who celebrates
without the principal sacred vestments, v. g. the albe or
stole, sins grievously, even in a case of necessity, v. g., in
order that a sick man may receive the viaticum: so authors
generally decide: to celebrate in any urgent necessity, with-

out some one of the minor vestments, v. g., the maniple or girdle, appears lawful to many. When the priest puts on the sacred robes, he ought to recite the prayers prescribed by the rubrics, not, however, under pain of mortal sin, as Neesen pretends; whom Pauwels justly contradicts. The sacred garments lose their benediction when they no longer retain the form under which they have been blessed; so that they now are unfit for the functions of the ministry: and thus the blessing of the albe ceases, if the sleeve is torn off or separated from it; not, however, if the sleeve is fastened to the body with cords. The blessing of the girdle equally ceases, if it is so torn that neither part which remains, is fit for girding; not, however, if the one part is sufficient for girding; and then Collet says, for the sake of greater convenience, the other part may be tied to it. Neither is it sufficient to mend vestments thus torn, that they may dispense with the blessing, but when mended, they need a fresh benediction. Sacred vestments, so much worn that they can no longer subserve their proper use, are not according to the canons, to be applied to common purposes; but others are either to be made out of them, which may subserve the use of the Church, or they must be burned, and the ashes must be laid aside in the sacristy, or in the wall, or in the interstices of the pavements, that they may not be trampled upon by the feet of those who enter. It is to be observed respecting all the aforesaid things, to wit, altars, vestments, &c., that it is more probable, that they are not consecrated or blessed by the mere use, but only by the rite and ceremonies prescribed by the Church."

The reader will observe that our author has not been quite so precise in defining nice points, in sacred casuistry, in this instance, as in most cases which we have reviewed; this is to be regretted, as there are several questions, which naturally suggest themselves to an inquisitive mind, in connection with this interesting, intricate, and most solemn and momentous subject. It is true we are told, that if the sleeve of the albe be tied to the body with *cords*, the blessing does not forsake it; but *what if it be fastened with pins?* And in this case *must the pins be blessed or consecrated, before they can be applied to this holy use?* And if thus blessed, *may they be employed for profane or common purposes, after the sleeve has been regularly stitched to the albe with sacred thread?* Again; we are satisfied, if a girdle has been torn, and both pieces are like the Dutchman's rope, that they may be reverently tied together, and thus comfort and sustain the bowels of the holy priest, who wears it; *but the question is, what if the one part, which has been laid aside as insufficient to encircle the loins of its former owner, should be found ample for a stomach of smaller circumference, may this rag of a girdle in such case, be used as a proper belt by another? And if so, will it need another benediction?* And again, supposing a priest celebrates mass in an alb, which has but one sleeve, so that the faithful are scandalized by the apparition of one arm of his sacred shirt, or his still more sacred skin; *will the sacrament be invalidated by this irreverent display, and by the sacrilegious disregard of the custom and ceremony of the Church?* These and similar questions, grievously torment our mind, but being in bad odour with the bishop, we apprehend that our perplexity will never be relieved. But to return:

It is not in itself wrong to celebrate mass in a vernacular tongue, but the church has forbidden the practice for the sake of preserving uniformity. In offering mass, it is requisite that there should be a minister to respond to the priest, unless some urgent necessity should excuse, such as administering the viaticum to a sick person. The rubrics require that the person officiating be in all cases, a male; in case of absolute necessity in some instances a female may be permitted to respond. (No. 17.)

CONCERNING THE PRECEPT OF HEARING MASS. (No. 18.)

"Among the five precepts of the church, the second is that of hearing mass on Lord's days and other festival days, expressed in these words: '*Reverently hear the sacred office of the mass on festival days*': this office includes not only the essential or integral parts of the sacrifice, but the whole liturgy from the beginning to the end. But this is a principle of ecclesiastical law, founded however upon natural and divine right. *Who are obliged by this precept?* All the faithful of both sexes after they have attained to years of discretion, which generally takes place about the seventh year of the age, and therefore children of such an age are to be compelled to go to the mass. *How great is the obligation of this precept?* It is important, because it is a weighty matter the object is most important, in order, says Pauwels, that the memory of the passion and resur-

36*

rection of the Lord Jesus Christ, and in order that God may be honoured with the sacrifice, in as much as the people present at the mass unite their affections and devotion with the priest, who is celebrating. Hence the sin of its omission is from its nature mortal : therefore he who with sufficient deliberation omits mass on a festival day, or a considerable part of the mass, sins mortally. It may, however, become venial, not only from the want of deliberation of the action, v. g. if any one out of merely venial ignorance of the festival omits hearing mass; but also from the smallness of the matter, so that he sins only venially who omits merely a trifling part." The amount which is to be regarded as considerable depends both upon the quality and the quantity of the omitted portion. Thus he sins mortally, who is absent at the consecration, or who suffers his thoughts to be distracted at the time, or who is not present at the communion, because in these the essence and integrity of the sacrifice consist. A considerable part is detracted from the quantity, when a large part of the prayers, orations and ceremonies, which take place in the performance of the mass is lost, according to some the third, according to others the fourth part of the mass. If a person who has been present from the commencement goes out immediately after the communion, he is by common opinion excusable. The dignity and importance of the omitted portion, and the state of the heart are also to be taken into consideration. The faithful are to be admonished to be present betimes at catechism and preaching from beginning to end. Several small omissions in the same mass coalesce, and therefore, if in the aggregate they constitute a considerable omission, they induce mortal sin, &c. &c. (No. 18.)

Actual intention, and devout attention are required, in all who would hear mass. Sacramental confession is strongly recommended as an act preparatory to the mass. (No. 20.)

Four causes are usually assigned as affording sufficient excuse of absence from hearing mass; they are *inability, charity, duty, and custom.* Inability may be *physical, spiritual,* and *moral.* Those who are in prison, or sick in bed, or at sea, or living in a heretical country, in which the mass is not celebrated, are excused on the score of *physical* inability. So too, one who omits the duty through inculpable inadvertence or ignorance. But the sick must use the necessary means for recovering strength, else they are guilty of the omission of the mass. If the sick person has a chapel, and can attend without much inconvenience, he ought to see to it that some priest celebrates mass there. *Spiritual* inability proceeds from censure, by which any one may be hindered from hearing mass; hence the faithful are excused if there is no other priest at hand except an interdicted one, or one who has been excommunicated by name. *Moral* inability excuses those, who cannot hear mass except with great danger, inconvenience, or some considerable injury, either of body, reputation, or fortune. On this ground, the sick, who are apprehensive of aggravating their disease, or of incurring a relapse, also they who cannot leave their work or flock on account of danger of theft, or incursion of the enemy, may be excused. So too a respectable girl, who is pregnant from secret fornication, is excusable. Difference of sex and constitution is to be regarded, in deciding whether the case is really one of moral inability. *Charity* to a neighbour excuses from attending mass; v. g., waiting on a sick person, by your presence preventing homicide, serious injury, grievous sins or quarrels. *Official Duty* also excuses; thus a soldier may not leave his station, nor a general his army, in order to hear mass. So also persons engaged in glass or iron works, after the furnace has been kindled, may absent themselves from mass, if they cannot leave without serious inconvenience or loss, and are unable to procure substitutes, &c. The claim of *custom* obtains until their purification in the case of women lately delivered. Billuart observes that he who in good faith believes himself to be excused from mass, although the reason be not sufficient, sins only venially. The case is the same if the mass be omitted contrary to intention through some slight neglect. Travellers who go from a place, where there is a festival, are bound to hear mass before they leave; not, however, if they merely pass through such a place. Yet they are excused, if by hearing mass they would lose the opportunity of going in a certain ship, or forfeit the society of a travelling companion, who is indispensable, because without him they cannot find the road, or because robbers infest the country.

There is no rite of which the Church of Rome boasts more loudly, than the mass, and yet we need not be surprised at this, as she always glories in her shame! Of all the blasphemous and idolatrous ceremonies, which Satan has ever invented, the mass is the most abominable. Such another compound of silly trumpery and audacious impiety, is not to be found on earth. The substance of the following sketch of the matter, form and ceremony of the mass, is prepared from an authorized missal of the Romish Church, printed at Lyons, A. D. 1520, from the Rationale of Durandus, &c.; and I give it to my reader with a few, merely verbal alterations, as I find it in a work published in London, 1735. First, the priest who is to officiate, puts on his head an amice, a thing, which signifies the veil that the Jews put on Christ; then over the rest of his clothes an alb, a white linen garment, which betokens a garment of that colour, which Herod is said to have put upon Christ; then he puts on his girdle, signifying the cord with which our Saviour was bound in the garden; next he puts a stole about his neck, as an emblem of the cord with which Christ was led to execution; and another contrivance called a maniple, something like a fetter on his left hand, in allusion to the cord with which Christ was bound to the pillar when scourged. Over all this sacred apparatus, a rich vestment variously figured, is thrown. Some have the picture of God, or of the Holy Ghost; others, some passage in sacred history, or a cross curiously wrought behind and before; and this we are to understand, as significant of the purple garment with which the Jews clothed our Saviour.

Thus accoutred, cap-a-pie, forth comes his reverence with solemn dignity, and moves his sacred person towards the altar, which, be it remembered, represents the cross, and is covered with a white cloth, denoting the linen that shrouded the body of the Lord. On this, stands the chalice or cup, which is a symbol of the sepulchre in which Christ lay, whilst the Patin or plate that holds the cake and covers it, represents the stone which was laid on his grave. On the altar stands a lighted candle, emblematical of the light of Christ, and of the rays of his divinity; also a flagon of wine and water, and the cake made of a wafer. The clerk, or sometimes a boy, who responds to the priest, is in attendance, bell in hand. The priest crosses himself on the forehead and on the breast; and after advancing towards the altar, retreats with three motions, significant of Christ's prostration in the garden. He then begins the confiteor, or confession, which is made to the Virgin Mary and other saints, desiring them to pray for him. Whilst repeating this, he bows very low, in

order to provoke the people to humility; though they generally know
no more what he says, than if it were wild Irish, and many of them
not near as much. At the words, *meâ culpâ, meâ culpâ, meâ maximâ
culpâ*, he strikes himself violently on the breast, to show that sin lies
in the heart. Then he gives the absolution; and coming close to the
altar, makes a cross upon it and devoutly kisses it. Then he begins
the Introit, or office of the mass, commencing, *Command me, O Lord,
to speak well*, &c., which he speaks aloud, of course, in Latin; and
answers himself, "Dominus sit in corde," &c.; *the Lord be in my
heart and in my mouth*, &c. Then he says the *Kyrie Eleison*, (two
Greek words, signifying, Lord have mercy; which are repeated nine
times in honour of the Trinity, three times to each person.) Upon
this, advancing to the middle of the altar, and looking upon the pax,
the cross on which the sacramental bread is hung, he makes a pro-
found courtesy, and says the "Gloria in excelsis;" then wheeling
round, he says, "Dominus vobiscum;" *the Lord be with you;* and immediately returning to the altar, goes over sundry collects, the substance of most of which is, that he desires to be heard for the sake
of the merits and intercession of certain saints. This part of the
service, duly and reverently performed, he reads the epistle, still of
course in Latin; then follows the gradual, or as it is sometimes called,
for brevity's sake, the grail, and after this the hallelujah. Next come
the tract and sequence, a pair of short prayers, which are soon mum-
bled over; which done, his Reverence takes up the mass-book, goes
to the end of the altar, uncovers the chalice, and looking into it,
makes a solemn bow to the pax, and then reads the gospel in Latin,
which being finished, the faithful cross their breasts, *that the devil
may not steal away the good seed out of their hearts*, although there is
no doubt that they might as well save themselves that trouble. After
this, the priest kisses the book, and rehearses the creed; then turning
to the people a second time, he says, *Dominus vobiscum*, and going
again to the altar, he proceeds with the offertory or offering, which is
dispatched by taking up the chalice, with the wafer upon the cover of
it, lifting up his eyes, and saying, *Suscipe sancta Trinitas*, &c. "Take,
O holy Trinity, this oblation, which I, unworthy sinner, offer in honour
of thee, of the blessed Virgin Mary, and of all thy saints, for the salvation of the living, and for the rest and quiet of all the faithful that
are dead." Then setting down the chalice, he says, *acceptum sit*, &c.
"Let this new sacrifice be acceptable to Almighty God." Then going
to the other end of the altar, he washes his hands, and with a bow to
the pax, turning to the altar, he makes a cross over it, and kisses it;

upon this he requests the prayers of the people, and again facing the altar with a bow, he begins the *secret prayers* in behalf of the people; for which, however, they are none the wiser nor better. These being concluded, he bursts out into a loud exhortation to the people to lift up their hearts, be thankful, &c. &c. Then he reads the preface, and in pronouncing the *sanctus*, " Holy, holy, holy, Lord God," &c., they lift up their hands and voice, and suddenly the priest kisses the mass-book again.

Now comes the Canon of the mass consisting of a string of litanies and prayers; here with frequent crossings, he prays for the Pope, &c. and after this, the people go to pray for all whom they can remember of their friends and benefactors; desiring that for the merits of such and such saints, they may be saved from evil. Then again he crosses the wafer and chalice, standing with his back to the people, and takes up the wafer in his hands, when the boy rings the bell, which invites the people to look up, whilst the priest repeats the consecration in Latin as follows : " *The day before our Lord suffered, he took bread into his holy and adorable hands, and lifting up his eyes to heaven to God, and giving thanks, he blessed,* (here his reverence crosses and re-crosses the wafer,) *brake and gave to his disciples, saying, Take, eat ye all of this, for it is my body.*" These last five words are those in which the transubstantiating virtue lies. Then with a world of circumstance the priest lifts it over his head, for the people to see it; (this is called the elevation of the host;) and they fall down on their knees and worship it. This done, he takes up the cup, saying : *In like manner, after supper, he took this noble chalice into his holy and adorable hands, and after thanks to the Father, he blessed,* (here he crosses again,) *and gave it to his disciples, saying, Take ye, and drink you ALL of this : for this is the cup of my blood, a new and everlasting testament, a mystery of faith, which shall be shed for you and for many, for the remission of sins: so oft as you do this, you shall do it in remembrance of me.*" These words as well as those spoken over the bread are uttered softly and with a low voice. Then the priest holding up the chalice in his hand, breathes upon the wine, and kneels down to it and the bread; then rising up he holds the cup over his head that the people may likewise worship it. This ceremony over, he sets down the chalice and covers it with the cloth, and then kneels down again before the host and cup, and with outspread arms kisses the altar. All this is done with the proper quota of crosses and bows. Then follows the second memento or prayer for the dead; after which the priest takes up the wafer, shakes it up and down about the chalice, saying, *per ipsum, et cum ipso, et in ipso*, takes up the cover of the chalice, and crosses himself on the breast, forehead, and crown; this uncovering of the cup is to be considered emblematical of the rending of the veil of the temple at the death of Christ; he then crosses the chalice three times over the top to typify the three hours during which Christ hung upon the cross; and twice on the brim to show the overflowing of his blood, and then by laying down the host on the altar cloth, he professes to represent Christ's being taken down from the cross. Then his reverence takes up the host, which he breaks into three pieces, two of which he holds in his hand over the chalice, and the third he puts into it; (sometimes however, this ceremony is omitted;) upon this, the priest kneels down and says the agnus to the bread, which is this prayer: "O lamb of God, who takest away the sins of the world, have mercy upon us"; this must be rehearsed three times. Then he takes the pax (i. e. kisses an image of a crucifix in the missal,) and saying *Peace be with thee*, gives it to the clerk or boy, who carries it about to the people to kiss. Meanwhile the priest drinks up the wine, and eats the wafer, and then prays: "*Quod ore sumpsimus*, &c. That which we have taken with our mouth, Lord grant that we may receive with a pure mind, and that it may of a temporal gift be made an everlasting remedy, &c." By this time, the boy has come back with the pax; and his reverence holds out the cup for more wine, which he drinks off three times, then wipes his mouth, goes to the lower end of the altar, washes his hands, comes back to the altar, takes up the chalice, and does his best to extract every drop, that he may with a clear conscience say that he has drunk ALL of it. This done, he goes to the upper end of the altar, reads certain prayers and collects, and says to the people the third time, The Lord be with you. *Ite, missa est;* "Depart, the mass is over." Then he kneels down at the altar, says a prayer to the Virgin Mary, and rising up, repeats in his way the beginning of St. John's gospel, crossing himself to admiration; lastly, his reverence closes the book, folds up the corporal, (or altar cloth,) shuts the chalice, disrobes himself in due method, puts out the candle, makes his honours, and *exit*." This picture does not profess to present all the sacred antics and gesticulations, &c., which are practised on such occasions, nor are they at all times in all places exactly the same, but it is believed that it affords a fair representation of the principal scenes, which may be witnessed at the ecclesiastical exhibitions, in which the Romish priests are the principal *dramatis personæ*. This is a specimen of the mode of worship practised in a church which claims to be exclusively the church of Christ; the mem bers of its communion are *the faithful*, the true worshippers who worship *the Father in spirit and in truth!*

Although the absurdity of the mass is self-evident, yet a few suggestions may perhaps not be unacceptable to the general reader. We remark then,

1. This pretended sacrifice of the body and blood of Christ, is contrary to the institution of Christ. He did not stand at the altar to offer himself a sacrifice to God, that the disciples might adore it, but sat at a common table to set apart bread and wine to sacred use, and to distribute them to his disciples, that they might take, eat, and drink them. He says, *Take ye, eat ye, drink ye;* he does not say, " sacrifice my body and blood," or " make an unbloody oblation of me !"

2. It is directly contrary to the positive injunctions of Scripture, which expressly declare that Christ need not offer himself, or be offered OFTEN, but that the offering he ONCE made, is sufficient to the end of the world. " Nor yet that he should offer himself often, as the highpriest entereth into the holy place every year with blood of others; (for there must he often have suffered since the foundation of the world ;) but now once in the end of the world hath he appeared, to put away sin, by the sacrifice of himself." (Heb. ix. 25, 26.) And again, " By the which will we are sanctified, through the offering of the body of Jesus Christ once for all. And every priest standeth daily ministering, and offering oftentimes the same sacrifices, which can never take away sins: but this man, after he had offered one sacrifice for sins, for ever sat down on the right hand of God; &c. For by one offering he hath perfected for ever them that are sanctified." (Heb. x. 10, 11, 12, 14.) Therefore if Christ cannot be sacrificed again, according to the word of God, it is an insolent sacrilege to speak of the mass being a *propitiatory sacrifice for the sins of the living and the dead.* This argument Peter Dens professes to notice and to refute ; and of course adopts the favourite Romish method of *distinction.* He distinguishes between the *one oblation* of Christ as of sufficient price to purchase the redemption of the world, but not as sufficient for the application of its benefits. But this is a mere quibble, which does not mend the matter. For according to Peter Dens, the mass avails only for believers, but if Paul is to be believed, Christ has by this " one offering FOR EVER perfected them that are sanctified," and consequently they have no need of the mass, which professes to be a repetition of this sacrifice.

But we are demurely told, Melchisedec was a type of Christ; and the bread and wine he brought forth to Abraham, was a real, proper sacrifice. Hence when the Scripture says, in allusion to Christ, " thou art a priest for ever, after the order of Melchisedec," there is an allusion to the mass, and a warrant for the *unbloody sacrifice*. To this we reply, that there is neither truth, sense, nor probability in this argument.

1. It is not true that the bread and wine, which Melchisedec brought forth, was a proper sacrifice; the Scripture does not call it such, and from its nature it was incapable of being a sacrifice, as it had neither life, nor blood, which every expiatory sacrifice must have; and transubstantiation had not then been thought of. Melchisedec is called a priest, from the fact of his blessing Abraham, which was part of his priestly office, and not because he brought out bread and wine, which as an act of beneficence pertained rather to his kingly office. Besides, it is said, " he *brought forth* bread and wine," not he *sacrificed* them. He simply entertained Abraham and his servants.

2. If there *was* any sacrifice, to whom was it made? To God? Surely not; for as before remarked, every propitiatory sacrifice required a living victim, and as Melchisedec did not transubstantiate the bread and wine into the body and blood of the Saviour, this could not have been an expiatory offering, and therefore serves but badly as the prototype of the mass. Did he sacrifice to Abraham? Was Abraham a God? Besides, did not Abraham pay tithes to Melchisedec, and thus acknowledge his inferiority, according to the apostle's own inference; and how then should Melchisedec sacrifice to Abraham?

3. It is not probable; for can it for a moment be imagined, if there had been any such mystery in this bread and wine of Melchisedec, that the Apostle Paul, who speaks of Melchisedec as a type of Christ, but for reasons very different from those which Papists assign, would say not one word about Melchisedec's sacrifice? Yet he neither mentions that nor anything else that could furnish so much as an iota of evidence to sustain the doctrine of the mass, or remotely insinuate that the bread and wine had any allusion to the unbloody sacrifice of the Roman Church.

Another passage which Peter Dens cites in favour of the mass, is Mal. i. 11. " *From the rising of the sun to the going down of the same, my name shall be great among the Gentiles, and in every place a* SACRIFICE *shall be offered in my name for a pure offering*." Now as this prophecy relates to Gospel times, of course there must be some sacrifice in the Christian Church, that may be offered up in every place, and what can this be but the mass? Sure enough! To this we answer; the reading of this text is bad, but the interpretation is worse: the word, which in the Doway is translated *sacrifice*, properly signifies

37

incense, or any spiritual oblation, and so it is rendered in the Holy Bible. Now both *sacrifice* and *incense* are figuratively used in the word of God to denote a purely spiritual oblation. " Let my prayer be set forth before thee as incense, and the lifting up of mine hands, as the evening sacrifice ;" the Psalmist (Ps. cxli. 2.) here speaks of the incense and sacrifice of prayer ; why, therefore, must the word here be understood as alluding to a proper expiatory sacrifice ? In Rev. v. 8. we read ; " the four-and-twenty elders fell down before the Lamb having every one of them harps, and golden vials full of odours, which are the prayers of the saints." By odours we are to understand incense, which is a sweet perfume, and signifies that the prayers of the saints are sweet and acceptable to God. But wherever Christ has a church, " from the rising of the sun to the going down thereof," there the "pure offering," and the " incense" of prayer ascend to the mercy seat ; so that this prophecy is literally fulfilled, even though we repudiate the mass, as an *unbloody* ABOMINATION !

CHAPTER XXXIX.

TREATISE CONCERNING THE SACRAMENT OF PENANCE.

APPROBATION.

" Many truly excellent theologians have hitherto thoroughly discussed the matter of the Sacrament of Penance, according to rule ; so that it might appear superfluous to submit it again to the press. They have indeed proposed principles and foundations ; but (saving their peace be it spoken,) the most of them have insisted on speculation rather than on practice. The venerable and most learned D. Archpresbyter, President of the Archepiscopal Seminary," (PETER DENS,) " being especially solicitous to train for pastoral duties, the theologians committed to his care, insists upon practice more than speculation. And therefore retrenching very many questions of little utility, he teaches the way by which his pupils may be able to lead to true penitence. Turning neither to the right hand nor to the left, and hence avoiding on the one hand, the rocks of Scylla, of too great severity, and on the other, the Charybdis of undue indulgence, he pursues the middle way, or the safe path of salvation, and insists steadfastly upon the doctrine of holy mother Church, and the decrees of the apostolic See ; and according to his own and my judgment, whatever he has written or said, he submits entirely to the censorship of the supreme Vicars, of the same holy Mother, and of Christ. In reliance, therefore, upon these foundations, I think without hesitation, that this treatise on penance, and the other connected topics, will be worthy of the public light, and profitable to the readers. Mechlin, September 18th, 1758.

"J. F. FOPPENS,

"S. T. L. Metropol. Mechl, Eccl. Canon. Grad. et Archidiac. Libr. Censor."

PREFACE.

DECREE OF THE COUNCIL OF FLORENCE, FOR THE INSTRUCTION OF THE ARMENIANS.

" The fourth sacrament is penance, of which the acts of the penitent are, as it were, the matter, and these are distinguished into three parts ; of which the first is, contrition of heart ; to which pertains, that he be sorry for the sin committed, with the purpose of not sinning in future. The second is, the confession of the mouth ; to which pertains, that the sinner confess entirely to his priest, all the sins of which he has any recollection. The third is, satisfaction for the sins according to the judgment of the priest ; which, indeed, is made principally through prayer, fasting, and alms-giving. The words of absolution, which the priest pronounces, when he says, *I absolve thee*, &c., are the form of this sacrament. The minister of this sacrament, is the priest having either the ordinary authority of absolving, or by the commission of a superior. The effect of this sacrament is absolution from sins."

Canons of the Council of Trent, concerning Penance.

" 1. Whoever shall say that penance in the Catholic Church, is not truly and properly a sacrament for the reconciliation of the faithful to God, as often as they fall into sins after baptism, instituted by Christ our Lord ; let him be accursed !

" 2. Whoever confounding the sacraments, shall say, that baptism itself is the sacrament of penance, as if these two sacraments were not distinct, and that, therefore, penance is not rightly termed, *a second plank after shipwreck ;* let him be accursed !

" 3. Whoever shall say, that those words of the Lord and Saviour : Receive the Holy Ghost ; *whose sins you shall forgive, they are forgiven them, and whose sins ye shall retain, they are retained :* are not to be understood of the power of remitting and retaining sins in the sacrament of penance, as the Catholic Church has always understood, from the beginning : but shall falsely apply them against the institution of this sacrament, to the authority of preaching the gospel; let him be accursed!

" 4. Whoever shall deny, that three acts are required in the penitent for the entire and perfect remission of sins, constituting, as it were, the matter of the sacrament of penance, viz : contrition, confession, and satisfaction, which are called the three parts of penance; or shall say, that only two are parts of penance, to wit : the terrors by which the conscience is smitten by the sense of sin, and faith, produced by the gospel, or by absolution, whereby the person believes that his sins have been remitted to him by Christ; let him be accursed!

" 5. Whoever shall affirm, that the contrition, which is produced by examination, enumeration, and detestation of sins, by which any one recounts his years in the bitterness of his soul, pondering the weight, multitude, and baseness of his offences, the loss of eternal happiness, and the desert of eternal damnation, with a resolution of leading a better life, is not true and profitable sorrow, and does not prepare for grace, but makes a man a hypocrite and a greater sinner, and that it is only a forced sorrow, and not free and voluntary; let him be accursed!

" 6. Whoever shall deny that sacramental confession has either been instituted by divine command, or is necessary to salvation; or shall say that the mode of secretly confessing to a priest alone, which the Catholic Church always has observed from the beginning, and still observes, is foreign from the institution and command of Christ, and is a human invention; let him be accursed!

" 7. Whoever shall affirm, that in the sacrament of penance, it is not necessary by divine command, for the remission of sins, to confess all and every mortal sin, of which recollection may be had, with due and diligent premeditation, including secret offences, and those which are against the two last precepts of the decalogue, and the circumstances which change the species of sin : but that this confession is useful only for the instruction and consolation of the penitent, and was anciently observed, only as a canonical satisfaction imposed upon him : or shall say, that they who endeavour to confess all their sins, wish to leave nothing for the divine mercy to pardon; or finally, that it is not proper to confess venial sins; let him be accursed!

" 8. Whoever shall say, that the confession of all sins, such as the Church observes, is impossible, and that it is a human tradition, to be abolished by the pious; or that all and every one of Christ's faithful, of both sexes, are not bound to observe it once in the year, according to the constitution of the great Lateran council, and that for this reason, Christ's faithful should be advised not to confess in the time of Lent; let him be accursed!

"9. Whoever shall say, that the sacramental absolution of the priest is not a judicial act, but a mere ministry to pronounce and declare, that sins are remitted to the person making confession, provided that he only believes that he is absolved, even though the priest should not absolve seriously, but in joke; or shall say, that the confession of a penitent is not requisite, in order that the priest may absolve him; let him be accursed!

"10. Whoever shall say, that priests who are living in mortal sin do not possess the power of binding and loosing; or that the priests are not the only ministers of absolution, but that it was said to all and every one of Christ's faithful: *Whatsoever you shall bind upon earth, shall be bound also in heaven; and whatsoever you shall loose upon earth, shall be loosed also in heaven; and whose sins you shall forgive, they are forgiven, and whose sins you shall retain, they are retained:* by virtue of which words, any one may forgive sin; public sins, by reproof only, if the offender shall acquiesce; and private sins, by voluntary confession; let him be accursed!

"11. Whoever shall say that bishops have not the right of reserving cases to themselves, except such as relate to the external polity of the Church, and therefore that the reservation of cases does not hinder the priest from truly absolving from reserved cases; let him be accursed!

"12. Whoever shall say that the whole penalty, together with the guilt, is always remitted by God, and that the satisfaction of penitents is nothing else than the faith by which they apprehend that Christ has satisfied for them; let him be accursed!

"13. Whoever shall say that satisfaction is by no means made to God, through Christ's merits, for sins as to their temporal penalty, by punishments inflicted by him, and patiently borne, or enjoined by the priests, though not undergone voluntarily, as fastings, prayers, alms, or also other works of piety, and therefore that the best penance is nothing more than a new life; let him be accursed!

"14. Whoever shall say that the satisfactions by which penitents redeem themselves from sin through Jesus Christ, are no part of the service of God, but traditions of men, obscuring the doctrine concerning grace, and the true worship of God, and the actual benefit of Christ's death; let him be accursed!

"15. Whoever shall say that the keys of the Church were given
37 *

only for loosing, not also for binding, and that therefore, the priests when they impose punishments upon those who confess, act against the design of the keys, and contrary to the institution of Christ; and that it is a fiction, that when by virtue of the keys the eternal penalty has been removed, the temporal punishment may still often remain to be suffered ; let him be accursed !"

Penance is defined as "*a sacrament of the new law, by which absolution of sins is given by a priest having juris-diction, to baptized persons who have relapsed, are contrite, and have made confession.*" This sacrament is known by various names ; the Council of Trent terms it, *the second plank after shipwreck ;* and it is also commonly called *con-fession,* from its material part. (No. 1.)

It is PROVED to be a sacrament, 1. From the Councils of Florence and of Trent, by which an anathema is inflicted on all who deny that penance is a sacrament. And 2. From the words of Christ ; *Receive the Holy Ghost : whose sins you shall forgive they are forgiven to them, and whose ye retain they are retained.* John xx. 22. In which words Christ designated all things that are essential for the sacra-ment of penance ; he designated the *minister,* when he con-ceded this power to the apostles only, whom he addressed ; the *form* of the sacrament is indicated in the words, *you shall forgive,* by which is intimated that the remission should be effected by the words of the priest ; the remote matter is expressed by the word, *sins ;* contrition, or the dis-position is insinuated by the fact that the sins of some peni-tents are to be forgiven, but of others to be retained ; lastly, the confession of every sin in particular is taught by this, that the priests are there constituted judges ; for it is entrusted to their judgment to remit or retain all sins ; but now no one can be a judge in a case that is unknown to him ; therefore he ought to know the offences ; but he cannot become acquainted with them except through the sinner's own con-fession ; because the sinner alone knows the offences, inas-much as they are in his conscience ; therefore his confession is requisite in order that the confessor may judge of the of-fences as they are in the sinner's conscience. To the objection that God alone can forgive sins, the reply is made that God alone can remit principally, and by his own au-thority ; but the priests forgive ministerially. (No. 2.)

This sacrament was instituted on the very day of the resurrection.   (No. 3.)

The *proximate* matter of the penitent, consists of the three acts of contrition, confession and satisfaction.   The *remote* matter comprises any sins whatever, committed after baptism.   (No. 5.)

The remote matter is divided into *necessary*, and *optional*, or *sufficient*.   The *necessary* remote matter consists of all mortal sins, and the *optional*, (so called because it is left to the choice of the penitent, whether he will express them or not in confession,) includes all *venial* offences. (Nos. 6 and 7.) It is considered beneficial to confess these also.   (No. 9.)

The *form* is, *I absolve thee from thy sins, in the name of the Father, and of the Son, and of the Holy Ghost.* The essential words are, *I absolve thee.*   (No. 13.)

" The sense is this : I judicially confer upon thee the grace of the remission of thy sins, or grace in itself procuring the remission of thy sins, in so far as respects my ministry. This sense of the form cannot be admitted : *I declare thee absolved ;* because it was condemned by Council of Trent." (No. 14.)

It is proper to use " these and similar conditions, as the case may require ; *If thou art alive, if thou art baptized, if thou hast sinned, if thou art capable of the use of reason;* Daelman adds, *If thou art a Catholic :* but it is enough to understand these internally and intentionally."   (No. 16.)

This sacrament is necessary in fact or in desire, as a means to justification and salvation for those who have relapsed into mortal sin, after baptism.   (No. 21.)

Penance may be repeated till seventy times seven, that is, as often as the sinner sins and repents.   (No. 22.)

Public penances, which were formerly customary, were distinguished as *ceremonial* and *not ceremonial;* the latter were frequently repeated, but the former was performed only once in a lifetime.   (No. 23.)

The ceremonies which are observed at the sacrament of penance, are as follows ; " First, the confessor in imparting his blessing to the kneeling penitent, says: *The Lord be in thy heart, and in thy lips, that thou mayest worthily confess thy sins : in the name of the Father, and of the Son, and of the Holy Ghost.*   Presently the confessor may inquire, how long it is since he has confessed, &c. Having heard the confession, and the necessary questions and examination being finished, the confessor will endeavour to excite the penitent to true sorrow of contrition, above all from the motive of the love of God. Thus the pastorale. Lastly, he will enjoin salutary and convenient satisfaction.

"Afterwards let the priest say : *May Almighty God have mercy on thee, and having remitted thy sins, lead thee through to eternal life. Amen.* Then, having raised his right hand towards the penitent, let him say : *May the Almighty and merciful Lord give to thee the indulgence, absolution, and remission of thy sins, Amen. May our Lord Jesus Christ absolve thee :* Thus far the prayers and invocations are preparatory : the absolution from censures follows : *And I, by his authority, loose thee from every bond of excommunication, suspension, and interdict, in so far as I am able and thou hast need.* If the penitent is a layman, the word, *suspension*, is omitted. Then follows the sacramental absolution, or the form of the sacrament : *I absolve thee from thy sins, in the name of the Father, and of the Son, and of the Holy Ghost. Amen.* The confessor subjoins the following prayer. *May the passion of our Lord Jesus Christ, the merits of the Blessed Virgin Mary, and of all the saints, whatever good thou hast done, or whatever evil thou hast suffered, be to thee for the remission of sins, the increase of grace, and the reward of eternal life. Amen.* The rituals permit that, for certain reasons, the said prayers and invocations may be omitted ; so that in extreme necessity it may briefly be said : *I absolve thee from censures and sins in the name of the Father, and of the Son, and of the Holy Ghost. Amen.*" (No. 24.)

There are six *grades* by which sinners are ordinarily led to repentance. The first is a motion of divine grace, according to Jer. xxxi. 19. *After thou didst convert me,* I DID PENANCE. The second is a motion of faith, according to Heb. xi. 6. *He that comes to God must believe.* The third is the fear of punishment : Eccle. i. 27. *The fear of the Lord driveth out sin.* The fourth is an act of hope : Matt. ix. 2. *Son, be of good heart, thy sins are forgiven thee.* The fifth is an act of the love of God, *by which they begin to love God as the fountain of all jus-*

tice : Conc. Trid. The sixth is the proper act of penance, viz., *Sorrow, or contrition, through some hatred and detestation against sins,* as injurious to God, with a resolution of beginning a new life, to which in the New Law, the desire of baptism or of the sacrament of penance is necessarily to be connected." (No. 27.)

The effects of penance are : " 1. The remission of sins, and of eternal punishment, and of all temporal punishment. 2. The revival of virtues, and of good works, or merits. But besides the abovementioned these effects are assigned. 3. Sanctifying grace which is imparted by the power of the sacrament through the due administration. 4. Also, sacramental graces from the due administration, or actual graces ; also such as are to be given subsequently in order to perform works of penance, to avoid sins, to overcome temptations, &c. 5. There is wont at times, says Council of Trent, sess. 14. c. 3. to follow peace and security of conscience with very great spiritual consolation." (No. 29.)

So long as a man is in the state of probation, all sins whatever may be remitted through penance. (No. 30.)

When a fault is forgiven, the guilt of eternal punishment is always removed ; but the whole temporal penalty is not always remitted, and must be expiated here, or in another period, or in purgatory. This point sectarians assail, because it involves the necessity of admitting purgatory, indulgences, and works of satisfaction. As proofs of the truth of the Romish doctrine, we are referred to the Council of Trent, and 2 Sam. xii. 18, where David was punished for adultery with the death of the child, after it had been said to him : *the Lord hath taken away,* or hath forgiven, *thy sin;* so also ch. xxiv. 15—for the sin of numbering the people he suffered the plague ; thus Moses, Numb. xxvii. 13, was shut out from the promised land : thus Adam was sent out to suffer many calamities, Gen. iii. 17, 18, 19. Sometimes, however, with the fault, all temporal punishment may be remitted. (No. 36.)

The faithful may be delivered from temporal punishments : " 1. By baptism, by the sacrifice of the mass, and by sacramental penances by their own power ; also by martyrdom ex privilegio. 2. By indulgences, by the intercessions of the saints in heaven, and by the prayers and satisfactions of just men on earth.

" 3. By our own good works, and sufferings, disease, and punishments endured from the love of Christ, in a state of sanctifying grace: which may avail, not only by way of pure suffering or satisfaction, but also by way of merit and imputation. The dead in purgatory are freed from their temporal penalties. 1. By their own personal suffering or endurance of punishments: but this endurance does not avail for them by way of merit, but only of satisfaction. 2. By the sacrifice of the mass, and indulgences, by the intercessions of the saints, and by the good works of just men. Infer from these things that temporal punishments may more numerously, easily and abundantly be taken away in this life than in purgatory: and that he is enriched more than by usury, who takes care to make satisfaction in this life." (No. 37.)

The remains of sin, such as depraved habits and customs, corruption, or indisposition of the appetite, passions, fancy, and spirits or humours, ignorance, dulness, blindness of mind, lethargy in respect to spiritual things, trouble of conscience, dread of the future state, &c., are not removed by penance. (No. 38.)

CONTRITION is defined as " a sorrow of mind, and detestation of a sin committed, with a resolution of not sinning in future." Amongst the rest it is said; " Our heretics contend, that penance does not consist in sorrow for, and detestation of past offences, but in a mere reformation for the future: and they bring forward as objections certain passages of sacred Scripture. Is. i. 16. *Cease to do evil;* Ps. xxxiii. 15. *Turn away from evil and do good."* (No. 43.)

The next twenty sections treat of the various divisions, and subdivisions of contrition, and present questions of little or no general interest.

OF SACRAMENTAL CONFESSION. (No. 63.)

" *What is sacramental confession?* It is the voluntary accusation of one's own sins made to a priest having jurisdiction, in order to obtain remission of them by virtue of the keys."

"*By what authority has confession been introduced?*" By positive, divine command, inasmuch as it was instituted by Christ the Lord. It is proved by tradition, and by the definition of the Council of Trent. It is proved also by the words of Christ, John xx. 23, as was proved above. Some with St. Thomas, understand the text, James v. 16 : *Confess one with another*, of sacramental confession. "The Calvinists object that auricular confession was introduced by human authority in the *4th Lateran Council*, under Innocent III. in the thirteenth century. The fathers of the Council of Trent, sess. xiv. c. 5, reply, that this is an empty calumny of the heretics ; but in that council only the time of the annual confession, was determined and commanded ; which had before been already observed in the church. Just reasoning refutes this objection : because it is not conceivable neither is it possible that all men would without any contradiction have tolerated so heavy a burden as the confession of secret sins, unless holy church had practised it from the beginning by divine command: now no history makes mention of a contradiction ; therefore, &c.

The fact that we find no objection to auricular confession in any early ecclesiastical historian effectually establishes one of two things ; it proves either that the church generally was satisfied that it was a divine institution, or else, *that nobody knew any thing at all about it* ; of the two we suppose the latter to be the more probable.

"*Obj.* Nectarius the bishop of Constantinople abrogated confession in the fourth century ; as Socrates and Sozomenus relate: therefore confession is not of divine institution. *Ans.* Baronius accuses their histories of falsehood. The usual answer is, that in this instance sacramental confession was not abrogated, but public confession before the people, or perhaps only the public confession of secret sins, or the mere mention of an accomplice; from the occasion that a certain noble woman through an indiscreet zeal had publicly confessed a sin with a deacon in the temple, from which public confession, scandal and murmuring of the people had resulted. In the west however, the practice of public confession lasted till beyond the sixth century."

"*What benefits does the confession of sins afford?*" Beside the effects mentioned (No. 29.) it affords the following advantages : 1. Proper counsels and remedies against sins are received from the confessor. 2. Through the shame and humiliation of confession, it serves usefully for some little satisfaction for past offences, and for restraining from future sins. Sacramental confession was prefigured in this that Christ, Matt. viii. 4, sent the lepers to the priests: also that under the old law, sinners were compelled to go to the priests to offer sacrifices for their sins. And what is more, Corn. à Lapide thinks that under the old law there was an obligation to confess all sins to the priests: and he proves this by the variety of the sacrifices for sins. The multifarious expiations and purifications in the old law were figures of the sacrament of penance."

Sacramental confession is enjoined both by a divine and ecclesiastical precept. It is obligatory upon every baptized person who is conscious of having committed mortal sin. (No. 64.)

According to a decree of a Lateran council: "*Every one of the faithful of both sexes, after he (or she) shall have reached the years of discretion, must faithfully confess all his (or her) sins, alone, at least once a year to the proper priest, &c.* Which the council of Trent has confirmed, sess. xiv. c. 5 and 8, and which is commonly recited among the five precepts of the church." (No. 16.)

It is sufficient if this is done in any part of the year; but the custom of the faithful fixes the time at Easter, and the synod of Mechlin has resolved that they cannot be admitted to the sacrament who have not confessed in Lent, and this mode of confessing in Lent the council of Trent approves. (No. 67.)

"*Who are under obligation by the ecclesiastical precept of confession?* All baptized persons who have attained to years of discretion and have sinned. *When may they be presumed to have reached those years of discretion?* When they have attained to such a use of reason that they are able to discern between moral good and evil, &c."

"Boys are presumed to have reached this period of the use of reason, usually about the seventh or eighth year of their age: some sooner, others later: for a discrepancy occurs according to the development of the brain, and education and practice: Greg. Bk. iv. Dial. c. xviii. tells of a

boy five years old condemned for blasphemy : so that sometimes it may be proper to say with St. Augustine : *So little
a boy, and so great a sinner.* Therefore even very young
children may profitably be sent to a confessor, in order that
the priest may judge of their discretion, and the boys themselves may learn and become accustomed to confess. In
truth this is a great part of the pastoral care, that a pastor
on every Lord's day, should allure some of the little children
to the confessional, whom he may hear whilst others who
are adults do not come ; for he who wishes to reform a parish
and bring it to better fruit, must begin with the children.
" *Are children therefore of eight or nine years to be sacramentally absolved every year ?* Yes, and oftener, if they
are found to have committed actions mortally sinful." - The
precept of confession is obligatory at an earlier period than
that of communion. (No. 68.)

If a child concerning whom it is doubtful whether he has
attained to years of discretion, is in danger of death, he should
be absolved on the condition, *If thou hast sinned,* or *if thou
art capable,* and in a similar condition the sacrament of
extreme unction, may also be conferred. But if the sins of
a child are such as to be mortal, and he has attained to years
of discretion, it is necessary to endeavour to produce the
proper disposition, and absolve him on the condition, *If thou
hast sinned,* &c. (No. 69.)

Deaf and dumb persons are also obliged to confess by
signs, &c. (No. 70.)

Whether the precept of annual confession is of obligation
in the case of those who have committed only venial offences,
is a controverted point ; but the affirmative opinion is to be
practically followed. (No. 71.)

" *What is the punishment of those who transgress the
ecclesiastical precept of annual confession ?* These things
are decreed in the chapter, *Every one of both sexes, &c.
Living, let him be sequestered from the threshold of the
church, and dying, let him be deprived of Christian burial :*
that is to say, when these two things concur, that this omission is notorious, and that at the close of life he has given
no signs of sorrow ; which is inferred from the Roman
ritual. The punishment of one who does not commune at
Easter is the same. This punishment is not, properly speak-

38

ing, excommunication, but as it were, a certain part of it, as Steyaert says." (No. 72.)

Frequent confession is advised. (No. 73.)

"Sixteen conditions of a legitimate confession are wont to be mentioned by St. Thomas, and the doctors, which are contained in these four lines——

> "Sit simplex, humilis confessio, pura, fidelis,
> Atque frequens, nuda et discreta, libens, verecunda,
> Integra, secreta, et lacrymabilis, accelerata,
> Fortis, et accusans, et sit parere parata.

Let the confession be simple, humble, pure, faithful,
And frequent, naked and discreet, ready, modest,
Entire, secret, and tearful, rapid,
Bold, and accusing, and let it be PREPARED TO OBEY." (No. 75.)

"*How great a sin does he commit who speaks a falsehood in confession?* If he lies, accusing himself of a mortal sin which he has not committed, or denying a mortal sin which he has committed, and which ought to be expressed in this confession, he commits a mortal sacrilege; because, in a serious matter he perverts sacramental judgment. However, the sincerity of scrupulous and good minds is not to be at once severely blamed: for those persons wishing not to deceive, but to choose more securely, accuse themselves more severely. If any one lies in confession, saying that he has committed a venial sin which he has not committed, and that venial offence is the only matter of absolution, he commits mortal sacrilege: because he renders absolution, or the sacrament invalid. But if in the same confession he confesses other sins which he has committed, with due contrition for them, the sacrament seems to be valid, and this falsehood to be only venial sacrilege: because the deception is not in an important thing, neither in the entire nor in the proximate matter." (No. 76.)

Hypocrisy in confession is a mortal sin. (No. 77.)

The integrity of the confession is distinguished as material and formal. "That confession is called materially entire, in which all and every mortal sin committed after baptism, as well internal as external, not yet directly and legitimately subjected to sacramental absolution, is exposed to one and the same confessor, in order to one and the same sacramental absolution. A confession is called formally entire, when after a diligent examination of the conscience, all mortal sins committed since baptism, and not yet directly and legitimately subjected to the keys, and which must and may be expressed here and now in this confession, are revealed to one and the same confessor; although, perhaps something may be omitted for a legitimate cause; v. g., when any one confesses two sins, and from blameless inadvertency, omits a third." " *Formal* integrity is sufficient, and this is also absolutely necessary; so that a confession not formally entire, is invalid and sacrilegious." (No. 78.)

An accomplice in crime must be revealed in confession, when the integrity of the confession requires it; but if he can confess his own sins without it, the penitent ought not to mention an accomplice. (No. 80.)

The examination of a conscience is defined thus: It is the reconsideration of committed sins, by a diligent discussion of the conscience, by applying the understanding to know, and the memory to recollect. (No. 81.)

" *Why ought the number of sins to be expressed in confession?* 1. In order that all sins may be revealed; 2. And that the condition, custom, affection, danger, &c., of the penitent may be learned." He does not confess properly, who says, *I have sometimes,* or *often committed this sin,* because he does not express a fixed number. If he does not know the precise number, he ought to express the more probable one, by saying, v. g., *I have done it twenty times, more or less.* If the penitent is ignorant, and cannot even tell the probable number, the confessor must help him, by inquiring, how often in a month, or in a week, or in a day, he has committed the sin; and then for how many days, months, or years, he has continued in those sins, &c. In a case of hatred, he ought to declare the number of persons whom he hates; so in a case of detraction, because there are just as many sins as there are persons. (No. 84, and corollary.)

All CIRCUMSTANCES which change the kind of the sin, and which materially aggravate or diminish it, are to be mentioned in confession; because, unless this is done, sins are not entirely declared by penitents; and the confessors, who are judges of the grievousness of crimes, cannot ascertain their degree without it, nor impose the proper penance; besides, a person concealing such a circumstance, may omit a mortal sin in confession; suppose, for instance, that some one who is bound by a vow of chastity, confesses fornication, but is silent on the circumstance of his vow. (No. 86.)

THE CONFESSOR MUST INTERROGATE THE PENITENT, for this his office of physician, judge and counsellor, requires. The Mechlin pastorale cautions priests not to detain any one, particularly young people of both sexes, with inquisitive or useless questions: and not imprudently to interrogate others about things of which they know nothing, lest they might occasion scandal, and their penitent might learn to sin. "If the priest observes that the penitent is silent from shame or fear, it is proper to begin the interrogations from the greater, by proposing to the same, the question, v. g., whether he has committed homicide, or adultery, or a sacrilegious theft, &c., because then the penitent will promptly reply, that it is not so enormous a crime, and he will venture to make known his sin, which is less, that he may avoid the suspicion of the greater. But if the penitent may be supposed to omit the sin from ignorance or simplicity, questions are put from the less, lest perchance, he may learn to sin. Schema 8, affords an example of this. *How shall a confessor conduct himself towards those, who confess nothing unless they are asked?* If this happens through neglect of examination, they are ordinarily to be sent back to a diligent examination of conscience, and they are to be admonished to be sorry, and blame themselves for the neglect. But if it proceeds from bashfulness, timidity, simplicity, or from the rudeness of uncultivated nature, they are to be kindly and patiently received and assisted. Hence, those confessors commit no small deviation from the path of prudent judgment, who, when some simple, and perhaps pious person, says in confession; Sir, I do not know what to confess, confound and ironically insult him, by saying; I will put you on the altar, because you are holy, for you have not sinned," &c. (No. 90.)

OF INTERROGATIONS IN PARTICULAR.

"*Concerning what things may the confessor interrogate a penitent?* 1. How long ago, or since what time he has confessed? 2. What is his condition, (unless it should be known), that is to say, whether he is married, bound by a vow, the master of a household, a merchant, labourer, &c., in order that he may be interrogated about sins usually committed in such a state. 3. Whether he has performed the penance imposed. 4. Whether he has regularly and entirely confessed at other times. 5. Whether he has previously, diligently scrutinized or examined his conscience as he ought. 6. Whether he has learned the rudiments and articles of faith, and other things necessary to be known. 7. If the penitent has not expressed the number, and kinds, and circumstances, of the sins necessary to be explained, let the priest prudently ask him. Moreover, lest the confessor should be embarrassed in investigating the circumstances of any sin, let him have this little line of circumstances in readiness.

" Who, what, where, by what helps, why, how, when.

"But what may be denoted by each of these particles, is compendiously explained at the close of the practical Schemata, at the end of this volume." (No. 91.)

Probably the very best idea of the character of the Romish doctrine and practice of confession, will be afforded by the translation of these practical exemplifications of the orthodox mode of ransacking the conscience of a *penitent.* I shall, therefore, present them without delay. But first observe:

" Sacramental confession ought regularly to be made by *proper word of mouth ;* because this mode is the most perfect, and involves greater humility and bashfulness : add to this, that it has been the perpetual practice of the Church. When, however, the penitent has not the use of his tongue, or some other reason exists, a confession by writing, or by any kind of nods and ·signs, is sufficient," &c. A confession may also, in case of necessity, be made by an interpreter; but a penitent is not obliged to make such a confession. (No. 93.)

38 *

PRACTICAL MODELS.

" A method of interrogating a penitent, who confesses in an ignorant manner, not sufficiently explaining the object, number and circumstances.

The penitent confesses : I have sworn.

CONFESSOR. What words did you say ? PENITENT. By my soul what I assert is true : I did not use any other forms of swearing. CONF. How often ? PEN. Seven times from the time of the last confession, made at the festival of the Lord's nativity. CONF. Did you say it from habit ? or from an unpremeditated impulse ? or deliberately ? PEN. Deliberately enough, but not from habit.

Examination concerning the addition of truth.

CONF. Did you swear contrary to the truth ? PEN. I have once confirmed a falsehood by a positive oath. CONF. Did you know that it was false, when you swore? PEN. Yes, I knew it. CONF. You have committed a grievous sin of perjury; besides if you can and ought to foresee or fear that losses, scandals, or any bad results will follow, declare them, and tell which of them have already resulted : make amends for the injuries inflicted, remove the bad results, and if some will still follow, you ought to prevent them. PEN. Nothing of these, for it was a lie spoken in jest, which I confirmed with an oath. CONF. Have you fulfilled your promissory oaths, with which you swore that you would do something ? PEN. Once I did not fulfil, through negligence. CONF. What had you sworn? PEN. I had sworn to pay a debt of ten florins, within three days, and I delayed it beyond a month. CONF. Did not the other consent to the delay, at least implicitly ? Or did not other claims excuse you, by which the obligation of an oath sometimes ceases ? PEN. No. CONF. You have sinned grievously, and you will pay the debt as soon as possible. PEN. I will do so. CONF. Could it be foreseen that any injuries or other bad results would follow ? PEN. None. CONF. When you swore, had you the intention of fulfilling the oath? PEN. I thought it would be impossible within three days. CONF. Therefore accuse yourself farther of formal perjury from the defect of formal virtue.

Examination concerning the addition of justice.

CONF. Did you swear anything unlawful or not decent ? v. g., that you would inflict injury on any one ? PEN. Yes, once. CONF. What was it ? PEN. I swore that I would break my neighbour's arm.

Conf. Had you the intention of doing it, when you swore ? Pen. Yes. Conf. You have grievously offended against religion and against justice : it is not lawful for you to fulfil what you have sworn : in addition, tell for what length of time you persisted in this bad intention of doing injuries, and what harm must be apprehended as likely to result. Pen. &c.

II.

CONCERNING HABITUAL SWEARERS.

Pen. I have sworn in saying : Par Dieu. Conf. How often ? Pen. Two hundred times, more or less, in the time of two months, during which I have not confessed. Conf. Therefore you labour under the habit of swearing ? Pen. Yes. Conf. Did you use other words or forms ? Pen. No. Conf. Do you swear indiscriminately truth and falsehood, things lawful and unlawful ? Pen. From habit I speak for the most part before I maturely examine them. Conf. Therefore the most of your oaths are mortal sins, on account of the danger of swearing that which is false or unlawful. How often have you sworn contrary to truth ? Pen. Certainly at least ten times, and once I swore knowingly to a falsehood, by a positive oath. Conf. Did you fulfil what you swore you would do ? Pen. Five times I did not fulfil it in a small matter ; but people did not accept my oaths, because they knew that I swear habitually. Conf. How often have you sworn something unlawful, or not decent, in addition against justice ? Pen. About six times, that I might vindicate myself for refusing the common offices of charity to another. Conf. Did any, and what injuries or losses ensue, or were they to be apprehended, especially scandals in regard to children and domestics, who usually hear and imitate ? Pen. None, except perhaps general scandal in the hearers ; for I have no children or domestics. Conf. How long has this habit continued ? Pen. Now, five years. Conf. How often have you confessed in that time ? Pen. Three times every year. Conf. What means have confessors prescribed to you ? Pen. That I should read one Ave Maria as often as I swore. Conf. Did you observe this ? Pen. Whenever I remembered : very often. Conf. St. Francis Sales teaches that absolution must be delayed, because you do not stretch every nerve to eradicate the vicious habit. Therefore return after eight days, and meanwhile use these more efficacious means, &c. Besides, the preceding confessions are to me very doubtful as to their value, and must therefore be repeated, because in the whole time of the voluntary habit, you have persevered in the intention and desire of sinning, and thus you have committed as many sacrileges as you have received sacraments. Therefore you will institute an examination of your conscience concerning them, and a general confession from the time that the habit has commenced. Did you not certainly sometimes do better for a considerable time after confession, by very great anxiety to eradicate the habit? PEN. I did not pay special regard."

More efficacious means against the habit of swearing.

" They are those, which remove precipitation, and produce deliberation. 1. At every oath, let him immediately say openly : I retract what I said, I am sorry for it, and I will say so no more, &c. This is best if it can be obtained, because by thus publicly retracting, the person swearing repairs the scandal, which he occasioned. 2. Let him immediately recite *Pater noster* and *Hail Mary*, kneel down, or do some other work of penance. 3. Let him immediately put aside from one pocket into another, a farthing, that he may give it to the first poor man whom he meets. 4. Let him ask, that others, companions or servants may immediately reprove him. 5. Every week let him return to the same confessor."

III.

OF BLASPHEMIES.

" PEN. I have said : *Mort Dieu* and *Sacré Dieu*. CONF. From custom, and how often ? PEN. Both, three times, not from custom, but from levity. CONF. Did you commit six crimes of blasphemy ? PEN. I have sometimes heard it said that these are enormous oaths. CONF. Did you say these things by way of oath, in order to affirm or deny something, and this in addition against truth and justice ? PEN. No. CONF. Did scandal, or any other evil follow, or was it at least to be feared? PEN. No.

" If the penitent is an habitual blasphemer, let him be treated as in Schema II.; if bad results have followed, &c., as in L"

Appendix.

" PEN. I have said : *Par Dieu* and *Mort Dieu*.

" In this case each must be examined separately : for *par Dieu* denotes a simple oath : *mort Dieu* also contains blasphemy, therefore the confessor will ask : How often did you say, *par Dieu*? How often *mort Dieu*? &c. But if this swearer is such a one who babbles out indiscriminately, *mort Dieu*, or *par Dieu*, whichever first comes into his mouth, without any difference, he will be guilty of blasphemy in each act, even when he pronounces only *par Dieu*, because in every act, he was ready for either one or the other."

IV.

OF A PROXIMATE OCCASION.

" Pen. I have been drunk. Conf. How often?   Pen. I am accustomed to be drunk five or six times in a month. Conf. Were you quite drunk, destitute of the use of reason? Pen. So that I was incapacitated even for common business. Conf. From what occasion do these drunken excesses happen? Pen. From frequenting the tavern. Conf. Frequenting the tavern is to you the proximate occasion of sin. How often did you thus enter the tavern, even if you were not drunk? Pen. About ten times a month: for I am accustomed to enter the tavern sixteen times every month, and out of these I am used to be drunk six times more or less. Conf. In these ten times also, you are guilty before God of the sin of drunkenness, because you exposed yourself to danger. You may elicit fresh contrition for these, and accuse yourself of them in confession. Have bad results followed, or will they follow, or were they at least to be feared, which you could and should have foreseen? Or indeed do any usually follow? Pen. No: for when drunk, I am good and peaceable. Conf. For how long a time have you frequented the proximate occasion? Pen. Now for a year. Conf. Therefore, for a year you have lived in the desire or intention of sinning mortally : therefore you will institute a general confession of this time; you will accuse yourself besides of having sacrilegiously taken the sacraments, &c."

A VOLUNTARY OCCASION.

" Conf. Do you frequent from necessity, or indeed without any just cause? Pen. My profit is from it, for I am the agent of another man's affairs, which must be carried on in the tavern. Conf. Have preceding confessors prescribed to you efficacious means that this occasion might become remote? Pen. Yes : but I know from experience that I cannot be kept from these drunken excesses by any means. Conf. Therefore you will absolutely quit frequenting taverns : and for this reason you will give up that office, and assume another business to gain a livelihood : if you will not I can not absolve you. Besides you will institute a general confession from the time at which you voluntarily retained the proximate occasion, &c. Pen. Ought I therefore to retrench my mode of living? Conf. You must retrench it : because just reasons for retaining a voluntary proximate cause can not be given."

AN OCCASION MORALLY INVOLUNTARY.

"Conf. Do you frequent from necessity, or indeed without any just cause? Pen. From necessity, because I am an agent, and in this way only do I know how to gain the livelihood necessary for my wife and children, so that I cannot give it up except to my serious loss: and I may fall perhaps into greater dangers. Conf. Have you in the mean time confessed, and have means been prescribed to you? Pen. No. Conf. Therefore, employ means by which the occasion may become remote: you must not drink in the tavern, or you must drink only a single pint, and you must mix with it if you conveniently can, bitter herbs, or you must drink water under another pretext. If drink be offered you by others, you must refuse, or else PRETEND THAT YOU ARE DRINKING IT. You must return after eight days. Meanwhile pray earnestly to God, &c."

V.

CONCERNING DETRACTION.

"A method of interrogating a penitent in sins of detraction, who confesses without expression of object or circumstances.

EXAMINATION CONCERNING A FALSE STATEMENT.

"Pen. I have spoken slander. Conf. Is what you have said true or false? Pen. What I said is false. Conf. Is it a very disgraceful defect: or is it materially against the fame or good reputation of this person? Pen. I think so. Conf. What then did you say? Pen. That a certain respectable girl had committed fornication. Conf. How often did you say this? and to how many persons? Pen. To three persons at one time. Conf. Have they divulged it to others? Pen. It is so: for they are talkative and loquacious, and receive slander greedily. Conf. To how many persons? Pen. I do not know; perhaps to ten people. Conf. You will immediately hinder any farther infamy, and personally or through others restore the good name with all those, to whom you or others have divulged it. Pen. How shall I do this? Conf. By recalling it, and asserting that you have spoken that which was false, and that you are prepared to take an oath upon it, and to bring witnesses, &c. Will you do it? Pen. Yes I will. Conf. Could and must any losses or other evils be foreseen and feared, and have in reality any followed or will they still follow? Pen. Yes. Conf. Tell what they are, and also those which have not yet followed and which will not follow, but which you could and must fear will follow: but those which have followed, amend, and take away the evils: just as you will be obliged to make restitution for what will follow, unless you prevent them : meanwhile take care that you prevent. PEN. It is well, &c. CONF. Did the detraction or infamy extend to some others, so that they were injured in their reputation also ? PEN. Yes truly, I mentioned an accomplice with whom she had committed fornication. CONF. Of what condition, quality and reputation was this accomplice ? PEN. He was not situated in high life, but a married man ; an honest citizen of the common sort, having a respectable wife and children. CONF. This is another slander. You must make restitution, &c. The rest must be investigated as above."

EXAMINATION CONCERNING A TRUE STATEMENT.

"CONF. Is what you have said true or false ? PEN. What I said is true. CONF. And was it public by the publicity of the fact or right ? Had you just reasons for revealing it ? PEN. No. CONF. Is the failing very disgraceful with respect to that person ? PEN. It seems so. CONF. What then have you said ? PEN. That a certain girl had committed fornication. CONF. Is she is a respectable girl or of good reputation in this respect ? Or is she considered infamous in this thing, because she has frequently committed it ? Or is she a harlot ? &c. PEN. She is acknowledged as respectable. CONF. To how many persons did you reveal it ? PEN. To three at one time. CONF. Have they told it to others ? Or must you not at least fear this danger ? PEN. No : because I knew them to be prudent, and they reproved me. CONF. Notwithstanding this, you have sinned against justice with regard to the girl, and against charity in regard to the hearers by giving them on your part, scandal or occasion that they might sin in listening to your detraction. Could actual injuries or other evils be foreseen as likely to result ? PEN. No. CONF. You must restore the reputation you have injured. PEN. It has already become public and known everywhere. CONF. If it has become public through injury, you are still obliged to make restitution. Has it perhaps become public in some other way ? PEN. It is public, because a child has notoriously been born. CONF. You are liberated from the duty of restitution, but you have certainly sinned because at the time in which you revealed it, the fact was secret, nor was it known that it would be public."

VI.

OF PERSONS HEARING SLANDER.

PEN. I have heard slander. CONF. Did you reprove the slanderer ? Or did you hinder the detraction in some other way ? Or did not the

others do this? Pen. No. Conf. Had you just reasons for not reprov
ing or not hindering, v. g. because it was public, or because no hope
of good effect appeared : or because you feared other injuries or evils;
or because it was lawfully denounced in order to hinder the evil? &c.
Pen. I had not any reasons to excuse me. Conf. Was it a very disgraceful fault with respect to this person? What was related? And
what evils and injuries were to be feared as likely to follow? Pen. It
was told of a servant known to us, that he once stole a silver box;
but no danger of loss or evil seems to be feared from the statement.
Conf. How did you behave during this detraction? Were you
silent? Did you listen willingly, and were you secretly pleased?
Did you take part by externally asking, conversing, laughing? &c."

Against justice.

"Pen. I asked in an inquisitive manner about the circumstances
and evidences of the truth of the fact, which the detractor also added.
Conf. How many persons were present hearing it? Pen. We were
four who heard it. Conf. Did you communicate it to no one farther?
And did not the others who heard it do so? Pen. No. Conf. 1. You
have sinned against charity with respect to the slanderer, and the
hearers on account of the scandal. 2. You have sinned against justice as co-operating, with respect to the person who was slandered,
and, therefore, you are bound to make restitution of the character,
losses, &c., if the slanderer or the principals fail, or do not make restitution."

Against charity.

"Con. Did you join in externally by asking, conversing, laughing? &c. Pen. By no means, but I was silent and kept myself negatively. Conf. Were you obliged ex officio or from justice to hinder
those sins or the infamy? Pen. No. Conf. You have certainly sinned against charity; 1. in respect of the slanderer, and the hearers,
because you did not hinder the sins; 2. with regard to him, who was
slandered, because you did not prevent the injury to the reputation,
and the loss of your neighbour; all of which you could and should
prevent from charity."

VII.

EXAMINATION CONCERNING THEFT OR INJUSTICE.

Pen. I have committed theft. Conf. What have you stolen?
Pen. Seven florins. Conf. Did you take them from necessity, or from

some other cause? Pen. No: but I unjustly took them from a gentleman whose servant I am. Conf. Did you steal them at one time, or many by small thefts? Pen. At several times in the space of four weeks. Conf. In how many times? Pen. I do not know. Conf. How much did you take at every time? Or how often in the week? Pen. A shilling, at every time. Conf. Was there the desire or inclination of stealing more at each time, if occasion had offered? Pen. No: but I wished to take a shilling only at each time. Conf. Had you the intention, indeed, from the beginning of attaining to a considerable sum through small thefts? Pen. Yes. Conf. To how great a sum? Pen. To the sum of six or seven florins, in order that I might be able to buy a new cap and hose. Conf. Therefore, from the first time you have sinned mortally. During this time, were the internal acts of desire to steal often repeated or renewed, when the deed did not follow? Pen. Yes, perhaps, fifty times: but I forbore, lest I should be detected. Conf. Have other losses or injuries followed? Or must you fear and foresee that they will perhaps follow? Or are other bad circumstances known to you? Pen. Nothing of these. Conf. Have you made restitution? Pen. I have not; nor have I anything which I can restore, except the cap which I have bought. Conf. You have sinned also in this, that you have made yourself unable; see, however, if you cannot get back the price by returning the cap; otherwise you must every day lay aside something from your daily wages, and you must not enter a tavern unless you have first made restitution. Pen. I will do so. Conf. For how long a time have you remained in this state without interruption, or without intention of making restitution? Pen. For six weeks, namely, until yesterday. Conf. Meanwhile, you have not confessed? Pen. No. Conf. For so long a time, you have persisted in the desire of the mortal sin, which has been continually done, &c."

VIII.

METHOD OF PRUDENTLY EXAMINING CONCERNING IMMODEST THOUGHTS.

" Pen. I have had immodest thoughts. Conf. Did you afford cause or occasion for them by look, words? &c. Pen. No. Conf. Did you endeavour to repel them? Pen. No. Conf. How long did you voluntarily persist in them? Pen. Through five Pater et Ave. Conf. How often did this happen? Pen. Once. Conf. Did you take pleasure in them? Pen. I did so. Conf. Did you give your

39

consent to any bad action, or was there any desire or intention of doing a bad action if the opportunity had been offered? PEN. No: but it was merely a lingering delight, to which I gave my consent. CONF. About what object, and about what thing was this delight? PEN. Circa copulam cum filia honesta libera, mihi nulla cognatione vel affinitate juncta!

CONF. What are you, single, married, or bound by a vow? PEN. I am a single young man. CONF. An inde secutæ sunt aliquæ commotiones carnales in corpore? PEN. Yes. CONF. Did you endeavour to resist these impulses and to repel them? PEN. No: but I simply permitted them. CONF. An secuta est pollutio? PEN. Yes. CONF. Did you afterwards persist in the thoughts and pleasures? PEN. No: but I immediately trembled with horror, restrained my emotions, abandoned these thoughts, betook myself to God, and invoked the names of Jesus and Mary."

AN ADDITION TO SCHEMA VIII.

" It sometimes happens that young men or girls, attired in a somewhat vain manner, and addicted to pleasure and voluptuousness, confess nothing of the temptations of licentiousness, by which however, persons of this kind are went to be assailed. These the confessor will interrogate prudently and by a roundabout method (as St. Thomas advises) beginning with general things thus :

CONF. Do not indecent thoughts sometimes occur to you? If the penitent answers affirmatively, the confessor may proceed according to the schema ; if negatively, perhaps from ignorance of the wickedness, he must proceed to external things more known to the penitent in this mode : Do you sometimes visit persons of the other sex or parties? PEN. Yes. CONF. Are immodest words or remarks sometimes exchanged at such places? PEN. It is so : concerning" * * * [kind reader, excuse me I would give you the Latin, that you might carry it to some holy confessor and ask him to put it into good Saxon for you, but it is too bad to offer even in the original.]

" CONF. What part did you take? PEN. I laughed with others, and sometimes added a word. CON. How often did this happen? This is asked that the number of sins, which is in the actions, may be known. Before what persons? This is asked because it destroys so many souls, by affording them so many scandals, or at least by positively co-operating with them in laughing and speaking. CONF. Before what kind of persons? This is demanded that the circumstances of the scandals may be exposed : which if they have taken place with a person bound by a vow will be sacrilege; if with a married one, injustice : because he himself becomes guilty of those sins to which they might be induced on account of the scandals.

CONF. Did any desires, carnalities, or improper liberties, kisses, &c. follow? These things are asked, because they are frequently connected with the preceding sins. Children are usually asked in this matter: whether they have played indecent games with themselves, or with others? &c.

IX.

EXAMINATION CONCERNING DISTRACTIONS IN PRAYER.

"PEN. I confessed a month ago. CONF. Very well: what has happened meanwhile? PEN. I have often been distracted in prayer. CONF. Were these distractions directly voluntary, or indirectly, by affording an occasion or cause? PEN. I gave occasion by staring about. CONF. In the prayer of obligation? PEN. Once in the mass of obligation on the Lord's day. CONF. How long did this distraction last? PEN. Through half the time of the mass. CONF. Did you not certainly endeavour to attend to the principal parts of the mass, viz. to the offertory, consecration, and reception? Or did you not endeavour to break off the distraction, and how often? PEN. Two or three times in a lukewarm manner, but not efficaciously enough. CONF. Did you hear another mass on that day? PEN. No: because it was the last mass. CONF. Are you therefore in the habit of being negligent in prayer and in divine service, and in attending preaching? PEN. No: but this happened only once; otherwise, I always frequent preaching in my parish, and I endeavour to fulfil the obligations of my station. CONF. Does nothing else oppress your conscience? PEN. Nothing. CONF. You ought to avoid those places and causes of distractions in the temple. PEN. I will do so. CONF. Therefore you are sorry that you have offended God whom you love above all things, and you are resolved not to sin in future? PEN. I am sorry. CONF. You must elicit an act of contrition. Afterwards at the time when the penitent renews the contrition, the confessor says : may Almighty God have mercy, &c. Do you accuse yourself of all those things inasmuch as you are guilty before God? PEN. Yes. CONF. For sacramental penance at a proper time, you will hear mass, and give to the poor one farthing. These things being done, he absolves the penitent sacramentally."

X.

THE EXAMINATION OF LABOURERS.

PEN. Confessors are in the habit of putting questions to me. CONF. My friend, have you not examined your conscience? PEN. Yes: but I recollect better, when I am questioned. CONF. Have you regularly and honestly confessed at other times? Have you omitted something about which you were perhaps not asked? PEN. I never knowingly have omitted any thing. CONF. How long is it since you have confessed? PEN. Three months. CONF. Of what state, condition, or trade are you? PEN. I am a stone cutter and unmarried. CONF. When you work for daily wages, do you perform the proper labour? Do you not sometimes spend time idly? PEN. Sometimes, in talking. CONF. How often, and how long a time have you thus spent? PEN. Nearly every day, four or five times, so that daily, this time put together may amount to an hour, one day more, another less. CONF. How much wages do you earn every day? PEN. One florin. CONF. Therefore, every day you have committed injustice to the amount of about two stivers? PEN. So it is. CONF. Have you laboured thus daily for others for day wages? PEN. Yes, on every week day now for three years. CONF. Have you been the cause that other labourers have also neglected their time like yourself? PEN. Yes; and this with respect to two: for I am in the habit of relating some new or ridiculous things, the others whilst listening desist from work. CONF. Do you know that you have sinned in the way of scandal by giving them occasion of sinning? Besides that you have sinned against justice, and that you are bound to make restitution or compensation by other works according to the proportion of the time neglected? Moreover you ought to admonish your other associates: if, however, they neglect to make restitution, you are bound to do it. PEN. It is true; I have sometimes been reproved by the master for it. CONF. Did this same thing happen before the last confession? PEN. Yes. CONF. Did you confess it? PEN. No, because the confessors did not ask me about it. CONF. For how long a time have you remained in this state? PEN. Now for three years. CONF. Friend, through all this time, you have been in continual sin, and your confessions have been invalid; for which reason you ought to institute a general confession of this time. How often in this time have you made confession, and communed? PEN. Three times in the year. CONF. So often you have received the sacraments unworthily; therefore, examine your conscience more rigidly concerning other sins with which you are probably burdened, and accuse yourself of them all, as well as of the omission of acts of the supernatural precepts of charity, contrition, and of annual confession and communion. You will return eight days hence, meanwhile amend your ways, and pray to God daily. You will also admonish the others about making restitution."

XL

EXAMINATION OF A GENTEEL MAN.

"Conf. Are you in the habit of attending preaching, and of sometimes reading spiritual books? Pen. No. Conf. Do you remember the mystery, which we call to mind at this time of Easter? Pen. I do not remember. Conf. What mystery is fulfilled in Christ on the first day of Easter, after his passion? Pen. That I do not know. Conf. What do you believe concerning Christ: how was he born, how did he die, and where is he now? Pen. He was born of Mary, and was crucified. Conf. How many natures has Christ? Pen. I do not know. Conf. Is Christ God and man at the same time? Pen. Yes, so it is. Conf. How many divine Persons are there? Pen. Only one, because there is only one God. Conf. Do you not therefore believe the mystery of the Most Holy Trinity? In what does it consist? Pen. Children know these things; I have forgotten them. Conf. My dear sir, children learn these things because they are indispensable to salvation, through the necessity of means; and unless you explicitly believe these things, you cannot be saved, although you might be invincibly ignorant of them; but you, an intelligent man, are culpably ignorant of these things! From what time have you begun to live thus negligently? Pen. From my twentieth year; for ten years until the present time. Conf. It is necessary that you institute a general confession from the twentieth year of your age: for during this whole time you have been in a state of mortal sin, and the confessions you have instituted are invalid; neither have you fulfilled the precepts of annual confession and communion; but before you can be absolved, it first behooves you to learn the rudiments of the faith, which must be believed through the necessity of means. For which purpose, you must buy a Mechlin catechism, and in it you will daily read four lessons, and you will return after eight days."

Examination of one of the common people.

"Conf. Are you in the habit of attending preaching, and of sometimes reading spiritual books? Pen. No. Conf. Why not? Pen. Because I am a servant; time is not given me for attending preach-

39 *

ing, and I do not know how to read.   CONF. How many Gods are there?   PEN. There is one God.   CONF. How many divine Persons are there?   PEN. Three, viz., God the Father, God the Son, God the Holy Ghost.   CONF. Which person of them became incarnate, and suffered for us the death of the cross?   PEN. The Second Person, who is called Jesus Christ.   CONF. What reward will the good receive after this life, and what the bad?   PEN. God will give the eternal life of the kingdom of heaven to the good; but the wicked will be sent into hell.   CONF. Why do you believe all these things?   PEN. That I may be saved.   CONF. I do not ask the final, but the formal reason of your faith; namely, why do you believe these things to be true?   PEN. Because our pastor has taught me so.   CONF. Whence does your pastor know that these things are true?   PEN. From his books, for he has a great many.   CONF. But whence have those books, or the writers, learned these mysteries?   Have they fabricated them?   PEN. They have had them from ancient time, from the Church.   CONF. Who manifested and revealed them to the Church?   PEN. God.   CONF. Why do you believe God, who reveals?   PEN. Because he is the highest and eternal truth.   CONF. How many and what are the sacraments in the Catholic Church?   PEN. They are baptism, the Eucharist, and confession; the rest I do not know.   CONF. Do you know, and do you sometimes recite Pater noster, Ave Maria, Credo, &c.?   PEN. I recite daily, just as I have learned.   CONF. Leave that family, unless they concede to you time for learning those things which it becomes a Christian man to know.   Besides, do you resolve to learn the other things which ought to be known as soon as possible, and will you bestow greater care on the salvation of your soul, Eh?   PEN. I will do so.   CONF. Proceed in the confession of your sins, that you may be absolved."

NOTES UPON SCHEMA XI.

" Therefore those who are ignorant of the mysteries, which ought to be believed by necessity of means, cannot be absolved so long as they labour under this ignorance : whether this is vincible, or invincible; and all confessions made in such ignorance, are invalid, and ought to be repeated, because without faith it is impossible to please God. Heb. xi.

" Blameless ignorance of other articles of the faith does not render them invalid; but if it has been mortally bad, they have been invalid and sacrilegious at the same time, on account of the defect of contrition, which cannot consist together with negligence that is mortally bad, or with actual mortal sin. But lest an occasion for pretended indignation should be afforded to some, especially the more genteel, if the examination should be begun from common things, the following course may be taken with them.

"Conf. Through whose merits do you hope for the remission of sins? If the penitent replies aptly, v. g., if he says: through the merits of Jesus Christ, the Son of God, offered on the altar of the cross, that he might satisfy for us sinners; you know the lion by his claw, and that he is sufficiently instructed; but if he cannot reply, you will descend to less things, as above. However an examination would be made foolishly in this manner: Do you believe that there is one God? Threefold in Persons? Do you believe that the Second Person became incarnate for us? &c.; because the very thing which must be answered is manifest, and thus the question is rendered useless."

COROLLARY.

Of interrogatories.

From the Roman ritual, and the Mechlin pastorale, the following ought ordinarily to be made. 1. How long it is since the penitent has confessed. 2. Of what condition he is, in order that he may be interrogated concerning the sins which are usually committed in that condition. 3. Whether he has fulfilled the imposed penance. 4. Whether he has regularly and honestly confessed at other times. 5. Whether he has first diligently examined his conscience as he ought. 6. Whether he has learned the rudiments of the faith, and other things necessary to be known. 7. If the penitent has not mentioned the number, and kinds, and circumstances of the sins necessary to be explained, let the priest prudently interrogate him."

Of denying absolution.

"In the same place also they are mentioned to whom absolution is to be denied on account of the defect of the proper disposition, namely · 1. Who give no signs of sorrow, or not sufficient. 2. Who will not lay aside their animosities and enmities. 3. Who will not restore another's property, if they are able. 4. Who will not leave the proximate occasion of sinning. 5. Who will not relinquish sins in any other way, and amend their life for the better. 6. Who have given public scandal, unless they publicly make satisfaction, and remove the scandal. To these the Lovanians add such as are ignorant of the articles of the faith; but this cause the rituals mention afterwards. Yet it is to be observed that in a sin, the following things may concur, and ought to be exposed : 1. Of what kind the external, and of what kind the internal act is ; and of what kind that was which was voluntary. 2. The kind of sin with the expression of the particular object or individual. 3. The number of acts and objects : the habit and proximate occasion of sinning. Then the circumstances : 1. *Who*, the quality or condition of the person acting. 2. *What*, the quality of the object, the quantity of the action, and the accidental effects of loss, scandal, danger, &c. 3. *Where*, the quality of the place, namely, sacred or public. 4. *With what aids*, the instruments, means, companions. 5. *Why*, the aim and intention of the acting person. 6. *How*, ignorance, passion, earnestness, contempt, command, counsel, consent, &c. 7. *When*, the quality and quantity of the time, or, the extraordinary duration of the sin : also the duration of the desire towards the sin, before and after it."

THE MINISTER OF THE SACRAMENT OF PENANCE, is the priest only, who has jurisdiction over the penitent; the choice of a confessor is a highly important matter; it is not lawful to confess to a deacon or layman. The power of giving absolution, belongs to the priest by virtue of his ordination, through these words: *Receive the Holy Ghost, whose sins ye shall forgive*, &c. There is no reservation in the article of death, and thus all priests may absolve any penitents whatsoever, from any sins and censures; and in such a case, every priest is bound to absolve from an obligation of charity. Even an excommunicated priest has this authority, according to the common opinion of the Church.

The article of death is understood, as signifying not only the time of the death agony, but " such a danger of death, that unless he confesses to this priest not approved, some danger may threaten, that perhaps he may never have an opportunity of confessing, or at least of confessing entirely to one who is approved; v. g., if it may be apprehended that the sick man will perhaps lose his sense or speech, before an approved priest who has been sent for, can arrive." The qualities requisite in the confessor, are these three : *goodness, knowledge*, and *prudence*. He ought to have such a knowledge of theology, as to be acquainted with the common principles, and he should be able to resolve common cases ; but if he does not possess proper knowledge, his absolution is still valid ; unless it should become invalid, through the wrong disposition of the penitent, who knowing the confessor's want of skill, chooses him in order to escape the proper judgment for his sins.   In order to be able to apply special remedies, the confessor must always ascertain the *root* of the disease.   (Nos. 99—113.)

OF THE SEAL OF CONFESSION.   (No. 159.)

The seal of sacramental confession, is the obligation of concealing those things which are learned from sacramental confession.   This contains the mystic signification that God forgives sins and blots them out, as if he did not remember them.   The sacramental seal is obligatory from *positive divine commmand;* from *natural right,* which enjoins, that secrets be preserved ; and from ecclesiastical law, which is to this effect : " But let the priest beware, that he do not by any means, betray the sinner, by word or sign, or by any other mode ; but if he is in want of prudent counsel, let him cautiously inquire, without any mention of the person ; since we decree, that he who shall presume to reveal a sin detected by him in penitential judgment, shall not only be deposed from the priestly office, but shall also be thrust into a closed monastery, to perform perpetual penance."

THE VIOLATION OF THE SACRAMENTAL SEAL is a sin of sacrilege against the virtue of religion : also a sin of unfaithfulness against a neighbour : because a secret committed to another, is obligatory from fidelity.   This treachery is a mortal sin, no matter how small the affair itself may be.   No circumstances can justify the disclosure of any thing learned at the confessional ; " ALTHOUGH THE LIFE OR SALVATION OF A MAN, OR THE RUIN OF THE STATE SHOULD DEPEND UPON IT ; NOR CAN THE POPE GIVE ANY DISPENSA- TION IN THIS CASE ; SO THAT THIS SECRET OF THE SEAL, IS THEREFORE MORE BINDING, THAN THE OBLIGATION OF AN · OATH, VOW, NATURAL SECRET, &c. ; and this from the positive will of God.

" *What, therefore, must a confessor reply, who is asked concerning the truth, which he has learned through sacramental confession alone ?*

" HE MUST REPLY THAT HE DOES NOT KNOW

IT, AND IF IT IS NECESSARY, HE MUST CON-
FIRM THE SAME WITH AN OATH.

"OBJ. *In no case is it lawful to lie : but this confessor
would lie, because he knows the truth ;* therefore, &c.

"ANS. I deny the minor ; because such a confessor is
interrogated as a man, and answers as a man : BUT NOW
HE DOES NOT KNOW THIS TRUTH AS A MAN,
ALTHOUGH HE MAY KNOW IT AS GOD, says St.
Thom., &c. : and this sense is naturally in the answer : for
when he is questioned or replies out of confession, he is considered as a man.

"*What if it be directly asked from the confessor, whether he knows this through sacramental confession ?*

"ANS. In this case he need answer nothing ; so Steyaert
with Sylvius ; but the question is to be rejected as impious :
or also, he might say absolutely, not relatively to the ques-
ton : *I know nothing :* because the word *I*, restricts to human
knowledge.

"LIKEWISE, IF A CONFESSOR BE CITED IN A
JUDICIAL CASE, THAT HE MAY GIVE HIS REA-
SON FOR REFUSING ABSOLUTION ; HE MUST
PROTEST THAT IN THIS CASE, HE ACKNOW-
LEDGES NO SUPERIOR, EXCEPT GOD. *What will
the confessor reply, who is asked whether he has absolved
such a one ?* He will reply that he has fulfilled his duty.
He might sometimes testify that he has absolved him, if from
it suspicion would not follow, that any other person, to whom
the relation is made, had been dismissed without absolution.

"Observe that the seal of confession does not hinder the
use of human knowledge received from another source : thus
the confessor, if he has seen or heard, that certain faults
have been committed by those whose confessions he has
received, might speak of those faults, in so far as he has
heard or seen them, adding nothing of the knowledge
obtained in confession ; and for this reason, he will prudently add the cause of this human knowledge, by saying,
I have heard, I have seen, &c. : if any things are related,
which he knows from the mere knowledge of confession to
be false, he ought not on this account to argue that they are
false." (No. 160.)

This duty of secrecy, obtains, in respect to every sacramental confession; and it is sufficient, that it is sacramental in the intention of the party confessing. (No. 161.)

A confessor who relates what he has heard in confession, but in such a way, that the person confessing, cannot be ascertained, and that no prejudice can result from it to the penitent, does not violate the seal. But confessors are admonished to abstain from such narrations, except for the sake of asking counsel. "A priest does not violate sacramental secresy, by saying, This man has confessed to me : nor by declaring, I have absolved this man; unless suspicion might, in that case, arise from it, that some one else had not been absolved. To say, I have not absolved this man, is more odious, because it usually denotes his want of disposition. *What kind of a certificate will a confessor write, concerning the confession of him whom he does not absolve?* One of this kind :

"I, the undersigned, declare that John N——— has sacramentally confessed to me, this ——————— day of ——————— month, ——————— 1794. N. N., confessor in the Metrop. Church, S. Rum. Mechl."

"It is proper, however, always to write this certificate under the same form, even when absolution has been denied or delayed; because it is true, that he has sacramentally confessed. It is also safer not to mention that absolution has been given, in order that when it is not added, no suspicion may arise that absolution has been denied." (No. 163.)

All those to whom the knowledge of any thing said in confession comes, whether mediately or immediately, lawfully or unlawfully, are bound by the sacramental seal to keep it secret. (No. 165.)

If permission to reveal the secret is obtained from the penitent, v. g., if the penitent says; "those things which I have confessed, I tell you out of the confession;" then the priest knowing it as a man, may mention it, only let there be no scandal. Without the permission of the penitent, it is not lawful for a priest to speak out of the confession, to the individual, about the sins which he has confessed. He may speak of them to the penitent after he has given absolution, and so long as they are in the confessional. (No. 166.)

Neither is it lawful to make any use of the knowledge acquired from confession, when there is danger that something would be directly or indirectly revealed, concerning the confession. "Thus Clement XVIII. prohibited the use of the knowledge of confession for external government, May 26, A. D. 1594, in these words: As well superiors, as confessors, who have subsequently been promoted to the rank of superior, must most carefully beware, lest they make use of that knowledge of the sins of others, which they have obtained in confession, for external government." Hence an abbot may not depose the prior of a monastery, whom he knows to be unworthy from confession alone. "The knowledge obtained from confession, may be used when the sinner is no way exposed, when no injury results either to himself or another; and in short, when nothing intervenes which renders the confession odious. Thus it is lawful for a confessor to pray for the penitent, it is proper for him to consult books and more learned men, also to observe certain things, which, under another head, he is bound to observe: v. g., a confessor understanding from confessions, that he speaks in too loud a voice, that he is negligent in his duty, in visiting the sick, &c., might amend those defects. In those things which the penitent considers favourable to himself, the use of the knowledge of confession, is not thought so much to violate the seal, as on account of that part by which the confession might be rendered odious. Likewise, if through confession, he knows that heresies are scattered in his parish, that certain vices and sins are skulking about, he may by general instructions and admonitions, fortify the faithful against such sins: so as it does not betray the person." (No. 170.)

A priest if asked to administer sacraments to a sick man, whom he knows to be unworthy, from mere knowledge obtained in confession, must administer the last sacraments of the holy Viaticum, and extreme unction.

"*What must be done by a confessor, who hears the confession of a girl, who is pregnant, and near to death, which thing is unknown to all?* He ought to induce her to declare her pregnancy to some one out of the confession; in order that, if she should perhaps die, the foetus may be baptized; if she refuses, she is not to be absolved; however, the confessor, without leave of the penitent, may not reveal this to any one, although the foetus should perish without baptism.

" *What shall the confessor do, who from confession alone has understood that poisoned wine will be offered him to drink, in the celebration of the mass?* Such a confession will often be not sacramental, because it is not made with the intention of the sacrament, but with a spirit of unjust menacing : and the confessor might immediately reply to such a person confessing, that he does not receive this declaration as a sacramental confession. But if it be supposed sacramental, (which it might more readily be, if the evil was threatened by another than the person confessing,) and the person confessing will in no way consent to the use of the knowledge of the confession : Neesen and Pauwels resolve that the confessor may not omit the celebration of the mass, if other causes of omitting do not occur : for this makes very much for the reverence of the sacrament, and at the same time for the increase among all of the security of the seal : so that in this case it would be necessary to trust to Divine Providence. And this must be indubitably maintained, if from the omission of mass the person of the one committing the crime, or the person of the penitent would be revealed, or any difficulty happen to them.

" Sylvius, Conink, and others teach, that the confessor may lawfully omit the mass, having feigned some other cause. And this resolution seems plausible enough in a case in which no one, not even the penitent, can observe that the confessor omits mass from the knowledge of the confession : because no revelation of the confession is made, nor is any difficulty created for any one, nor any odium on the sacrament : indeed some suppose, that the confessor in this case would be bound to abstain from the celebration of the mass, in order to hinder evil results."

So much for the priests' belief in their own doctrine of transubstantiation ! No better evidence could be desired to prove that they know full well that the bread and wine are not changed into the body and blood, soul and divinity of Jesus Christ. Few Papists have any ambition to suffer martyrdom for the sake of transubstantiation ! Let the priest find out that there is any foul play about the wafer, or the wine, and he is not quite such a fool as to put the virtue of

40

his potent charm, " hoc est corpus meum," to a practical
test.   No, no : he would smile as sweetly as innocence itself,
put the poison into the *sacred sink*, with the proper intention too, and mutter, very complacently, " distinguo, distinguo."

" According to the aforesaid doctrine the following cases
may be resolved : whether a confessor may desist from a
journey in which he has learned from confession alone that
he is to be killed ; whether a confessor may dismiss a servant, whom he knows to be a thief, from her confession
alone." (No. 171.)

OF SATISFACTION FOR SINS IN GENERAL. (No. 172.)

" *What is satisfaction ?*   It is the voluntary endurance
of punishment, in order to make amends for an injury offered
to God. It is called *voluntary*, through the acceptance of the
will.

" *Obj.* By the affliction of diseases we can satisfy, but
they are not voluntary ; therefore, &c.

" *Ans.* I deny the inference : because to endure patiently
and penitentially, is voluntary : but we then satisfy by their
voluntary endurance, not only on account of the internal act,
but also through the external or real suffering accepted by
us."   To the heretical objection that Christ has fully satisfied for our sins, and that therefore our works of satisfaction
are useless, the reply is made, that his satisfaction must be
applied by us in such a way as to profit us : and to this purpose our satisfactions tend, and are therefore not superfluous.
The advantage and practice of satisfactory works is proved
by the examples of the Ninevites, of David, and of all the
saints of the New Testament.   The doctrine that one man
may satisfy for another, is founded on the communion of
saints ; but it is not possible that one should fulfil sacramental
satisfaction for another.   " Hence this 15th proposition was
condemned by Alex. VII.   A penitent may, by his own authority, substitute for himself another, who may fulfil his
penance in his stead."   The penitent may profitably be admonished to seek to have works of satisfaction performed for
him by others, but these works done by others are not a part
of the sacrament; but the act of the penitent, who makes pro-

vision for the performance of these works for himself, is a part of the sacrament. Satisfaction is distinguished as *sacramental*, and *not sacramental; perfect* and *imperfect; public* and *private;* satisfaction IN *punishment,* and satisfaction FOR *punishment,* which is called *satisfaction,* or *sufficient suffering,* as takes place in purgatory. (No. 172.)

Sacramental satisfaction is the voluntary endurance of punishment enjoined by the confessor for the compensation of voluntary injury done to God. This satisfaction is commonly called PENANCE. The confessor is under solemn obligation to impose sacramental satisfaction whenever he absolves. Even upon sick persons, and those who are at the point of death, some penance must be imposed, which they must endure or perform immediately, before death, lest overcome by the disease, they should forget it. (No. 173.)

The penitent is under solemn obligation to accept any reasonable penance imposed on him by the confessor; if he deems it unreasonable, he may decline it, and absolution also, and go to some other confessor. It is a sin of sacrilege to omit the performance of a penance : the opinion that it is only a venial offence to neglect the penance when the matter is in itself a trifle, is expressly repudiated, unless a small and unimportant part of the penance is omitted, in which case it may sometimes be a venial offence. Satisfaction is imposed as chastisement for past sins; as medicine for present offences, and as a preservative against future transgressions. (No. 175.)

Sacramental satisfactions ought according to the council of Trent to be *salutary and convenient according to the quality of the crimes and the ability of the penitents.* All works of satisfaction may be reduced to these three kinds, *prayer, fasting and alms-giving.*

"Lest a confessor who is a novice should perhaps hesitate, what he may enjoin as satisfaction, we here subjoin the individual works of satisfaction now practised in the church, according to that which P. Tombeur et P. Bossuyt observe. Thus under the class of *prayers* the following may be enjoined once, or several times, or for several days, or weeks :

1. "To say five *Pater Noster,* and *Ave Maria,* in memory of Christ's five wounds, either on his bended knees, or with extended arms, or before a crucifix.

2. " To recite the rosary, or litanies of the blessed Virgin Mary, or of the Saints, &c.

3. " To read the psalm *Miserere* (51st. ?) or seven penitential psalms.

4. " To hear masses, or lauds, or *preaching*.*

5. " To read a chapter in Thomas à Kempis.

6. " To visit the churches to pray before the tabernacle.

7. " At stated times, early, at evening, or through the day, or as often as they hear the sound of the bell, to repeat orally or in the heart, ejaculatory prayers, acts of contrition, or of charity : v. g. I love thee, O God, above all things ; I detest all my sins : I will sin no more : Jesus, crucified for me, have mercy upon me.

8. " On the appointed day to confess again, or at least to return to the confessor."

To the class of *fasting* is referred every thing which pertains to the mortification of the body : thus either a perfect fast, or a part of a fast, may be enjoined ; v. g.

1. " Let him fast on the sixth day of the week, or oftener.

2. " Let him fast only till twelve o'clock.

3. " Let him not drink before noon, or after noon, except at dinner, or supper, although he may be thirsty : let him abstain from wine and strong beer.

4. " Let him eat less, at evening let him take only half a meal.

" The above mentioned abstinences are properly imposed on workmen, because they may be connected with labour, because otherwise they are wont to excuse themselves on account of their work. St. Jerome confirms the same, when he says : *scanty food, and a stomach ever hungry, is better than a three days' fast.*

5. " Let him rise out of bed earlier : let him kneel more frequently and for a longer time : let him endure cold : at a certain time let him observe silence : let him abstain from games and from recreations, &c.

" To the class of *alms* is reduced whatever is expended for the advantage of a neighbour : v. g.

1. " To make presents of money, clothes, food, &c.

---

* Let no one suppose that this is a small penance. I once, and but once, heard a priest preach, and from such endurance of rhodomontade and fustian may I ever be delivered !

2. "To afford personal helps, to wait upon the sick, to pray for the conversion of sinners, &c., and works of any other mercy, whether corporeal or spiritual." (No. 176.)

OF THE AMOUNT OF SATISFACTION TO BE IMPOSED.
(No. 179.)

The confessor must impose so much penance as is proportionate to the sins and to the persons : in order that by it the purposes and effects above prescribed may be attained ; council of Trent, sess. xiv. c. 8. *Lest by enjoining certain very light works for very serious offences, they may become partakers of the sins of others.* In a doubtful case it is more safe to impose a less penance than is due, than to impose a greater : because such defect will be supplied in purgatory. (Comfortable, very !)

" *What penance is it therefore proper to impose for mortal sin, v. g. for voluntary drunkenness without scandal ?* ANS. That he read on two days with bended knees the psalm *Miserere : (Have mercy upon me, &c :)* that he fast twice in this week : and that he distribute to the poor, twice as much as he consumed in drink.

" *What if he is a poor man, and a labourer in heavy work ?* ANS. For three days in succession let him repeat five *Pater et Ave,* (our Father and Hail Mary,) on his bended knees : for two days let him not drink before noon, and at evening let him eat only half a meal ; on the two following Lord's days let him not enter a tavern : but in the afternoon let him walk to preaching and lauds. Generally with Steyaert sect. v. &c., it is proper to appoint, that for some mortal sins, neither very grievous, nor many, a penance may be imposed continuing through several days, through one or two weeks, or until the next confession. It is generally expedient that a previous penance should be finished with the following confession, lest the penances of the penitent should accumulate, and lest, overwhelmed by their multitude, he should forget them, or, becoming weary, negligently omit them. For many and serious sins especially when a general confession of a vicious life is instituted, a penance may be imposed continuing through months, half a year, or a whole year, or longer ; and in this case it is proper that the penance be discontinued, so that if it be hin-

40 *

dered by one work it may be supplied by another: v. g. if on some day, he should be hindered from hearing daily mass, let him supply it by alms or some other work," &c.

It is therefore not expedient to impose a penance of seven years for adultery, according to the ancient penitential canons.   S. Carol. Borr. admonishes confessors that they enjoin heavy and difficult penances upon blasphemers. (No. 179.)

The following causes will justify the occasional application of smaller penances.   *Inability*, arising from sickness, weakness, labour, &c.   *Indulgences* earned by the penitent; *spiritual infirmity*; and the *pusillanimity* of the penitent, lest he be too much dejected.   It is not lawful to impose a greater penance than is justly due, if the relation be made with respect to all the three purposes of penance; (viz. as chastisement, medicine, and as a preservative;) but it is lawful if done with reference to only one object.   Thus, v. g. rigid restitution is imposed upon boys at first for slight theft, and a severe and longer penance as a preservative and restraint against relapse; although the purpose of expiating the temporal punishment would not require so great a one for a venial sin.   From this it appears, how sometimes a severe penance may be imposed for venial sin, and a greater than for mortal sin.   (No. 180.)

The most convenient time of enjoining penance is before absolution.   (No. 181.)

The obligation of sacramental satisfaction ceases, when the sacrament is not valid; when the penance enjoined is impossible; when the penitent entirely forgets it; in the latter case Suarez, Neesen and others, liberate him entirely on account of inability; but others maintain that he is bound to perform some other penance.   (No. 183.)

The confessor may change the sacramental satisfaction for something else.   (No. 184.)

Of Canonical Penance.   (No. 186.)

" *Which penance is called canonical?* Ans. That which was performed according to the canons, or laws, or statutes of councils, bishops, or churches; v. g., wearing a sack sprinkled with ashes, standing before the church doors, fasting on bread and water, &c.   The penitential canons took their origin in the third century, on occasion of the heresy of the

Montanists and Novatians, who denied penance: at which time also, the four grades of penitents were instituted; the weeping, the hearing, the prostrate, and the standing. The observance and practice of these penances, sensibly declined from the ninth century, in consequence of admitting their redemption by alms, flagellations, psalteries, &c. Subsequently, still more on the occasion of the Jerusalem expedition, for the recovery of the Holy Land. Afterwards, in the twelfth century, and finally in the thirteenth, the obligation ceased through the use of indulgences; which were granted for the sake of munificent alms, or some other work, from which, at that time, magnificent temples were constructed and built."

These canonical penances were imposed only on account of the more enormous sins; though, sometimes people assumed them without obligation, from a voluntary humility. These public penances pertained to the external discipline of the Church, and were not sacramental, as they might be remitted by a deacon.

CHAPTER XL.

Treatise concerning Indulgences.

" *What is an indulgence?* Ans. It is the remission of temporal punishment due to sins remitted as to their guilt, made by the power of the keys, apart from the sacrament, by the application of satisfactions which are contained in the treasury of the Church. *What is meant by the treasury of the Church?* It is an accumulation of spiritual blessings remaining in divine acceptance, and whose disposition is entrusted to the Church.

" *From what does this treasury coalesce?* It coalesces primarily from the superabundant satisfaction of Christ, then from the supereffluent satisfactions of the blessed Virgin Mary, and the other saints. This treasury is the foundation, or the matter of indulgences, and these resources are infinite, by reason of the satisfactions of Christ, and therefore never will be exhausted; besides the superabundant satisfactions of pious men are daily added."

The objection that all the good works of the saints are abundantly remunerated by God in heaven, and that therefore there can be no superabundant satisfactions from them, is thus answered: " All the good works of the saints are rewarded, in so far as they are meritorious, but not inasmuch as they are satisfactory; for many saints had not so great a debt of temporal punishments, as the price of their satisfactions: for, v. g., the blessed Virgin Mary never contracted any debt of punishment, and yet she underwent the most grievous anguish: John the Baptist sanctified in the womb, led an austere life, which he crowned with martyrdom: thus the apostles, martyrs, anchorites, and other innumerable saints and saintesses, suffered more than their sins required, according to the manner which God observes, in exacting punishments. But the satisfactions of the saints concur, not only by way of impetration, as some pretend, but also by way of payment; as appears from the proposition condemned in the case of Bajus, No. 60. By the sufferings of the saints communicated in indulgences, our faults are not properly redeemed, but through the communion of love, their sufferings are shared by us, that we may be worthy, who are delivered by the price of Christ's blood, from the punishments due for sins. It is plain from these remarks, that the effect of indulgences is the remission of the temporal punishment, remaining after the remission of sin as to its guilt; but the guilt itself of the sin, is not directly remitted through indulgences.

" OBJ. Popes sometimes say in bulls, that they grant indulgences of sins : therefore, &c. ANS. The cause is put for the effect, and an indulgence of the punishment from the sin is signified: in which sense it is said, 2 Macc. xii. 46. ' It is therefore a holy and wholesome thought, to pray for the dead, that they may be loosed from sins.' Also, when an indulgence from the guilt and penalty is said to be granted, the power of absolving from any fault whatever, in the sacrament of penance, and of relaxing temporal punishments is meant; as Lezana teaches, together with others. But indulgences avail not only in the court of the Church, but also in the court of God; that is, they not only liberate from punishments, inasmuch as they would otherwise be enjoined by the Church; but also, inasmuch as they are due to God, and would otherwise have to be expiated, either here or in purgatory, as will be shown more at length hereafter." (No. 236.)

THE DIVISION OF INDULGENCES is as follows: (No. 237.)

" 1. Into *local*, *real*, and *personal*. 2. Into *plenary*, and *not plenary:* some also are *more full ;* others are *most full.* 3. Into *perpetual* and *temporal.*

" *Perpetual* are those which are granted for ever, without limitation of time. *Temporal*, are those which are conceded only for a limited period, say for seven years, which having elapsed, they cease. *Local* indulgences are such as are appointed for some place, say a temple, altar, &c. *Real*, are those which are annexed to any material thing, v. g., a rosary, a coin, an image, &c.: very often, however, such are carried about, which do not in truth subsist." (Beware of counterfeits !)

" *Personal*, are those which are directly granted to a person, without limitation to a thing or place.

" *What indulgences are plenary ?* Those which are granted for the remission of all the temporal punishment which the person owes : those are called *more full*, which in addition to this, give the power of absolving from cases and censures reserved to the pontiff: and those are called the *most full*, to which is added, besides the aforesaid things, according to Collet, the power of commuting vows, or of dispensing in certain irregularities. Observe, that although plenary indulgences are sometimes given under this expression : *Indulgences in the form of a jubilee*, they never have privilege to the extent of absolution, from reserved cases, &c., unless it is formally and expressly contained in the bull. For these words are not added, in order that the more ample effect of the indulgence may be expressed, but that the greater desire and abundance of the cause may be implied, and that anxiety may be excited in the faithful, of earning the indulgence." So Suarez and others.

" *What indulgences are called not plenary ?* Those which are not conceded for the remission of the entire temporal punishment, but are usually limited through certain days or years, according to the mode in which the canonical penances were formerly prescribed; after these were abrogated, the use of indulgences began to be more common, and as it were, succeeded in their place : and thus the mode was introduced of measuring, or determining indulgences, not according to months or weeks, but by days and years, as the canonical penances prescribed.

"*What, therefore, is signified by an indulgence, v. g., of a hundred days?* ANS. It is not meant, that by this indulgence a person is liberated from a punishment in purgatory, that will last precisely one hundred days, as the common people suppose; but that he, who obtains this indulgence of a hundred days, may obtain so great a remission of temporal punishments in this life, or of those which are to be expiated in purgatory, as he would have obtained, if he had really performed a penance of a hundred days, such as was wont to be imposed, according to the canons, regarding it indeed, merely inasmuch as it is satisfactory : but the remission of how much temporal punishment, or of how many days to be expiated in purgatory, may correspond to this penance or indulgence of one hundred days, is not altogether known; perhaps not even ten days.

"Hence also, is understood what is meant by an indulgence of one or more *quadragenæ*, which is sometimes granted : a *quadragena*, according to the canons, was a fast to be continued through forty days; but when it was performed on bread and water, it was called *carena*, from wanting other food. (Carendo aliis cibis.)"

"*But what is to be said of indulgences of a thousand or even more years, which are recorded as having sometimes been granted?* I answer with Steyaert : the same as of plenary indulgences, which are still more copious; for some one might have been a debtor of so many years of penance, if he had sinned to such an extent, that so great a penance was due to him. Neither ought it to appear wonderful, that so many years of punishment were due to the sins of any one, according to the canons, although he could not live so long : because this length of time, says Boudart, might be diminished by the earnestness and fervour of charity, by which the works enjoined, and other works of virtues might be produced : hence, some persons have unjustly inveighed against these indulgences of many years, as though framed by those who disposed of them, and never granted by the Church; on which account, Steyaert admonishes, that this is one of the passages to be cautiously read in Estius. Meanwhile, BENEDICT XIV. may be consulted," &c.

That the Church has the power of granting indulgences, is proved by a decree of the council of Trent; by Matt. xvi. 19. *I give unto thee the keys of the kingdom of heaven*, &c.; and John xxi. 17. *Feed my sheep;* also by 2 Cor. ii. 10, where Paul remits a part of the temporal punishment, which the incestuous Corinthian owed!! (No. 238.)

The Pope is the supreme dispenser of indulgences; and he has plenitude of power with respect of the whole Church. The bishop may grant indulgences in his diocese, and the archbishop through a whole province, of one year, at the dedication of a church, and of forty days, at the anniversary of the dedication, &c. The bishops have this authority only from ecclesiastical right, the Pope by divine right. (No. 239.)

The person enjoying an indulgence, must be baptized and in a state of grace. (No. 240.)

If conceded without just cause, it is invalid. "It is to be observed with Bellarmine, that a just cause for the most part, embraces two things, viz.; some object acceptable to God, and some work enjoined, in order to obtain that object; so that the attainment of the object may be more acceptable to God, than the satisfaction itself, which is relaxed through the indulgence. Thus an indulgence is frequently conceded to men, who have deserved well of the Church, without actual works." (No. 243.)

In No. 244, it is gravely asked "whether indulgences are worth as much as they sound?" And what is stranger still, the question is answered affirmatively, " because otherwise, the concession of indulgences would contain a fraud, and the Church or ecclesiastical superior, proclaiming or pronouncing the indulgences, might be accused of *lying or falsehood*, WHICH IS ABSURD."

Who ever heard of a lie or a falsehood, or any thing of the kind, being for a moment tolerated in the Church of Rome? Such a supposition would verily be *absurd!*

There is this difference between an indulgence for the living and one for the dead; an indulgence for the living, is not only a payment, but an absolution: whereas, an indulgence for the dead, is merely a payment. That indulgences may be applied to souls in purgatory and profit them, is quite certain.

"1. Because private believers may apply their own satisfactions to souls in purgatory; therefore the Pope may apply to them the satisfactions of Christ and the saints, from the treasury of the Church. 2. The Pope may apply indulgences to the living; therefore, also to the dead, as they are members of the same body." To the somewhat formidable objection, that "the power of conferring indulgences, is founded on the words of Christ, *Whatsoever ye shall bind upon earth, shall be bound in heaven;* but the souls in purgatory are not *upon earth,* therefore, &c:" the answer is given; "1. These words *upon earth,* according to many, are not referred to the object of the loosing, or to those who are loosed; but to the Superior loosing, who only can loose, so long as he is upon earth. 2. The Church only does concerning the dead, what the faithful do, who offer prayers and satisfactions to God, that souls may be freed from punishments; thus also, the Church offers the satisfactions of Christ and the saints, in payment of punishments due by them." Indulgences may be applied to the dead, "then only when it is expressly signified, that the indulgences are so made, that they may be applied to the dead: the reason is, that indulgences are valid, only for those for whom they are granted: but when they are conceded for the dead, particular mention is usually made: therefore, if this mention is not made, they cannot be applied to them. For the same reason, no one can apply indulgences to another living person, unless this is expressly granted; which is not wont to be done." (No. 245.)

Whether indulgences for the dead infallibly have their effect or not is a mooted point; but the Romish doctors generally opine that they have the same value for the dead as for the living, in which conclusion every Protestant will heartily concur.

" An altar is said to be privileged, to which a plenary indulgence is annexed for that soul for which mass is said at that altar." Whether the soul is by this very act liberated from purgatory, whilst mass is said for it at the privileged altar is uncertain ; besides it is also not known whether the cause of the concession is fully sufficient, whether the celebrant offers with sufficient fervour in order to obtain what he asks, and finally whether God here and now accepts the satisfactions offered to him in payment of the remaining debt. (No. 248.)

By the Jubilee " is properly signified that plenary indulgence, which is granted with a certain solemnity by the Roman Pontiff with various favours and particular privileges to those who have performed the prescribed good works. A two-fold Jubilee is usually distinguished : one ordinary, which is granted only every twenty-fifth year to persons visiting the designated churches at Rome, and performing the other things requisite ; and it is called the Jubilee of the holy year : the other extraordinary, which the Pontiffs concede for important reasons occurring out of the 25th year ; such as every Pope is wont to concede at the beginning of his pontificate for a happy reign."

" The Jubilee of the holy year at Rome lasts through the whole year, beginning from the first Vespers of the Lord's nativity with the ceremony of the opening of the Sacred Gate ; which in the vigil of the nativity of the following year is shut up with a new wall, and remains thus closed until a holy year again recurs." (No. 249.)

In order to know what privileges are granted, the bull of concession must always be consulted : because they are not always the same, but sometimes more, sometimes fewer. (No. 250.)

There is scarcely any peculiarity of the Romish church which awakens more painful feelings than the general topic which has been discussed in the last two chapters. It is degrading to human nature to find men of general intelligence who can nevertheless so far forget themselves as to bow down to a fellow-mortal, and breathe into his ear the confession, which should be made to God alone. The priest claims the prerogative of God; literally sits in the temple as God, and thus perfectly fulfils the sure word of prophecy, which designates this as a striking feature of the Romish apostasy. As man he knows nothing

41

that is stated to him by the penitent: so long as the husband or wife, or child is at his feet in the confessional, he sits upon the throne of God as a spiritual judge! This is literally the arrogant claim of every Romish priest who professes to absolve his fellow-creatures from their sins! Is it not inconceivable that any mortal should dare to usurp this prerogative? and, above all that men should be found willing to recognize the claim and actually to prostrate themselves at his feet that they may obtain the Holy Father's blessing and absolution?

There are passages in Peter Dens' Treatise on Penance, &c., which I have been obliged from a regard to decency to pass by. I would not outrage the feelings of my reader by stripping them of their Latin disguise, and their deformity is such that even this covering would be insufficient to hide it from an English reader. Paul tells us that it is a shame to speak of certain things that were done among the Gentiles, but it is actually a shame even to think of some of the topics which are discussed with the most obscene discrimination by Roman theologians, and with which their minds must be familiar before ever they can hear confessions. Every form of imaginable and unimaginable bestiality is investigated with the closest scrutiny, and questions are propounded, which to use the language of a living member of the Romish church, " are enough to make the hair of one's head stand up." There is nothing connected with the matrimonial state, nothing too sacred or secret in the virtuous intercourse of those whom God has joined, which is not made a subject of impudent inquiry. No matter whether the penitent be male or female, the priest may propound what interrogatories he chooses. We cannot say we pity the man, who will suffer his wife and daughters to be thus tortured and trodden down by a Popish priest; if it ever can be lawful to turn with loathing from a fellow-creature, we might be pardoned for an expression of disgust at the sight of such an object; but when we remember the force of education, the deadly influence of Popish superstition which is the rankest form that fanaticism has ever assumed; the power of the strong delusions that can bind the soul of man with a chain of ada-mant, and fetter every noble principle, we bless God that we were not educated in the nurture and admonition of the church of Rome, and we pray for our deluded brethren, Father forgive them, they know not what they do!

Satan could not possibly have devised a scheme, which more com-pletely subverts the principles and the design of the gospel than this fatal system. The poor Papist is taught to regard his prayers, (such as they are,) the reading of the Scriptures, &c., as *punishments;* when he wishes to make *satisfaction* for his sins, he goes over the rosary or the litany of the Blessed Virgin. If he has been drunk six times, in as many days, he gets absolution, and is ready to run up a new score with the landlord and his Maker, so soon as with due preparation, he has read the seven penitential psalms on his bended knees, with arms extended before a crucifix! What if the priest does charge him to keep away from the tavern? If he can obtain forgiveness at so cheap a rate, he will get drunk again, and do penance for it with a hearty good will.

Who does not see that the practical result of this spiritual, or rather *carnal* discipline, will be to fill him with the most determined and inveterate hatred for prayer, and for the Bible? He will love them just as soon, and as much as the schoolboy loves the rod! We may be told that in many instances the operation of the confessional is beneficial; that stolen property is frequently restored to its rightful owner, and that the mere fact that the Papist acknowledges his obligation to confess his sins against God and his neighbour, will make him careful not to commit such transgressions, especially when, in addition to the dread of the *humiliation* of a minute confession, he is deterred by fear of the sacramental satisfaction or penance which his confessor may and *must* impose. But even supposing that all the advantages are gained for which the most strenuous advocates of this Romish practice contend, they are too dearly purchased. The price is the surrender of the penitent's liberty as a man, the recognition of a blasphemous assumption of a divine prerogative, and the fatal delusion that sins can be blotted out of the book of God's remembrance, by means of a paltry penance, imposed at the option of the confessor! Satan would rejoice to see all the stolen property in creation, restored on such terms!

If the Romish priests were pure as angels, and as fully proof against the seductive influences of temptation as the marble pillars in their cathedral, it would still be unpardonable idolatry to confess to them, because this is an act of worship, which belongs to God alone. But, alas! their reverences are most unfortunately, at best, only earthen vessels; and though they sit as God, in temples professedly dedicated to the Most High, they do occasionally afford lamentable evidence that they are *men of like passions* with the rest of their fellow-mortals. We might remind our readers of facts illustrative of this remark, but they are neither so few nor far between as to render specifications very necessary. Let it not be supposed, however, that we are so prejudiced against Romish priests as to be unwilling to accord to them the praise that is due; we may as well acknowledge in this connection, the disinterested zeal of the holy *fathers* in the endowment of orphan asylums, and the special and almost paternal regard which they entertain for the nephews and nieces, with which a kind Providence bountifully supplies the defect of sons and daughters ; for of course it is known that the reverend confessors are bound by a vow of perpetual celibacy, which under pain of sacrilege they may not forget.

But there is another view of the practical operation of the confessional, which is calculated to awaken alarm. We are not surprised at the strict injunction of secresy, because it is the only preservative of the confessional. Penitents would not resort to the priest, if this injunction were removed. But we call attention to the presumption which makes the authority of the confessional superior to all civil or judicial authority, and which absolves the priest from all guilt in concealing anything which he has learned in confession, *although the life or salvation of a man, or the* RUIN OF THE STATE should be involved in his silence. To cap the climax, if questioned concerning it, to use the language of Dens : " *He must reply that he does not know it, and if it is necessary,* HE MUST CONFIRM THE SAME WITH AN OATH ! Again : " *if a confessor be cited in a judicial case, that he may give his reason for refusing absolution, he must protest that in this case, he acknowledges no superior except God !*" If we are not mistaken, a case in point was tried some years ago in the state of New York, in which the court actually recognized the priest's scruples ; it is doubtful, however, if a confessor were detected in a flat perjury by a Philadelphia Court, whether his reverence would not have an opportunity of preparing a treatise on *fasting*, according to the rules of the Moyamensing Manual. The results of his experience would perhaps be very nearly as valuable as the brilliant dissertations of Pope Benedict XIV., on the drinking of chocolate, and the smoking of segars on a fast day ; and, (which is a very great consideration,) the materials for the work would be collected at the expense of the state, so that, if the priest chose to be generous, he might devote the profits to the support of St. Joseph's Orphan Asylum. The case as yet, however, is altogether hypothetical, and we would not be understood as presuming to dictate to a *conscientious* confessor.

CHAPTER XLI.

TREATISE CONCERNING THE SACRAMENT OF EXTREME
UNCTION.

PREFACE.

" THE names of the sacrament of *extreme unction*, are various: from
the matter, the Greeks call it *holy oil*; from the matter and form together, it is called by the same, *prayer with oil*; from the subject,
upon whom it is conferred, it is called by the Latins, the *anointing of
the sick*, also, the *sacrament of the departing*; from the effect which
it produces, it is called by the Council of Trent, the *consummating sacrament of Penance.*   We preface according to our custom

*The Decree of the Council of Florence for the instruction of the
Armenians.*

" The fifth sacrament is extreme unction, the matter of which is
olive oil, blessed by the bishop: this sacrament ought not to be dispensed except to a sick person whose death is apprehended; who is to
be anointed on these parts: on the eyes, on account of vision; on the
ears, on account of hearing; on the nostrils, on account of scent; on
the mouth, for taste or speech; on the hands, for touching; on the
feet, for walking; on the reins, for the pleasure, &c. &c. — The
form of this sacrament is: *Through this unction, and his own most
gracious mercy, may God pardon thee, whatever thou hast done amiss
through sight*, &c., and likewise in the other members.   The minister
of this sacrament is the priest: but the effect is the healing of the
mind, and in so far as is expedient, also, of the body itself.   Concerning this sacrament, the blessed Apostle James says, ch. v. 14, 15: ' Is
any sick among you? Let him bring in the priests of the church, and
let them pray over him, anointing him with oil, in the name of
the Lord; and the prayer of faith shall save the sick man, and the
Lord shall raise him up; and if he be in sins, they shall be forgiven
him.'

Canons of the Council of Trent concerning Extreme Unction.

" 1. Whoever shall say that extreme unction is not truly and properly a sacrament, instituted by Christ our Lord, and promulgated by
the blessed Apostle James, but only a rite received from the fathers, or
a human invention; let him be accursed!

41 *

" 2. Whoever shall say that the sacred anointing of the sick does not confer grace nor remit sins, nor raise up the sick, but that it has now ceased, as if the gift of healing existed only in past ages : let him be accursed !

" 3. Whoever shall say that the ceremony of extreme unction, and the practice which the holy Roman Church observes, are repugnant to the meaning of the blessed Apostle James, and that therefore they are to be changed, and may be despised by Christians without sin ; let him be accursed !

" 4. Whoever shall say that the elders of the Church, who the blessed James advises should be sent for to anoint the sick, are not priests ordained by the bishop, but those who are the more advanced in age, in any community ; and that on this account the proper minister of extreme unction is not the priest alone ; let him be accursed !'"

Extreme unction is defined as a sacrament in which the sick man is anointed with holy oil by the priest, under a prescribed form of words, for the healing of the mind and body.   It is proved to be a sacrament from the words of James above quoted, from the definition of the councils of Trent and Florence, and from the constant practice of the Church, as well the Latin as the Greek : indeed, the Greek schismatics themselves, admit this sacrament : but Luther and Calvin have rejected it.   That all the essentials of this sacrament are designated by James, is demonstrated thus :

" By saying, (v. 14.) *If any one is sick*, he designates the subject to be a person dangerously sick, and that he is baptized ; by adding *among you*, that is the faithful : by saying, *let him bring in the priests*, he intimates that the minister is a priest ; by these words, let them pray over him, and the prayer of faith, he denotes its deprecative form ; by the word anointing, he intimates that the proximate matter is the unction, and by the following words, *with oil in the name of the Lord*, that the remote matter is oil that has been blessed : in the words, *shall save the sick man, and raise him up*, &c., it explains the effects of this sacrament.

" Obj. In this epistle, the question is discussed, merely concerning the natural efficacy of the oil for healing bodily diseases, and concerning the gift of healing, conferred gratuitously ; therefore, &c.

" Ans. 1. I deny the antecedent ; because he would not, in that case, have commanded the elders to be called, but thè physicians, or those who have the gift of healing; which was not given to all the elders, nor to them only.

" 2. The gift of healing was not given only for the sick, of whom St. James treats, but also for the blind, the lame, &c.

" 3. The remission of sins, which St. James places as the effect of this anointing, cannot be attributed to the natural virtue of the oil, or to the gift of healing. The anointings applied by the apostles, Mark vi. 13, " they anointed with oil many that were sick, and healed them," were not sacramental, because they referred only or principally, to the healing of bodily disease : but the sacraments in themselves, pertain to the soul, to the body by accident, and at most secondarily : and hence, these anointings were only figures, by which this sacrament was insinuated, as the council of Trent says, sess. 14, concerning extreme unction, ch. 1."

Was this sacrament instituted immediately by Christ ? " Yes : (!!!) it is inferred from the council of Trent, sess. 14, &c., in which it teaches, that it was promulgated by St. James ; it judged therefore, that it was instituted not by him, but immediately by Christ. *When did Christ institute it ?* The time is uncertain : probably however, he instituted it after his resurrection, in the period of forty days, in which he spoke to his disciples concerning the kingdom of God, or concerning the affairs of the Church, and in which, as S. Leo says, the great sacraments were confirmed. Probably also, he instituted it after the sacrament of penance, of which it is the perfection and consummation, had been instituted."

" The oil of the sick, which is the matter of this sacrament, together with the chrism and the oil of catechumens, is solemnly blessed by the bishop, every year on the day of the Lord's supper, who distributes them to the archpresbyters, and they to the pastors ; for this purpose each pastor brings three silver or pewter vessels, marked with letters for the sake of distinction, in which silk or some other spongy matter is usually deposited, in order to avoid the danger of spilling. When fresh oils are brought, the old ones are burned, and the ashes are sent into the sacristy, or if the quantity is considerable, it may be consumed in a lamp, before the adorable sacrament," &c.

In case the oil blessed by the bishop should fail before the annual period for preparing new has arrived, oil that has not been blessed may be mixed with it, but the quantity must be less than the holy oil which remains. The proximate matter of the sacrament of extreme unction, is the anointing, or the use and application of the oil. Although the council of Florence requires the sick and dying to be anointed on the loins, yet for modesty's sake, the breast, or in females, the lower part of the throat has been substituted; so that the unction is applied to the eyes, ears, nose, mouth and hands, and then to the breast and the feet.

Here there appears to us to be something of a dilemma. Why has the recommendation of the council of Florence been changed? Was it not an infallible, œcumenical council? So the Church of Rome would have us believe; and yet for modesty's sake, the mode of administering this *sacrament* of Christ's own institution, has been changed! Therefore the council of Florence has recommended a practice, which is too indecent even for Romish priests to perform, without material modification; and thus by their own act, they prove that the council of Florence was immodest, and hence not infallible. If the mode enjoined by this council, was suggested by the holy Spirit, what right have the priests to modify it? We apprehend, that serious injury must be done to the souls of the faithful, by this unwarrantable innovation. If I were a believer and an advocate of extreme unction, I would insist upon the literal fulfilment of the injunction of the council of Florence, in order to obviate all risk of invalidating the sacrament. The anointing upon the loins, has a special local signification, which is entirely lost in the application of the holy oil upon the throat.

The feet are anointed on the upper part, lest the holy oil might seem to be trodden under foot. The anointing of the eyes is not done on the pupil, but on the eyelid; the anointing for the sense of taste is performed on the lips, not on the tongue. When the sick man has neither hands nor feet, the unction must be made on that part of the body which is nearest to where they ought to be. The back of the hands must be anointed. Those who have been born blind must also be anointed, on account of vision; for though they have never seen any thing, and consequently could not sin by the organs of vision, yet they may have sinned by desiring to see improper things. The unction may be performed either with the thumb, or with a rod, at the option of the minister. If there is danger of infecting the oil, a fresh bit of wood may be used at the time of each anointing, and these must afterwards be burned. As for the wiping off of the anointed organs, the pastorale prescribes—that the minister or priest, after each unction, must wipe the anointed parts with a fresh wad of silk or tow, and deposit them in a clean vessel, and burn them; but if there is no fire ready, the burning is entrusted to the servants. The five unctions of the five senses are alone essential. The anointing of the breast or feet is not essential ; so that the Mechlin pastoral directory teaches, that when the five former have been applied, the mind of the priest may be easy, as the sick man has now received the sacrament." (No. 4.)

The form of the sacrament of Extreme Unction is given in the decree of the Council of Florence.

" Is the distinct expression of the sight and the other senses essential ? The affirmative answer is probable : hence, if the priest should say *whatever thou hast sinned by means of the senses*, the sacrament would be doubtful ; just as it would be improper to administer baptism in this form : *I baptize thee in the name of the most Holy Trinity*. The following form, however, will be sufficient, in case of necessity : Through this holy unction, and his own most gracious mercy, may the Lord pardon thee whatsoever thou hast done amiss by sight, hearing, smell, taste, and touch." The proper subject for extreme unction is a sick person who has attained to years of discretion, and who has been baptized, and sacramentally absolved.

The effects of this sacrament are—1. Sanctifying grace. 2. Sacramental or actual graces. 3. The wiping off of the remains of sins, and comfort of mind, by exciting in the sick man great confidence in the divine mercy. 4. Remission of sins. 5. Healing of the body. This latter effect is merely secondary, and the impediments to its taking place are—1. " The indisposition of the recipient. 2. The want of faith or confidence in the recipient. 3. The want of faith in the minister. 4. The too great progress of the disease, so that health could not be restored except by a manifest miracle, and against nature ; for although the healing of the body through this sacrament is performed by supernatural efficacy, yet it ought not to be called ·miraculous, because it is effected by an ordinary and mild operation, in a mode of operation similar to that of corporeal medicines. 5. The ordinance of divine providence and justice otherwise disposing."

Extreme Unction may be repeated as often as any one falls into a deadly sickness, but not in one and the same danger of death : i. e. the sickness must be at different times. The priest is the proper minister of this sacrament, and is bound under pain of grievous sin to administer it to the sick of his parish.

The *sacrament* of extreme unction, is an *extreme* absurdity. The practice of anointing with oil in the Jewish Church, was a common sign by which an extraordinary influence was designated. When Christ first sent out the apostles to preach the gospel, we learn from the divine record, that he gave them power to cast out unclean spirits, and to heal the sick, and this latter faculty was connected with anointing of oil. " They cast out many devils, and *anointed with oil* many that were sick, and healed them." Mark vi. 13. What connection there was between the anointing and the healing, we cannot pretend to determine; but it was manifestly significant, and was probably intended to illustrate a part of the Jewish ritual. This power was continued to the apostles after the Saviour's ascension; and they had not only received the heavenly unction of the Holy Ghost, but they could impart his influence to others, on whom they laid hands for that purpose; and in this manner, elders of churches were appointed. The Apostle James wrote his epistle to the Christian converts from Judaism, and he informs them that the divine influence, with which some of their nation had been favoured, from the institution of the Jewish Church, was still continued in the overseers of the Church, who were endowed with certain miraculous powers, and that the exercise of these powers, was accompanied by the familiar sign of anointing with oil. This ceremony, to the mind of a Jew, would be important and significant, though it might not be to us. The converts then are exhorted to avail themselves of this extraordinary power, whilst it was continued among them; and are directed to use it in sickness, that they might be healed. The *saving of the sick*, according to James, evidently means their restoration to health, for it is immediately added, *the Lord shall raise him up.* Here then is the vast and irreconcileable discrepancy between the ceremony described by the apostle, and the Romish sacrament of extreme unction. The apostolic rite was performed with a view to the restoration or healing of the sick; the popish sacrament is administered to those only who are in danger of death; and as Peter Dens informs us, with a view to their restoration to health, although in consequence of divers impediments, this latter object is usually not attained.   In the apostolic practice, the anointing of oil *never* failed in connection with the prayer of faith, to raise up the sick.   James speaks of sickness in connection with sins, and in the primitive church, such expressions of divine displeasure were not uncommon, as we see from the history of the Church at Corinth; 1 Cor. xi. 30.   This power of healing diseases, with which Christ himself uniformly connected the forgiveness of sins, was a fulfilment of the Saviour's promise.   "These signs shall follow them that believe : in my name shall they cast out devils; they shall speak with new tongues; they shall take up serpents; and if they drink any deadly thing, it shall not hurt them; *they shall lay hands on the sick, and they shall recover.*"   These miraculous endowments were to be conferred on *those that shall believe*, not on the apostles alone; they were gifts which belonged to the Church in that age, and were given for her establishment.   If the priests have this power, let them show it.   They will not taste a poisoned wafer after its consecration, nor will they drink wine in which poison has been mixed, although the ancient promise, upon part of which they have based the sacrament of extreme unction, assures them that believe, that "if they drink any deadly thing, it shall not hurt them."   If the priests can cast out devils, (and I know any one of them professes to be a match for a whole legion of them, when he is armed with a pot of holy water), and handle serpents, and drink poison without being hurt, and heal the sick by laying hands on them, they may then with propriety, employ the significant sign of the anointing with oil; but if they can not perform these miracles, the ceremony of the unction becomes *extreme* mummery!

ECCLESIASTICAL BURIAL is to be denied according to the Roman ritual, to the following classes of unhappy human beings.   To Pagans, Jews, and all infidels, heretics and their abettors, apostates from the Christian faith and schismatics; and some assert that a strong suspicion of heresy or infidelity, is sufficient to exclude from ecclesiastical burial.   Those who have been publicly excommunicated by the greater excommunication; so too such as have been by name interdicted; suicides, unless they have given signs of penitence before death; manifest and public sinners, such as usurers, and those who have notoriously failed to receive the sacraments of confession and communion at Easter, and who have departed without any signs of penitence, as well as persons killed in a duel, and infants which have died without baptism, unless still in the womb of the mother, are all excluded from consecrated ground.   Whether Catechumens may be ecclesiastically interred, is a controverted question.

CHAPTER XLII.

TREATISE OF THE SACRAMENT OF ORDERS.

Decree of the Council of Florence for the instruction of the Armenians.

" The sixth sacrament is that of orders, whose matter is that by the delivery of which, the order is conferred; as the priesthood is conferred, by the delivery of the cup with the wine, and of the plate with the bread; the deaconship by giving the book of the gospels; the subdeaconship by the delivery of the empty cup with an empty plate put upon it; and likewise of the rest by the indication of the things pertaining to their peculiar ministries. The form of the priesthood is: Receive the power of offering sacrifice in the church for the living and for the dead in the name of the Father and of the Son and of the Holy Ghost; and so of the forms of the other orders as it is contained at length in the Roman Pontifical. The ordinary minister of this sacrament is the Bishop. The effect is an increase of grace, so that the person may be a proper minister.

Canons of the Council of Trent concerning Orders.

1. " Whoever shall say that in the New Testament, there is not a visible and external priesthood: or that there is not any power of consecrating and offering the true body and blood of the Lord, and of remitting and retaining sins: but only the office and naked ministry of preaching the gospel; or that they who do not preach are surely not priests; let him be accursed!

2. " Whoever shall say that besides the priesthood there are not other orders in the Catholic church, both greater and inferior, by which as by certain steps, the priesthood may be attained; let him be accursed!

3. " Whoever shall say that orders, or sacred ordination, is not truly and properly a sacrament instituted by Christ the Lord; or that it is a certain human invention, devised by men ignorant of ecclesiastical things, or that it is only a certain ceremony of choosing the ministers of the word of God and of the sacraments; let him be accursed!

4. " Whoever shall say that by sacred ordination the Holy Spirit is not given, and that therefore the Bishops say in vain, Receive the Holy Ghost : or that by it character is not impressed : or that he who has once been a priest may again become a layman : let him be accursed !

5. " Whoever shall say that the sacred unction which the church uses in holy ordination is not only not required but is contemptible and pernicious ; likewise also the other ceremonies of orders ; let him be accursed !

6. " Whoever shall say that in the Catholic church there is not a hierarchy instituted by divine appointment, which consists of Bishops, priests, and ministers ; let him be accursed !

7. " Whoever shall say that Bishops are not superior to priests, or that they have not the power of confirming and ordaining ; or that that which they have is common to them with the priests ; or that orders conferred by them without the consent or call of the people or the secular power are null and void ; or that they who have been neither duly ordained nor sent by ecclesiastical and canonical power, but come from some other source, are lawful ministers of the word and sacraments ; let him be accursed !

8. " Whoever shall say that the Bishops who are appointed by the authority of the Roman Pontiff, are not lawful and true Bishops, but a human invention ; let him be accursed !"

CHAPTER XLIII.

TREATISE CONCERNING MARRIAGE.

Decree of the Council of Florence for the instruction of the Armenians.

" The seventh is the sacrament of Marriage, which is a sign of the union of Christ and the Church, according to the Apostle, who says, Eph. v. 32, This is a great sacrament ; but I speak in Christ and in the church. The efficient cause of marriage usually is the mutual consent expressed by words, &c. A threefold advantage of marriage is assigned. The first is, receiving and educating children for the worship of God ; the second is faith, which the one of the married persons should preserve for the other ; the third is the indivisibility of

42

marriage, because it signifies the indivisible union of Christ and the Church; although on account of fornication it may be lawful to make a separation from the bed, yet it is not proper to contract another marriage: as the bond of matrimony legitimately contracted is perpetual."

Canons of the Council of Trent concerning Marriage.

1. " Whoever shall say that marriage is not truly and properly one of the seven sacraments of the Evangelical laws instituted by Christ the Lord, but that it is invented by men in the church and does not confer grace; let him be accursed!

2. " Whoever shall say that it is lawful for Christians to have several wives at once and that this is forbidden by no divine law; let him be accursed!

3. " Whoever shall say that only those degrees of relationship and affinity, which are expressed in Leviticus can hinder marriage from being contracted, and annul the contract; and that the church cannot dispense in any of them, or appoint that more may hinder and annul; let him be accursed!

4. " Whoever shall say that the Church could not constitute impediments annulling marriage, or that in constituting them, she has erred; let him be accursed!

5. " Whoever shall say that the bond of marriage may be dissolved on account of heresy, or mutual dislike or voluntary absence from the husband or wife, let him be accursed!

6. " Whoever shall say that a marriage solemnized, but not consummated is not annulled by the solemn profession of a religious order by one of the parties; let him be accursed!

4. " Whoever shall say, that the Church errs, when she has taught and teaches that according to the evangelical and apostolical doctrine, the bond of marriage cannot be dissolved on account of the adultery of one or the other of the parties, and that neither of them, not even the innocent party who has given no cause for the adultery, may contract another marriage, whilst the party is living, and that he commits adultery, who marries another after putting away his adulterous wife, or she, who marries another after putting away her adulterous husband; let him be accursed!

8. " Whoever shall say that the Church is in error, when for many reasons she decrees that a separation may be made between married persons as to the bed, or as to intercourse either for a certain or an uncertain time; let him be accursed!

9. " Whoever shall say that the clergy constituted in sacred order

or regulars, who have solemnly professed chastity may contract marriage, and that the contract is valid, notwithstanding ecclesiastical law, or vow, and that to maintain the opposite is nothing else than to condemn marriage, and that all may contract marriage who do not think that they have the gift of chastity, even though they have vowed it; let him be accursed: as God does not deny this to those who seek it aright, nor does he suffer us to be tempted above what we are able to bear.

10. " Whoever shall say that the married state is to be preferred to a state of virginity, or celibacy, and that it is not better and more blessed to remain in virginity or celibacy, than to be joined in marriage; let him be accursed!

11. " Whoever shall affirm that the prohibition of the solemnization of marriage at certain times of the year is a tyrannical superstition, borrowed from the superstitions of the pagans, or shall condemn the benedictions and other ceremonies, which the Church uses at those times : let him be accursed!

12. " Whoever shall affirm that matrimonial causes do not belong to the ecclesiastical judges; let him be accursed!"

The Treatise on marriage is a developement of the peculiar views contained in the decree of the Council of Florence and the canons of the Council of Trent,—and a translation would not repay me for the labour of writing, nor the reader for the trouble of perusing such chapters as are fit for the public eye. Topics are discussed in this connection, to which decency almost forbids me even to allude. I should disgust every modest person and for ever forfeit his good opinion, if I were to spread before an English reader the abominable obscenity in which Peter Dens wallows with perfect self-complacency. I will, however, give a few extracts in Latin, and if the priests think proper they may supply an English translation for the benefit of the curious. The following questions among the rest are gravely and systematically discussed.

An copula carnalis inter conjuges licite habetur propter solam voluptatem ? Quantum est peccatum exercere actum conjugalem ob solam voluptatem ? An licet actum conjugalem exercere partim ob debitum finem, putá generationem prolis, et partim ob delectationem ? An licitum est petere debitum conjugali ex solo fine vitandi propriam incontinentiam, non concurrente fine generationis prolis, vel redditionis debiti ? * * * * * * * *

Colligitur ex dictis, petitionem debiti esse venialiter malam, si uxor sit senex, aut sterilis, idque sive vir, sive uxor petat; quia non potest intendi prolis generatio : licite tamen reddi potest, quia redditio excusatur ob bonum fidei.   *   *   *   *   *   *

Certum est conjuges inter se peccare posse, etiam graviter, contra virtutem castitatis, sive continentiæ ratione quarumdam circumstantiarum. In particulari autem definire quæ sint mortales quæ solum veniales, perobscurum est, nec eadem omnium sententia; ut vel ideo sollicite persuadendum sit conjugatis, ut recordentur se esse filios sanctorum, quos decet in sanctitate conjugali filios procreare.   Quidam auctores circumstantias circa actum conjugalem præcipue observandas, exprimunt his versibus.

> Sit modus et finis, sine damno, solve, cohære,
> Sit locus et tempus, tactus, nec spernito votum.

1. Ergo debet servari *modus*, sive *situs*, qui dupliciter invertitur : 1. Si non servetur debitum vas, sed copula habeatur in vase præpostero, vel quocumque alio non naturali : quod semper mortale est, spectans ad sodomiam minorem seu imperfectam : idque tenendum contra quosdam laxistas, sive copula ibi consummetur, sive tantum inchoetur, consummanda in vase naturali.

2. *Modus* sive *situs*, invertitur, sic tamen, ut servetur debitum vas ad copulam a natura ordinatum, si v. g. fiat accedendo præpostere a latere, stando, sedendo, vel si vir sit succubus.   Modus is mortalis est si inde suboriatur periculum pollutionis respectu alterutrius : sive quando periculum est, ne semen perdatur, prout sæpe accidit, dum actus exercetur stando, sedendo, aut viro succumbente : si absit, et sufficienter præcaveatur istud periculum ex communi sententia id non est mortale.   Est autem veniale ex gravioribus, cúm sit inversio ordinis naturæ.   Estque generatim modus ille, sine causa taliter coëundi, graviter a CONFESSARIIS reprehendendus.   Si tamen ob justam rationem situm naturalem conjuges immutent, secludaturque dictum periculum nullum erit peccatum, &c."   The following question is also asked :   "An uxor potest se tactibus excitare ad seminationem, si a copula conjugali se retraxerit maritus, postquam ipse seminavit, sed antequam seminaverit uxor ?"

"Confessarius potest etiam conjugatos interrogare sub his terminis : Confidis, quod utaris matrimonio honesto modo, non plus faciendo quam necessarium est ad generandam prolem ?   Non habes specialia dubia quæ te angunt ?   Si autem pœnitens det occasionem ulterius interrogandi, inquirat confessarius, an sibi vel comparti causaverit periculum pollutionis, vel perditionis seminis."

The atrocity of these extracts will appear infinitely more flagrant when it is remembered that the confessor institutes inquiries in relation to all these things in order that he may ascertain the amount of guilt which his penitent has contracted! Language cannot portray the deep indignation and abhorrence with which every enlightened and virtuous mind must regard the ineffable arrogance and impudence of the Romish priesthood. Would to God that the Roman Catholic laity for whom as individuals we would cherish no other feelings than those of the utmost kindness, could but view these things in the light in which we see them!

CHAPTER XLIV.

In the Treatise which treats of the four last things, viz. death, judgment, hell and heavenly glory, we find in No. 15, the following remarks:

CONCERNING ANTICHRIST.

"Who is here meant by Antichrist? Ans. Some particular very wicked man, who will arise in the last days, saying that he is Messiah, and showing himself as God, 2. Thess. ii. 4. As to his rise and country nothing certain is held, except that Damascenus hands down the tradition that he will be born from fornication, and the ancients supposed that he will arise from the tribe of Dan, because Rev. vii. the tribe of Dan is not numbered with those who are to be saved.

"He will excite terrible persecution against the Church, and will perform many lying wonders and signs, as is said, 2 Thess. ii. 9. in order to confirm the false doctrine. His persecution will last as is thought for three and a half years according to Dan. vii. 25: 'And they shall be delivered into his hand until a time, and times, and half a time.' At length the Lord Jesus will kill him with the spirit of his mouth, 2 Thess. ii. 8.

"From these remarks it is plain how foolish is the calumny of heretics of our time, who are not afraid to say that the Roman Pontiff is Antichrist. For:

I. "Antichrist will come at the end of the world; the Roman Pon-

42 *

tiff rules the church now upwards of 1800 years, by a continuous succession. 2. He will be a particular person: there is a great series of Popes. 3. He will call himself Christ; the Pope calls himself Christ's vicar. 4. He will exalt himself above all that is called God: The Pope calls himself the servant of the servants of God. 5. The advent of Antichrist will be in all power, and signs, and lying wonders: no history relates this of the Roman Pontiffs. Some of them indeed have shone forth by true miracles, but many other saints by greater: nor among the Pontiffs was any distinguished by greater miracles than St. Peter: will they peradventure say that Christ himself appointed Antichrist over his own Church?

"It is plain also, that they are in error, who have supposed that Nero or Mahomet was Antichrist; because he will come only at the end of the world.

"*Obj.* 1. John ii. 18, it is said: ' Ye have heard that Antichrist cometh; therefore he will not come at the end of the world.'

"*Ans.* *Cometh* in the present is put for *will come* on account of the certainty of the event.

"You will reply: Immediately after the words cited it is maintained, Even now there are many Antichrists; therefore, &c.

"*Ans.* By many Antichrists, John means heretics, on account of their resemblance to Antichrist; for, Antichrist signifies one who is contrary to Christ."

N. B. Our reasons for conferring the title of Antichrist upon his Holiness will be seen at the close of this chapter.

OF PURGATORY. (No. 25.)

"What is purgatory? ANS. It is the place in which the souls of departed just people, which were obnoxious to temporal punishments, endure sufficient suffering. It is said, *endure sufficient suffering*, because as souls there are beyond the state of probation they can merit no longer, nor properly satisfy for the punishment that is due, but they satisfy only in punishment, or expiate the appointed penalty: so that they cannot help and liberate themselves from punishment, except by enduring sufficient suffering. What ought we to believe concerning purgatory? The council of Trent, sess. 25, in the commencement of the decree concerning purgatory, has settled two things which are to be believed, namely that there is a purgatory, and that the souls there detained are assisted by the suffrages of the faithful, chiefly, however, by the acceptable sacrifice of

the altar. This faith the Greeks also professed in the council of
Florence. In relation to the remaining questions concerning purgatory, nothing has been settled."

The proof texts of the existence of purgatory are, 2 Macc. xii. " It
is therefore a holy and wholesome thought to pray for the dead that
they may be loosed from sins." Eccli. vii. 37, " Restrain not grace
from the dead." Tobias, iv. 18, " Lay out thy bread upon the burial
of a just man." Matt. xii. 32, where Christ says of the sin against
the Holy Ghost: " It shall not be forgiven him either in this world or
in the world to come." 1 Cor. iii. 12, " Now if any man build upon
this foundation, gold, silver, precious stones, wood, hay, stubble ;——
and the fire shall try every man's work of what sort it is ;——if any
man's work burn, he shall suffer loss, but he himself shall be saved,
yet so as by fire, i. e. by the punishment of fire. By wood, hay and
stubble, venial sins are denoted: although indeed the text may seem to
treat directly of the fire of conflagration, nevertheless purgatory is
rightly evinced from it by parity of reason : for if then the souls of
the just must be purged from the guilt of the punishment of venial
sins by that fire, the souls of the just obnoxious to a similar guilt ought
likewise to be purged by fire."

" St. Augustine wrote a whole book concerning care for the dead,
in which he teaches, both that there is a purgatory, and that the souls
there detained, are helped by the suffrages of the faithful : nor did he
only teach it, he practised it also, in respect to his deceased mother,
S. Monica, as he himself relates, Bk. 9. conf. cap. 13. The aforesaid
doctrine may be proved also by the following reasons.

" First ; when a fault has been remitted, there frequently remain
temporal punishments to be expiated; and if these are not paid, in
such a case justice demands, that a person expiate them after this life ;
lest otherwise they should be equal, who die with a great debt of punishments, and those who die with none.

" Second ; it may happen that a man dies in venial sin : but in such
a case this sin will indeed be remitted, as to the fault, by the act of
charity which the soul elicits at the first instant of its separation from
the body, as S. Thom. teaches. But by this act of charity, the liability
to punishment will be neither removed nor diminished ; and therefore
satisfaction ought to be made for it in purgatory. St. Thomas in the
passage quoted, gives as a reason, that as after this life there is no state
of meriting, this act of delight in them, takes away indeed the impediment of venial sin, yet it does not merit either absolution or a diminu-
tion of punishment, as in this life."

" *Where is purgatory?* The ordinary place of purgatory, which is properly and commonly understood by the name of purgatory, is under the earth, near to hell." The punishment of purgatory is twofold: one *of loss,* the other of *sense,* but both temporal. The punishment of loss, is merely a delay of the beatific vision, as a punishment of sins. " *Is the punishment of sense in purgatory caused by material fire?* The opinion of the Latins is steadfast, and is to be retained, that in purgatory there is material fire, similar to the fire of hell; hence the Church asks for the souls of the faithful, not only a place of light and peace, but also of coolness against the heat of the fire. However, this opinion is not of the faith, as the Greeks in the council of Florence maintained, that in purgatory there is not real fire, but that it is only a place full of hardships and sorrows, and that by these, the punishment of sense is occasioned, and yet they were not condemned either in the council of Florence or of Trent.

" *How great is the punishment of purgatory?* St. Thomas teaches, that both punishments of purgatory, as well of loss as of sense, exceed all the punishments of this life. S. Bonaventure and Bellarmine, teach that the greatest punishment of purgatory, is indeed more severe than the greatest punishment of this world; not however, that the least punishment of purgatory is greater than the greatest of this life. At all events, although this thing is uncertain, it is still certain that the punishment of purgatory is very grievous and bitter: as is plain, both from the solicitude of the Church, which exhorts us to works of satisfaction, and to earn indulgences, and because the future world is a world of retribution and punishment; also from the opinion of the holy Fathers. The punishment of purgatory is more mild than that of hell. It is also greatly alleviated by the friendship of God, and the certainty of obtaining glory, as also by the resignation of the sufferers to the most righteous will of God. St. Thomas teaches that the souls in purgatory are not harassed by devils, because they have triumphed over them; nor also by the good angels, because they would not so grievously afflict their own citizens."

All are not equally punished in purgatory: but according to the debt, the punishment both of loss and of sense, will be greater or less. Whether the punishment gradually becomes less severe, is uncertain; Bellarmine and Sylvius maintain that it does. The length of time during which souls are detained in purgatory is not known; neither are all souls punished equally long; the duration of their suffering is graduated in proportion to their guilt. They are certain of their salvation, and are confirmed in grace, so that they cannot lose it. They suffer with consummate patience, and are constantly exercising acts of charity, faith and hope, but they *merit* nothing by these acts. There can be no doubt that the souls in purgatory pray for themselves; whether they pray for us is doubtful; but Bellarmine, Estius and Sylvius, affirm that they do, especially for those who pray for them; and although these souls do not know who of us prays for them, this is no objection, because they may pray for all who pray for them in general; besides they have the knowledge which they had gained before their departure, and may be guided in some measure by that. Whether the souls in purgatory may be invoked, is not altogether clear, Steyaert says *nay*, Bellarmine says *yea*.

The communion of saints shows very evidently, that souls in purgatory may be assisted by the suffrages of the living. The militant and the suffering Church sympathize with each other. Besides the constant, perpetual, and universal practice of the Church, abundantly proves that the suffering Church is assisted by the prayers, &c., of the faithful upon earth. The principal means of assisting the souls in purgatory, are, above all—the sacrifice of the mass; then indulgences applied to the dead; and finally, prayers, alms, and any other good works performed from charity. It is very probable that the suffrages infallibly benefit those deceased souls for whom they are offered; but it is not so clear whether the whole benefit is thus applied. The objection that the souls of the rich are in a better condition in purgatory, than those of the poor, is obviated amongst the rest, by the suggestion, that *perhaps* the deficiency of masses, &c., for the poor, " is compensated by this, that God applies to them the suffrages made for those, who are either damned, or already in heaven," to neither of which classes, suffrages can be of any benefit. Suffrages are not made for baptized children, who have died before the use of reason. When masses are said for them, it is only by way of solemn protestation of the belief of their resurrection, and as an expression of thanks for the benefit conferred on them.

The belief of purgatory is enjoined upon the members of the Romish Church as an article of faith, according to the bull of Pope Pius IV. in which the following confession is made : " I do constantly hold that there is a purgatory, and that the souls there detained are helped by the suffrages of the faithful." The word *purgatory* is derived from the Latin verb *purgo*, I cleanse, purge, refine, &c. Now in this strict and literal sense the blood of the Lord Jesus Christ is the true *purgatory*—for he is said, Heb. i. 3 ; " by himself to have purged away our sins." And again, 1 John i. 7 ; " The blood of Jesus Christ cleanseth us from ALL sin." But in an inferior sense, afflictions, and faith, and the influences of the Holy Spirit and the preaching of the word, are said to purge and purify.

Amid all the uncertainty with which this subject is invested, we are told that there are two things, which the faithful must believe, the one is that there is a purgatory, and the other that the souls of the faithful there detained are aided by the suffrages of their brethren on earth. The first proof which Peter Dens offers is the passage from Judas Macchabæus. "It is therefore a holy and a salutary thought to pray for the dead that they may be loosed from sins." To this we answer:

1. The book is apocryphal, and therefore of no authority in any matter of faith.

2. This act of Judas, even supposing it were precisely what Papists affirm, cannot justify prayers for the dead, any more than the suicide of Rasias, xiv. 41, which Judas applauds, (v. 42,) proves that it is " a holy and salutary thought," for a man to kill himself, when he is in danger of being taken prisoner.

3. In the original Greek Text the words are προσάγειν περι άμαρτιας θυσιαν, which are rendered in the vulgate pro peccatis mortuorum sacrificium &c., which is a most unwarrantable liberty, for literally the original means *to offer a sacrifice for sin*; which may very properly be understood as implying that Judas made a propitiation for the dead, lest for their sin God should punish the rest of the army, and if so, the words " that they may be loosed from sins," would refer not to the dead, but to the living. Now Judas did this either against the Law or in accordance with it; if against it, he is not to be imitated; if according to the Law, we ask the erudite priests to show us the authority in the Levitical law, for their sacrifices for the dead.

The next passage we notice is from Tobit, iv. 18, where Tobias requires bread and wine to be placed on a righteous man's sepulchre; i. e. we suppose, he called together the poor, and gave them alms that they might pray for the soul of the deceased.

The advocates of purgatory must be sorely pressed for evidence if they look for it in this passage of the Book of Tobit; for they ought to know that it was customary among the Jews to comfort the poor mourning relatives of the deceased by giving them a kind of funeral banquet; hence the force of the language, Jer. xvi. 5, 7; " Thus saith the Lord, Enter not into the house of mourning, neither go to lament nor bemoan them: for I have taken away my peace from this people, neither shall men give them the cup of consolation to drink for their father or their mother."

" Another argument for purgatory is based upon the language of Christ, Matt. xii. 32; "Whoever speaketh against the Holy Ghost, it shall not be forgiven him, neither in this world, nor in the world to come." In reply, we remark :

1. The words "seculum futurum," or the world to come, are never used to denote the time between death and the last day, but invariably designate either the gospel dispensation, or the last day, or the condition subsequent to the judgment, Luke xx. 35, &c.

2. It is not logical to infer an absolute affirmative from two negatives; v. g. "this sin shall be forgiven neither in this world, nor in the world to come," therefore, some sins shall be forgiven in the world to come. This is a specimen of the close reasoning of Romish theologians.

3. The meaning of these words is evident from the parallel passages in Mark iii. 29, and Luke xii. 10, where it is said that this sin " shall never be forgiven ; " and again " shall not be forgiven." And at all events the passage will not sustain the Romish doctrine, because in purgatory sins are not *forgiven* but *expiated* by suffering.

" What," says Archbishop Tillotson, " have we here to do with remission of sins? Purgatory is a place not where sins are remitted but where they are punished with the greatest severity. Nay, what is still more, punished after they are remitted, nay, what is still more extraordinary, therefore punished, because they are remitted ; for if the guilt were not remitted, the sinner could not go to purgatory, nor have the favour of being punished there."

In concluding this work, I cannot offer anything more appropriate than the evidences, which conspire to prove that the Head of the Romish Church is really par excellence the Antichrist spoken of in the word of God. The Greek preposition ἀντι admits of a two-fold interpretation; it sometimes signifies for, or in the place of, implying a *vicegerency* or *subordination*; thus in profane authors we read of ἀντι βασιλεὺς and ἀντιστρατηγος, which designate the officer next to the King or Captain. This signification Peter Dens carefully omits, lest Antichrist might be found after all to mean Christ's *vicar*. The word is, however, more frequently employed as signifying *against*, and as denoting *opposition*. In either of these senses, and in both conjointly, the Pope is emphatically ANTICHRIST. We admit that the name may be used in its common acceptation to denote all the adversaries of Christ, and thus as the Apostle John says, there may be " many Antichrists," but it is evidently employed with special reference to some particular apostasy eminent for wickedness and for the bitterness of its opposition to Christ. The fanciful theories of Romish authors on this subject show the difficulty which it presents to them. One maintains that Antichrist will be born of a Virgin by the agency of the Devil; another that he will be a devil incarnate, assuming false flesh from a false virgin; another that he shall be a devil-man, partaking of the nature of Satan and man; another that Nero shall rise again and become Antichrist. Some have said the Turk is Antichrist, and others have imagined that he shall be a Jew, the son of Satan, and of a woman of the tribe of Dan. But these are certainly not the characteristics, which the word of God designates as the peculiarities of Antichrist, our enemies themselves being witness. Now, when we affirm that the Pope is Antichrist, we do not mean all the Bishops of Rome from the times of the Apostles, but only since the defection of the Church. This apostasy commenced in the fourth century, which was a period of gross corruption of the Church. Jerome, A. D. 390, complains of the avarice and corruption of the clergy, and of the PROHIBITION of MARRIAGES and MEATS: and Augustine laments, A. D. 399, that the Church was fallen from her purity. But these were only the preparations for the rise of the Man of Sin. The Pontiff had not yet gained supreme power; the civil authority of the Roman state still hindered, and therefore was *first to be taken out of the way,* 2. Thess. ii. 6, 7. When Jerome heard of the capture of Rome by Alaric, the King of the Goths, he expected the coming of Antichrist. In his epistle to Ageruchia he says: *He that letteth is removed, and shall we not know that Antichrist is near at hand?* Some designate the year 606, as the period of the first revelation of Antichrist, when Pope Boniface III. by the help of the rebel and murderer Phocas, assumed the title of UNIVERSAL BISHOP. Others refer it to the times of Pepin and Charlemagne about the year 750. We call the Pope, Antichrist, by way of distinction, as he is the head of the Antichristian apostasy; and it will not be denied that it is a common thing in Scripture to designate a body politic, state, or succession of men by a particular person or individual. Thus Deut. xvii. 14, 20; *the king of Israel* is used to denote *all* the kings of Israel. Num. xxxv. 25, 28; by *the* High Priest is to be understood any High Priest in a regular course of succession. In Daniel vii. 1, 3; each beast signifies a multitude of men in a succession under one government, which lasted for ages. Rev. xii. 1; the state of the Church is indicated by the figure of a woman in travail, and afterwards by a woman in the wilderness, &c., and thus the Popes in succession are designated in the word of God as the head of the Antichristian apostasy, although there have been *a great series of Popes;* and thus we dispose of Peter Dens' second objection. The rest shall be attended to in due season, though for convenience sake we may notice them in an order different from that in which they are stated. We proceed to show that the great characteristics of Antichrist as delineated by the Holy Spirit in the word of God, are ALL found in the Romish apostasy.

1. Is Antichrist denominated "the MAN OF SIN, the SON OF PERDITION," 2 Thess. ii. 3? Witness the horrible lives of most of the Popes, and the encouragement they give to sin by their indulgences, jubilees, &c.

2. *Does he sit in the temple of God AS GOD, and exalt himself above all that is called God?* Witness the language of the Romish theologians; the priest does not know the confession of a penitent as man, though he may know it AS GOD! Hear the blasphemous adulation of the Pontiff's vassals, who accost him as OUR LORD GOD the Pope! Look at the title, which the Head of the Romish Church claims as his prerogative. HIS HOLINESS, the Pope! But, says Dens, "the Pope calls himself the servant of the servants of God," hence he cannot be the Antichrist of whom Paul speaks! He calls himself the servant of the servants of God, and permits others to accost him as their LORD GOD! He calls himself the servant &c., and yet claims to be above all law; exalts himself above all civil authority; puts his foot upon the neck of kings, and makes Emperors kiss his holy slipper; professes to hold the keys of heaven and hell, to have power to absolve subjects from their oath of allegiance to their lawful rulers; acts as the King of Kings and Lord of Lords, and then with the utmost complacency plumes himself upon his vast humility in assuming a title, which is belied by every official act which he performs! In fact by styling himself the servant of the servants of God, he verifies another characteristic of Antichrist, who is to be known by "*speaking lies in hypocrisy!*"

3. The antichristian apostasy is to be characterized by "giving heed to doctrines of devils." The word rendered *devils*, here might have been translated *demon-gods;* it is the same word that is used in repeated instances in profane authors, to designate the spirits of departed men, who were declared *gods* by an *apotheosis* not unlike the Pope's *canonization* of saints; and there can be no doubt, that the invocation of the Romish saints, is the very abuse which is thus designated by the Holy Spirit.

4. Antichrist shall FORBID TO MARRY. Who does not see the verification of this prediction in the celibacy of the Romish priesthood?

43

If this be denied, show us the sect professing to be Christian, (for remember, it must be a departure *from the faith*, 1 Tim. iv. 1, not a heresy, which originated like the Moslem delusion, entirely apart from the Church;) which at all forbids marriage, except the Church of Rome !

5. Antichrist shall COMMAND TO ABSTAIN FROM MEATS; not to *fast*; but to *abstain from meats;* see this verified to the very letter in the discipline of the Romish apostasy, which permits men to eat any thing but MEATS on a fast day; according to Peter Dens on a day of solemn ecclesiastical fast, the faithful may be two hours at the table, before the guests are to be admonished to abstain from eating; but they may not eat MEAT under pain of mortal sin.

6. The coming of that WICKED ONE " is after the working of Satan." The chief attributes of Satan's character are *falsehood and cruelty*. And has not the apostasy, whose head is the Pope, introduced false doctrine, false worship, and a false religion into the Church, and thus become the great murderer of souls? Satan shows that he is a liar, when he deludes souls into a false worship, and changes *the truth of God into a lie;* (Rom. i. 5.); and he has never done this more effectually, than in the establishment of the idolatrous worship of Rome. The Church of Rome for centuries, has worn out the saints of the Most High. The blood of sixty millions of souls, cries from earth to heaven, against her. Her coming is truly after the working of Satan, with all power, secular and spiritual !

7. Antichrist is to come with " signs and lying wonders." Strange that our theologian should assert that this cannot be substantiated of the Popes, some of whom he asserts, have been distinguished by the power of working real miracles, though many of the saints have wrought greater. It is the boast of the Romish Church, that she still retains the power of working miracles. Even in our own city, and in the present year, legends have been published, containing reputed miracles of St. Francis Xavier, St. Ignatius, &c., which in absurdity are not to be surpassed by any work of fiction or romance, that has ever appeared in print; the adventures of Gulliver and Baron Munchausen, are far more probable than the insane stories that are told about these saints. Here is a specimen of the " lying wonders," which are actually detailed and retailed in this enlightened community. On one occasion, St. Francis Xavier whilst at sea, leaning over the side of the ship, lets a precious crucifix fall overboard. The saint, as may well be supposed, is overwhelmed with grief at the loss, and for a season is almost disconsolate. In due time the saint is set ashore, and whilst walking along the beach in company with some friends, they observe

at a distance a crab moving towards them; and as it approaches nearer, something is discerned in its claws; it proves to be the saint's crucifix; the crab lays the crucifix at the saint's feet with the utmost reverence, and then demurely walks back into the sea. A large volume of upwards of 400 pages, is filled with such stuff as this. Shall we be asked HERE, where is the evidence that the Romish Church deals in " lying wonders ?"

But the objection is offered, that antichrist shall reign but three years and a half; whereas the Popes have filled the chair of St. Peter for upwards of eighteen hundred years. This, by the way, is not true. For it was in the year 606, that the bishop of Rome first claimed and usurped *universal supremacy.* So that if Peter ever was bishop of Rome, we cannot be said to include the apostle in the Romish apostasy. The text in Daniel ch. vii., to which allusion is made, is sometimes referred to the tyrant Antiochus, who is considered as a type of Antichrist; besides, the years are prophetical; hence each one of them contains 365 years, so that this is equivalent to the period of 42 months, Rev. xi. 2., or a thousand two hundred and threescore, or 1260 days, mentioned Rev. xii. 6, according to the key furnished in Ezek. iv. 6. " I appoint thee each day for a year." This period of 1260 years, added to the 606, when the title of Universal Bishop was assumed, brings us to the year 1866, when we anticipate the overthrow of his spiritual supremacy. For a masterly and succinct view of this subject, I refer my reader to Dr. Brownlee's Introduction to my lectures on Romanism. The objection that antichrist will call himself Christ, whereas the Pope calls himself Christ's vicar, is already answered. One meaning of *antichrist,* is literally CHRIST'S VICAR ; just as ἀντι βασιλεὺς means viceroy.

I bless God that I have been spared to finish this synopsis; may the Lord whom I desire to serve, use it to counteract in some measure at least, the wiles and delusions of the Man of sin, and to his great and holy name, shall be all the glory ! If Protestant ministers find it of service to them in combating the errors of antichrist, I shall be amply repaid for the labour which it has cost me. They are required to testify against this apostasy ; for Paul after specifying the characteristic marks which we have just reviewed, adds these words : " If thou put the brethren in remembrance of these things, thou shalt be a good minister of Jesus Christ, nourished up in the words of faith and of good doctrine, whereunto thou hast attained." May the Lord, by his grace, help us to do this in a spirit of love, and with a sincere desire to save souls from death !

THE END.